SHAKESPEARE
AS A DRAMATIC ARTIST

SHAKESPEARE
as a
DRAMATIC ARTIST

*With an Account
of His Reputation
at Various Periods*

THOMAS R. LOUNSBURY

FREDERICK UNGAR PUBLISHING CO.
NEW YORK

Republished 1965

Reprinted from the 1901 edition
published by Yale University Press

Library of Congress Catalog Card No. 64-25561

GENERAL INTRODUCTION *

"WILL it do to say anything more about Chaucer?"
It was with this query that one of the most brilliant of
modern essayists began an article upon that poet. If such
a man as he could feel hesitation about adding further
comment to the comparatively little which has been
made upon the earliest of our great authors, how much
more ought one far inferior to feel it, when purposing
to bring out not merely a single volume but a series of
volumes about the greatest of them all.

For if there is any belief held by the common consent
of critics as thoroughly established, it is that Shakespeare is a writer about whom can no longer anything
new be said, — that is, anything which, while being new,
has also a right to be termed rational. Of new things
which are irrational, we are warranted in asserting that
the supply will never fail. Probably no other author
in any speech has indirectly contributed so many illustrations as he to the vast variety of ways in which
human idiocy manifests itself, whether it take the
shape of emendation of his language, or of interpretation of his meaning, or of the exploiting of every sort of
fanciful view about his life and writings which perverse
ingenuity can concoct or addled brain evolve. It seems,

---

*The original edition of this volume was a part of a series
known as *Shakespearean Wars*.

therefore, almost like a renewed assault upon his reputation and the interest inspired by his works to seek, at this late day, to contribute anything more to the accumulation of matter which has been heaped up by generations of scholars, or to repeat in inadequate phrase what has already been better said by scores of men possessed of keenest insight, of profoundest intellect, and of exquisite taste.

Yet the subject, however worn, continues to retain its freshness. In numerous ways Shakespeare has broken all literary records; but it is to be doubted if among his many triumphs there is one more striking than the fact that, in spite of the best or the worst that men have done to make him uninteresting by writing about him, his hold upon us has deepened instead of decreasing with the course of the centuries. He remains not merely an object of reverence to the few, but of intelligent curiosity to the many; and that too in a world in which the lamentable state of affairs exists, that the things we ought to want to know are as a rule very apt to be distinct from the things we actually want to know. Nor does this general desire to learn all that can or cannot be learned about him show the slightest sign of abatement. In truth, it is this very interest in the dramatist which gives whatever vitality it possesses to the theory which denies his existence as a dramatist at all.

But has everything been said about Shakespeare which can properly be said? That there are points connected with his life and writings which have been exhaustively examined and discussed, few will be found to deny. Is this statement, however, true of all of them? It may be ignorance, it may be folly, it may be presumption, it may be all these combined, but it seems to me that there is a field of Shakespearean research which, though frequently entered, has never been thoroughly explored. At all events, its story has never been fully told. There are controversies affecting the name and work of the dramatist which have never been made the subject of detailed recital. Some of them were going on at the very beginning of his career; certain of them have gone on from that day to this, nor do they yet show signs of ultimate subsidence. Even echoes of those which may be considered as finally settled still continue to fall upon our ears. To all of them there have been or are frequent allusions. Scattered episodes in the history of some have been given in full. But, so far as I am aware, no attempt has been made to record in continuous narrative the whole story of these discussions; to bring to view and to contrast the different opinions held about Shakespeare as a dramatist and a poet, which at times have come into collision, and to trace their varying fortunes; to give a description of the disputes which have been carried on in regard to the proper method of settling the text of his works; and furthermore, to furnish some slight portrayal of the men, whether well or little known, who were concerned in these various conflicts, and to relate the precise part they took. It is these controversies which it is the aim of the present series to chronicle.

They naturally fall into two distinct and sharply defined classes. One of them is limited to the consideration of the art displayed by the dramatist, the other to the methods taken to establish the text of his works in its original purity. There are matters of dispute in regard to Shakespeare which do not range themselves under either of these heads; but, comparatively speaking, they are of minor importance. It is the controversies about the text of the poet which suggested originally the general title which has been given to the series, and formed the real occasion of its being. It soon became apparent, however, that the two classes, slight as seemed the relation between them, were after all inextricably bound together; and that in order to understand the one completely some knowledge must be possessed of the other. The attitude taken towards Shakespeare as a writer for the stage affected in the past not only the alterations made in his plays, but to some extent also the manipulations to which his text was subjected, and even the character of the corrections proposed or adopted. The consideration, therefore, of the controversies of this first class, though in a sense entirely independent of those of the second, rose naturally out of the latter. Accordingly in this series the history of the views entertained about Shakespeare as a dramatic artist, including as it does the varying estimates taken of him at different periods, assumes precedence of controversies on all other topics.

The discussion of Shakespeare's position as a dramatic artist necessarily involves reference to, or rather discussion of, various questions at issue between what we now call the classical and romantic dramas. Strictly speaking, this should imply a consideration of

the differences between the ancient and the modern
stage, between the French and the English stage, and
between the practices which have prevailed at different
periods on the English stage to which playwrights willingly or unwillingly conformed. The field, however, is
by no means of this unrestricted nature and extent.
By classical, it hardly needs to be said, is not meant
here the Greek or Roman drama, but the modern which
assumed that title, which professed to be a direct de-
scendant of the ancient, and was not unfrequently disposed to believe that it had improved upon its parents.
Its enemies, on the contrary, have been fond of applying
to it the term pseudo-classical. Between its methods
and those of the romantic drama controversy has raged
with violence for fully three centuries. Upon Shakespeare, as the chief representative of the latter, the
brunt of the attack almost from the outset has fallen.
National feeling has been aroused by it, and there have
been times when the conflict of opinion threatened to
assume something almost of the character of an inter-
national quarrel.

It is the English sentiment at different times which I
have sought to portray, and not the foreign, save so far
as the latter affected the attitude exhibited towards
Shakespeare by Shakespeare's countrymen. In one way
the difficulty of this task cannot well be overrated. It
is never an easy matter to ascertain the prevailing state
of mind of a whole people in regard to any author or
subject, even when ample testimony exists for contemporaries in the opinions of all sorts which are put forth
in profusion by persons occupying various points of

view. Far less easy is it when the evidence transmitted from the past is scanty and imperfect, and as a consequence almost invariably one-sided. In such a case there is always special danger of being unduly impressed by the little which chances to have come down. Scattered remarks, of no particular weight in themselves, have formed the foundation of many misleading statements in regard to Shakespeare's popularity at different periods. They have had the luck to survive the oblivion which has overtaken the others, and frequency of repetition has at last conferred upon them among the many an authority to which they are not in the least entitled. It is only by a full examination of the whole field that we can correct the erroneous inferences drawn from the assertions of individuals. In particular, it is only by the careful study of the critical writings, now often deservedly forgotten, of the men who took part in the controversies which went on between the adherents of the two dramatic schools, that we can get any real insight into the nature of the conflicting views which were held from time to time in regard to Shakespeare.

One exception there is to the statement that this work does not pretend to deal directly with foreign opinion. It is in the case of Voltaire. This author occupies a most conspicuous position in the controversies that took place in regard to Shakespeare's dramatic art ; and in the varying views entertained about it, the words he said, and the influence he exerted not only on the Continent but in England itself, can never be disregarded. It was my original intention to make the part he played the subject of a chapter in the present volume. But the mass of matter accumulated speedily rendered it manifest that it could not be satisfactorily compressed in so short a space. For Voltaire not only affected the opinions of others in regard to Shakespeare, his own reputation in turn suffered in the reaction which his hostile criticism of the poet provoked. No small share of the derogatory opinion expressed of him in England was due not so much to his attacks on theological belief as to his attacks on Shakespeare. The feeling showed itself early and grew in strength as time went on. For the adequate representation both of his own state of mind, and of the state of mind in reference to himself which he called into being, a separate treatise became indispensable.

So much for the controversies belonging to this first class. It was to those of the second, as has been said already, that the title of Shakespearean Wars was intended to be applied. These deal generally with the efforts to establish the text of the dramatist and with the linguistic and literary quarrels to which they have given rise. There was, however, enough of bitterness displayed in the controversies about his art to make the title not inappropriate to them also. Still, as the discussion was here mainly of general principles, it had nothing of the virulence which inevitably attends the discussion of words and meanings. The quarrels of Shakespearean critics and commentators have left enduring records of themselves in English literature. In them have been engaged some of the greatest authors of our speech, and for that reason, if not for themselves, they must always be of interest to educated men.

The moment, in truth, we take up the story of the
settlement of Shakespeare's text, we are entering into a
region of peculiarly embittered controversy. The *odium
philologicum* has always worthily maintained its place
alongside of the *odium theologicum* as a grand fomenter
of the evil passions which assail the human heart. Perhaps, indeed, unsoundness on a point of etymology or
syntax may be rightly deemed by the judicious to
betoken on the whole a profounder depth of depravity
than unsoundness on a point of doctrine or church dis-
cipline. At all events, I doubt if in the house occupied
by the *odium philologicum* there is a mansion roomier
and fouler than that given up to the *odium Shakespearea-
num.* Jealousies have been awakened by it and long-
continued friendships broken; unfounded calumnies
have been spread abroad which have never ceased to
follow their unhappy victim; and the course of its whole
history is strewn with the wrecks of reputations which,
when not wrought by personal wrongdoing, have been
occasioned by revenge, envy, malice, hatred, and all
uncharitableness.

Of these quarrels of Shakespeare's commentators and
critics it has always been the correct thing to express
disapprobation, when it has not been the object to
satirize. Speaking for myself, I am far from looking upon them as the unmixed evil which it is the
fashion to regard them as being. Critics and commentators, indeed, would rarely be selected as constituting
the ideal of a happy family. It is not from such a nest
of hornets that one expects to gather honey. But if
sweetness does not come from that quarter, penetration

frequently does. Few, in truth, appreciate the incalculable services which have been wrought by wrath in behalf of the advancement of learning. Love of an author will do much to promote inquiry and stimulate research; but in the case of no commentator will it ever operate with its fullest efficiency save when it is reinforced by a hearty hatred of another commentator, and a hearty contempt for the ridiculous opinions which he has seen fit to express. As little in the mental as in the material world can light exist without heat. At least this has been true of the past; and there seems little reason to think that it will be otherwise in the immediate future. When in the physical world some instrumentality shall have been devised which will illuminate and at the same time not burn, then we may have faith that in the intellectual and spiritual worlds men will learn to perform not merely the comparatively easy duty of loving their enemies, but the much harder task of bearing patiently with and even forgiving the imbecility which puts an interpretation upon an author's words and ideas entirely different from their own.

On this very point one announcement it is desirable to make. In no volume of this series shall I attempt to carry the account of these controversies down later than the beginning of the nineteenth century. It is a natural termination. No sharp dividing line exists, it is true, between periods in which belief in one thing ceases and belief in another begins. But with the close of the eighteenth century the old faith and the old assertions about Shakespeare's dramatic art may be said, in a general way, to have gone out; with the beginning of the nineteenth the new and now reigning faith came in. A statement not essentially dissimilar may be made in regard to the history of the text. In respect to its treatment there is a marked contrast between the general critical attitude of the two centuries. The general critical attitude, I say; for in both there are particular exceptions. But with this limitation it is correct to state that with the eighteenth century disappeared the violent treatment to which the language and versification of Shakespeare had been subjected; the calm assumption of editors that the transmitted text was a sort of dead substance, upon which they could operate at will, adding to it or rejecting from it or cutting it up in any way that suited their own pleasure. Such practices, to be sure, continue still; but they no longer continue to be looked upon with respect, still less with approval.

A specific statement I may be permitted to make in regard to my own treatment of certain phases of the subject. I have studiously refrained from resorting to comparisons between Shakespeare and the great dramatists of other nations, whether of ancient or modern times, so far as the degree of their achievement is concerned. In the history of opinion there is naturally frequent occasion to recount utterances of such a nature made by others. But comparisons of this sort, even when coming from men of highest genius, seem to me, as a general rule, to belong to criticism of a peculiarly valueless type. The cases are extraordinarily few in which they can be considered at all adequate; for the knowledge possessed by any one man of two contrasted authors is rarely equal as regards both, nor are the conditions the same which give him the means and capacity to appreciate each fully. Furthermore, such comparisons almost always reflect national prejudices when they do not personal tastes. Something of the same reticence I have observed in the discussion of the different methods employed by different dramatists, though this is a matter which falls legitimately within the province of the work, and is indeed essential to its completeness. No one, in fact, can write a treatise of this kind without having very definite opinions of his own upon the questions in dispute. It is right to give them, for they indicate to the reader the author's point of view. Still the expression of them here is incidental, not specifically designed. This is to say that the work is primarily a history of critical controversy, and not itself a critical estimate.

One further remark. The separate volumes of this series are intended to form complete works in themselves, so far as the particular subject is concerned. To all of them belongs the unity of a common interest; but each of them will constitute a treatise entirely independent of the others.

CONTENTS

CHAPTER   PAGE

I. THE DRAMATIC UNITIES — I 1

II. THE DRAMATIC UNITIES — II 37

III. THE DRAMATIC UNITIES — III 87

IV. THE INTERMINGLING OF THE COMIC AND THE TRAGIC 129

V. REPRESENTATIONS OF VIOLENCE AND BLOODSHED 174

VI. MINOR DRAMATIC CONVENTIONS 209

VII. LATE SEVENTEENTH-CENTURY CONTROVERSIES ABOUT SHAKESPEARE 257

VIII. ALTERATIONS OF SHAKESPEARE'S PLAYS . . . 293

IX. CONFLICTING EIGHTEENTH-CENTURY VIEWS ABOUT SHAKESPEARE 339

X. SHAKESPEARE AS DRAMATIST AND MORALIST . 379

BIBLIOGRAPHY 419

INDEX 437

SHAKESPEARE AS A DRAMATIC ARTIST

CHAPTER I

THE DRAMATIC UNITIES

I

" HE said that Shakespeare wanted art." This is the criticism of his great contemporary which Drummond of Hawthornden gives us as having come from Ben Jonson. There is no reason either for doubting that the man who reported the words reported them correctly, or that the words themselves correctly represented the belief of the one to whom they were attributed. In 1618 Jonson had made a journey to Scotland. While there he visited Drummond at his estate of Hawthornden. His host, who anticipated Boswell's conduct, though without Boswell's feelings of reverence, took notes of the conversation of his guest. Among the remarks of the latter were numerous comments upon his contemporaries, uttered with great freedom. The sentence quoted above expressed from one point of view his opinion of Shakespeare.

It was an opinion which with more or less of modification prevailed till within a hundred years past. In accordance with it the two great dramatic writers of the Elizabethan period were long regularly differentiated. The literary criticism of the seventeenth and eighteenth centuries with almost wearisome iteration depicts Jonson as the representative of art and Shakespeare as the representative of nature. This perhaps did not come to be the universally accepted estimate till after the Restoration. Still, the distinction, if not fully formulated before that time, was in process of formation. It may not be absolutely implied in the well-known reference in 'L'Allegro' to the " native woodnotes wild " of Shakespeare and the " learned sock " of Jonson. But in Milton's lines prefixed to the folio of 1632 there can be little question that, in asserting that the former writer's ease of composition was to the shame of slow-endeavoring art, the great Puritan poet had also the latter writer in mind. At any rate, as time went on, this distinction cropped out more and more in the critical judgments which contrasted the two men. Thus, in the commendatory verses to Fletcher, which were prefixed to the Beaumont and Fletcher folio of 1647, Sir John Denham assumes this difference between them as an accepted fact. As was proper in such a place, he gave to the poet he was celebrating the credit of having united in himself the varying merits of the two. But the characteristics which common consent had attributed to each are plainly marked in the following lines : —

> " When Jonson, Shakespeare and thyself did sit,
> And swayed in the triumvirate of wit, —
> Yet what from Jonson's oil and sweat did flow,
> Or what more easy nature did bestow
> On Shakespeare's gentler muse, in thee full grown
> Their graces both appear, yet so that none
> Can say here nature ends and art begins."

All through the following century this same view was expressed. Jonson's art, Shakespeare's nature, turn up almost as regularly as their names are mentioned in criticism. It was echoed and re-echoed by scores of persons who had the dimmest possible conception of what was meant by the words they were saying. How completely this method of characterizing the two men had become the merest commonplace we find indicated by Pope in his epistle ' To Augustus,' which came out a little less than a hundred years after the utterance of Denham that has just been given.

> "In all debates where critics bear a part,
>   Not one but nods, and talks of Jonson's art,
>   Of Shakespeare's nature,"

is the somewhat contemptuous comment he makes upon the now well-worn and conventional comparison. It is evident in truth, from the remarks scattered up and down the literature of the century and more following the Restoration, that a distinction of some sort was felt to exist between nature and art in dramatic composition. In the abstract such a distinction might seem without foundation. To some, indeed, it may even then have appeared absurd. Why should art be unnatural? That art should not represent some things in nature is a position perfectly defensible. But why should art be opposed to nature? Why should nature not be in accordance with the highest art? In the concrete, however, the question was invariably answered in one way, and it was answered in a way that for generations profoundly influenced the estimate taken of Shakespeare as a dramatist.

3

Let us, however, try first to ascertain what it was that the original users of this distinction intended to express. What in particular did Jonson mean when he declared that Shakespeare lacked art? He surely could not have intended to say that the great dramatist of all time was ignorant of the very things which were essential to success in his profession. In fact, in the glowing tribute which he subsequently paid to the memory of his friend he took care to insist upon his proficiency in the very particular which in the conversation with Drummond he is reported as having denied. He asserted that after Shakespeare the ancients — tart Aristophanes, neat Terence, and witty Plautus — please no longer, but lie antiquated and deserted, as if they were not of nature's family. Then he goes on to say, —

> "Yet must I not give nature all. Thy art,
> My gentle Shakespeare, must enjoy a part.
> For though the poet's matter nature be,
> His art doth give the fashion. . . .
> .   .   .   .
> For a good poet's made as well as born.
> And such wert thou. Look how the father's face
> Lives in his issue, even so the race
> Of Shakespeare's mind and manners brightly shines
> In his well-turned and true-filed lines,
> In each of which he seems to shake a lance,
> As brandished at the eyes of ignorance."

Jonson was not a man to use words at random or to indulge in meaningless compliments. Could any intention of the latter kind be conceived to have influenced his action, the responsibility of his position as the then acknowledged head of English men of letters would

4

have prevented their utterance. Clearly, therefore, the art spoken of in these lines is something quite distinct from the art which he told Drummond that Shakespeare lacked. What this latter was becomes apparent when we study with care one phase of the literary history of the Elizabethan period which has rarely received the full attention it deserves.

There seems to be a common belief that criticism is an art of comparatively late growth. It is frequently implied, and occasionally asserted, that the farther we go back in literature, the less we have of discussion of its principles, and that if we go back far enough we shall have no discussion of them at all. Genius, it is said, contents itself then with producing; it never stops to consider whether what it produces is in conformity with authorized canons of taste, even if it be aware that such canons exist. This happy condition of ignorance or indifference, assumed to be characteristic of early times, belongs to the realm of fiction rather than of fact. A critical age may not be creative; but a creative age is always critical. It has to be so by the very law of its being. The new experiments it is constantly making, the new forms it is introducing, the new methods of expression to which it is resorting, — all these compel it to give a reason for their employment to itself, if not to others. Whatever it does will be made the subject of comment, and consequently of attack and defence. Controversy, therefore, is always going on in a creative age. That the record of it does not come down to us at all, or at best comes down scantily, is due to other causes than lack of discussion at the time, or lack of interest in the subjects discussed. In early days there are no official organs existing for the purpose of recording the conflicting views and beliefs which divide men into hostile camps. Far the greatest part of the most thoughtful criticism then expressed dies away with the breath that utters it. From chance allusion only, or at best from occasional pamphlets, do we get any conception of the arguments that once tasked the intellects of the disputants and sometimes aroused their passions.

Naturally, therefore, but little critical discussion has reached us from the Elizabethan age. Still, enough of it has survived to make it clear that it was an age of keen literary controversy. During the whole of that period a furious war raged between the partisans of what we should now call respectively the classical and the romantic school. Though no such names were then known, the realities flourished as potently as they have at any time since. In certain ways the battle was then fought and won on ground which has never since been contested. It is easy to understand how the conflict should have arisen. The Latin and Greek literatures were the only ones with which the educated men of that day were familiar as a class. The steadily increasing attention paid to the two, which went on during the whole of the sixteenth century, developed at last a body of scholars who sought to make everything conform to the rules and practices which classical antiquity had established, whether suited or not to modern conditions. It met with determined, though to a certain extent blind, resistance from that new life which was running almost riot in the veins of the men who

6

were creating the literature which ir some respects we look upon as the proudest in the records of our speech. One phase of this long-continued struggle was the resolute attempt made to discard "rude and beggarly ryming," as it was called, and for it substitute in English poetry the metrical forms of the ancients. Hence in the literature of that period we come across dolorous sapphics, lame iambic trimeters, and lumbering hexameters; and in this slough of pedantry we find men of genius like Sidney and Spenser occasionally wallowing. Little success attended the attack on ryme, though it is possible that it may have had indirectly some influence in strengthening the tendency to make blank verse the favorite measure for dramatic composition.

A far more determined effort, however, was put forth to compel the drama of that period to conform to the rules which were supposed to govern the ancient stage. Conditions then existed which it might seem would contribute materially to the adoption of these. A movement of a similar kind had been begun some time before in Italy. There it had achieved a triumph. The example thus held out was full of encouragement to those who sought to rescue the English stage from what they chose to call barbarism. During the latter part of the sixteenth century and the beginning of the seventeenth, Italian literature exercised over English an influence greater than it has ever exerted since. Furthermore, the dramatic ideal set up by it came reinforced with the plea that it embodied the conceptions and followed the practice of the ancients. In this movement for the so-called reformation of the English stage we find the key to

7

explain Jonson's words. In his statement that Shakespeare lacked art is concentrated the issue which has been in controversy between the adherents of the classical and the romantic school since the birth of the modern drama. In this issue are involved several distinct questions. The one which has played far the most important part in the conflict has naturally the first claim to consideration. This is the doctrine of the unities.

It is outside the design of this work to enter into any account of this doctrine save so far as it concerns the English stage. For three centuries controversy in regard to it has raged with only occasional cessation. About it volumes have been written and further volumes are yet to be written. Even among its supporters there has been wide disagreement as to the exact scope of its rules. Here only so much needs to be said about it as bears directly upon the way in which, and the extent to which, it came to affect the English theatre, and as a result of that, the influence it exerted upon the estimate taken of Shakespeare as a dramatic artist. Scholars will forgive what will strike them as the obtrusion of the commonest of commonplaces when they find here a definition of the doctrine. In the varying interpretations which have at times been put upon the rules constituting it, the better course seems to be to furnish at the outset a statement of the precise meaning given to them in the following pages. They will be set forth as briefly as possible. The doctrine of the unities, it may then be said, consists in the three following points: —

First, the events occurring in the play acted upon the stage must be represented as having taken place within a period of twenty-four hours or less; that is to say, they must not extend over the space of one natural day. This is the unity of time. The reason given for the rule is that the duration of the action which goes on in the play should come as near as possible to the duration of the period in which it is represented. As the latter rarely covers more than three hours, the drama in which the events depicted as occurring come nearest to this space can be deemed the nearest imitation of nature. The time, however, has been occasionally lengthened beyond the limits here specified. Aristotle reported that such was occasionally the practice of the ancients. Corneille, who felt keenly how hard upon the modern author was the pressure of this rule, was disposed to prolong the time to thirty hours. This extension was assented to reluctantly, whenever assented to at all, by the stricter advocates of the doctrine. It was a concession to human infirmity which they might be forced to put up with; but they made no pretence to look upon it with approval. Furthermore, between those who were willing to prolong the duration of the action somewhat beyond the twenty-four hours, and those who sought to restrict it as nearly as possible to the exact duration of the representation, sprang up a third party, which insisted that the time should be confined to the artificial instead of the natural day. The period between sunrise and sunset was all that in their eyes could be properly allotted. Differences such as these, it will be seen, are mainly over details; they do not concern the justice of the rule itself. They are controversies simply between what is allowable and what is praiseworthy.

The second point is that the series of events that are represented in the play must be limited to one place. This does not ordinarily mean — at least in the English theatre — one room or one house. But just as the ideal attempted to be reached was to have the time of the action no longer than the time of representation, so also at certain periods, and especially in certain countries, a strenuous effort was put forth that nothing should take place in the performance of the play which would necessitate any change of scene whatever. The nearer an approach was made to this condition of things, the more it was felt that Art was justified of her children. Still, on the English stage this was an ideal rarely insisted upon, and less often attained. Much oftener was the requirement carried out that there should be no change of scene in any one act. But these are limitations which meet with favor or disfavor according to the opinions or prejudices of individuals. In general the rule means that the places in which the scenes are laid shall not be so remote from each other that the characters cannot be supposed to pass from one to the other in the limited time allowed for the action of the play. Consequently various localities in the same town may be used for separate scenes in accordance with this rule. On the other hand, it is impossible that cities in different countries — such for instance as Rome in Italy and Alexandria in Egypt — can be looked upon as being in conformity with its requirements. This is the unity of place.

The third point is the unity of action. About the precise signification to be given to this rule, about the nature and extent of its requirement, there has been even wider divergence of opinion than about the scope of either of the others. Certainly there have been wider divergences in its application. It is sufficient to say that as used in this work it means that there should be but one plot. Furthermore, the development of it must be orderly. Any matter that would interfere with this ought not to be brought into the play. This limitation does not necessarily involve the abolition of subordinate plots, though the rejection of any such has sometimes been proclaimed as essential. It requires no more, however, than the observance of the rule that if they are introduced they are to be made subservient to the main plot, and to help carry on its action and bring about its denouement. Were this not the case, we should be having, in reality, two plays instead of one.

These three requirements — of time, of place, of action — constitute, then, the doctrine of the unities. Upon them in the eyes of the classicists hang all the law and the prophets that have to do with the drama. Upon their exact observance depends the salvation of every man, not necessarily as a poet, but as a dramatic artist. The three unities, it has been said; but only two of them need much to be considered. Nobody seriously questions the propriety of the rule requiring unity of action. No adherent of the romantic drama ever denied its binding force, — at least as he understood it, and not as some one else defined it. Unlike the other two, it carries on its face the necessity of its being. As a con-

11

sequence, in the controversies which have gone on in regard to the unities, this particular one, though first in importance, has been the one least considered. In fact, it has usually been dropped out of the discussion entirely. It is the unities of time and of place to which alone attention has been directed. It is with them only that critical literature deals to any extent. It is they that are almost invariably specified when any attempt is made to test any particular play as to the degree of its conformity to the general doctrine. So regularly is this the case that when violation of the unities is spoken of in the following pages, those of time and place will ordinarily be the only ones intended, unless special attention is called to that of action.

It is hardly necessary to say that Shakespeare rarely conforms to these two. In the so called Histories they are absolutely disregarded. In them the period of time extends over many years, and so little attention is paid to the unity of place that successive scenes in the same act are sometimes supposed to occur in cities and countries scores and even hundreds of miles apart. These Histories indeed have generally been credited with being a law unto themselves. This was a feeling which showed itself at the very beginning. As early as 1591 Florio represented the views of the severer school of critics in saying that the plays the English stage possessed were neither right comedies nor right tragedies. He described them specifically as "representations of histories without any decorum." [1] The line of

---

[1] Quoted by Malone in his ' Historical Account of the English Stage,' Shakespeare Works, variorum of 1821, vol. iii. p. 41.

defence which has often been taken for these productions would strictly be inapplicable to the tragedies. Yet from some of these they differ in degree rather than in kind. The greatest of the latter, such as 'Hamlet,' 'Lear,' 'Macbeth,' and 'Othello,' disregard utterly the unities of time and place. In the comedies, while there is generally much closer conformity to these canons, there is wide variation from any strict compliance with their requirements. The time of the action is usually two or more days in those where the rules appear to have been most rigidly observed. In some instances it extends to weeks and months. In the case of 'The Winter's Tale,' an interval of sixteen years elapses between the third and fourth acts. In so doing, Shakespeare was only acting as did most of his contemporaries, though even among his fellow playwrights there were not wanting men to denounce the course usually followed as opposed to the example of the ancients, and therefore obviously reprehensible.

It is equally evident that it is Shakespeare's practice which is the one followed upon the modern stage. Stress is no longer laid upon the unities of time and place. In regard to these the doctrine is now so thoroughly discredited in theory and discarded in practice that there are playwrights of our day who, so far from accepting it, do not even know of its ever having had an existence. Accordingly it might seem an unnecessary slaying of the slain to consider it here at any length. Such an impression, however, would be a mistake. The weight which the belief in it has had upon the estimate formed of Shakespeare has been so unmeasured that a careful examination of its influence in English critical literature must always be a matter of first importance in the eyes of the special student of his career and reputation. Nor indeed can absolute confidence be felt that, at some period in the revolution of the ever-changing canons of taste and criticism, the doctrine of the unities may not, for a while at least, come again into fashion. It is improbable, to be sure; it is by no means impossible. The field of battle is at present held by the romanticists; but it cannot be forgotten that for nearly a century and a half even of the English drama it was occupied by the classicists. In France its sway over the belief and conduct of men was, from the middle of the seventeenth century, almost unmeasured. It was not, indeed, until 1827 that Victor Hugo, in the preface to his drama of *Cromwell*, sounded the trumpet blast that shook for the first time the literary traditions of his native land; for though at intervals inveighed against before, they had never lost perceptibly their hold. Yet even in spite of the triumph which he and his associates subsequently achieved, it is clear that the doctrine of the unities, though no longer held imperative, is still dear at heart to educated Frenchmen; that many of them look back regretfully to the days when submission to its behests was deemed absolutely essential to the highest art, and feel that the liberty now enjoyed is only another name for license.

Of any such sentiment there is now little exhibition among the members of our own race. Some modern English writers, it is true, have occasionally constructed dramas in which the unities have been strictly preserved.

14

They may have produced them for the sake of experiment, or possibly in accordance with their own convictions. Browning is a case in point. Three of his plays — 'The Return of the Druses,' 'Colombe's Birthday,' and 'Luria' — are all limited to one day and one place. Even 'Prince Victor and Prince Charles' and 'A Soul's Tragedy' — the last far the best of all — are divided into two parts; and in both each part strictly observes the unities of time and place. But plays like these — never acted or unsuccessful if acted — are not representative of the dominant influences which now affect the English stage. In general, these requirements, once deemed essential, are at present systematically ignored or contemptuously disallowed, even when they are not ignorantly disregarded. They are looked upon as trammelling the freedom of legitimate movement. If we are right now in this view, it is needless to add that Shakespeare was right long before. Was he therefore really wanting in art, as Jonson asserted, and as men continued to repeat for nearly two hundred years after Jonson was dead? In order to answer this question satisfactorily, as well as to understand the nature of the estimate in which the great dramatist has been held, it will be necessary to give a brief outline of the history of the doctrine of the unities, so far as it relates to the English stage. Then we shall be in a position to comprehend whether Shakespeare's violation of these rules was due to carelessness or design; whether his so-called lack of art sprang from ignorance or indifference on his part, or from an entirely different view of what constitutes art.

Aristotle, it is to be said in the first place, is the one usually credited with formulating the doctrine of the unities, basing it upon the practice of the Greek trage-dians. His name is almost invariably mentioned in connection with it. Accordingly, it is apt to strike readers with surprise when they find that in the treatise on 'Poetics' — the only work in which Aristotle touches upon the matter at all — it is the unity of action alone upon which he lays stress. About the unity of time there is but one sentence, and the observation in regard to it occurs almost incidentally. He is led to refer to it by his discussion of the distinction that exists be-tween dramatic and epic poetry. "Tragedy," he says, "is especially bounded by one period of the sun [that is, one entire natural day], or admits but a small variation from that period; but the epopee is not defined within a certain time, and in this it differs from tragedy, though at first tragedy, no less than epic poetry, was not confined to any portion of time."

This is the somewhat slender basis upon which the doctrine of the unities has been built up, so far as the one great authority credited with formulating it had any thing whatever to do with its creation. It is worthy of notice that Aristotle does not hold the action down rigidly to four and twenty hours. He allows a small variation from it, basing this privilege probably upon the occasional modification of the rule that was prac-tised upon the Greek stage. Nor does he even mention the unity of place; though it is just to admit that this is an almost inevitable sequence from the unity of time. But throughout there is nothing to indicate that he lays much stress upon the latter as a principle of vital importance. His language is not at all that of a lawgiver; it is merely that of an observer. He is simply registering the practice prevalent upon the Greek stage. He describes it in precisely the same way as he might have put on record a point of linguistic usage, about the abstract right or wrong of which he entertained no opinion, or at least expressed none.

It seems as if it must have been students of Aristotle, rather than Aristotle himself, who are to be credited with the responsibility for the great weight which was placed upon the doctrine of the unities and for the belief in its obligatory observance. It was in Italy that it had its birth, though in France it found finally its cherished home. Its history outside of the English stage does not specially concern us here. It is sufficient to say that the credit or discredit of having been the first modern writer to construct a drama in which the unities of time and place are regularly observed, is generally given to Giovanni Giorgio Trissino, a scholar and poet of the court of Leo X. He was born at Vicenza in 1478 and died at Rome in 1550. The play referred to is the tragedy of *Sofonisba*. It is commonly said to have been written in 1515, and was printed about ten years after. The example of Trissino speedily found imitators in his own country. It was not long, however, before the influence of the principles he advocated and of the methods he adopted began to be felt in foreign lands. Their progress was assisted by the increasing veneration which was paid to the works of classical antiquity, especially of Greek

17

literature. In time these rules came to play the same vigorous and damnatory part in the drama which the Athanasian creed has done in theology. It is hard indeed for us now to realize the importance that was once attached to the doctrine of the unities, how fervently or rather ferociously it was insisted upon, and how much opprobrium fell upon those who through carelessness about it, or ignorance of it, or disbelief in it, failed to conform to its requirements.

In England the doctrine was early advocated. Long before the coming of Shakespeare it had been preached as the only true dramatic gospel. For its disregard of it the English stage was taunted with barbarism. In the dedication of his comedy of 'Promos and Cassandra,' printed in 1578, George Whetstone expressed himself with earnestness on this very topic. He attacked the drama of Italy, France, Spain, and Germany, as deviating from the practice of the ancients in various particulars. That of his own country he held up to special censure for its disregard of the unities of time and place. "The Englishman," he said, "in this quality is most vain, indiscreet, and out of order. He first grounds his work on impossibilities : then in three hours runs he through the world; marries, gets children, makes children men, men to conquer kingdoms, murder monsters, and bringeth gods from heaven and fetcheth devils from hell."

Whetstone, however, was far from being a stickler for any rigid enforcement of the doctrine. He himself observed it with a looseness which would have brought down upon his head the heaviest censure of

its later advocates, had his work ever been brought to
their attention. In each of the two parts of 'Promos
and Cassandra' the time extends over several days; and
in the second part the place in one instance is transferred from the city, in which the scene is laid, to a
goodly distance in the country. One further comment
is to be made upon the value of the information supposed to be contained in the passage which has just
been quoted. When so much of our early drama has
perished, it is hardly proper to deny the veracity of
any statement made about it by a writer then living.
Still we may be permitted to doubt whether many, if
indeed any, plays were produced which correspond
closely to the description here given of the way in
which, and the extent to which, the unities were
violated. It seems a piece of rhetorical exaggera-
tion employed to emphasize an opinion rather than a
calm statement of fact. Ben Jonson in a similar
manner boasted that he had not made a child just
born at the beginning of a play become a graybeard
at its end.[1] No dramas corresponding either to his
or to Whetstone's account of the passage of time have
been handed down. Perhaps they never existed. At
any rate, it will not do to take this sort of criticism
too literally. During the eighteenth century Voltaire
gave his readers the impression that about twenty-five
years were wont to elapse between the beginning and
the end of a play of Shakespeare's. He repeated the
assertion so often that he probably came at last to
believe it himself; and certainly his disciples among

[1] Prologue to 'Every Man in his Humor.'

his countrymen had no suspicion that it was a mere figment of his own imagination.

But a far greater name than Whetstone lent its authority to this kind of attack upon the English stage. Sir Philip Sidney's 'Apology for Poetry' was not published until 1595, nine years after his death; but the date of its composition is usually ascribed to 1581. It could not have been later than 1585, the year of his departure to the war in which he fell. In this work he furnished ample evidence of the strength of the hold which the doctrine of the unities had taken upon the men of the critical school to which he belonged. Language is hardly contemptuous enough for Sidney to express his scorn for the neglect then prevailing upon the English stage of what he deemed the decencies of time and place. There is no hesitation in his utterance, no hint of uncertainty that he, and those who thought with him were not the people, and that wisdom should die with them. He first praised 'Gorboduc' as a noble play, which as it was in part the work of a noble lord, he was in all courtesy bound to do. "Yet in truth," he went on to say, "it is very defectious in the circumstances; which grieveth me, because it might not remain as an exact model of all tragedies. For it is faulty both in place and time, the two necessary companions of all corporal actions. For where the stage should always represent but one place, and the uttermost time presupposed in it should be, both by Aristotle's precept and common reason, but one day; there is both many days and many

20

places inartificially imagined. But if it be so in Gorboduc, how much more in all the rest, where you shall have Asia of the one side and Afric of the other, and so many other under-kingdoms that the player, when he cometh in, must ever begin with telling where he is; or else the tale will not be conceived. Now ye shall have three ladies walk to gather flowers, and then we must believe the stage to be a garden. By and by we hear news of shipwreck in the same place, and then we are to blame if we accept it not for a rock. Upon the back of that comes out a hideous monster with fire and smoke, and then the miserable beholders are bound to take it for a cave. While in the mean time two armies fly in, represented with four swords and bucklers, and then what hard heart will not receive it for a pitched field?"

This passage from Sidney is particularly interesting because it shows with what difficulties the early dramatist had to contend in designating place in a period when movable scenery was unknown. Still Sidney is just as earnest on the subject of time, in which the presence or absence of movable scenery is rarely a matter to be much considered, so far as concerns comprehension. He made it a point of special ridicule that a play should open with two persons falling in love with each other, and end in the space of two hours with the marriage of their child, including of course numerous adventures that had taken place between birth and maturity: "which," was his comment, "how absurd it is in sense, even sense may imagine, and art hath taught and all ancient examples justified." If we did not know that these words were written before Shakespeare made his appearance as a dramatist, we might almost fancy that the latter was the very writer Sidney had in view; for what the one described as absurd bears a reasonably close resemblance to what is represented as taking place in ' The Winter's Tale ' of the other.

Opinions such as these which have been quoted would hardly have been expressed, had not controversial discussion preceded their utterance. It is manifest that at this early period the thoughts of men had been directed to the question of the unities. A party certainly existed then in England which recognized and loudly proclaimed the obligation of their observance. Probably it was not large in numbers ; it was certainly feeble in influence. It did not affect appreciably the action of the great body of playwrights. The prominent earlier dramatists, Lyly, Greene, Peele, and Marlowe, — university graduates though they were, — paid no heed to this doctrine. The disregard of the unities which they displayed could hardly have been owing in all cases to ignorance. At any rate, in so doing they followed the general practice of their time. The situation was materially changed, however, when Ben Jonson threw the weight of his name in favor of the observance of these rules. Several things contributed to the influence he exerted. He was a scholar as well as a dramatist, and great learning often overawes contemporaries more than great talents, and sometimes even more than great genius. But talents and genius Jonson had in addition to his learning. During the latter half of his life, down even to his very death in 1637, he was the literary autocrat of his time. Both his influence and his unpopularity were augmented by the peculiarities of his character. In particular, besides his purely intellectual qualities, he had to a pronounced degree that pugnacity of disposition which in the case of many serves as an ample equivalent for actual ability, and as regards success in life frequently more than takes its place.

I am not forgetting the fact that long before the period of which we are now speaking, plays had appeared in which the unities are fully observed. There are indeed certain subjects, or certain ways of treating a subject, which may be said to exact this course. The plot of 'Gammer Gurton's Needle,' produced full thirty years before Jonson had written a word on this particular matter, almost compels the action to take place, as it does take place, in the space of a few hours; just as the plot of Randolph's 'Muses' Looking-Glass,' produced more than thirty years after Jonson began his propaganda, absolutely requires that the time of action shall be no longer than the time of representation. These are both plays which by the very nature of their being are obliged to observe the unities. Furthermore, before this same period there was a school of writers for the stage who in comedy professed to follow the practice of the ancients and in tragedy took as their model the dramas attributed to Seneca. In the latter pieces the chorus was retained after a fashion, monologue prevailed, and deference was paid to the unities, though they were not in all cases exactly observed.

23

But the influence of the writers of these productions was neither extensive nor lasting. The plays they produced were academic exercises rather than dramas. They are the outcome of the scholarly, or it would be better to say, the pedantic spirit, as opposed to the popular, or again it would be better to say, the national spirit. However much tragedies of this sort came to flourish elsewhere, they had in England only the sickly growth of an exotic, transplanted to an unsuitable soil and an ungenial clime.

Among the writers of this school were numbered some persons of scholarly attainments and one or two men of genius. Spenser pretty certainly belonged to it, though the comedies he produced have been lost, probably with little loss to his reputation. But the only name of eminence connected with it, whose work survives, is that of Daniel. It is significant of the immense sweep and force of the national movement which turned most literary activity in the direction of the drama, that it inspired or rather forced this poet to attempt a kind of writing for which he was totally unfitted. His two tragedies have the title and external form of dramas: they are really little more than discourses in the form of question and answer, with the questions very short and the answers very long. The first of these was 'Cleopatra,' printed in 1594. It is patterned upon that depressing Senecan model, in which everybody talks a good deal and nobody does anything at all. It is mostly written in quatrains, and consists largely of long speeches. The only ostensible reason for any one to ask a question is to furnish the one questioned with an opportunity of setting off on the production of another long series of quatrains. The piece was never acted; it hardly seems as if an English audience of any period could have endured its well-sustained tedious-ness. In it the unities are observed, though here, as frequently, exists that vagueness which arises from nothing ever being said about the time at all. Daniel's second tragedy, 'Philotas,' which appeared in 1605, is, as a drama, a distinct improvement. The dia-logue is wearisome, to be sure, but it does not always degenerate into monologue, and its quatrains are occa-sionally relieved by blank verse. But it fails unexpec-tedly in what the classicists would have deemed its most important feature. In the very middle of the third act three days avowedly elapse. The age had been too much for the poet.

But none of this class of writers had any real influ-ence over the practice, and possibly not over the belief of their contemporaries. It was quite different with Jonson. He plays, in fact, so important a part in the early history of the doctrine of the unities in connec-tion with the English stage, that it becomes a matter of consequence to determine his precise attitude. It is not an altogether easy task. Especially is it dif-ficult to ascertain it at the outset of his career. One indeed gets the impression that his views were for a time unsettled; at least that they had nothing of the positiveness which he came later to feel. Certainly his practice at first was far from indicating rigid obedience to these rules. One play of his — 'The Case is Altered' — was not admitted into the collection of his works brought out under his own supervision in 1616. Yet it was written as early as 1599, in which year there is a distinct reference to it by Nash. In this comedy the time of the action extends over several weeks, if not months, and the unity of place is very far from being strictly observed. But besides this play, which has come down to us, there are others of his which have perished. By Meres in 1598 Jonson is mentioned among the writers who are best for tragedy. But no tragedy of his produced as early as that year survives. Between December, 1597, and June, 1602, the manager Henslowe records the payment of various sums for six plays which Jonson was concerned in preparing for the Lord Admiral's company. They were written either singly or in conjunction with others.[1] Not one of these has been preserved. Nor is it impossible that he was producing at the same period pieces for other companies. Whether he was unable or unwilling to include any of these in his own collection we have no means of ascertaining. Yet it is no improbable supposition that he did not care to be held responsible for them, simply because they violated the doctrine of the unities of which he had come to be the declared champion. This is an impression which is made by his failure to include 'The Case is Altered.' It was a play of which he had no reason to be ashamed; yet not only did he omit it from the folio edition of his works, but he seems to have had no concern with its publication in quarto in 1609.

[1] See Henslowe's Diary, under dates of Dec. 3, 1597, Aug. 18, 1598, Oct. 23, 1598, Aug. 10, 1599, Sept. 2, 1599, and June 24, 1602.

At any rate, whatever his practice may have been originally, it is clear that, while still comparatively young, Jonson had begun to look upon the preservation of the unities as essential to the proper construction of the drama. Not only did he govern his own conduct accordingly, but he set out by precept as well as example to reform the English stage. The first of the plays included by him in the folio of 1616 was the one entitled 'Every Man in his Humor.' In that volume it is seen in its revised form; in its original form it had been published in quarto in 1601. In both versions the unities of time and place are observed. The play was first acted, as Jonson tells us himself, by the Lord Chamberlain's servants in 1598, and there is a contemporary reference to a performance of it in a letter of September 20 of that same year.[1] As found in the folio of 1616 it is preceded by a prologue in which the author criticised

[1] Letter of Tobie Matthew to Dudley Carleton, dated September 20, in Calendar of State Papers, Domestic Series, 1598–1601, p. 97. This date disposes of the theory that Jonson had fallen out with the Lord Admiral's company, in consequence of his killing one of its actors in a duel, and had on that account transferred his services to the Lord Chamberlain's company. Jonson's own statement that the play was first acted in 1598 is confirmed by the letter-writer who speaks of it as "a new play." This date for its first production would never have been seriously controverted, had not Gifford found the selection of another year essential to the support of the view he was advocating. He therefore not only followed Malone's conjecture that the 'Umers' of Henslowe's Diary was perhaps Jonson's play, but assumed that there was no doubt of it. His fictitious date of 1596 has ever since been treated with a respect to which it never had the slightest claim. Gifford was utterly unscrupulous in his assertions when he thought a view of his needed bolstering. He first stated something as probable, and then proceeded to argue from it as certain.

the evil practices of composition then prevalent. The disregard of the unities of time and place naturally received attention. The date of the composition of this prologue is unknown; but it is safe to say that it was never spoken when the piece was first acted. There was little limit, indeed, to Jonson's self-assertion and arrogance. Still he was not likely at the beginning of his career to put in the mouth of an actor of the company performing his play a criticism of the pieces they were in the habit of bringing out. But the prologue undoubtedly represented the feelings which he was then coming to entertain, and which later he took frequent pains to express. That portion of it which refers to the unity of time is comprised in the following words : —

> " Though need make many poets, and some such
> As art and nature have not bettered much :
> Yet ours for want hath not so loved the stage,
> As he dare serve the ill customs of the age,
> Or purchase your delight at such a rate,
> As for it he himself must justly hate :
> To make a child, now swaddled, to proceed
> Man, and then shoot up in one beard and weed
> Past threescore years ; or with three rusty swords,
> And help of some few foot-and-half-foot words,
> Fight over York and Lancaster's long jars,
> And in the tyring-house bring wounds to scars."

The unity of place is referred to further on in a line in which he assures the audience that the chorus shall not waft them over the seas.

The unities are not so rigorously observed in the second comedy which appeared in this collection. It was entitled 'Every Man out of his Humor,' and was brought out the year following the production of the preceding play. In it, as printed, Jonson not only supplied the text of the comedy, but set out to save the reader the trouble of criticising it by furnishing a running comment for his benefit. This work is intrusted to two characters called Mitis and Cordatus. The business of the former, as indeed his name suggests, is to raise feeble objections and to subside meekly the moment they are controverted. In all cases they are brushed aside instantly and almost contemptuously by the strong-minded Cordatus. He, as the author's friend, shows how silly and frivolous must be those who presume to find fault with anything which has been done. In the course of the dialogue between the two, which is entirely independent of the play itself, there occurs, among other things, a discussion about the unity of time and of place. This has an interest of its own, for the light it throws upon Jonson's opinions at that particular date. It had then evidently dawned upon his mind that as there had been an advance in the development of the drama among the ancients themselves, there might be an advance also after the time of the ancients. In the dialogue upon this subject Mitis insists that the whole argument of the play must fall within the compass of a day's business. The necessity of this Cordatus denies. He points out how in various ways the privileges of comedy had been enlarged from time to time by the Greek and Roman playwrights. "I see not," he adds, "but we should enjoy the same license and free power to illustrate and heighten our inventions as they did; and not to be tied to their strict and regular forms which the niceness of a few, who are nothing but form, would thrust upon us."

These words reveal to us the existence at that time of a class of critics who sought to restrain the liberty of the playwright by rules of severest strictness. With these sticklers for regularity, as it was afterwards styled, Jonson did not sympathize, at least then. He says of them somewhat contemptuously, that they are nothing but form; we hardly need his testimony that they must have been few in number. It is indeed noteworthy that Jonson, while a believer in the doctrine of the unities, ranges himself at this period distinctly upon the side of those who give to its requirements a liberal interpretation. This he does in practice as well as precept. The time of this particular play is not clearly defined. It is apparently rather more than a day and a half; though things are performed in it which in real life would have occupied several days. There is something of the same latitude shown in the matter of place. The scene announced as the Fortunate Island is actually London and its vicinity. In the course of the play it shifts from the country to the city, from the city to the court, and again from the court to the city. A passage in the dialogue between Mitis and Cordatus is here worth quoting in full, partly because it shows the extent of the privilege which Jonson was then willing to accord the playwright, but also because it is the first statement in our tongue of the assumed incapacity of the auditor to comprehend change of scene. This was subsequently to be echoed and re-echoed for centuries by the advocates of the unity of place. The words are as follows: —

" MITIS. What's his scene ?

CORDATUS. Marry, Insula Fortunata, sir.

MITIS. Oh, the Fortunate Island; mass, he has bound himself to a strict law there.

CORDATUS. Why so ?

MITIS. He cannot lightly alter the scene without crossing the seas.

CORDATUS. He needs not, having a whole island to run through, I think.

MITIS. No! how comes it then, that in some one play we see so many seas, countries and kingdoms passed over with such admirable dexterity ?

CORDATUS. O, that but shows how well the authors can travel in their vocation, and outrun the apprehension of their auditory."

The sea, it will be observed, was an insurmountable barrier; to cross it was license, not liberty.

In another class of productions Jonson went much farther than in this comedy as regards the freedom given to the dramatist. When a few years later he came to write his tragedy of 'Sejanus,' he gave up all thought of adhering to the unity of time. He acknowledged it in his address to the reader. It was impossible on the modern stage to conform to the practice of the ancients and at the same time interest a modern audience. "If it be objected," he wrote, "that what I publish is no true poem in the strict laws of time, I confess it; as also in the want of a proper chorus, whose habit and moods are such and

31

so difficult, as not any whom I have seen, since the ancients, no, not they who have most presently affected laws, have yet come in the way of." Two things are brought out distinctly by this remark. One is the existence at that time of a body of men who, to use Jonson's phrase, affected laws. The other is that in his opinion there was no hope of success for him who strove to revive the practices and customs of the past. "Nor is it needful," he continued, "or almost possible in these our times, and to such auditors as commonly things are presented, to observe the old state and splendor of dramatic poems with preservation of any popular delight." This was Jonson's position when 'Sejanus' was published in 1605. Nor does it seem to have undergone any change when six years later he brought out the tragedy of 'Catiline.' In that not only is the unity of time disregarded but also the unity of place. The same state of things would also have been true of the unfinished 'Fall of Mortimer,' the last work that came from his pen, if we can trust the argument prefixed to the fragment that has been preserved.

But, after all, these instances are exceptional. It was comedy to which Jonson devoted his main attention ; and comedy he held down unflinchingly to the requirements of time and place. His course of conduct follows, too, the common experience of men. When he republished in the folio of 1616 the play of 'Every Man out of his Humor,' he allowed the remarks about the unities to stand as they appeared in the quarto of 1600. His opinions in theory were the same as before ; but his later practice, for a while at least, became much more rigid. There is always a tendency to make restrictions voluntarily adopted into one's creed much more strict. An artificial regularity, the assumed beauty of which consists in its regularity, recommends itself more and more to the favor of those who admire it, the more closely its lines are drawn. Jonson, who in his comedy of 'Every Man out of his Humor' was theoretically willing to give his characters a whole island to disport in, and found practically that he had sufficiently satisfied the requirements of time and place in varying his scenes between the country, the court, and different parts of the city, soon began to manifest a disposition to subject himself to much more rigorous limitations of these laws. His three greatest works are usually reckoned 'Volpone, or the Fox,' 'Epicene, or the Silent Woman,' and 'The Alchemist,' brought out respectively in 1605, 1609 and 1610. The first is well within the rules, but the latitude employed in it is altogether restricted in the case of the second and third. In 'The Silent Woman' the time of the action is hardly more than that of the representation, and the change of place does not extend farther than the opposite side of the same street. Even this is surpassed by 'The Alchemist.' There the scene is confined to one house and the space immediately in front of it, while the time is no longer than that required to perform the play. In his subsequent productions Jonson did not conform to requirements so severe; but the ones just mentioned exhibit the ideal which he had in mind.

Nor, as we have seen, was he satisfied with enforcing the doctrine of the unities by his practice. In season and out of season he proclaimed its binding force. His position as its great expounder and champion was recognized by his contemporaries. In the commendatory verses which Beaumont wrote upon the play of 'The Fox,' that dramatist bears testimony to his friend's knowledge of

> " The art, which thou alone
> Hast taught our tongue, the rules of time, of place."

It was Jonson alone, it is to be observed, who had brought back to the English stage the simplicity and perfection of the ancients. To the same effect speaks Selden in some Latin verses addressed to the poet on his plays. Jonson himself proudly assumed the distinction. In his recommendatory verses to 'The Northern Lass' of Brome, published in 1632, he plumed himself upon it. He praised his old servant, now turned playwright, for the skill he had displayed in writing for the stage, and the favor he had justly gained in so doing,

> "By observation of those comic laws
> Which I, your master, first did teach the age."

Praise of the same sort followed Jonson when he was laid in his grave. It by no means limited itself indeed to his advocacy of the unities. The volume of commendatory verses to his memory, published the year after his death, contains several tributes to the various efforts he had put forth to purify the theatre from the ill practices of all kinds which he had found prevalent when he came to write for it. Cleveland spoke of him as the one " who first reformed our stage with justest

laws." To the same effect, but with more detail, wrote
Jasper Mayne. He commended Jonson's scene as being
free from monsters. No deity was called in to loose
the knot of improbabilities in which the action of the
play was involved. His regard for the unity of place
and his avoidance of the tumultuous scenes of the romantic drama were further indicated in the following
lines : —

> " The stage was still a stage, two entrances
> Were not two parts of the world disjoined by seas.
> Thine were land-tragedies; no prince was found
> To swim a whole scene out, then o' the stage drowned;
> Pitched fields, as Red Bull wars, still felt thy doom;
> Thou laidst no sieges to the music room."

Owen Feltham poured himself forth in a similar strain.
To the observation that with the career and death of
Shakespeare, of Beaumont, and finally of Jonson, the
stage had witnessed both her glory and decay, he added
this declaration of the influence which the last-mentioned
dramatist had exerted : —

> " Whose judgment was 't refined it? or who
> Gave laws by which hereafter all must go,
> But solid Jonson?"

Too much stress need not be put upon the exact accuracy of complimentary phrases paid to a dead man whom,
now that he was out of the reach of either praise or censure, all could unite in honoring. Still, there is no mistaking the meaning of the opinion generally entertained
about him both while he was living and after his death.
Respect could never have failed to be paid to the lofty
conception he had of the poet's mission, and to his un-

flinching determination not to allow his necessities to drag him into doing anything unbecoming the art he professed. Even those who did not accept his judgment and were offended at his arrogance must have admired the independence of his spirit. He represented worthily his side of the controversy which went on then between classicism and romanticism. Men at that time, as later, belonged consciously or unconsciously to the one party or the other. They did not dignify their differences by the assumption of titles; none the less did the realities exist. It is clear in the history of the early drama that Jonson was to his contemporaries as distinctly the protagonist of what we now call the classical school as Shakespeare has been to all succeeding times the protagonist of the romantic.

CHAPTER II

II

JONSON in the course of time became the literary
autocrat of his age. He was disliked by many; but
there was no one to dispute his supremacy. As he
was conspicuously identified with the cause of the
unities, it was inevitable that his advocacy of it and
his example should affect in some measure the belief
and practice of his contemporaries. The extent of the
influence he exerted in enforcing the obligation of
observing the doctrine he championed has never been
accurately determined. To ascertain it precisely would
require an exhaustive examination, with reference to
this particular point, of the extant dramatic production
of the seventeenth century down to the closing of the
theatres in 1642. A somewhat superficial examination
leads to the impression that the obedience paid to the
rules he proclaimed was exceptional rather than general.
A theoretical assent was perhaps given to their requirements, and respect professed for them as exhibiting the
only correct method of stage composition. But in
actual practice Jonson's example found few imitators
outside of that circle of younger writers who in his
latter days recognized him as their master. He himself was apparently not able to influence the action of

37

those in conjunction with whom he wrote. The comedy of 'Eastward Ho' carried on its title-page, when printed in 1605, the names of Chapman, Jonson, and Marston as its authors. Jonson's part in the production of this piece has been frequently declared to be slight. It is an assertion that can be safely made, as no evidence exists either to confirm or to confute it. But whether he shared much or little in its composition, he shared in the punishment inflicted upon its composers. Yet in this very play for which he suffered imprisonment, it is noticeable that neither the unity of time nor of place is observed.

Still there is no doubt that his teachings bore fruit, and to some extent speedily. Even early in the seventeenth century the preservation of the unities was an ideal which certain of the writers for the stage had come to cherish, and there is little question that in most cases this came to pass through his influence. Its actual achievement was regarded as something redounding to the credit of the author. At least that was the assumption on his own part. There was, for instance, published in 1611 a lively, bustling, coarse comedy entitled 'Ram Alley or Merry Tricks.' It was the work of a certain Lodowick Barry, who only exists for us as its author. In this play the unities of time and place are strictly regarded. The writer prided himself upon the fact. In his prologue he spoke of himself as

> " Observing all those ancient streams,
> Which from the Horse-foot fount do flow,
> As time, place, person."

In truth, not merely was the practice affected of those who looked up to Jonson as their leader, but occasionally that of his opponents. This can be seen in the literary duel that went on between him and Dekker. In 1602 the latter produced his 'Histriomastix or Player's Scourge' as a reply to 'The Poetaster' of the former. In it, very likely for the first time in his life, and probably for the last time, Dekker confined the action of his play to one place and one day.

It is manifest, however, that there was no general assent to the doctrine. To it, from the outset, there must have been not only vigorous but successful opposition. Few of the great names connected with our early drama conformed to its requirements save in occasional instances. Against it could always be cited at that time, as in later days, the practice of Shakespeare, even then reckoned by the multitude as the greatest name of all. Furthermore, those who pretended to observe the doctrine observed it very loosely. They cast a certain discredit upon it by the latitude they gave to place. They cast upon it still further discredit by enveloping the time of the action in a vagueness which renders its precise length very difficult to ascertain even now on careful reading, and must have made it impossible to detect in representation. That this was sometimes done intentionally there can hardly be any question. The writer sought to shelter himself from the tyranny of laws which he felt he must obey by shrouding in misty language the period required for the development of the plot. More than this, some of those who ranged themselves distinctly under Jonson's banner failed to live up to the austerity of his precepts. Brome, his old servant, tried, for instance, to conform to his doctrine in the comedy of ' The Northern Lass,' and succeeded well enough, as we have seen,[1] to receive commendation for it from his master. Yet in a play which speedily followed — ' The Sparagus Garden,' brought out in 1635 — the time of the action, though much wrapt in mystery, cannot be less than seven days.

It was not, indeed, until after the Restoration that conformity to the doctrine of the unities came to be accepted by the leading playwrights of the age as the only correct practice. French tastes and French critical canons had come in with Charles II. These tastes and these canons dominated English opinion in many ways for more than a century; but nowhere so much as in the theories held about the stage. In France the doctrine of the unities had established itself triumphantly. All opposition to it had been crushed. It was now about to extend its dominion over England. Its progress there was assisted by the authority of the purely classical school. From the period of the Renaissance there has always been a body of critics who have been disposed to look upon everything produced since the fall of the Roman empire as partaking somewhat of the nature of the frivolous. In their eyes any practice of the moderns disagreeing with that of the ancients is objectionable; or if not strictly objectionable, it is of an inferior character. These men are to be found now; but they were far more numerous one or two

[1] See p. 34.

hundred years ago. To them everything done by the Greeks or written in the Greek tongue was redolent of the odor of peculiar sanctity. All the influence they exerted was naturally given to the support of the doctrine of the unities; and among them are to be found one or two of the greatest names in our literature. In 1671 Milton published his tragedy of ' Samson Agonistes.' In it he added the weight of his authority to the critical views that were then beginning to be generally accepted. In the preface to his play he took pains to censure the modern stage for several things which are now regarded as redounding to its credit. Naturally the matter under consideration did not escape his notice. The unities he supported as earnestly as if he were a member of the French Academy. "The circumscription of time," are his closing words, "wherein the whole drama begins and ends, is, according to ancient rule and best example, within the space of twenty-four hours."

Not but that after the Restoration there were plenty of dissenters in practice, and a few in theory. To the former state of things both previous example and the natural indolence of man would contribute. There were authors who had little reputation to gain or lose. These did not care to burden themselves with requirements to which it was hard to conform, and for which the audiences they appealed to cared little or nothing. They knew, too, that they had on their side the great writers of the former age with the exception of Jonson; and Jonson, who observed the rules, was then no more popular with theatre-goers than Shakespeare, who disregarded them, and much less so than Fletcher, who observed them but rarely. But no indifference of this sort prevailed among the dramatists who were daily rising into prominence and favor. They took pains to conform to what was called regularity. Dryden bears witness to the feelings that existed on the part both of poet and of public in his comedy of ' Secret Love or the Maiden Queen.' This was brought out in March, 1667. In the prologue he boasted of it as having been written in exact conformity to the rules. In the preface to the published play he added similar testimony. "I would tell the reader," he said of it, "that it is regular according to the strictest of dramatic laws; but that is a commendation which many of our poets now despise, and a beauty which our common audiences do not easily discern."

This feeling about the necessity of observing the unities of time and place grew steadily from the period of the Restoration. During the eighteenth century it increased rather than diminished. By the middle of it Voltaire had become acknowledged as the supreme literary legislator of Europe. His attitude towards Shakespeare, and the English attitude towards him in consequence, will demand a treatise of its own. Here it is sufficient to observe that upon the propriety of conforming to the unities his opinions were of the most decided character. He had argued vigorously for their observance in the preface to the edition of his *Œdipe*, which was published in 1730. This preface was largely an answer to the attack of La Motte upon the unnaturalness of the French stage. That writer had shocked to the very soul the feelings of his countrymen by asserting that tragedy could properly be written in prose. He had gone farther. He had denied the binding force of the unities, and pleaded for their abolition. Such heretical views Voltaire felt called upon to combat, and, if possible, to crush. The French, he claimed, were the first to revive the wise rules of the ancient theatre. Other nations had for a long time refused to submit to the restrictions these imposed; but as the laws were just, and reason must finally triumph, they too had yielded. "Even in England," he continued, "at this day authors give a notice at the beginning of their pieces, that the time employed in the action is equal to that in the representation, and thus go farther than ourselves who taught them." It was a consequence that those ages, in which the practice was unknown to the greatest geniuses like Shakespeare and Lope de Vega, were beginning to be looked upon as barbarous. These opinions Voltaire held with increasing fervor till the day of his death. He never wavered in the view expressed in his letter to Lord Bolingbroke that the fundamental laws of the theatre were the three unities. He was of course mistaken — on matters of fact he was very apt to be mistaken — in his assertion that it was in France that the doctrine of the unities had originated, or from it had been introduced into England. But he was to this extent right that it was the French influence which came in with the Restoration that converted into positive obligation what had hitherto been deemed by most writers merely a matter of choice.

But the English never took kindly to the doctrine of the unities. The audience cared nothing for it: the writers for the stage, while generally accepting it, while professing to regard it as the only true gospel, invariably fretted under it. It was with them a belief of the intellect rather than of the heart. In the days of its greatest vogue this doctrine never gained in England any such foothold as it had in France. Many will see in this little more than a characteristic difference between the two nations, — one submitting impatiently to any restraint which hinders the freedom of its movements, grumbling at laws which it recognizes the propriety if not necessity of obeying; the other not only liking to be governed, but liking to feel itself governed. There may be a certain amount of truth in such a view. But it will hardly do to accept it as a full explanation. Experience shows that in literary fashions there are few practices or beliefs, no matter how unimportant or unreasonable in themselves, which any people under proper conditions cannot be trained to regard as of greatest moment. No better illustration of the fact can be found in the dramatic history of our own tongue than the attitude once taken by the public towards a mere accessory of stage representation, in itself absolutely unessential.

In general, at earlier periods, but during the whole of the eighteenth century in particular, every dramatic piece produced in England had to be preceded at its first appearance by a prologue and followed by an epilogue. It was not a matter of choice; it was one of necessity. The greatest play ever written, composed by the most popular dramatist that ever wrote, would hardly have been allowed, unless under exceptional conditions, to be brought on the stage without these accompaniments. Mrs. Centlivre, in her preface to the comedy of ' The Perplexed Lovers,' tells us of the resentment expressed by the audience because, owing to circumstances, there was no epilogue the first night. The requirement was often felt to be a hardship; and the freedom of the French stage from the obligation was many times remarked upon to its credit. But no disposition manifested itself to release the dramatic author from this exaction. These pieces were eagerly waited for by the spectators. Later they were regularly printed in the periodicals of the time. They were sometimes discussed as seriously by the critics as the play itself. Certain writers gained a special reputation by their success in composing them. A good prologue contributed directly to the success of the performance which followed; and while a good epilogue could not bring about a result which had already taken place, it affected to some extent the future of the piece. It served to send the audience home in good humor. We are told that Dr. Francklin's tragedy of ' The Earl of Warwick,' produced at Drury Lane in 1766, would have been condemned if it had not been relieved by a most admirable epilogue of Garrick;[1] and the assertion, whether true or not, bears witness to the popular belief. These appendages, therefore, in themselves of no real consequence, and having no bearing upon the

[1] Life of Francklin, in London Magazine, 1784, vol. iii. (enlarged series), p. 179.

merits of the piece, were elevated in public opinion to matters of essential importance. The custom died out in time because there was no real justification for its living. Still it continued to be kept up long after the taste which demanded it had disappeared. When in the early part of the nineteenth century the manager of one of the London theatres ventured to put a play upon the stage without prologue or epilogue, he did it with fear and trembling, and was agreeably surprised to find that their omission had excited no attention whatever.

Just so it was in France with the doctrine of the unities, only much more so. The public was trained to regard the observance of these rules as a matter of vital importance. No variation from them, no modification of their restrictions was allowed. To demand conformity to their requirements became so much a French critical practice that it may fairly be said to have in time become part of the French nature. But it was never thus in England even in the days when the unities of time and place were most strictly insisted upon in theory and observed in practice. Though the leading writers generally submitted to the rules, they did not do so rejoicingly. They felt the hardship much more than they appreciated the assumed æsthetic result. Shadwell, for instance, tells us in the preface to his comedy of ' The Sullen Lovers,' brought out in 1668, that as near as he could he had observed the unities. The place was a narrow compass, and the time did not exceed six hours. But "you cannot expect," he concludes with saying, "a very correct play, under a year's

pains at the least, from the wittiest man of the nation."
If such words could come from a professed follower and
enthusiastic admirer of Ben Jonson, we can easily get
an insight into the feelings of those who gave the preference to Jonson's greater contemporary. As time
went on, Shakespeare came more and more to the front.
His plays, and an increasing number of them, were
more and more acted. They not merely kept before
the minds of men other ideals than those then in
fashion, but the name of their author served as a standard of revolt about which the disaffected gathered.

For there was disaffection from the very outset.
Dissent in practice there always was; but dissent in
theory also continued to break out at intervals until it
became strong enough in time to supplant the established
faith. It was manifested early. No one who has fa-
miliarized himself with the critical controversies of the
Restoration period is ignorant of the fact that Dryden
and Dryden's brother-in-law, Sir Robert Howard, differed as widely about the unities as they did about
the use of ryme. The same arguments were then employed on both sides, which, as we shall discover, had
been implied, if not directly stated before, and were
to do frequent duty later. Howard insisted that one
stage cannot represent two rooms or two houses any
more truly than it can two countries. Twenty-four
hours cannot be crowded into two hours and a half any
more than can twenty-four months. All these things
are impossibilities; and impossibilities are equal and admit of no degrees.[1] The reply of Dryden was essen-

[1] Preface to 'The Duke of Lerma' (1668).

tially to the effect that though impossibilities are in reality the same, they are not the same to our conceptions. It is more in consonance with our feelings to accept a business of twenty-four hours as having happened in three, than a business of twenty-four years. Furthermore, one real place can easily represent two imaginary places, provided it be done in succession.[1] Dryden did not seem to be aware that in this last modification of the rules he was practically giving up his own cause. Still, most of the rising generation of dramatists ranged themselves on his side. Howard's was little more than a solitary voice; for while others doubtless thought as he did, few had the courage to say so. The weight of critical opinion was and long continued to be the other way. Moreover, it was positive in the expression of its views up to the point of arrogance and insolence. However much individuals might therefore dislike the doctrine of the unities or be disposed to deny its truth, they felt the pressure put upon them to submit to its requirements.

For all that, it was no few scattered persons whom Howard represented. They constituted a party, and it was a party which never ceased to exist. It may be said to have had the secret sympathy of most of the spectators; at least it never incurred their hostility. It was not, indeed, dread of the hearers that made the English playwright observe the unities; it was dread of the critics. This was a fundamental distinction between the English and the French theatre. It arose largely from the fact that in France the

[1] Defence of an Essay of Dramatic Poesy (1668).

audience was made up of a select class, while in England it was made up of all classes. But furthermore, in the critical world of the latter country there was always to be found a number who in theory at least did not bow their knees to this particular Baal. Some of them, too, were men who occupied a high position in literature. Early in the eighteenth century the dramatist Farquhar attacked the doctrine in his ' Discussion upon Comedy in reference to the English Stage.' Neither the men who originated it nor the men who defended it were spared. He spoke with the utmost contempt of the plays produced by scholars in exactest conformity with the rules, but lacking every quality that could interest or excite. Aristotle, moreover, fared hardly at the hands of Farquhar, not so much for what he had said himself as for what others had said that he said. The force of this special attack was largely impaired by his contention that inasmuch as the great philosopher was no poet, he was incapable of judging what constitutes poetry. This is of course a principle which, if fully carried out, would leave only to a cook the power of determining whether a dinner is good or bad. But his vigorous argument against what he spoke of as the folly of the unities was not weakened by the adoption of this ancient fallacy.

In regard to time, Farquhar maintained that if writers extended, as they ordinarily did, to twelve or twenty-four hours the action of a play which took but three hours in representation, there was no reason why they should not also extend it to days. Adherence to precise fact had been violated in the one case and had been authoritatively sanctioned. There was no reason in the nature of things why the same privilege should not be accorded to a further as yet unsanctioned violation of exactly the same character. A similar argument prevailed as to place. How can you carry me with you? he represents the objector as asking. Very easily, replies Farquhar, if you are willing to go. You enter the theatre, and as soon as the curtain rises you are told that you are in Grand Cairo, though the moment before you were in England. This is a most outrageous improbability, but you consent to it without difficulty. Then the curtain rises on a second scene, and you find yourself in Astrachan. Intolerable, you say. No more so than in the other case, is the reply. If you let your mind travel, it will perform the journey with perfect ease without the slightest disturbance to your person. There was of course nothing novel in this argument. It did no more than repeat what we shall see had been said by Shakespeare himself.

This was the protest against the observance of the unities put forth by a leading dramatist at the very beginning of the eighteenth century. In the middle of it views of the same character were expressed by two men of eminence, one of whom was a man of genius. These were Foote and Fielding. In a guarded way the former expressed contempt for the doctrine. "In general," said he, "these bonds do not hit the taste and genius of the free-born luxuriant inhabitants of this isle. They will no more bear a yoke in poetry than in religion." He added that Shakespeare, by heeding only

the unity of character, disregarded by the writers of
other countries, "had produced more matter for delight
and instruction than could be culled from all the starved,
strait-laced brats that every other bard has produced." [1]
It was almost to be expected that the doctrine in question should be spurned by the robust intellect of Fielding. Such was certainly the fact. In the critical chapter
prefixed to the fifth book of 'Tom Jones,' he took occasion to sneer at the authority which had been adduced
to bolster it up. "Whoever demanded," he wrote, "the
reasons of that nice unity of time and place which is
now established to be so essential to dramatic poetry?
What critic hath ever been asked why a play may not
contain two days as well as one? Or why the audience
(provided they travel, like electors, without any expense)
may not be wafted fifty miles as well as five?"

Incidental utterances like these could not be expected
to affect profoundly public opinion. An assertion of
this sort, however, would not be true of two fuller discussions of the subject which were made a little later.
In this controversy more weight should be given than
has yet been the case to the influence of Henry Home,
who in 1752 had been appointed one of the Scotch
judges of session, and had taken his seat as Lord
Kames. Ten years later — in 1762 — he brought out
a work in three volumes entitled ' Elements of Criticism.' It is not a treatise which, strictly speaking, can
be called exciting. Indeed Goldsmith is credited with
the assertion that it is one easier to have written than

[1] Foote's ' Roman and English Comedy Considered and Compared'
(1747), pp. 21–22.

to read. The ideas of Kames were often acute and suggestive; but in his way of expressing them he was almost invariably prosaic and dry. This characteristic, however, had its compensations. He got that reputation for being profound which comes to the author who makes the reader share in his own labor. Still, for a production of its kind the work was fairly successful, if, indeed, it is not entitled to be called popular. Before the death of its author in 1782 it had gone through five editions. It had early been translated into German. Even at this day it may be said still to survive after a fashion. There is no question that during the latter part of the eighteenth century, owing to the position of its author and the philosophical nature of the work itself, it exerted a good deal of influence, especially with the critical fraternity. This makes the opinion expressed by Kames about the unities a matter of some importance in the history of the controversy.

In regard to the doctrine, he took what was in some respects advanced ground for his day. His line of argument may be briefly stated. The unity of action is the only thing essential to dramatic composition. The unities of time and place stand upon an altogether different footing. Observance of these two latter had indeed been inculcated as absolutely necessary both by French and English critics. Such they were even acknowledged to be by the very dramatists who in their practice frequently disregarded them. These, however, made no pretence to justify their conduct. This task Kames proceeded to do for them. In requiring the modern theatre to conform to the ancient in the matter of the unities, he insisted that modern criticism was guilty of a gross blunder. The Greek drama was a continuous representation without interruption. Continuous representation gave no opportunity to vary the place or prolong the time. These unities were therefore with them a matter of necessity and not of choice. In the modern drama, on the other hand, obedience to this doctrine was a matter purely of choice and not at all of necessity. In it the stage is emptied at regular intervals, and the spectacle suspended. When the action is renewed, the mind easily accommodates itself to the variations of time and place that may have been introduced.

In some particulars Kames had anticipated the line of reasoning by which Lessing was a little later to demolish the foundations upon which the doctrine of the unities was built. In other ways he had not worked himself clear from the beliefs and prejudices of his time. He clung to the division of the play into five acts as something peculiarly sacred. Consequently, while time and place might be varied from one act to another, it could not be within the acts themselves. He further failed to comprehend the very strongest argument which Lessing subsequently brought against the obligation of the unities, and even went on to argue against its force. There is, however, a good deal of justice in his contention that unbounded license on the subject of time is faulty, not necessarily in itself, but because it tends to destroy the first and only important unity, that of action. The judicial attitude of mind which Kames preserved throughout his whole discussion of the subject undoubtedly contributed much to the favorable reception of his conclusions. His very moderation of utterance on certain points would recommend his views on others to many who would have been unwilling to cast off at one stroke the burden of traditional beliefs which had been brought down from the past.

But the most effective opponent of the unities during the eighteenth century was Dr. Johnson. It was in one of his essays in 'The Rambler' that he first considered them.[1] In that it was merely a part of a general attack upon dramatic beliefs current in his day. He specifically mentioned certain rules, then or formerly accepted as governing stage productions, as being nothing more than the " accidental prescriptions of authority," which, he added, " when time has procured them veneration, are often confounded with the laws of nature." As their origin was frequently undiscoverable, they were supposed in consequence to be coeval with reason. One of these laws peremptorily decreed by ancient writers — by Horace in particular — was that but three actors should appear at once upon the stage. This rule, for which there was no real reason, it had been found impossible to observe in the crowded modern scene. It had therefore been violated without scruple, and, as experience had shown, without the least inconvenience. In this instance Johnson found his own opinion supported by the opinion of his age. But hostility was manifested by him to the rule, then regularly observed, that the number of acts should be five. For this practice he could find no justification. The intervals in any given play, he

- No. 156, Sept. 14, 1751.

said, might be more or fewer than that number. Usually indeed they were different from it. As a consequence the rule was constantly broken on the English stage in effect, while a most absurd endeavor was made to observe it in appearance. Modern practice sustains Johnson's contention. Regard is no longer paid to this rule which Horace had authoritatively declared should never be trangressed in stage representation. To the unprejudiced observer, indeed, there seems no more reason that a drama should be in five acts than a novel in three volumes.

With independent views upon these points it is not surprising to find Johnson questioning the authority of the doctrine of the unities. At this time, however, he did little more than record his dissent. But when fourteen years later he brought out his edition of Shakespeare he was much more outspoken. In the preface to that work he not only examined the doctrine at considerable length, but he made no pretence to veil the contempt for it he felt. He ridiculed the idea that any representation is ever mistaken for reality, and summed up the situation by declaring that the spectators are always in their senses, and know from the first act to the last that the stage is only a stage, and that the players are only players. They do not believe for a moment that the place, where the scene is supposed to be, is Athens or Vienna or Venice or Verona, and still less that the persons who are speaking the words they hear are actually Theseus or Mariana or Shylock or Romeo. Delusion, if delusion be admitted, has no limitation. If a man, when the play opens at Alexandria, really imagines himself to be at Alexandria, he can readily imagine more. If at one time he can take the stage to be the palace of the Ptolemies, he can a little later as easily take it for the promontory of Actium. This, it will be seen, is essentially Farquhar's position. Yet while Johnson laid down principles like these, which seem to us almost commonplaces, he did it with a certain hesitation. He acknowledged that the weight of authority was against him and that he was almost frightened at his own temerity. These words are significant. Strongly intrenched indeed must have been the belief which could make Johnson falter about attacking it, whether it was held by few or by many, by great men or by little men.

Yet he must have met with views not essentially different in works with which he was familiar. Dissent pervades a good deal of the critical literature of the eighteenth century. It was to some extent encouraged by the wavering action of the advocates of the unities, which naturally did not tend to inspire implicit confidence in the justice of these rules. Dryden argued for them. In his earlier plays he had more than once pointed out how careful he had been to observe them with a strictness which the audience did not demand. The views expressed by him in the preface to 'The Maiden Queen,' he repeated in the preface to 'Tyrannic Love,' published three years later. In it he said that "the scenes are everywhere unbroken, and the unities of time and place more exactly kept than are perhaps requisite in tragedy." These words represent his earlier attitude. In his later plays

he was far from manifesting this scrupulous respect.
He sometimes regarded these rules; at other times he
disregarded them, and disregarded them deliberately.
Shakespeare, whom he had come more and more to
admire, was influencing both his views and practice.
In 'The Duke of Guise,' written in conjunction with
Lee and brought out in 1682, the unities of time
and place are not observed. It was not the intention of the authors, he declared in his vindication of
the play, to make an exact tragedy. "For this once,"
he wrote, "we were resolved to err with honest Shakespeare." The habit of erring is apt to grow upon men,
and this particular one certainly did so with Dryden.
He not only repeated the offence, but ceased to apologize for it, and in fact became somewhat defiant. In
the preface to 'Don Sebastian,' brought out in 1690,
he unblushingly declared that he had not kept the rules
exactly. These for some time previous he had begun,
rather disparagingly, to term mechanic. "I knew them,"
he said, "and had them in my eyes, but followed them
only at a distance; for the genius of the English cannot
bear too regular a play: we are given to a variety, even
a debauchery of pleasure." Accordingly he had lengthened the time of the action to two days, on the avowed
ground that it is lawful for a poet to sacrifice a lesser
beauty in order to secure a greater. This same heretical state of mind, expressed in about the same language,
can be found exhibited in the preface to 'Cleomenes,'
produced some two years later.

Even the professional critics themselves could not
be trusted to maintain the orthodox view, when it

suited their convenience to disown it. In the last decade of the seventeenth century Thomas Scott, a young graduate of Cambridge University, had caused considerable fluttering in the critical dovecotes by declaring that he who wrote by rule would have only his labor for his pains. This monstrous sentiment appeared in the preface to a play entitled 'The Mock Marriage,' which is said to have met with a good deal of success. The utterance of such an opinion aroused the indignation of Dennis, who took pains to point out that while one man may write irregularly and yet please, and another may write regularly and yet not please, still he who writes according to the rules will, other things being equal, always please more than he who transgresses them.[1] Dennis proved his faith by his works. The remarks with which he introduced his plays are interesting for the revelation they furnish of the strong hold which the doctrine of the unities had then gained. In the advertisement to the reader prefixed to his comedy of 'A Plot and no Plot,' he called attention to the fact that the action takes place inside of four hours. Yet to obtain this result he had sacrificed throughout the truth of life by representing the characters of the play as pursuing a course of conduct which could never have been followed by any persons outside of Bedlam. Had this been the work of another, no one would have been quicker than he to comment upon its absurdity. A little later in the preface to his 'Iphigenia' he took

[1] Dennis's letter of Oct. 26, 1695, to Walter Moyle, in 'Letters upon Several Occasions.'

pains to assure the readers of that tragedy that his aim had been to reconcile variety to regularity; "for irregularity in a drama," he observed, "is like irregularity in life, a downright extravagance, and extravagance, both on the stage and in the world, is always either vice or folly and usually both."

But the moment Dennis subjected to rigid examination the work of another who had conformed to these same rules, his eyes were opened to their impropriety, not to say enormity. In 1713 he published his remarks upon the 'Cato' of Addison. Never was a more merciless exposure made of the improbabilities and absurdities into which a writer can fall by strict adherence to the unities of time and place. It was the reading of this somewhat famous critique, while still a boy, which first led Jeffrey, as he said in 1822, to feel the contempt for these vaunted rules which he had ever after retained.[1] No answer could be made to it, and Pope's vulgar abuse of the author was itself a confession that its arguments could not be met. But it shows how great a revolution had taken place in the mind of the critic that by this time regularity had lost for him its charm. Dennis recognized the difficulty of applying the rules of the ancient drama to the government of the modern. He pointed out that the chorus rendered the unity of place a necessity to the Greek stage. But as the chorus had ceased to exist, there was in his opinion no longer any compulsion to preserve this unity. It was indeed desirable to do so, if it could be done without destroying the probability of the

[1] Edinburgh Review, vol. xxxvi. p. 423.

incidents. But if it could not be kept without making them seem unreasonable and absurd, far better that it should be discarded.

It would be an error to assume that utterances of the kind which have been quoted were confined to those whose intellectual superiority or peculiarity of character was sure to be attended with a certain degree of intellectual independence. During the whole of the eighteenth century disbelief in the unities can be found expressed by writers, some of them entirely unknown to fame now, and certain of them not too well known then. A few of them are worth noting. An anonymous treatise upon the tragedy of ' Hamlet,' published in 1736, denounced the rules as arbitrary and absurd. If they prove anything, said the writer, they prove too much; "for if our imagination will not bear a strong imposition, surely no play ought to be supposed to take more time than is really employed in the acting; nor should there be any change of place in the least." So far therefore from deploring, as was then the usual and correct thing to do, Shakespeare's disregard of the unities, he denied that there was any obligation on his part to observe them. He further pointed out that there were certain conventions to which we all assent without being in the least shocked by their inconsistency with the facts of real life. Change of time and place in the same play is no more absurd, for instance, than that all the men of all nations should speak English.[1]

[1] This pamphlet has been ascribed to Sir Thomas Hanmer by Sir Henry Bunbury, the editor of his ' Correspondence ' (p. 80). His authorship of it is so improbable that it may be called impossible. The sentiments expressed in it are not Hanmer's sentiments.

A more signal example of revolt was furnished by the commentator Upton. He was steeped in the literature of the classics; yet he spoke somewhat contemptuously of Ben Jonson for his deeming it a poetical sin to transgress the rules of the Greeks and Romans. He was himself not inclined to look with disapprobation upon the disregard of the unities which had been exhibited by Shakespeare. Dramatic poetry was, in his opinion, the art of imposing. Accordingly, if the story is one whole — that is, if the unity of action has been preserved — the spectator does not take into consideration the length of time necessary to produce the incidents that occur. It is the same with the unity of place. The artificial contrivance of scenes equally imposes upon the audience. It enables the hearer to accompany without difficulty the poet in the transitions he makes from one spot to another. But it is characteristic of the timidity of his age that Upton, after showing that neither the unity of time nor of place is essential, proceeded to remark that he was unable to determine whether they are essential or not. All he professed to do was to question the justice of insisting upon them as necessary. Others there were, however, who were bolder. Daniel Webb, a writer who had then some vogue, brought out in 1762 a work entitled 'Remarks on the Beauties of Poetry.' In it he maintained that to Shakespeare's neglect of the unities is due the singular energy and beauty of his style; that regard for these rules is sure to end in substituting narration for action, the tumidity of declamation for the excitement of passion.

After Johnson had given the weight of his authority to the denial of the obligatory nature of the unities, the number of those protesting became greater, and their expression of opinion much more decided. A perusal of the periodical literature of that day shows that dissent was steadily increasing in volume and energy. It manifested itself also in formal works, and in some instances where it could hardly have been expected. A writer of miscellaneous productions, named William Cooke, who flourished at that time, published in 1775 a treatise on the 'Elements of Dramatic Criticism.' On many of the questions at issue between the classicists and the now encroaching romanticists, he took very conservative ground. Still he did not consider unity of time and place as essential to the modern drama. All that he insisted upon was that the time should not be exceptionally long, — that, for instance, a child at the beginning of the play should not appear a full-grown person at the end. This was no uncommon view on the part of the disbelievers in the unities; it had been expressed but a little while before by Kames. But the extent to which the revolt against the doctrine was now beginning to go was evidenced in the biographical history of English literature which still preserves, so far as it is preserved, the name of Berkenhout. This work was published in 1777. The independence of its author was exhibited by one peculiarity. Berkenhout was an ardent admirer of Voltaire. There was little limit to the homage which he paid to the character, the genius, and the philanthropy of that writer. In this very volume he spoke of him as the scourge of sancti-

fied tyranny, and the advocate of oppressed innocence
who deserved the thanks of all mankind. On the subject of the unities, however, he considered that Voltaire
was wholly wrong. Of these rules Berkenhout spoke
in terms of vituperation rather than censure. According to him they were the inventions of dulness, and
served merely as leading-strings for puny poetasters.
Shakespeare was perfectly right in rejecting them. The
result of obeying them led, in Berkenhout's opinion, to
nothing but the production of monstrosities. "I never
saw or read," he asserted, "a tragedy or comedy fettered
by the unities, which did not seem improbable, unnatural,
or tedious." [1]

As the century approached its close this voice of
dissent became bolder and louder. The critical world
gradually ranged itself into two distinct parties; but
it is plain that the one opposed to the unities grew
steadily more numerous and aggressive. Some there
were who sought to take a middle course, such as
Chesterfield had advocated at an earlier period. The
time was to be somewhat extended, and change of
place allowed to spots adjacent to the principal scene
of the action.[2] But compromises never satisfy in time
of war. In general the old belief was stoutly maintained by the writers for the periodical press, and
these were not unfrequently reinforced by men occupying prominent positions in the learned world.
Shakespeare's "inattention to the laws of unity" was

[1] Biographia Literaria, Preface, p. xxxii.
[2] See Chesterfield, Letter to his son, Jan. 23, 1752; and 'Observations on Tragedy,' appended to Hodson's 'Zoraida' (1780), p. 87.

lamented by Richardson, professor of humanity in
the university of Glasgow. This author was in many
ways an enthusiastic admirer of the poet. But the
wish to keep the public taste from becoming tainted,
the hope to remove all obstacles which retarded the
improvement of dramatic writing, compelled him to
do violence to his feelings by censuring the grave
fault Shakespeare had committed in disregarding these
rules. This same conduct on the part of the poet
naturally fell under the condemnation of Richardson's
fellow professor in the neighboring university of Edinburgh, Hugh Blair, a perfectly conventional critic of the
old and now rapidly disappearing type.

In Scotland, indeed, due possibly to the influence
of Hume, belief in the unities seems to have lingered
longer than elsewhere in the United Kingdom; as if
the ancient military alliance with France had been
replaced by a literary one. Still it is fair to add
that Beattie from his northern university joined the
forces of those opposed to the doctrine, by taking the
ground that conformity to its requirements was not
an essential but a merely mechanical rule of composition. He had not made the acquaintance or gained
the patronage of Johnson in vain; and in his 'Dissertations Moral and Critical,' which he brought out in
1783, he followed the footsteps of his leader. He
attacked the necessity of five acts.[1] He repeated with
variation of phrase and feebler speech Johnson's argument against the unities.[2] So some years previously
had the Italian Baretti done in the reply which he

---

[1] Dissertations, p. 180.   [2] Ibid. p. 188.

had made to Voltaire's attack upon Shakespeare before the French Academy. At a still later period we
find the historian and essayist, Belsham, insisting that
the unity of action was the only thing of importance
in the drama; that the supposed necessity of imposing upon the hearers was a pure illusion; that in
the representation of a tragedy not only are we not
deceived, but we should be miserable if we were.[1]
These are the sort of ideas which were becoming
more and more prevalent. By the time the century had
reached its close, belief in the doctrine of the unities
had largely faded away. It did not actually die with
its expiring breath, but it was in a dying condition.

Yet for nearly the whole of the latter half of the
eighteenth century all this dissent, all these attacks
had but little influence upon the practice of the prominent playwrights of the time. These accepted the
unities sometimes gladly, sometimes grudgingly; but
in any case they accepted them. Those who found
most difficulty in conforming to their requirements
might hope that relief was coming; but if so, it was
not advanced by any action on their own part. In
truth, they lived in perpetual awe of the adherents
of the classical school. These men still held the post
of control in the official organs of critical opinion, and
they generally stood ready to fall foul of the venturesome author who did not heed strictly the proper observance of time and place. It was the one thing
over which these petty critics kept constant watch.
Other offences might find palliation, if not forgive-

[1] Essays Historical and Literary (ed. of 1799), vol. ii. p. 551.

ness; this was the one unpardonable sin. Berkenhout, whose bold denunciation of the unities has just
been quoted, was cautioned by a friendly reviewer that
he ought to pay greater deference to public opinion.
His words showed that he was as heterodox in the
matter of the drama as he was in that of divinity.[1]
Such was the attitude taken generally by the body
of professional critics. Now and then, as we have
seen, a voice was raised in opposition. This occurred
more frequently as time went on; but for a good
while the current ran too strongly to be successfully
resisted. References to this condition of things are
not unfrequent in the dramatic literature of the time.
Dr. John Brown's tragedy of 'Athelstan,' for instance,
was brought out in 1756. Garrick wrote the epilogue
to it, and in that commented upon the various kinds
of taste which the writers for the stage felt bound to
consult. Among others he specified the " Greek-read
critic," who speaks with contempt of modern tragedy,
but

> " Excuses want of spirit, beauty, grace,
> But ne'er forgives her failing — time and place."

It is in the prologues to plays that we find reflected most clearly the varying beliefs not only of
different men but of different periods during the
eighteenth century. But amid the ebb and flow of
opinions about dramatic art expressed in these productions, one view remains fixed. This is the invariable deference paid to Shakespeare. The concession
was frequently, almost constantly, made that he was

---

[1] Kenrick's 'London Review,' May, 1776, vol. v. p. 350.

exempt from the operation of those laws by which
the action of others was held in check. But though
the possession of boundless genius entitled him to
pardon, no mercy was shown to the admirer who ventured to imitate his practices. Such a one must not
seek to shelter himself under the sovereignty of Shakespeare. That dramatist had received a sort of divine
right to act wrong. The prologues expressing this view
embrace other differences between the classical and
the romantic drama than the question of the unities;
but still this was the one upon which the principal
stress was almost invariably laid. To diverge from
its requirements might be permitted to the genius of
Shakespeare, overriding all rule; but no such liberty
was permitted to the modern writer. He could not
hope to approach the excellence of the great dramatist.
It was therefore all the more incumbent upon him,
since he was sure to lack Shakespeare's positive merits,
to free himself from that author's faults or supposed
faults. As examples both of the view itself and of
the occasional protests made against its enforcement,
it may be well to select certain passages from the
prologues to three plays produced at different periods
during the century.

In 1712 Ambrose Philips produced at Drury Lane
an adaptation of the *Andromaque* of Racine under
the title of 'The Distrest Mother.' The prologue was
written by Sir Richard Steele. It took up the question
of the unities, enlarged upon the necessity of the rules,
and censured particularly those who conveyed their
audience where they chose, and made the stage rep-

resent all countries the sun visited. The inevitable
objection based upon the conduct of Shakespeare necessarily came up for consideration; and it is in this
way that it was summarily disposed of by Steele: —

" But Shakespeare's self transgressed; and shall each elf,
  Each pigmy genius, quote great Shakespeare's self!
  What critic dares prescribe what 's just and fit,
  Or mark out limits for such boundless wit!
  Shakespeare could travel through earth, sea and air,
  And paint out all the powers and wonders there.
  In barren desarts he makes nature smile,
  And gives us feasts in his enchanted isle.
    Our author does his feeble force confess,
  Nor dares pretend such merit to transgress;
  Does not such shining gifts of genius share,
  And therefore makes propriety his care.
  Your treat with studied decency he serves ;
  Not only rules of time and place preserves,
  But strives to keep his characters entire,
  With French correctness and with British fire."

This is the point of view of the early part of the
eighteenth century. By the middle of it men had
begun to long for the freedom which they did not
venture to assume. Colman, in his prologue to Dr.
Francklin's 'Earl of Warwick,' brought out in 1766,
declared that, in times of old, scholars only durst presume to judge. Now, he adds, every journalist has
turned Stagirite. The modern writer, in consequence,
while envying and admiring the freedom of Shakespeare, does not venture to follow in his footsteps, so
much does the fear of little men hold in check the
courage of the ablest and boldest. It is in these
words that Colman pictures the situation: —

" In Shakespeare's days when his adventurous muse,
A muse of fire ! durst each bold license use,
Her noble ardor met no critic's phlegm,
To check wild fancy or her flight condemn.
Ariels and Calibans unblam'd she drew,
Or goblins, ghosts or witches brought to view.
If to historic truth she shap'd her verse,
A nation's annals freely she 'd rehearse ;
Bring Rome or England's story on the stage,
And run in three short hours thro' half an age.
Our bard all terror-struck, and filled with dread,
In Shakespeare's awful footsteps dares not tread :
Through the wide field of history fears to stray,
And builds upon one narrow spot his play,
Slips not from realm to realm, whole seas between,
But barely changes twice or thrice his scene,
While Shakespeare vaults on the poetic wire,
And pleased spectators fearfully admire."

Thirteen years later Jephson, in the prologue to his own
'Law of Lombardy,' contrasts the liberty of the ancient
stage with the restrictions placed upon the modern.
The only toil of the old writers, he said, was to achieve
with success dialogue and ryme.   The unities either
they did not know, or if they knew they despised.
They could open a piece in Mexico, if they chose,
and end it in Greece. Now all was changed. The
author appears now before a learned tribunal, quick
to detect violation of law and ready to condemn it.
" Nor," he adds,

> "Let presumptuous poets fondly claim
> From rules exemption by great Shakespeare's name;
> Tho' comets move with wild eccentric force,
> Yet humbler planets keep their stated course."

If authors anticipate the rod for deviation from rule,
it is hardly in human nature that critics should refrain

from disappointing their expectations. The result was that the practice of observing the unities in dramatic productions continued to prevail a good while after faith in them had generally died out. By the beginning of the nineteenth century the belief maintained but a lingering life in England. Johnson's dictum that the stage was only a stage, and that the spectators knew it was only a stage, carried its truth on its face; otherwise the scenes of suffering represented would not awaken pity but pain. Minds not already prepossessed by mechanical criticism, he had observed, feel no offence at the extension of the intervals of time between the acts. Equally was this true of change of place. The maintainers of the old doctrine never stopped to ask whether the hearer was actually disturbed by the alteration of the scene. As a matter of fact he was not. Still, according to their view this was no justification. It was his business to be disturbed. If he failed to be, his conduct was reprehensible. To the existence of fictitious states of mind like this the believers in the unities clung to the last. In truth, to how late a period the doctrine continued to keep its hold over the minds of superior men can be inferred from the preface which Walter Scott furnished to Dryden's 'All for Love.' In this driven from the position that the argument in favor of the unities depends upon preserving the deception of the scene, he proceeded to maintain that it was necessarily connected with the intelligibility of the piece. Scott gravely informed us that it is a cruel tax, both upon the spectator's imagination and his power of

comprehension, to transfer him from a scene which
he has made up his mind to let pass temporarily for
one place to another far distant with which he has
to form new associations.[1] Did any one ever actually
feel this tax upon his imagination or comprehension?
Scott never asked. He assumed it, and then asserted
it. In the character of his criticism we see the belief
in the unities in its dying agonies.

Towards the end of the century the playwrights at
last began occasionally to pluck up courage. From the
outset, while the critical opinion had been nearly all one
way, the popular opinion, as we have seen from Dryden's
words, was largely another. The bolder or more impatient spirits even among its believers were in consequence prompted to transgress these rules, and did
not always withstand the temptation. Early in the
eighteenth century Mrs. Centlivre, in the preface to
her comedy of 'Love's Contrivance,' informed us that
the audience cared nothing about their observance; and
therefore, while admitting their justice and the desirability of heeding them, she had not taken the pains to
do so in this instance. The same view of the public
indifference was implied by Aaron Hill a little later.
In the preface to his 'Elfrid,' brought out in 1710,
he remarked that he had observed the unities to a greater
nicety than an English audience would probably think
necessary; for the scene was confined to a house and
garden, and the time was no more than the play required
for its representation. About the middle of the century
the tragedy of 'Philoclea' was produced at Covent Gar-

[1] Scott's Dryden, vol. v. p. 287 (1808).

den and met with a fair degree of success. It is only worthy of notice here from the fact, commented on at the time, that its author, McNamara Morgan, boldly disavowed allegiance to one of the then established laws of the drama. "The unity of place," he said in his preface, "I have disregarded, because I have observed such regularity has seldom pleased an English audience."

Courage and conduct like this were rare. The usual state of mind is exemplified by Dodsley, who was careful to prefix to his tragedy of 'Cleone,' brought out in 1758, that the time of the action was that of the representation. But aversion to the doctrine, which had always been latent among the playwrights, slowly spread. In the last quarter of the century it broke out into open revolt. Not only were the unities occasionally violated, but what was more significant, a contemptuous opinion was sometimes expressed of their importance. Here, as before, the prologues reveal the change that was coming over the minds of men. In January, 1785, Kemble brought out 'The Maid of Honor,' altered from Massinger. It met with no success and it was never printed. But the prologue remains. The remarkable thing about that is the view expressed in it of the unities. These were no longer held up as things desirable in themselves to be observed, even though it were not done. They were something rather to be shunned. This was a sort of view which had not unfrequently been taken in the case of Shakespeare; but it was certainly very unusual, if not absolutely unprecedented, to apply words like the following to the work of an inferior dramatist: —

> " Fired by the subject, the nice bounds of art
> His muse o'erleaps, and rushes to the heart.
> Disdains the pedant rules of time and place,
> Extends the period and expands the space;
> From state to state, without a pause, does run,
> Whilst with a thought, ' the battle 's lost and won:'
> Impetuous fancy rides the veering wind,
> And actionless precision leaves behind." [1]

This was an old play revamped; but a few years later the same liberty of action was taken with one entirely new. In 1792 the dramatist, Thomas Morton, rejected the observance of the unities in his historical play of 'Columbus.' He did it designedly. It is in these words the prologue announced his intention:—

> " The rigid laws of time and place our bard
> In this night's drama ventures to discard;
> If here he errs — he errs with *him* whose name
> Stands without rival on the rolls of fame;
> *Him* whom the passions own with one accord
> Their great dictator and despotic lord."

Even this attitude, little apologetic as it was, did not long continue. In time not only were the unities violated, but all reference to the fact ceased. When that omission became general, it was clear that belief in them had lost all its vitality. It was only a question of time when disregard of their requirements would become the merest matter of course. It was only a matter of a little longer time when playwrights would arrive at the situation which it was long supposed

---

[1] This prologue was written by the Hon. Henry Phipps, afterward Lord Mulgrave. It can be found in the 'European Magazine,' vol. vii. p. 142, and in the 'London Magazine,' vol. iv. (new series) p. 137.

that Shakespeare himself had occupied. They would violate the rules in happy unconsciousness that any rules ever existed.

There was, however, a good deal more to be said on this subject than had been said. But it was not then said in England; nor was the demolition of the scientific basis upon which the doctrine of the unities pretends to rest, due to English criticism. In that country the champions of Shakespeare had stood, as regards this particular point, almost entirely on the defensive. They did not deny the perfect propriety of the rules, if one chose to observe them, no matter what was the character and conduct of the piece; what they denied was merely the necessity of their observance. Even in the case of the very few who went farther, it was to the feelings they appealed and not to the reason. Berkenhout's attack on the doctrine, for instance, is pure denunciation. He offers no argument; he simply expresses a personal opinion. It was reserved for the man of another country to proclaim Shakespeare as the true modern inheritor of Greek art. It was left for him to assume the offensive and carry the war into the enemy's territory; to maintain that the vaunted deference to the requirements of the unities boasted of by the French dramatists, was due to imperfect comprehension or wilful perversion of the principles laid down by the ancients; that these dramatists had mistaken the incidental for the essential, and even then, after making it essential, had gone about, not to conform to it honestly, but to evade it, to circumvent its plain-

est provisions by devices which enabled them to keep
up a show of obedience to the doctrine while violating its spirit. Little did the men of that time
either in France or England suspect, even less would
they then have been disposed to acknowledge, that
in Germany had arisen a dramatic critic far greater
than either Voltaire or Johnson. Yet this is the
position which few will now be disposed to deny
to Lessing. His recognition of Shakespeare's superiority to modern dramatists, not merely in poetic
achievement but in poetic art, had been proclaimed
several years before; but it was not until 1767, in
the successive numbers of the *Hamburgische Dramaturgie*, that he gave the reasons for his faith. Much
has been written since on the subject, and much more
in quantity than he wrote; but Lessing's comparatively
brief discussion of it still remains unsurpassed. To him
belongs the credit of being the first to demonstrate the
inapplicability of the unities to the modern drama except under special conditions, — conditions which the
modern author is generally unwilling to observe.

Germany has often shown a disposition to assert
that it was she who first appreciated the greatness
of Shakespeare. No assumption has been more indignantly scouted by English and American students
of the poet. In one way there is a great deal in the
claim that is peculiarly ridiculous. At the time at
which we have arrived Shakespeare was no better
known in Germany than he was in France, if in fact
so well. He was not so much depreciated, indeed, as
he was ignored. What acquaintance existed with his

writings was confined to a very small body of men. There had been a few scattered translations of single plays. Of twenty-two of them Wieland had published a version between 1762 and 1766. But this had not made Shakespeare known. The work was but little read. To this fact Lessing himself bears testimony that cannot be impeached. He commented on the indignation he aroused by his perpetual insistence upon the superiority of the great English dramatist to Corneille and Racine. "Always Shakespeare, always Shakespeare!" he represents his impatient countrymen as exclaiming, "and we cannot even read him." He therefore took the opportunity to inform them of something which they apparently preferred to forget. It was that a translation of the poet already existed. It is not yet completed, he added, and yet no one troubles himself any longer about it.[1] This would be decisive, if indeed any proof of it were needed, against the pretence that appreciation of Shakespeare had its origin in Germany. That country indeed was at this time dragged hand and foot at the car of French criticism; and there is something almost pathetic in the way in which Lessing occasionally refers to the intellectual servitude under which his countrymen were so far from groaning that they hugged their chains. To strike off the shackles by which they were fettered was his constant aim; yet at times there clearly came over his spirit a feeling of doubt and almost of despair at the apparent hopelessness of the task.

[1] Hamburgische Dramaturgie, No. 15, June 19, 1767.

But though England owes nothing to Germany for the appreciation of Shakespeare as a poet, the latter country may justly claim that it took the lead in establishing upon solid ground his supremacy as a dramatic artist. The admiration expressed for him in his own land was then, and to some extent has since remained, a blind admiration. On the question of his art his most enthusiastic advocates spoke ignorantly when they did not speak hesitatingly. Such was not the case with Lessing. There was neither lack of insight nor of knowledge on his part, nor of the confidence which is based upon them. Beside his keen analysis and masterly exposition of principles, most English criticism of that day seems peculiarly shallow and inconclusive. In the consideration of the doctrine under discussion he laid down at the outset the principle that the unity of action was the only thing the ancient dramatists really cared about, and that the other unities were mere incidental consequents of it. To these latter they would have paid no heed, had not the introduction of a body of persons, constituting the chorus, who were always present on the stage, or absent from it only for brief intervals, necessitated the selection of a limited time and place for the action. Even under such conditions there was no rigid observance of these requirements. There was no scruple about disregarding them, if higher effects could be procured. But as a general rule the Greeks accepted the situation honestly. They made use of the restriction of time and place as the reason for simplifying the plot. They cut away everything that was superfluous. They reduced the action to a singleness which rendered it independent of events that required for their accomplishment length of time and change of place. This was their ideal. It was not always attained, to be sure; but it was always kept in mind.

Now the French — and this was equally true of the English who had both preceded and followed them in their practice — had not honestly observed the rules. The action of the play was no longer simple. On the contrary, it was made exceedingly complex. The chorus was abandoned; but the unities of time and place, which the chorus had alone made of importance, were lifted from their subordinate position and treated as indispensable to the proper representation of the play. As in the crowded modern stage these rules in their practical working were too oppressive to be followed in their strictness, expedients of various kinds had been set up to evade the rigidity of their requirements. A spurious unity of place was established. The scene was supposed to be one and the same spot. Actually, however, the spot was indefinite enough to represent, under the changing conditions of the drama, several distinct places. Again, for the unity of a single day was substituted the unity of indefinite duration, in which no one spoke of the events that marked the passage of the twenty-four hours.

It was this mechanical unity against which Lessing protested. It was, according to him, not in conformity with the rules of the ancients, still less binding upon the practice of the moderns. But he took much more

advanced ground. In combating the delusion which
then prevailed among his countrymen in regard to the
regularity of the French drama, he struck a blow at
the unity of time as observed in most modern plays,
from which it has never recovered. His argument has
certainly not yet been met successfully; perhaps it
would be truer to say that no attempt has been made
to meet it. Does a man, Lessing asked, necessarily
regard unity of time because he represents a certain
number of acts as taking place within twenty-four
hours? The answer is obvious. It will depend entirely on the nature of the acts performed. Are they
such as can properly take place within the period specified? The word "properly" is here of utmost importance. There may perhaps be no physical impossibility
of the commission of the acts in the time allotted. But
the physical possibility is not the main consideration.
Is there a moral possibility of the events happening in
a single day which in the drama are credited to that
day? In a world of rational beings — and this is the
world with which the stage is supposed to deal — could
the actions represented as performed in twenty-four
hours have been really committed? The physical unity
of time is not enough. It is the moral unity which demands much more consideration. The violation of the
former will often be known but to few, while the violation of the latter comes home to the consciousness of
every one. All men are not acquainted with the geo-
graphical situation of places. If therefore a journey
between two points which it requires more than twenty-
four hours to make is represented in a play, the viola-

tion of the unity of time will be recognized only by those who are familiar with the distance traversed. But every person can feel the ridiculousness of portraying events as happening in a single day which from his own experience or observation he knows could not have taken place in several. The dramatist, therefore, who cannot preserve the physical unity of time save at the expense of the moral, has sacrificed what is essential in art to what is purely accidental.

Lessing's point of view was far from being a new one. For that it was too obvious. It had been indicated by Racine himself in the preface to his *Berenice*, in which he is supposed by many to have said what he did for the purpose of reflecting upon the multitude and variety of events found in the plays of Corneille. Whatever his motive, he insisted upon simplicity of action, and consequently denounced the introduction of a great number of incidents. " It is only truth to life," he wrote, " which affects us in tragedy. But what truth to life is there when in one day a multitude of things takes place which could hardly happen in several weeks? " Similar expressions of opinion can be met with not unfrequently. La Place, in the preface to his translations from the English drama, called attention to the habit, in which the French writers indulged, of compressing in their plays a vast variety of action into the space of a few hours. He pointed out the improbability of such representations as a serious objection to the doctrine of the unities. The same view was taken by Lord Chesterfield. He remarked, as one of the faults of the French stage, its disposition to crowd and cram things together to almost a degree of

impossibility from too scrupulous adherence to the unities.[1] Doubtless there were many others to whom the
same reflection must have occurred. It was Lessing,
however, who was the first to bring it out sharply and
distinctly, to enlarge its scope and importance, and to
reveal clearly its damaging character. By no one else
had it been stated so clearly as an argument against the
unities, or had been put so forcibly. In this sense he
may be called its originator.

The difficulty, therefore, which always besets the
writer who seeks to observe the unities, is to give
to the action taking place within the limits of the
time and place assigned the appearance of probability
or even of possibility. It is a difficulty which has
sometimes been successfully overcome. More often
it has been evaded, as there has already been occasion to point out, by a vagueness which leaves uncertain the length of time which has elapsed. More
often still it has been treated as no difficulty at all.
The large majority of modern plays which profess to
regard the unities cannot endure successfully the test
of Lessing's principle. There is no moral possibility
that the events represented as happening in them can
have happened in the time given; in some cases not
even the physical possibility. In order therefore to
conform to a mechanical rule, the reason of the spectator is outraged by being asked to believe that something has taken place in a certain number of hours
which he knows could never have taken place in twice
or even twenty times the number allowed.

[1] Letter to his son, Jan. 23, 1752.

It was in the course of his examination of Voltaire's *Merope* that Lessing formulated and delivered this damaging criticism. He applied it generally to the plays of the great French dramatists; but it is possible to apply it with equal success to the greater number of English pieces which set out to observe the unities. They constantly make a demand upon the credulity of the hearer for which no exactest observance of artificial rules can compensate. The fact can be illustrated by scores of examples. In this place it may be worth while to test by this principle a production of the man who was not only the stoutest upholder of the doctrine, but who was the first to announce that Shakespeare lacked art because he disregarded it. For this purpose it is fair to take not one of his poorest but one of his very best pieces. Let us select 'Volpone, or the Fox.' This comedy has received unstinted praise from the day of its first appearance. By some it has been regarded as Jonson's best play, and few will be found to deny that it deserves a goodly share of the praise it has received. Yet an analysis of the plot will furnish a striking proof of the justice of Lessing's criticism of the way in which the unity of time is nominally maintained, while really set at naught by its advocates.

Before proceeding to the main point, however, it is worth remarking that in this comedy the unity of action — the highest unity of all — has been but imperfectly preserved. The characters of Sir Politic Would-be and his wife, and of the gentleman traveller, Peregrine, have no vital connection with the rest of the play. The two former are tacked to it by what is the flimsiest as well as the clumsiest of fastenings. They contribute really nothing to the development of the plot. They have been dragged into it for no other purpose than to give Jonson an opportunity to attack English persons and practices that he deemed fair objects of satire. In one instance only does Lady Would-be do enough for a short time — when she comes forward to denounce Cœlia — to justify her having any place in the piece at all. Even that is lamely brought about. The last character, Peregrine, has no part whatever in the real business of the play, and the episode of the revenge he takes upon Sir Politic Would-be is a mere patch upon it. All these personages could be cut out of the comedy entirely without affecting the progress of events and with perceptible improvement to its perfection as a work of art. This is a consideration wholly independent of the skill or success with which they have been portrayed. To that all the praise may be given which any one is disposed to bestow. It is only from the point of view of art — upon which Jonson laid so much stress — that the introduction of these characters is criticised.

We now proceed to give an account of the events which are represented as taking place within the space of about twelve hours; for in this play the time extends from sunrise to sunset. Volpone, a Venetian magnifico, though in the enjoyment of vigorous health, has for years been pretending to· be at the point of death. The object of this course of conduct is to heap up wealth by gifts of money and valuables from

men who are flattered with the hope of inheriting his
vast possessions. Accordingly we have at the outset
a number of visits paid in succession to the supposed
dying man by several persons, — a lawyer, an old gentleman, and a merchant. Each one, under the impression
that he is likely to be the heir, brings a rich present.
After these have come and gone, Volpone learns from
his parasite of the beauty of Cœlia, the wife of one
of these greedy seekers after his fortune. She, however, is immured at her home and kept under jealous
guard from all approach. In order to obtain a sight
of her, he now proceeds to dress up as a mountebank
doctor, and then sets out to dispose of his wares in
the piazza directly under her window. She looks out,
and seeing her he becomes at once deeply enamored.
By the machinations of the parasite she is dragged
later to the house of the supposed helpless invalid
by her scoundrel of a husband. Left alone with Volpone, he shows himself at once in his real character,
and she is only saved from ravishment by the unexpected interposition of another personage, the son of
the old gentleman, who has been brought to the house
for a special purpose. The rescuer and the rescued
complain to the authorities. They in turn are complained of in a forged tale which imposes upon the
expectant greedy heirs themselves. A trial ensues.
The husband denounces his wife, the father his son.
In consequence the guiltless pair are sent to prison.

After the successful result of the trial Volpone
makes up his mind that he will pretend to die. He
draws up a will leaving his fortune to his parasite.

Then he places himself in hiding where he can watch the behavior of the persons who suppose themselves his heirs. These all appear at his house as soon as they receive the news of his death. From his place of concealment he amuses himself with the exhibition they make of their disappointment and wrath, as soon as the will is shown. To enjoy their vexation still more, he manages to dress himself in the garb of an inferior officer of the law. This his parasite has been enabled to secure for him by making its owner drunk enough to be stripped. In the disguise thus obtained Volpone waylays the men who had been seeking to inherit his riches, and taunts them with the failure of their hopes. But, as an unexpected consequence of this conduct on his part, the case is reopened through the agency of the irritated lawyer. A new trial takes place. After various turns of fortune in the course of it, the truth at last comes out. The innocent are freed, and justice is pronounced at once upon the guilty parties.

These are the main incidents of the plot. The mere recital of them is sufficient of itself to show that a series of events has been represented as taking place in the compass of a dozen hours which in real life could hardly be conceived of as having occurred in as many days. There are minor details, of which space forbids mention, which still further enhance the grossness of the improbability. Let it be conceded that there exists in this instance no physical impossibility of performing in the time given the various acts described. The greater moral impossibility of their accomplishment still remains. As one illustration out of several, no court of law which aimed at justice ever proceeded or could proceed in the rapid manner here indicated. In the space of what can be at best hardly three hours two separate trials are conducted. In each a state of facts is developed not merely different but entirely contrary. Yet the perplexing questions thus raised do not perplex the tribunal. It removes doubts and settles difficulties with a rapidity which puts to shame the proverbial charge of the law's delay. Yet all this and numberless other violations of the facts of life as we know them, we are expected to accept without protest, because the author has paid strict attention to certain artificial rules. Jonson himself was proud, and in some respects justly proud, of this play. Especially did he felicitate himself upon its regularity, upon its being constructed in accordance with the principles of highest art. In the prologue he boasts that in it he

> " Presents quick comedy refined,
> As best critics have designed.
> The laws of time, place, person he observeth,
> From no needful rule he swerveth."

Yet the gross improprieties which examination reveals as pervading this play owe their existence to the author's success in conforming the action to these very unities which he looked upon as needful to the perfection of the piece. The art it exhibits is of the kind which comes from the observance of the rules. It was the kind of art of which Shakespeare was ignorant or in which he did not believe.

CHAPTER III

III

IT was neither to the protest of Dr. Johnson against the doctrine, nor to Lessing's scientific demolition of its pretensions, that the stage owes its deliverance from the incubus of the unities. The criticism of the English author affected, without question, public opinion. As time went on, it affected it more and more. Still, as we have seen, it did not at the outset affect the practice of the prominent playwrights. Still less was any influence exerted by the German author. Faint echoes only of Lessing's reputation had begun to reach England in the eighteenth century. These, furthermore, celebrated him as a creative writer and not as a critical one. In truth, the great work, in which he had attacked the precepts of Voltaire and had exalted Shakespeare above all modern dramatists, was translated into French long before it was apparently heard of at all by Shakespeare's countrymen.

One can easily get a false impression from assertions of this sort. Lessing came in time to influence profoundly the critical estimate taken of Shakespeare. This was because he furnished men with solid reasons for a faith which, begot in the first instance of blind admiration, was held in uneasy defiance of what was

then loudly proclaimed as art. But it was an influence
which in the beginning was transmitted through others.
In Germany its action was direct, immediate, and far-
reaching. Not so in England. At the time of which
we are speaking, not only was Lessing little known in
that country, he was less regarded. It was not until
1781 that a translation of his *Nathan der Weise* appeared
at London. It was the work of a German exile, named
Raspe, who had left his country for his country's good,
but who has achieved a certain distinction in English
literature as the creator of Munchausen. If contemporary notices can be trusted, the version was a very indifferent one. But while in some instances Lessing, as
author of the original, was treated with respect, the
contemptuous attitude then frequently assumed towards
German productions in general was often exhibited
towards him personally with peculiar offensiveness.
The two leading reviews of the day commented upon
his play with scant courtesy. "Considered merely as
a drama," said one of them, "whatever may be its
author's reputation in Germany, it is unworthy of
notice."[1] This, however, may be deemed almost eulogy
when contrasted with the insolent tone in which the
other permitted itself to speak of a literature of which
it knew nothing, and of a great writer belonging to it
whose name it was not even able to spell correctly. It
began by describing the work just mentioned as "a heap
of unintelligible jargon, very badly translated from the
German original, written, it seems, by G. T. Lessling."
It then added that the author fell infinitely beneath all

[1] Monthly Review, vol. lxvi. p. 307.

criticism. It concluded by declaring that if the present time were, as the translator asserted, the golden age of German literature, "it appears by this specimen to put on a very leaden appearance."[1]

Nor did lapse of time seem to raise Lessing's reputation in the English critical world. An adaptation of his *Minna von Barnhelm* was brought out in 1786, under the title of 'The Disbanded Officer.' Like Shakespeare, he too, it appears, had come to have his blind and bigoted partisans. Another review felt called upon, in consequence, to fix for him his precise position. "Though Lessing," said the critic, "has probably little claim to the elevated rank that has been assigned him by his injudicious admirers, he is not, we think, entirely destitute of merit. . . . We are ourselves acquainted with some of his performances which we do not recollect with disgust." The reviewer was disposed to conclude that, on the whole, he was perhaps of not inferior brilliancy to Colman.[2] Of criticism of this sort it is hard to decide whether the arrogance or the ignorance be the greater. In no case, however, would much weight have been attributed to the opinions of a writer of whom the leading exponents of public opinion could venture to speak without rebuke in terms like these. There were, doubtless, a number of persons then in England, whom the reviewers would have felt justified in calling injudicious, who were impressed by the views Lessing put forth. He had, however, to wait until the next century before the

[1] Critical Review, vol. lii. p. 236.
[2] English Review, vol. viii. (1786) pp. 348–355.

justice of these views was widely recognized in that country.

But, in truth, the influence of the greatest names who were opposed to the doctrine of the unities was impaired by the fact that their practice did not harmonize with their precepts. The principles they inculcated could hardly be expected to control the conduct of others when it had not been able to control their own. Farquhar had argued against the necessity of observing the unities; nevertheless, he had observed them. Fielding ridiculed them; in his practice he respected them. Johnson spoke with contempt of the reasons given for regarding them; in the only play he ever produced, the action was limited to one day and to one place. By the two first-mentioned writers an insubordinate spirit was sometimes manifested in the way they obeyed these rules. They occasionally went as far in defiance of them as they dared. But however loosely they observed them, the fact remains that they kept up the pretence of observing them. Lessing, likewise, was the inspirer of a revolution in his own literature, in which he himself took no part. He had demolished the reason, or rather the lack of reason, upon which the support of the unities was based; yet his own plays are written in accordance with their requirements. The subservience of writers like these to practices they disliked and in truth despised shows how little the greatest men can hold their own against the spirit of their age. Each of them felt the tyranny of a public opinion which caused him to act as if he believed that to be true which he knew to be false.

The doctrine of the unities was not, indeed, broken down by elaborate disquisitions to prove that it was founded upon false assumptions. These, undoubtedly, contributed to the result. When the movement was under full headway, they did much to hasten the fall of the fabric which, however, they had not been the first to undermine. Long before Johnson's powerful voice had been lifted up against these rules, faith in them had been steadily sapped by the frequency with which the plays of Shakespeare were acted. During the eighteenth century, it must be borne in mind, only two places in London had ordinarily the right to exhibit theatrical pieces. That one circumstance forbade the prolonged repetition of the same play. Accordingly, to vary the performances, there was kept on hand a large number of dramas. To this collection of stock pieces Shakespeare furnished far the largest number. In the frequency with which plays of his were acted, no author, living or dead, rivalled the great dramatist. This was true of the whole century. Rarely was it the case that a month passed without the performance of several of his pieces at one or both of the two houses. Maimed and mutilated as they often were, they could not be so tortured out of shape as to hide from the general view the superiority of the dramatic laws he obeyed and the dramatic methods he followed. His so-called irregular plays interested men, inspired them; the so-called regular plays of others made them yawn. The existence of Shakespeare was, in truth, to the advocates of the unities a gigantic and somewhat unpleasant fact. He could not be ignored; he could not be set aside. He had violated the established rules of the drama and had succeeded. They conformed to them religiously and failed.

Let it not be imagined, however, that any attempt is made here to deny the merit of modern plays which observe the unities, or to maintain that a powerful drama cannot be produced upon the lines they prescribe. Such a contention would be only repeating on the side of the opponents of this doctrine the erroneous assumptions which its advocates put forth. He who ventures to take a position so extreme can hardly escape a feeling of serious discomfort if called upon, in consequence, to decry the productions of Corneille, Racine, and Molière, — to say nothing of some of the most brilliant pieces which have adorned the English stage. Nor, furthermore, need it be denied that there are conditions in which the observance of the unities may be a positive advantage. Especially will this be the case when the characters are few and all the incidents of the plot are directed to the accomplishment of a single result. The concentration of the action is likely to contribute, in such pieces, to the effect of the representation. He who sets out to imitate the simplicity of the Greek drama will usually find himself disposed to adopt, as far as possible, its form. Within its limitations great work can be accomplished by the drama which regards the unities, and, to some extent, it will be great work because of its limitations.

This fact, so far from being denied, has been fully acknowledged by many of those who have been foremost in denying the obligatory observance of these rules. Furthermore, it has not unfrequently been acted upon. Goethe, for instance, not only disregarded the unities, but characterized them as "the stupidest of all laws."[1] Yet he recognized the propriety and advantage of conforming to them under certain conditions. To him Byron, in 1821, dedicated in most flattering terms the volume containing ' Sardanapalus,' ' The Two Foscari,' and ' Cain.' In the preface to these plays the English poet avowed the most thorough-going devotion to the doctrine, which by that time had fallen into general disuse and disfavor in his own country. Without the unities, it was his opinion, there might be poetry, but there could be no drama. He was aware, he continued, "of the unpopularity of this notion in present English literature; but it is not a system of his own, being merely an opinion, which not very long ago was the law of literature throughout the world, and is still so in the more civilized parts of it." Goethe was a good deal affected by the tribute paid him in the dedication, coming from the man for whose genius he had the profoundest admiration. But it furnished him an equal amount of amusement — as it did also Byron's reviewer, Jeffrey — to find, at this late time of day, the one author who had set all ordinary conventions at defiance, who had raged at the restraints imposed by prevalent social beliefs and customs, not only submitting meekly to shut himself up inside the stone walls of the unities, but insisting that it was only within those penitentiary precincts that dramatic virtue could flourish. Yet while Goethe set no store by these rules,

[1] Eckermann's 'Conversations of Goethe' (under 1825).

he respected them wherever he found them of service. Early falling under the influence of Shakespeare, he had followed the freedom and boldness of his practice. But when he imitated the Greek tragedy, as in his *Iphigenie*, he naturally adopted the simplicity of its methods. In this play the characters are but five; the sole end aimed at is the restoration of the priestess to her own land. Hence the action does not need to take up but part of a day, and finds ample place for its representation in the grove before Diana's temple.

The distinction between the two methods is, in fact, fundamental. The drama which disregards the unities gives the widest possible scope for the display of the different passions which, by turns, agitate the heart and control the conduct. In it we behold men operated upon by the varying impulses and stirred by the varying feelings which affect, at times, the lives of us all. Their behavior is constantly modified or altered by new agencies that unexpectedly thrust themselves into the action of the piece. They fall, at intervals, under the sway of opposing motives. But the drama which regards the unities, when produced in accordance with the conditions of its being, lacks complicated situations. It is not so much complex man that is brought upon the scene, as man under the storm and stress of a single dominant passion. No conflicting interests distract our attention from the main one. Men, as we see them in the life about us, are not so single-minded. They may be ambitious, they may be revengeful, they may be jealous, they may be lover-like, but they are also sure to be something else; and it is this view of their nature which finds natural opportunity for its full expression in the ample field of the Shakespearean drama. Yet it is certainly reasonable to believe that one phase of character can be brought out much more adequately and effectively, if that can be made the one to which attention is wholly directed.

There are two plays in our literature, both written by men of genius on the same subject, which illustrate the distinction between these two methods of scenic representation. They are here of special interest, because in the development of their plots they deal with the same situation, and furthermore introduce some of the same leading personages. In the case of the two principal ones the difference of portrayal is peculiarly noteworthy. These are the characters of Antony and Cleopatra, as set forth by Shakespeare and by Dryden. No one, of course, would think of placing the latter author by the side of the former, least of all in dramatic power: the comparison, therefore, cannot fairly be extended to results, but must be limited to the methods employed. The time of Shakespeare's play of ' Antony and Cleopatra ' extends over a period of ten years. The scene is laid sometimes in Alexandria, sometimes in Rome, and occasionally wanders over portions of Europe and Asia. Dryden's play — styled ' All for Love ' — abounds in reminiscences and imitations of that of his great predecessor. But the time purports to be limited to the prescribed twenty-four hours. In the course of it Antony and Cleopatra are both represented as dying; and the action in no instance is carried on outside of Alexandria.

In certain ways the ' Antony and Cleopatra ' of Shakespeare is one of the most astonishing exhibitions of the many astonishing exhibitions the poet has afforded of that almost divine insight and intuition which enabled him to comprehend at a glance that complete whole of which other men, after painful toil, learn but a beggarly part. The student of ancient history can find in the play occasional disregard of precise dates. He can discover, in some cases, a sequence of events which is not in absolutely strict accord with the account of them that has been handed down. But from no investigation of records, from no interpretation of texts, will he ever arrive at so clear and vivid a conception of the characters of the actors who then took part in the struggle for the supremacy of the world. Nowhere in ancient story or song will he find, as here, the light which enables him to see the men as they are. It is a gorgeous gallery in which each personage stands out so distinct that there is no danger of misapprehension or confusion as to the parts they fill. Antony appears the soldier and voluptuary he was, swayed alternately by love, by regret, by ambition, at one moment the great ruler of the divided world, at the next recklessly flinging his future away at the dictation of a passionate caprice; Cleopatra, true to no interest, fascinating, treacherous, charming with her grace those whom she revolts by her conduct, luring the man she half loves to a ruin which involves herself in his fate; Octavius, cool, calculating, never allowing his heart to gain, either for good or evil, the better of his head, showing in early youth the self-restraint, the caution,

the knowledge of the world which belong to advancing
years; the feeble Lepidus, striving to act the part of a
reconciler to the two mighty opposites, with whom the
irony of fate has thrown him into conjunction: these
and half-a-dozen minor characters appear painted in
clear and sharp outline on the crowded canvass of
Shakespeare; while in attendance, like the chorus of a
Greek tragedy, stands Enobarbus, commenting on every
incident of the great world-drama which is acted before
his eyes, ominously foreboding the declining fortunes
of his chief in the moral ruin which carries with it
prostration of the intellect, and pointing to the inevitable catastrophe of shame and dishonor to which events
are hurrying.

Not a single trace of these characteristics, of these
conflicting currents of thought and feeling, is indicated, or even suggested, in the regular drama which
Dryden produced. His whole play is made to turn
upon the infatuation for Cleopatra which has taken
possession of the Roman commander, and against the
force of which the loyalty of Ventidius struggles to no
purpose. There are few things said and fewer things
done by Antony which remind us of the great general,
of the dishonored soldier, of the fallen master of half
the world. He is little more than a sentimental love-
sick swain, while the Egyptian queen has lost nearly
every one of the characteristics with which she has
impressed the ages, and is exhibited to us as display-
ing the behavior of a tender-hearted, affectionate, and
wholly romantic school-girl. Scott, who is at his worst
in his comparison of this play with Shakespeare's,

assures us that its plan must be preferred to that of the latter's on the score of coherence, unity, and simplicity; and, further, that as a consequence of the more artful arrangement of the story, the unity of time, like that of place, so necessary to the intelligibility of the drama, has been happily attained.[1]

It is the last assertion alone which concerns us here. How has this unity of time been attained? It has been preserved by the studious suppression of all reference whatever to its passage. Events are crowded into it which history is not alone in assuring the scholar did not happen in the space assigned: common sense further assures everybody they could not possibly so have happened. Numerous minor incidents, however important, are not necessary to be considered in the examination of the play. But in this one day Antony goes out to fight a great battle. We only hear of it; there is no representation of it. On his return he reports that five thousand of his foes have been slain. As battles go in this world, the mere despatching of so large a number of men would encroach heavily upon the time allotted. Further, at a later period in this one day, the Egyptian fleet sets out to attack the enemy. Instead of fighting the Romans it goes over to them. Then follow the consequences of defeat and despair. This is the happy attainment of the same old spurious unity of time which cheats our understanding at the cost of our attention. Yet, though marked by these and other defects, Dryden's play is, after its kind, an excellent one. There are in

[1] Scott's Dryden, vol. v. p. 288 (1808).

it passages of great power, which will explain the favor with which it has been held by many. Had its author been gifted with dramatic genius, as he was not, he would doubtless have made it far more effective. But under the limitations imposed by the critical canons he accepted, neither he nor any one else could have drawn the picture of life which we find in the wonderful corresponding creation of the great poet of human nature.

Men felt the force of scenic representation of this latter sort long before they were convinced of the justice of its claim to be considered art. The frequency with which Shakespeare's plays were acted in the eighteenth century could not fail to produce a steadily deepening impression upon the beholders. It was only a question of time when the truths they silently taught as to the value of his methods should be loudly proclaimed by many. It was only a question of a little more time when they should be accepted by all as the fullest exemplification of that art which seeks to hold the mirror up to nature. But it needed transcendent power like his to emancipate the mind from the tyranny of rules which cramped its energy and restricted its scope, and to give it the opportunity of becoming the exponent of the complex life we lead to-day. This is as true of other races as of ours. So long as Shakespeare's plays were unknown in Germany, Germany looked upon the French drama as the representative of the highest art. It accepted, submissively, the canons of French criticism. Acquaintance made with the work of the former was rapidly followed by repudiation of the practice of the latter. A greater triumph

— greater because achieved under much more unfavorable conditions — was gained by the English dramatist in the land where the doctrines of classicism had been held and practised most stoutly. It is not to be forgotten that it was under the banner of Shakespeare that Victor Hugo and his allies fought and won the battle of *Hernani*, and freed the French stage from the trammels which for centuries had cramped the freedom of its movements.

These successive conquests are justly deemed proofs of the excellence of his dramatic art. But a further question now arises: Was he himself aware of its excellence? Was the deliverance he wrought due, so far as he personally was concerned, to accident or to design? Did Shakespeare, in disregarding the unities, disregard them because he was ignorant of their existence, or because he saw that in most instances they were unsuited to the requirements of the modern stage? About this point there has been difference or uncertainty of opinion from the middle of the eighteenth century down to our own day. The Shakespeare editor, Richard Grant White, in one of his latest essays, insisted that the observation of the unities by the dramatist, so far as he did observe them, was a mere matter of convenience, and not at all due to purpose.[1] This is one of the very few positive pronouncements upon the subject. The large majority of critics — more especially in the eighteenth century, when the question

---

[1] Studies in Shakespeare, p. 28. Mr. White further says, that in 'Love's Labor's Lost' the unities of time and place are preserved *absolutely;* but the time of the play cannot be less than two days.

excited far greater interest than now — have not ventured to decide the point.   Dr. Johnson, who was the
first of Shakespeare's editors that presumed to deny the
obligation of observing the unities, proclaimed himself
as distinctly unwilling to express a definite opinion.
The sagacity of Theobald, as might have been expected,
did not fail him here.   As a classical scholar he took
the orthodox classical view.   But he had the insight to
see that Shakespeare's disregard of the unities was owing not to ignorance but to intention; though he drew
from the dramatist's words some unauthorized inferences as to his opinions.[1]   In the general opprobrium
which fell upon Theobald this observation of his
escaped the notice of nearly every one.   Steevens, however, who had a genius for discovering and not mentioning what his predecessors had found out, announced,
later, that he was disposed to believe that Shakespeare
was acquainted with the unities, and had disregarded
them consciously; and Malone, unheeding or ignorant
of Theobald's previous assertion, credited Steevens with
originating the view.

It was not, however, a view generally entertained.
The opinion on this point, held by those most favorable
to the dramatist, was rarely confident, and the expression of it was almost invariably guarded.   If Shakespeare knew of the existence of these rules, said his
advocates, he deliberately broke them; if he did not
know of them, he showed by his course how much supe-

---

[1] See Theobald's note in vol. ii. p. 181, of his Shakespeare, edition
of 1733, upon the remark found in act v. scene 2, of 'Love's Labor's
Lost,' that a twelvemonth was " too long for a play."

rior to art is genius. The attitude generally assumed by the critics of the time is best indicated by Johnson in the following words: "Whether Shakespeare," he wrote, "knew the unities, and rejected them by design, or deviated from them by happy ignorance, it is, I think, impossible to decide and useless to enquire." [1] Is it so useless to enquire? Upon the answer to the question depends the view whether the poet was a conscious artist, or whether he blundered by a lucky carelessness into the right method of procedure. This is certainly a matter of some importance in making up our estimate of the man. For if he was utterly unacquainted with these rules, the assumption of Voltaire cannot be successfully controverted that he was a barbarian of genius, with whom inspiration took the place of knowledge and reflection.

Again, is it so impossible to decide? Certainly a number of questions at once present themselves to the mind which render improbable, to say the least, this assertion of the impossibility of reaching a conclusion. Is it likely that the greatest dramatic genius of his time should have been ignorant of what must have been discussed by every playwright whom he was in the habit of meeting daily? Could the man, who built one of his own plays upon the 'Promos and Cassandra' of Whetstone, have failed to read the attack upon the English stage for its disregard of the unities which was made by Whetstone in the preface to that production? Could the intimate friend of Ben Jonson have been unacquainted with Ben Jonson's opinions, bearing in mind,

[1] Johnson's Shakespeare, vol. i. Preface (1765).

as we must, that Ben Jonson was not one of those retiring persons who are in the habit of keeping their opinions to themselves? Two of the comedies of that dramatist — ' Every Man in his Humor ' and ' Every Man out of his Humor ' — had been originally performed by the company of which Shakespeare was a member. He had taken a leading part in the first of them, in which Jonson strictly observed the unities, and must have read the second, in which he commented upon them. Would he not have been likely to gain a slight inkling, at least, of the nature of the dramatic laws which his contemporary had illustrated in act and directly discussed in words? Such inquiries carry with them but one possible answer. Indeed, if there be foundation for the story of the wit-combats which Fuller reports as having taken place between the two leading playwrights of the time, we can feel reasonably confident that the question of the unities was one of the very topics about which controversy raged most fiercely.

It is hard, in truth, to understand how any editor of ' King Henry V.' can miss not merely the recognition of Shakespeare's acquaintance with these laws, but also the perception of the hostile criticism to which the violation of them subjected the dramatist even then. This particular piece appeared near the close of the sixteenth century. That was the time in which Jonson was setting out on his mission of bringing the English stage into conformity, as far as possible, with the classical. One distinguishing feature of this play is that to every act is prefixed a prologue delivered

by a so-called chorus. The ostensible business of
the prologue is to inform the hearer of what is coming. But it does something more than impart information. It defends the romantic drama, or, if one chooses
to put it in another way, it apologizes for the practices
to which, from the beginning, the romantic drama had
been addicted. It is largely a reply to the criticisms of
that school of writers of which we have already had a
representative in Sir Philip Sidney. Naturally the
chorus takes occasion to defend the constant and glar-
ing violation of the unities of time and place which
occur in the course of the play. Its observations are
very much of the same sort as those we have found
made later by Farquhar and Dr. Johnson. The spectator is asked to perform the very easy task of travelling
with his mind. He is to suffer himself to be transported in imagination over periods of time and dis-
tances of space. The opening prologue prepares us for
this view. In it we are told that

> " 'T is your thoughts that now must deck our kings,
> Carry them here and there; jumping o'er times,
> Turning the accomplishment of many years
> Into an hour-glass."

In the prologue to the second act the same idea is
repeated. There the audience is specifically requested
to "digest the abuse of distance." The scene is to
be transferred from London to Southampton, and it is
added, —

> " There is the playhouse now, there must you sit:
> And thence to France shall we convey you safe,
> And bring you back, charming the narrow seas
> To give you gentle pass."

Again, in the prologue to the fifth act, those of the audience who are acquainted with the story of the play are desired

> " To admit the excuse
> Of time, of numbers, and due course of things,
> Which cannot in their huge and proper life
> Be here presented."

Words of this sort would never have been used, had there not been going on at the time violent discussion as to the propriety of the methods of representation then followed upon the English stage. The writer of the prologue was not seeking to impart unneeded knowledge to others, but to justify the course adopted by himself. His eye was fixed not upon the possible hearer who sought information about the coming incidents of the play, but upon the very tangible critic who objected to its form.

Nor had controversy on this same subject died out when, towards the close of his dramatic career, Shakespeare produced ' The Winter's Tale.' In this the defiance of conventional rules of every sort was carried to its farthest extreme. The novel from which it was taken, with its Bohemian seacoast and its island shrine of Delphos, was bad enough; but to the critics of the eighteenth century these seemed comparatively venial offences when contrasted with the numerous other violations of the everlasting proprieties with which the piece bristles. It must be conceded that the play carries the liberty of the romantic drama fairly up to the point of license. The jumbling together of ancient times and customs and countries with modern; in the same piece

Apollo delivering oracles and a puritan singing psalms to hornpipes; a pagan religion prevailing while a Russian emperor reigns, and a statue has just been executed by the rare Italian master, Julio Romano, — these and other not dissimilar details would tend to make the conventional classicist shudder and the most liberal-minded hesitate. Still, by nothing were the critics of this school so shocked as by the disregard of the unities. There is no question as to the audacity with which this is manifested. The action takes place in countries far apart. A child born at the beginning of the play appears on the stage at its close as just married. Compared with such improprieties, even the grave-diggers' scene in ' Hamlet ' was pardonable. The disgust which these violations of the rules caused the professional critics prevented them from doing justice to the skill with which the whole piece had been constructed. They did not see that what was in art strictly impossible had been accomplished by the genius of the poet; for the play within the play — apparently annihilating the unity of action — had been made to contribute to the development of the main plot.

At any rate, the work, whether well or ill done, was done as deliberately as it was audaciously. An examination of it leaves no doubt on that point. In his own mind the dramatist was clearly satisfied with the wisdom of his proceeding. It requires more dulness than rightfully belongs even to the dull to suppose that Shakespeare was not himself aware of the numerous ways in which he had trampled upon beliefs accepted by many. Yet it is noticeable that the only point where he thinks it worth while to justify his course is in the allowance of sixteen years to intervene between the third and fourth acts. This was the one thing which, more than all else, would subject him to the censure of contemporary criticism. Again, therefore, he calls in the chorus to his aid. This, assuming the character of Time, puts in his plea. "Impute it not a crime," he says,

> " To me and my swift passage that I slide
>   O'er sixteen years, and leave the growth untried
>   Of that wide gap."

If your patience will allow this, adds the chorus, I shall turn my glass and develop the plot of the play as if you had slept the interval between. There is no mistaking the meaning of these words; it is idle to pretend that Shakespeare did not know what he was doing. What possible crime could be imputed? There was but one. The unity of time had been violated.

What has now been said on this subject is sufficient to show that to whatever cause Shakespeare's rejection of the unities was due, it was not due to his lack of acquaintance with them.[1] But there is more direct evidence even than that already brought forward; and when we come to consider the date of its appearance with other accompanying circumstances, it will be found very significant. Disregard of the unities of time and place may spring from indifference or ignorance. Not

[1] I have not introduced any reference to the " scene individable or poem unlimited " of scene 2 of act ii. of ' Hamlet,' though I believe the words refer to the unities; but they are susceptible of a different interpretation, and, furthermore, the argument is not in need of their help.

so regard for them. Unlike the kingdom of heaven, that can never come save by observation. No man ever conformed to these laws in any original dramatic composition unless he did it consciously; to comply with their requirements demands unremitting toil and attention. Now, of the thirty-seven plays of Shakespeare there are two in which he observes the unities faithfully. One of these — ' The Comedy of Errors ' — may perhaps be thrown out of consideration. As it is based upon a play of Plautus, it naturally follows his treatment. Accordingly there would be nothing antecedently improbable in the fact that the modern author should, without thought, subject himself to the same limitations as did the ancient. But the case is different in the other of these two plays, — ' The Tempest.' This is purely Shakespeare's own. Any original of it has remained as undiscoverable as is the enchanted island where its action takes place. Like ' The Winter's Tale,' it is conceded to belong to the latest period of his dramatic activity. Unlike that play, it is remarkable for its strict observance of the unities. Even a superficial examination shows that this could not have been the result of accident; a close examination furnishes unmistakable proof of the existence of thoroughly meditated design.

The action of the comedy is represented as taking place in less than four hours, not much longer than would be required to perform it upon the stage. Not only is it thus limited, but there is a perfectly plain purpose to make prominent the fact that it is so limited. During the whole progress of the play the unity of time is something we are never allowed to forget. At the very beginning our attention is called to it; at the very end we are reminded of it again and again. In the second scene of the first act Prospero asks Ariel what is the hour of the day. "Past the mid season," is the answer. Two o'clock is then distinctly specified as the precise time; the interval between that and six, it is added, must by both be spent most preciously. Nor in the middle of the play is the time allowed to slip by unnoted. In the first scene of the third act Miranda tells Ferdinand that her father is hard at study, and that for three hours they will be free from his presence. At the end of the same scene Prospero says that he has much business appertaining which must be accomplished before supper-time. In the scene following, Caliban tells Stephano that he must take advantage of the opportunity offered; for it is his master's custom to sleep in the afternoon. At the opening of the fifth act Prospero again asks Ariel as to the time. "How's the day?" is his question. The answer given is that it is "on the sixth hour;" "at which time," continues Ariel, "you said our work should cease." Not long after, Alonso speaks of himself as having been wrecked "three hours since." A few moments later he discovers Ferdinand and Miranda playing at chess, and remarks to his son that the eldest acquaintance of himself and his companion "cannot be three hours." To confirm, still further, the impression of the brevity of the time, the boatswain, on his appearance, speaks of it having been but "three glasses" — that is, hours — since they had given up the vessel as split. There are other instances of the same general character, though not so distinctly marked, that could be cited. But surely the ones given are enough. Can it be assumed that these unnecessary references to the time — what Falstaff would have called the "damnable iteration" of it — are a mere accident? The strict observance of the laws found here, be it remembered, was not far removed, as regards date, from the lawless 'Winter's Tale.' Different impressions will be produced upon different minds by the same fact. To me it conveys satisfactory proof that Shakespeare, when he set out to produce 'The Tempest,' had deliberately determined to show to the adherents of the classical school that he could not only write what they called a regular play better than they could themselves, but could make it conform even more closely than they generally did to their beloved unity of time.

In the discussion of this doctrine there now remains one point that merits special attention. This is the prominence which the passion of love has come to assume in the modern drama, especially in comedy. It is something which of itself renders the observance of the unities utterly unsuited to the function of that drama in representing with fidelity the manners of modern life. Often discussed, as the subject has been, it has never met with the consideration to which, in this respect, it is entitled. True, the remark is familiar that the difference in the treatment of the passion of love and the consequent difference in the position and conduct of the female characters constitute a distinction which is fundamental between the ancient and the modern drama. The attitude taken by each towards woman is not merely dissimilar, it is practically opposite. The representation of love in any genuine sense of the word belongs to modern comedy alone. The earlier ancient comedy, as in Aristophanes, knows nothing of it at all; the later knows only a spurious form of it. What goes under that name is almost invariably lust. There is in none of the ancient plays any such personage as the heroine, in the sense in which we understand the word. The woman with whom the hero is supposed to be in love is usually in the power of a procurer or procuress. She is bought and sold as if she were a domestic animal. Even in the few instances in which, from the outset, the intent is honorable marriage, she who in the modern drama would occupy the foremost place continues in the ancient to keep her subordinate position. She has no control over her own destiny. She has no will, apparently, save that of those to whom her birth or the circumstances of her fortune have made her subservient. For any action likely to determine the fate of this passive instrument in the hands of others, the space of a day would furnish as ample time as that of a year.

Readers of Plautus and Terence will confirm the truth of this portrayal; and it is needless to say that the plays of these authors represent the character and plots of the lost Greek comedy. In them the female characters corresponding to the heroines of the modern drama belong, generally, to two classes. In the one, the place she takes is purely negative. Her business is to be and to suffer, but not to do. Often she never speaks or is spoken to; she is simply spoken of. One can hardly be expected to feel much interest in this helpless being, who never says anything to be remembered, and never does anything to be admired. In the case of the women of the second class, the one who would correspond to the modern heroine frequently takes an active part in the play; but her intellect gains at the expense of her character. She is almost invariably a courtesan. In her it is a mistress the hero is seeking, not a wife. Furthermore, if female characters are introduced who chance to possess virtue, they are usually disagreeable. It is the shrew, the scold, the jealous wife, the intriguing mother-in-law that comes upon the stage. To all this there are exceptions; but they are too few to counteract the prevailing impression the ancient comedy gives. Deserving of admiration in numerous ways, as are the works it has handed down, it is not its portrayal of womanly qualities that would recommend it to the modern reader. In scarcely a single one of these plays is there any attempt to depict the spiritual side of love as opposed to the sensual. In this respect Terence is perhaps worse than Plautus. In five of his six extant plays the woman, nominally an object of affection, has been either debauched or ravished by the man to whom she is finally given in marriage.

Modern comedy reverses completely the situation here depicted. In it the heroine occupies a position of prominence. She stands forth wholly, or in part, as the arbiter of her own destiny. In what she says or does we are as much interested as in what is said or done by the hero. Compared with her, the other female

personages of the play occupy a subordinate place. All
this is due not merely to the altered position of woman,
but to the fact that the passion of love in the highest
manifestation of the feeling has come to be the principal
subject of stage representation. This was an inevitable
result of the general line of development which the
drama took. It left, first, the region of political or
religious controversy in the stormy strife of which its
youth was nurtured, gave up the task of supporting a
side or advancing a cause, and passed on to the broader
domain of history and legend treated from the point of
view of art pure and simple. Even there it did not
tarry long. It began to deal more and more with the
social forces that operate upon the lives of us all. The
moment this became the prevailing tendency, the passion of love was sure in the vast majority of instances
to show itself as the underlying motive upon which the
unfolding of the plot turned. This was a course of
development impossible to the ancient comedy. In that
the helplessness of the heroine, or of her who should
have been the heroine, in disposing of her own fate,
and the conditions which encompassed her in the social
life then existing, cut off the possibility, and perhaps
the idea of a reciprocal interchange of lofty sentiments
of love, and limited the representation of the passion
itself largely to its purely sensual aspect. A suggestion of this same state of things, arising from the same
cause, can be found also in the Elizabethan drama.
But there is not enough of it to efface the picture of
love in its highest form, divested of all impurity, exalt-
ing the woman and ennobling the man.

This description of the difference between the ancient and the modern drama undoubtedly applies to comedy rather than to tragedy. In the latter there are both room and reason for the operation of many other feelings than that of love. Revenge, remorse, envy, hatred, pride, ambition, and scores of similar states of mind can easily be made the leading motive, about which the interest of the play centres. Any one of them may constitute the principal cause of the calamities which attend the development of the plot or wait upon its conclusion. But it is otherwise with plays which are bound by the laws of their being to end fortunately. In them the subject of love was certain, in time, to form the groundwork of the large majority of the themes selected for dramatization. The very nature of the feeling made such a result inevitable. It is the most universal of passions. It appeals to the widest circle of sympathies. It arouses the keenest interest in men of all ages and in minds of every class. So wide, indeed, is the sweep of the feeling, so powerful is the hold it has upon us all, that when once we find ourselves acquainted with the characters in the raggedest kind of a love-story, we cannot get wholly rid of the desire to see what becomes of them at last.

In this respect there has been a close analogy between the development of the drama and of the novel. Both of them have gone through what are essentially the same changes. The resemblance extends, indeed, to the feelings with which the result of these changes has been at times regarded. In the case of the novel the old tale of chivalry or adventure gradually gave way to the modern tale of society with the story of love as the leading feature. The other was not lost, to be sure, but it sank to an inferior position. This condition of things has been far from agreeable to some writers. A frantic effort has been put forth occasionally by the experimental novelist to get rid of the everlasting youth and maiden, to substitute some other interest for that of their sorrows and joys. He feels a sense of mortification and irritation that the world's regard should gather about the incidents of the story only so far as they bear upon the fortunes of two insignificant beings, whose sole claim to attention is that they care enough for each other to endure suffering and even encounter death rather than undergo separation. Yet efforts to introduce other motives have not often met with much favor. It is in but few instances that they continue to please. It is fairly safe to say that a general adoption in the novel of other interests than that of love will meet with permanent success about the time a radical reconstruction of human nature has been carried through to a successful completion.

Naturally, the playwrights of the Elizabethan age were quick to seize upon this theme. They recognized the possibilities that lay in appealing to feelings possessing an interest so universal. Love speedily came to take the place of prominence in scenic representation. In some plays it formed the exclusive subject of attention. It entered, more or less, into those that set out to deal with other motives. The use made of it, the predominant position it occupied, was noticed by Bacon in one of his essays which was first published in 1612.

"The stage," he wrote, "is more beholding to love than the life of man. For as to the stage, love is ever matter of comedies, and now and then of tragedies: but in life it doth much mischief, sometimes like a siren, sometimes like a fury." It was not the sort of siren that would ever have allured Bacon, nor the sort of fury that would have threatened his peace. In him the emotional nature, never very strong, was stifled by the excessive development of the intellectual; and though his mental greatness would enable him to comprehend fully the power which this particular passion exerted over the lives of men, it could not give him any sympathy with its spirit. But the remark is interesting as the comment of one of the acutest of observers upon the extent to which love had taken possession of the stage in his day.

Nor did its progress cease with the progress of time. It tended to intrude itself increasingly into tragedy, much to the disgust of the adherents of the purely classical school. This became especially characteristic of the French drama of the seventeenth century. Love took, then, complete possession of their tragic stage, and from that extended its sway over the English. The cause of its rapid spread is clear. In both countries the popular taste demanded it. The consequence was that men began to find unsatisfactory those pieces in which it did not appear. The influence of this feeling was fully exemplified, as we shall see later, in the changes that were made in Shakespeare's plays to fit them, in this respect, to the taste of the times. From them, as originally written, the passion of love was by

no means absent; but it had never been given the place
of absolute monarch.   But the men who criticised him
for his lack of art, and remodelled his dramas to make
them conform to it, foisted the subject into tragedies
from which he had properly left it out.   The most
flagrant example of this was the alteration of 'King
Lear.'   Yet the introduction into it of love was one of
the reasons why this abominable version so long held
the stage to the exclusion of the original.   By eliminat-
ing the French king, the adapter was enabled to represent a mutual affection as existing between Edgar and
Cordelia.   He thus lightened the tragic atmosphere
of the play by the alien interest of a love-story, and,
furthermore, of a love-story that ended happily.

No one will pretend that a love-story is essential to
comedy.   As we have seen, the passion plays a far less
important part in the ancient drama than in the modern, besides being there of a much more debased type.
From the former, even in its later period, it is sometimes absent altogether.   One of the most famous of
the plays of Plautus is the *Captivi*.   By many it has
been regarded as his very best.   Yet in it not a single
female character appears; not a word is said about love
between the sexes.   It is for this reason, perhaps, that
the prologue claims for it that there are in it no licentious lines unfit to be uttered.   The epilogue further
adds that the play is founded upon pure manners, that
there is in it no wenching, no intriguing, no exposure
of a child.   Still such plays are exceptional in the later
ancient comedy, and comparatively little known to the
modern.   In the latter, from almost the very outset,

the knowledge that interest could be most easily aroused in the audience by the introduction of a love-story put a pressure upon the writer from which he could with difficulty escape. We can see the working of this influence in 'The Comedy of Errors.' The *Menæchmi* of Plautus, upon which it is founded, shows no female characters but those of the courtesan and the jealous wife. When the English dramatist came to adopt the plot, he modified materially the tone of the whole play. A number of new personages were introduced. None of them appeal to the modern reader more than Luciana. If Shakespeare added to the farcical element of the comedy by furnishing the two closely resembling masters with two servants possessing the same characteristic, he added to its human interest by making Antipholus of Syracuse fall in love with the sister of his brother's wife.

There were, undoubtedly, authors of the time who looked with little favor upon the place the story of love had come to take in dramatic representation. This dislike was in part, due to the deference paid to the spirit that animated the ancient drama. This feeling was strengthened in some cases, however, by the conscious inability to portray the passion successfully. The subject is of universal interest, to be sure, but its delineation is often attended with peculiar difficulty. Unless conveyed with exceptional skill and force, the expression of intense feeling, where there is no necessary sympathy with it on the part of the hearer, tends to excite ridicule rather than respect. The fact is constantly exemplified in life. Under ordinary condi-

tions the perusal of love-letters in which one has no
personal interest arouses little other feeling than that
of amusement. Their extravagance, however real to
the writer, seems only laughable to him who reads them
in cold blood. Men who felt themselves unable to
depict the passion with felicity accordingly yielded with
reluctance to the pressure in this direction which the
wishes of the audience exerted. With the ancients
worthy of closest imitation, love, they argued, occupies
an inferior position. Why should not their example
be followed? The dramatists, so thinking, acted, as
far as they were permitted, upon this principle. Wherever possible, other interests were substituted. No
reader of Ben Jonson can fail to recognize the inconspicuous and almost contemptible part which love,
or rather the semblance of love, plays in his comedies.
The neglect of it as a leading motive in one way rendered easier, as we shall see, the task of conforming to
the unities. It has, however, affected the permanence
of his reputation. The lack of the interest of a love-
story in his plays has been one cause of the steady
decline of his popularity since the seventeenth century,
just as the presence of it in the plays of his greater
contemporary has been an element which has constantly
contributed to the increasing favor in which he has
been held.

Shakespeare himself could hardly have been ignorant
of the skill and power with which he depicted the passion. Of the extent to which he made use of it to
enhance interest there is no question. Not a single
comedy came from his pen in which it did not either

furnish the predominant motive or form a subordinate attraction. In every one of them is a love-story, and, unlike that of many of his contemporaries, it is a love-story almost invariably of a peculiarly pure and delicate kind. But in the representation of the feeling he did not limit himself to comedy. Love was rightly reckoned by him as one of the passions susceptible of tragic treatment, though he did not fall into the mistake of the French dramatists in making it extend to all plays of this character. Yet to two of his greatest it contributes a melancholy undertone. Of still another it is much more than a part. It is the whole. 'Romeo and Juliet,' as Lessing justly said, is the one tragedy in the world at which love itself has labored. There is in it no gallantry, no intrigue. From beginning to end the interest concentrates itself upon the fortune and fate of the two whose mutual passion gives a brightness, brief as the lightning flash, to the dark background of civil strife amid which it is born, and whose death is the sacrifice paid for the restoration of civil peace.

The foregoing facts make clear that Shakespeare gladly welcomed the delineation of love as the subject of scenic representation. But it is equally evident that the stage conditions under which the passion can be most successfully portrayed had not escaped his attention. As soon as love was made the principal interest in the modern drama, difficulties of a peculiar character beset him who aimed to observe the unities, — that is, if that drama were to live up to its professed ideal of holding the mirror up to nature. It is more correct to say they beset the writer of comedy. Of this it is an essential characteristic that the conclusion shall be happy. Under such a limitation the play, in nineteen cases out of twenty, is certain to end with either a betrothal or a marriage. But when the time of the action is limited to a single day, obstacles arise at once in the way of reaching satisfactorily a termination of this nature.

Two methods only have been taken or can be taken by the writer to extricate himself from the perplexities produced by conforming to the unities. The obstacles are either avoided altogether, or they are evaded. In the former case the series of events are so carefully arranged beforehand that we learn all the past proceedings from the speeches of the actors. We are simply called upon to be present at the dénouement to which weeks of previous preparation have been tending. This is a thing that can be done, and has often been brilliantly done, though it usually involves excessive pains on the part of the author. That requirement is indeed one of its main disadvantages. The strength of the writer must be largely spent in devising ingenious contrivances for bringing about the result at which he aims. But more than that, it gives him no adequate field for the display of his powers. It sacrifices, in particular, what are frequently the most effective scenes in representation, the gradual development of mutual passion, the removal or overthrow of the obstacles that stand in the way of the union of the hero and the heroine. Hence it is that brilliant plays of this kind, such, for instance, as 'Love for Love' and 'The Rivals,' appeal to the intellect much more than they do to the feelings.

In the other case the obstacles created by the observance of the unities are both disingenuously and inartistically evaded. All the circumstances that lead to betrothal and marriage are crowded into the space of a day or part of a day. Rapid work of this kind is not absolutely impossible in real life, but it is highly improbable; and the writer who draws his subjects from real life has no business to venture beyond the limits of the probable. In truth, such a course as the one indicated is so repugnant to our sense of propriety that the portrayal of it must be carefully disguised in order to prevent it from revolting the feelings. In the ancient comedy there was no such necessity. The audience would have been prepared, had it been necessary, to see, without protest, the future of the man or maiden arranged for with little or no consultation of their inclinations. But this is no longer possible. In modern life young people are not disposed of in marriage without at least going through the form of asking their consent. Their consent implies that there should be time enough for the two persons chiefly concerned to make each other's acquaintance, and to experience sensations to which they can feel justified in giving the name of liking, if not of love. But if the method under consideration is followed, all these sensations, in the drama which observes the unities, must be felt in the space of twenty-four hours or less. In that time two persons, who have never seen each other previously, must develop a wild desire to spend the rest of their lives together.

Now it might seem that no modern author would

venture to take the course just indicated. As a matter of fact, it will be found followed in some of our most celebrated comedies. The gross violation of propriety it implies frequently fails to excite disapprobation, because the attention is directed to some other interest in the play than that of the one which it nominally aims to represent. To illustrate how the observance of the unities works in practice, let us select for examination two noted specimens of this class of dramatic compositions taken from different periods in our literature. The first is the work of Ben Jonson, the great apostle who preached to a careless age the duty of obeying these laws. It is the one called ' Every Man in his Humor,' which there has already been occasion to mention. This play it is which Swinburne assures us, he is forced, in spite of his unqualified love for the greater poet, to characterize as "altogether a better comedy and a work of higher art than the ' Merry Wives of Windsor.' " [1] However true this may be, there is no question that in many respects ' Every Man in his Humor ' is a brilliant production. The attack contained in its prologue upon those who had neglected to observe the unities of time and place has already been given. But later in the same prologue occurs an assertion which is for us here of special moment. Jonson declares that the words and characters in this play are such as comedy would choose when she would show an image of the times. His satisfaction with what he had done cannot, therefore, be questioned. It is accordingly legitimate to test his conception of what consti-

[1] Swinburne's Study of Shakespeare, p. 121 (American edition), 1880.

tutes truth to life by an analysis of the plot of this work. From that we shall discover how just is Swinburne's praise of its art, how accurately Jonson has succeeded, to use his own words, in showing us an image of the time.

The scene of ' Every Man in his Humor' lies in London or its immediate suburbs, and the whole action takes place within the compass of a few streets. The time is just eight hours. The hero of the piece, young Knowell, is the son of an indulgent but somewhat anxious father, who loves him sincerely, and for whom he in return expresses and feels genuine affection. He leaves his parent's house early in the play in order to keep an appointment with his friend Wellbred, who is represented as the possessor, like himself, of high qualities of head and heart. Their place of meeting is the Old Jewry. There, at the beginning of the fourth act, young Knowell sees for the first time the sister of his friend. At least, no previous meeting is indicated or suggested. He immediately falls in love with her, and she goes through similar motions or emotions in reference to him. Through the agency of the brother a marriage is arranged, the two proceed to elope, and are united without the knowledge and consent of the relatives most directly and deeply interested. At the end of the play they make their appearance as man and wife. All this courtship and matrimony is therefore carried on and concluded in the space of four hours. There is no reason to suppose that the father would have opposed the son's choice, though, undoubtedly, in real life, if possessed of ordinary sense, he would have opposed this precipitate action. But even with the result regarded as a most desirable one, the hero of the piece has been guilty, not merely of an act of superlative folly, but also of a gross breach of filial respect and duty. No one needs to be told that we are not shown here an image of the times in the sixteenth century or in any century before or since. Men have done things as foolish and graceless as the actions just described, but not the kind of men that have been here brought upon the stage.

This is no solitary instance. In a number of Jonson's plays a similar condition of things is depicted. Two persons, who have never seen each other before, meet and agree to marry at once. But instead of confining ourselves to this period, let us take another example from a piece which holds, and justly holds, a place as one of the favorite comedies of our dramatic literature. It is Goldsmith's play of ' She Stoops to Conquer,' which was produced in 1773. In this the author, following the practice of his age, crowded all the events into a few hours. In the conduct of them, however, there is some respect paid to human nature and to the ordinary customs of life. The natural objections to precipitate action are obviated as far as possible. Two persons meet, who have never met before, to be sure, but they are dutifully prepared to fall in love with each other at first sight, so far as that result can be secured beforehand by parents and guardians. Accordingly, it does not come upon the mind with any particular sense of shock to find that the hero and the heroine have managed in less than half a day to fall in love with each other after a fashion, and are in consequence disposed to encounter the risks of matrimony. Nevertheless the absurdity exists. The reason we are not struck by it is that we are diverted from any consideration of the central improbability by the other incidents of the play.

No situations in the least resembling the two just described can be found in Shakespeare. The impropriety of such a representation of life was as apparent to him as it is to us. I have already tried to make it clear that ' The Tempest ' was undoubtedly written by him with his eye fixed upon the doctrine of the unities; and that he carried their observance through so unflinchingly that the time of the action is scarcely longer than the actual time of representation. It is therefore interesting to examine the method he took to meet the difficulties which confronted every writer who set out to comply with these artificial rules, how carefully he made his action in this particular conform to the natural feelings of the auditor or reader. In the first place, Ferdinand and Miranda belong to the station in life in which the wishes of the parties immediately concerned were rarely consulted then, and are rarely even now. They are of the class of rulers, and royal marriages are made to establish or cement alliances between states and not between persons. There is therefore nothing antecedently improper or improbable in the union. Yet even in so doing, Shakespeare defers to the practices which prevail in real life. Ferdinand pledges his faith to Miranda under the impression that his father had perished, and that he himself, in consequence, is a

126

perfectly free agent. But the dramatist is not content with mere conformity to these conventions. He not only makes the hero and the heroine personally attractive, so as to engage their inclinations to each other at first sight, but he also calls in to his help the aid of that potent magic which operates upon all the other characters in the play. Prospero himself attributes this rapid falling in love to the agency of Ariel. When he· sees how Miranda is impressed by the sight of Ferdinand, he adds, —

> " Spirit, fine spirit ! I 'll free thee
> Within two days for this."

A little later, after making the following comment on the lovers, —

> " At the first sight
> They have changed eyes, " —

he goes on to say, —

> " Delicate Ariel,
> I 'll set thee free for this."

In the two plays of Jonson and Shakespeare which have been examined we have had an opportunity to judge for ourselves which of the dramatists shows the higher art. In the one who looked upon himself and was celebrated by his adherents as its special representative, our feelings are outraged by having the hero portrayed in a matter which is to affect his whole future, as acting not merely the part of a fool, but of an ungracious and ungrateful fool. In the other, dealing with a similar situation, the work of the conscious artist appears in the minutest particulars. Every detail is in keeping with the demands of human nature.

No impropriety disturbs us, because everything which might tend to produce such an impression has been carefully eliminated. Miranda is to us the same peerless and perfect being, the same top of all admiration, which she appears to Ferdinand. Without the aid of Ariel's magic she conquers our hearts as completely and as rapidly as she did that of her lover. The same is true of her creator. He has been his own best advocate. The work of Shakespeare has triumphed over that of his contemporaries, has entered into the lives of us all, not because he lacked art, but because he possessed it.

CHAPTER IV

IT was his violation of the unities which constituted the most flagrant of the sins against art which were imputed to Shakespeare. Those who are familiar with the kind of criticism that for the hundred years and more following the Restoration not simply prevailed in England, but vaunted itself exceedingly, will be the least disposed to deny the importance which was then attached to the doctrine. The difficulties which attended its observance were held up as enhancing its merit. It is clear, from the reasons pointed out in the preceding chapter, that conformity to it not only tempted the dramatist to violate that highest art which consists in adherence to nature, but fettered in many ways his genius. One can hardly conceive the expenditure of time and toil that frequently became necessary to secure this artificial product. Yet, under the influence of the belief in this doctrine, men took pride in their chains. Writers for the stage deliberately went about to tie their own hands, and honestly persuaded themselves that the work so done was of an essentially higher grade than that which was accomplished with the hands at liberty. " Art," said Voltaire, "consists in triumphing over difficulties; and difficulties overcome give in every kind of

129

production pleasure and glory." The greater the difficulty, therefore, the greater the genius of the poet. This is a species of argument which, if carried out everywhere to its legitimate conclusion, would make the man who paints with his toes essentially superior to him who paints with his hands. Shallow as is the view, Voltaire's faith in it never wavered during the whole of his life.

From the period of the Restoration, therefore, the doctrine of the unities began to be accepted as the orthodox gospel to which all right-thinking persons were expected to conform. During the eighteenth century until towards its close it strengthened its hold. Belief in it received in England as well as elsewhere a mighty impetus from the preaching of Voltaire, its most ardent and effective apostle. The editors of Shakespeare, until Johnson came, assumed without question the correctness of the doctrine. Either by direct assertion or by implication they held the great dramatist censurable for his disregard of it. Most of the believers in it accepted the creed blindly. They rarely ventured to ask for the reason of the faith they professed. Everything had already been settled, it was assumed and asserted, by the wisdom of the ancients; though this, when subjected to close scrutiny, turns out now to be nothing more than the folly of the moderns. The men of the eighteenth century never seem to have had the idea that dramatic art consists in reproducing with fidelity the life we live or are capable of living; not in the observance of certain rules, which, however germane to the special development of the Greek stage, had no more binding authority upon the stage of later times than the ceremonial rites of the religion of the Jew upon the religion of the Christian.

It was not, however, disregard of the unities that constituted the only charge against Shakespeare. There were other precious things in which he had not attained to the standard the classicists set up. This failure on his part they imputed in a measure to ignorance, but mainly to lack of taste. Of that particular quality he had not a particle. Criticism of this sort began to show itself towards the close of the seventeenth century. By the middle of the eighteenth the opinion had assumed to many almost the nature of a self-evident truth. It is impossible to overlook the influence of Voltaire in extending in England itself the spread of this view. It did not owe its origin to him. It had been entertained and expressed in that country before he was born. But he gave it renewed vitality; above all, he gave it general currency. Men like Bolingbroke, Chesterfield, and Hume did not need to be converted to his views; but they were naturally confirmed more strongly in their own, when they found them sustained by the authority of the great literary autocrat of Europe. In fact so generally taken by professional critics was this estimate of the greatest of English playwrights that at one time it required not only independence, but a good deal of hardihood to run counter to a belief so widely accepted. Here, as in the unities, Shakespeare comes before us not only as the representative of the romantic drama but as its champion. It was its

131

methods which he exemplified; it was by his exemplification that they triumphed over hostile criticism
and were carried finally to victory.

There was one thing which the classicists professed
to hold especially dear. It constituted in their eyes an
essential distinction between their methods and those
of what we now call the romantic drama. It can
be designated by the somewhat vague general term of
propriety. This could be manifested in several ways.
When we come to the most generally discussed of its
various applications, we find that propriety required that
the bounds of tragedy and of comedy should be definitely determined and never transgressed. Accordingly there should be in the same production no mixture
of the pathetic and the humorous. The tragedy was
to be all tragic; the comedy was to be all comic. We
are able therefore to enter into the feelings with which
the adherents of the classical school looked upon the
practices in which Shakespeare indulged. His comedies
contained painful scenes; his tragedies humorous ones.
It was bad enough to violate the unities. But that
could be explained, even if it could not be pardoned,
by the assumed general ignorance of his age, involving
as it did his particular ignorance. But no such pal-
liating view could be taken, when the course adopted
by him depended, not on the possession or on the lack
of knowledge, but upon the presence or absence in his
nature of certain qualities. A man of genius is bound
in such matters to set an example to his age; not to
follow its ill example. This latter Shakespeare had
permitted himself to do. His action was explained

variously. The production by him of these mixed pieces was stated, negatively, to be due to nothing but the utter lack of taste; stated positively, to be due to barbarous taste. But whatever the precise cause, there could be no question as to the character of the result. He had been guilty of a gross violation of decorum.

Of the two ways in which propriety can be disregarded — the introduction of tragic scenes into comedy or of comic scenes into tragedy — it was perhaps impossible to decide which is abstractly the worse. It was the former, however, that was more common. In fact it was so very common that in the eyes of many of the classicists custom had shorn it somewhat of its theoretical native hideousness. Tragi-comedy was indeed one of the established forms of composition during the reigns of Elizabeth and the first Stuarts. Its popularity was so wide-spread that even adherents of the classical school were at times disposed to regard it with feelings hardly akin to disfavor. Some there were who accepted it as a kind of concession to human infirmity, very much on the same ground of hardness of heart which suffered the ancient Israelite to divorce a distasteful wife. No such countenance, however, did this mongrel production, as it was termed, meet with from the believers in art pure and undefiled. The gonfalon they marched under was to be absolutely spotless. It was the business of the comic muse to entertain, to delight, to fill our hearts with joy. Not once should the black shadow of care be permitted to overhang our spirits. Not under any pretext should the slightest thing be introduced calculated to arouse for a single moment feelings of grief or terror. Whatever else we fail in, was their cry, let us at least not fail in propriety. Whatever else we give up, let us not forget our first duty, which is to remain faithful to art.

And tragi-comedy, it came to be a general opinion, was not faithful to art. The arguments occasionally used to bolster up its pretensions were brushed away without ceremony. It had on its side the practice of the Elizabethan playwrights. But that of course was no authority. If these men were not rude and ignorant themselves, they were obliged to consult the taste of a rude and ignorant age. It had further on its side the continuous favor of the public. That was even less to its credit than the practice of the Elizabethan playwrights. So far from being evidence for either its correctness or excellence, its popularity aroused the suspicion that for that very reason it must be both inferior and wrong. That any work meets with general approbation has nearly always been proof positive to the superior person that it has failed to come up anywhere near to his own exalted standard. This attitude, taken from time immemorial towards all kinds of literature, was the one regularly assumed towards tragi-comedy. Unnatural inventions of this sort, it was said, might please the groundlings. The judicious would be only grieved or offended. He who thus sought to gain the applause of the ignorant must be content to dispense with the approval of the wise.

Again, tragi-comedy could boast on its side the authority of some men of letters. Even after the

Restoration it had had its advocates. Among them too could be reckoned the great name of Dryden. In his 'Essay of Dramatic Poesy,' published in 1668, he gave the views of both sides. One of the interlocutors in the dialogue, Lisideius — by whom is usually supposed to be meant Sir Charles Sedley — roundly denounced tragi-comedy. No theatre in the world save the English had anything so absurd. "'T is a drama of our own invention," he is represented as saying, "and the fashion enough to proclaim it so: here a course of mirth, there another of sadness and passion, and a third of honor and a duel; thus in two hours and a half we run through all the fits of Bedlam." When it comes to the turn of Neander — that is, Dryden — to speak, he maintains the propriety and excellence of this kind of composition. He denies that pity and mirth in the same piece destroy each other. As a matter of fact, in life as well as logic, contrarieties, when placed near, set each other off. It was to the honor of the English stage, he concluded, that it had invented, increased, and perfected a more pleasant way of writing than was ever known to the ancients or moderns of any nation.

But this defence of tragi-comedy availed little or nothing. No authority, however eminent, it was held could oversway the established principles of criticism which had set down this method of composition as monstrous. As in the case of the unities, the arguments denouncing their violation met for a long time with general critical assent, so it was with the proscription of the pathetic and the humorous in the same production. "There is no place in tragedy," wrote Gildon, "for anything but grave and serious actions." [1] Tragi-comedy fell completely under the ban of those who posed as the champions of true taste. The practice of writing it did not indeed die out; nor did the plays of that character produced fail of success. But however popular tragi-comedy might be with the public, it met with scant favor from the professed leaders of public opinion. It was the fashion to decry it as the ridiculous invention of an unpolished age. It was after this very manner that Addison spoke of it in one of his essays. In so doing he re-echoed the words put by Dryden into the mouth of Sedley. He described it as a production of purely native growth. The invention, however, so far from redounding to the honor of the English stage, was one of the most monstrous that had ever entered a poet's thoughts. "But the absurdity of the performance," he added complacently, "is so very visible that I shall not insist upon it." [2] From these last words it is clear that Addison was expressing the accepted view that had then come to be entertained by the men of the class to which he belonged.

Tragi-comedy, accordingly, though much liked by the public, met with scant favor from the professional critics. Even Dryden spoke of it at times disparagingly, and that, too, at the very moment he was exemplifying it in his practice. Certainly few there

[1] Essay on the Art, Rise, and Progress of the Stage (1710), in edition of Shakespeare, 1728, vol. x. p. 16.

[2] Spectator, No. 40, April 16, 1711.

were to put in any plea in its defence. Dryden's brother-in-law, Sir Robert Howard, who openly professed disbelief in the unities, found, though with some reluctance, that tragi-comedy was too much for him to approve.[1] Dennis, who under ordinary circumstances would far rather have died than fail to advocate the unpopular side of any subject, had nothing to offer in its favor. He commented, indeed, in no very amiable terms upon some of the statements made by Addison in the essay just mentioned. That writer was declared to be vilely mistaken if he fancied tragi-comedy was an outgrowth of the English theatre.[2] In this Dennis had been anticipated by Gildon, who about two years before had argued at great length against Dryden's defence of this "unnatural mixture," as he termed it, and had asserted that it belonged to the earlier and ruder period of both the Greek and the Latin drama, instead of being a modern invention.[3] But while Dennis himself did not denounce this species of dramatic composition, he made no attempt to justify it. There was indeed no one — at least no one of eminence — to say a good word for it until Dr. Johnson came forward to plead its cause. In the very same number of 'The Rambler,' in which he questioned the propriety of the unities, he professed himself inclined to believe that he who regarded no other laws than those of nature would take under his protection tragi-comedy. One of his sentences is

[1] Preface to Four New Plays, 1665.
[2] Essay on the Genius and Writings of Shakespeare (1712), p. 48.
[3] Remarks on the Plays of Shakespeare (1710), in Works, ed. 1728, vol. x. p. 426.

somewhat ambiguous; the end apparently contradicts the beginning. Tragi-comedy, he said, "however generally condemned, her own laurels have hitherto shaded from the fulminations of criticism." [1] His defence of this mode of composition he made still stronger in the preface to his edition of Shakespeare.

The account, which has here been given of the views of the eighteenth century, has so far gone upon the supposition that the men of that time attached to tragi-comedy precisely the same sense in which we ordinarily understand the word to-day. But this was not always the case. The critical estimate of that period is in consequence subject to an important modification. With us the term designates a play partaking of the characteristics of both comedy and tragedy, but having regularly a fortunate ending. Such was its use among the Elizabethans. So long as the final event of these two kinds of composition was kept perfectly distinct, so long as tragedy implied a tragic conclusion and comedy a happy one, the present sense is the only one in which the word could be properly employed. But after the Restoration this demarcation did not continue to exist. It was no longer essential that tragedy should have a tragic ending. Provided there had been a sufficient amount of misery in the course of the play, or provided that a reasonable number of the wicked characters had been done to death, the virtuous hero and heroine might be permitted to emerge from their troubles unscathed. This method of representing the result had in its favor the occasional support of an-

[1] No. 156, Sept. 14, 1751.

tiquity. The 'Electra' of Sophocles, the 'Iphigenia in Tauris' of Euripides, to select two examples, had each an ending, if not positively happy, at least satisfactory to the feelings. A similar treatment of the tragic theme developed itself upon the English stage. Tate's adaptation of 'Lear' is a noted case in point. It continued to be called a tragedy, though Cordelia came out triumphant, and saw her father privileged to reascend his throne. In the eighteenth century the term seems occasionally to have been applied to dramas hardly tragic at all, for no other reason apparently than that they were written in blank verse.[1]

The breaking down of this demarcation, however, was looked upon with little favor by many of the stricter sort; and controversy about its correctness lasted as late at least as the middle of the eighteenth century. But one consequence of it was the extension of the meaning of the term tragi-comedy. It came to be applied to dramas which had the most painful of catastrophes, provided they admitted anywhere humorous scenes. It was further applied to plays in which the comic element was almost wholly independent of the tragic. It was thus defined by Colman in the advertisement prefixed to his alteration of 'Philaster.' The term in question, he said, "according to its present acceptation conveys the idea of . . . a play, like 'The Spanish Friar' or 'Oronooko,' in which two distinct actions, one serious and the other comic, are unnaturally woven together." In the other and more limited sense it is, however, often employed. Consequently, when the eighteenth-century

[1] See, for illustration, Francis's 'Eugenia,' 1752.

critics speak of tragi-comedy, it is frequently and perhaps usually the introduction of humorous scenes into tragedy proper which they have in mind. This was in their eyes the grossest possible violation of decorum. The feeling that would banish what was painful from comedy could never be compared in intensity with that which shuddered at the introduction of comic passages into tragedy. Language at times seemed utterly inadequate to paint the absurdity, the grossness, and the barbarism of such a procedure.

The course was particularly objectionable because it conflicted with all the then established principles of dramatic art. These, it was felt, had come to be definitely settled for all time. Especially was it objectionable when the catastrophe of the piece was painful. In that case there was no room for anything which could be suspected of being even remotely jocular. Tragedy was to be throughout in a state of grief or terror. It was not really tragedy when there was any attempt put forth to lighten the generally pervasive atmosphere of funereal gloom. It must always be on the point of bursting into fits of tears or fits of rage. Anything that violently conflicted with these two engrossing occupations was regarded as detracting from its dignity. The monotony of wretchedness was never to be disturbed by anything which savored of the humorous, especially by that form of it which was called low. If any one resorted to such methods, and his venture was received with pleasure by crowded audiences, the professional reviewers took care to dispel any self-complacency in which the author might be disposed to indulge as a consequence, by assuring him that his work, however favorably regarded by the public, could not be expected to sustain successfully the ordeal of criticism. Shakespeare, in spite of the veneration in which he was held, had constantly to undergo castigation for the offences of this sort he had committed. Complaint was loudly expressed of the low nonsense, the misplaced buffoonery with which, in defiance of every principle of decorum, he had suffered even his best pieces to be disgraced.

These last words — which are taken almost literally from a periodical of the latter part of the eighteenth century [1] — are given merely as an illustration of the attitude assumed towards Shakespeare by those who regarded themselves as responsible for the preservation of pure and refined taste. Remarks of this regulation pattern can be found repeated again and again with positiveness in essays, in magazines, in reviews, in pamphlets of various kinds. The grave-diggers' scene in ' Hamlet ' came to be, in particular, the subject of attack. From it critics, even when otherwise favorable, turned away with averted eyes. The most fervent admirer of the great dramatist felt it incumbent to exhibit the impartiality of his judgment by falling foul of so manifest a violation of propriety. The anonymous author of ' Observations on the Tragedy of Hamlet,' which appeared about the middle of the eighteenth century, gave vent to sentiments which were so commonly expressed that they are worth quoting as representative of widely prevalent feelings in the class

[1] European Magazine, December, 1785, vol. viii. p. 417.

which assumed to itself the character of being specially cultured. After the usual lamentations about Shakespear~'s disregard of the unities, after the usual remarks that if he had only known the rules he would have risen to still nobler and sublimer heights than he actually attained, the writer let fall the full fury of his indignation upon the introduction of the grave-diggers. "Though this scene," he said, "is full of humor, and had not been amiss in low comedy, it has not the least business here. To debase his sublime compositions with wretched farce, commonplace jokes, and unmeaning quibbles, seems to have been the delight of the laurelled, the immortal Shakespeare. Some of his foolish bigoted admirers have endeavored to excuse him by saying that it was more the fault of the age than his, that the taste of the people was to the highest degree vicious when he wrote, that they had been used to buffoonery and would not be pleased without it, and that he was obliged to comply with the prevailing taste for his own emolument. This, instead of excusing, aggravates his crime. He was conscious he acted wrong, but meanly chose to sacrifice his sense and judgment to delight an injudicious audience and gain the applause of a herd of fools, rather than approach too near to purity and perfection. To mix comedy with tragedy is breaking through the sacred laws of nature, nor can it be defended." Those familiar with the writings of Voltaire will recognize at once how exactly these words reflect his opinions. The reference to the female sex with which the passage concludes bears, however, the unmistakable mark of the native soil. "This incoherent absurdity," adds the writer, "will forever remain an indelible blot in the character of our poet; and warn us no more to expect perfection in the work of a mortal than sincerity in the breast of a female."[1]

Fortunately for his peace during life, fortunately for his reputation after death, the writer of this little work remained anonymous. But to the list of undistinguished and indistinguishable mediocrities who found fault with this species of composition, can be added the great name of Milton. In the preface to his 'Samson Agonistes,' published in 1671, he spoke of the small esteem, or rather infamy, in which, according to him, tragedy was held in his day. It had all come about, he asserted, "through the poet's error of intermixing comic stuff with tragic sadness; or introducing trivial and vulgar persons: which by all judicious hath been counted absurd, and brought in without discretion, corruptly to gratify the people." This was the opinion of the man who looked at the drama from the point of view of classical antiquity. The French critics carried still further the stern repression of the comic element in tragedy. They found fault, indeed, with the ancients themselves for their deviations from this assumed standard of perfect propriety. The frivolous conversation, for instance, introduced by Euripides into his 'Alcestis' met with condemnation. If such could be their attitude towards a great writer of antiquity, it was inevitable that no mere modern like Shakespeare could escape the lash. His works were hardly brought to their notice till a third of the eighteenth century had

[1] Miscellaneous Observations, etc., p. 46, 1752.

143

gone. From that time on there was an almost unvarying uniformity of censure bestowed upon him for his mixture of comic and tragic scenes in the same production. This in turn affected English critical opinion, which in dramatic matters was then largely a mere echo of the French. It was rarely the case that Shakespeare's professed admirers attempted to defend his course in this particular. When Walpole did so in the preface to the second edition of his ' Castle of Otranto,' he was sneered at by the critics who were in good and regular standing. The ones favorably disposed towards the dramatist constantly shifted the burden of responsibility for his conceded excesses and absurdities from his shoulders to those of his age.

Nor was this all. Milton, in the passage just quoted, had done more than condemn the intermingling of the serious and the humorous in the same piece. His censure had further fallen upon the introduction into tragedy of low and trivial persons. One was not exactly a consequent of the other; but it was reasonably sure to be its accompaniment. Here was a peculiar aggravation of the original offence. A practice of this sort was contrary to all classical precedent; nor had it any support from the moderns who had followed classical models. At times exception had been taken to Ben Jonson's course in introducing into his two tragedies scenes below the dignity of tragedy. In ' Sejanus ' Livia and her physician satirize artificial helps to beauty. In ' Catiline ' there is a parliament of women. But in neither case do those who take part in the dialogue belong to a low class. This hostility to the introduc-

tion of men of an inferior social grade was based upon
the generally accepted doctrine that tragedy must never
deal with persons who belong to common life. If
otherwise, it could not properly bear Milton's epithet
of gorgeous. Its characters must hold the sceptre and
wear the pall. Any treatment of the theme that did
not conform essentially to this practice showed by that
very fact that it was deficient in art. There is a good
deal to be said in justification of the wide prevalence of
such a view when two authors, so great in genius and
so unlike in nature as Voltaire and Milton, agreed in
maintaining it. Under such circumstances the ordinary man may be pardoned for believing that it must
be true.

The belief in the necessity of preserving unimpaired
the dignity of tragedy by excluding from it all men of
the baser sort prevailed generally in the critical literature of the eighteenth century. To no small extent it
was affected by political considerations, especially by
the feeling entertained for the ruler. Even less on
the stage than in the court itself was there to be any
tampering with the dignity of so divinely an accredited
being. The moment a king appeared he must discover
himself in every word and sentence. Both thought
and language were to be in accordance with his high
position. Voltaire insisted that not only nothing common must be said by him, but nothing common could
be said before him. This was not merely in the play
itself, but in its representation in his presence. The
phrase, "not a mouse stirring," in the opening of ' Hamlet,' he asserted, might do for a guard-house; "but not

upon the stage, before the first persons of a nation, who express themselves nobly, and before whom men must express themselves in the same way." The French idea of the conduct of a tragedy seems, then, to have much resembled the conception which children have of the behavior of a king. In the eyes of these he always goes about with a crown upon his head. That he can act like other men, can share both their feelings and their failings, can enjoy the same pleasures and suffer the same pains seemed never to enter their minds. The French extended even to themselves the deference that was to be paid to their rulers. On their own account, as well as the king's, they objected to the introduction of inferior persons upon the stage. Like Hotspur's lord, they wished no rude, unmannerly knaves to come between the wind and their nobility.

Far otherwise had been the practice of Shakespeare. By him all these conventions so cherished by the classicists had been systematically violated. On his crowded stage men of all sorts and conditions of life appear. They talk to each other in the chamber, they jostle one another in the street. What was perhaps even worse was the introduction of the professional fools, holding conversation with the graver personages of the play, especially with the monarch. Such a course was against all classical precedent. It was one of the points of extremest divergence between the English and French theatres. Upon the latter, characters belonging to low life would never have been permitted by the audience to play their parts, had the author been audacious enough to introduce them. But to introduce them the author had no disposition. Voltaire tells us, in the preface to his tragedy of *Rome Sauvée*, that he was particular not to bring upon the stage the deputies of the Allobroges. It was their station in life that kept them from appearing before the cultivated audience to which his play was addressed. They were not really ambassadors of the Gauls, he tells us. In that case their presence would not have disgraced the distinguished assemblage before which they were to act. But, as a matter of fact, they were the agents of a petty Italian province, who were nothing but low informers, and therefore not proper persons to appear in company with Cicero, Cæsar, and Cato. As might be expected from a man holding such views, Shakespeare's course offered a favorite subject of criticism. He attacked the opening scene in ' Julius Cæsar,' where the lowest class of the populace are represented as exchanging speeches with the tribunes. It was not the character of the conversation that called forth his special censure. It was not because it abounded in dreadful quibbles and plays upon words — and in the wretchedness of this wretched practice, it must be admitted, Shakespeare surpassed all his contemporaries. But while these things aggravated the offence, they did not constitute it. That consisted in there being any conversation at all.

In all the numerous and varied censures which the professed guardians of taste passed upon the dramatist for his assumed violations of decorum, it never seemed to occur to any one of them that, from the point of view of dramatic art itself, he, the great master, might be right, and they, the critics, might be wrong. Being a man, he was liable in matters of detail to fall into error through haste, or carelessness, or even mistaken judgment. But being a man of genius, was he likely to err in the broad general methods which he had followed? A possibility that he knew much more than his censurers was never taken into consideration. His incorrectness was assumed as a matter of course. The only thing left was to explain how it came about. His severer critics did not impute his intermixture of tragic and comic scenes to ignorance. It was all owing, in their opinion, to his villanous taste. In this belief as to its origin they may be conceded to be right, even if we dispute the justice of the adjective applied to the noun. It would, indeed, be preposterous to take the ground that Shakespeare was not familiar with views which his practice shows that he did not accept. His remarks in ' Hamlet ' upon the many sorts of dramatic writing in vogue show that he knew perfectly well what he was doing. The course which he adopted was, without doubt, the course that had been common with his predecessors and was common with his contemporaries. But there is not the slightest reason to suppose that he followed it ignorantly or unadvisedly.

He had had, indeed, ample opportunity to learn the opinions of the school whose precepts he did not regard. There had been a number of plays written in accordance with its canons. They exist still, and are occasionally read, though read only by the painful student of the drama. There had also been a number of critical prophets going before him to point out the error of the

ways into which the earlier playwrights had fallen.
The same authorities, to say nothing of others, who
had come forward to instruct an unæsthetic generation
in the nature of the crime involved in the violation of
the unities, had also left their warnings as to the grave
impropriety of mingling comic matter with tragic.
"Many times, to make mirth," says Whetstone in his
comments on his contemporaries, "they make a clown
companion with a king. In their grave counsels they
allow the advice of fools: yea, they use one order of
speech for all persons: — a gross indecorum, for a crow
will ill counterfeit the nightingale's sweet voice." To
the same effect spoke Sidney in his 'Apology for
Poetry.' He declared that the plays of his time were
neither right tragedies nor right comedies. They mingle kings and clowns, he continued, "not because the
matter so carrieth it; but thrust in clowns by head and
shoulders to play a part in majestical matters with
neither decency nor discretion. So as neither the admiration and commiseration, nor the right sportfulness
is by their mongrel tragi-comedy obtained."

It is not unlikely that many, and perhaps the large
majority of the plays of that earliest period, had they
been preserved, would have been recognized by us as
justly falling under Sidney's censure, when he declared
that while no sort of poetry was so much used in the
England of his time as the dramatic, none was more
plentifully abused. But the abuse was not, as he supposed, in the method followed, but in the execution.
It was Shakespeare's triumph to prove by his practice
that the method was conformable both to nature and

the highest art. Kings and the professional fools of the household conversed together in real life. What inherent objection existed to their doing so in the drama which is supposed to represent real life? It was never their introduction into the same scene that merited censure. It was the way they conducted themselves after being brought together that would enhance or injure the effect of the play. It is one of Shakespeare's crowning distinctions that he recognized the possibilities that lay in the contrast of these opposed characters. He saw that it furnished opportunities for effective representation which did not and could not exist under the rigid rules of the classicists. Especially was he quick to seize upon the chances which the introduction of the household jester presented, to make acute and daring remarks on human life and motives that could not safely be put in the mouths of more serious characters; for it is the all-licensed fool that utters what other people think but are afraid to say.

What, indeed, is the objection to this mixture of the serious and the comic in the same play? By it is certainly represented, as it is not in pure comedy or pure tragedy, the life we actually live and the mingled elements that compose it. None of us exist in a state of perpetual joy or of perpetual gloom. We can go even farther. In the most tragical events there is usually somewhere an element of the humorous. In the most cheerful passages of life there always looms up before our eyes the suggestion, if not the reality, of sorrow. There is no one to whom existence is purely a pleasure. Those of us who have no great misfortunes to contend with, usually succeed in getting an adequate share of misery out of the little ones that fall to our lot. The lives of the happiest of us all are really tragi-comedies. In them painful episodes occur. They abound in events that wear upon the feelings, even if we are enabled to escape from calamities which sadden the heart, though they may not break the spirit. A single incident, or a series of closely connected incidents, may belong to the realm of comedy or of tragedy pure and simple. It is right enough to make matters of this kind the subject of a play. It is right enough to make the play in accordance therewith serious or humorous throughout. It would be, however, a most unjustifiable restraint upon the liberty of the dramatist to limit him either to incidents of this nature or to this method of treating them.

Yet this was something that was constantly attempted. A spurious reason, as we have seen, had been given for the maintenance of the unities. The spectator, we were told, suffered pain, or ought to have suffered pain, if they were violated. In being transported from place to place his ideas were confounded and his sensations dissipated. A line of reasoning, not essentially different, was adopted in regard to the mixture of serious and humorous scenes in the same play. As there was no question that sadness and mirth were constantly intermixed in real life, it was impossible to maintain that the illegitimacy of this form of dramatic composition was due to its improbability. Another sort of ground — already indicated in Dryden's essay — was taken. The two impressions were said to counteract each other. Their incompatibility destroyed the effect of the play when they were introduced together. This assumption, like many of the conventional assumptions of the classicists, was based upon the fallacy that the spectator feels the same degree of sorrow or joy that the characters in the play are represented as experiencing. No one seemed to think it worth while to controvert it; accordingly it turned up with invariable regularity in the criticism of the eighteenth century. Towards its close it was formulated and stated in fullest terms by Richardson, who was professor of humanity in the university of Glasgow.

Richardson was among the first, if he was not the very first, to enter upon the cultivation of a field which has since been worked almost beyond the capacity of production. This is the analysis of characters in Shakespeare's plays. Several of them were subjected by him to examination in two treatises which appeared, respectively, in 1774 and 1783. Both of these were creditable pieces of work. The style, to be sure, was somewhat labored and heavy; and an overpowering desire to scatter moral reflections on every imaginable pretext was not calculated to add to the charm of the matter. Still the author was a sincere and ardent admirer of Shakespeare. That, however, did not prevent him from contributing to his second treatise a short essay upon the faults of the dramatist. The criticism contained in it was very old and very shallow; nor was its ineffectiveness made any the less ineffective because clothed in pompous phraseology. According to Richardson, Shakespeare had been perverted by the dogma that the dramatist must follow nature; for while he possessed consummate poetical genius, he lacked philosophical discernment. In consequence, he had been misled by this belief into that practice of introducing comic scenes into his tragedy which so frequently disgusts. True, the passages of this sort to which exception had been taken were natural. But all things that are natural should not be represented. At this point was deployed the well-worn assumption which had been called upon to perform its part on so many previous critical battle-fields. We are once more told that the dissonant emotions produced by the tragic and the comic destroy one another, and the mind, during the contest, is left in a state of distraction.

The repute of tragi-comedy undoubtedly suffered from the presence of comic scenes which had no genuine connection with the play, and were brought in for no other purpose than to please the meanest class of the populace. An unsatisfactory effect can be and has been produced by such a course. It is the fault, for illustration, of ' Don Sebastian,' regarded by some as the best of Dryden's plays. It is even more in evidence in his last tragedy, ' Cleomenes,' where he avowedly admitted that he had introduced a low scene, not to help forward the action, but merely to gratify the rabble. Such a discreditable result is therefore liable to follow the concession of this privilege to the dramatist. But while it is possible, it is not in the least inevitable. In every instance, therefore, the particular work under consideration must be judged on its individual merits. If the comic scenes do not serve to advance the business of the play, or to heighten the effect of the tragic element, then their insertion is both an impertinence and an injury. It is exactly of the same character as the actor's wit extemporized in order to make laugh a quantity of barren spectators. That there is constant danger of the abuse of this privilege of introducing the comic may be conceded. That Shakespeare himself appreciated the peril is plain from the indignant comment made by him upon the pitiful ambition of those who take the part of the fool, and the stern direction Hamlet gives the players that the clowns shall speak no more than is set down for them. But while he recognized this risk, he recognized equally well the importance of the element of the humorous in relieving the strain upon the feelings of too prolonged consideration of the serious, as well as its adding by contrast to the effect of the serious. He knew better than did his critics how close life's tragedy stands to its comedy. It was a higher art than that of the schools which brought to our ears the conversation of the grave-diggers, and set before our eyes the ghastly preparations for burial. The stolid indifference of the world to private sorrow is a lesson that time brings home to us all; but nowhere has it been more strikingly conveyed than in the careless unconcern and trivial talk of the clowns to whom has been intrusted the charge of preparing the last resting-place of the hapless girl, who without fault of her own and without warning has been struck down, in the pride of youth, from love and happiness and high station into madness and doubtful death.

Exactly the same mingling of the comic and the tragic can be frequently observed in the art nearest

allied to the actor's, — that of the orator. In the very
highest efforts of the latter, the humorous, the pathetic,
and the sublime are often found in close juxtaposition.
They follow one another at the briefest of intervals.
For all that, no sense of incongruity jars upon our feelings, no inappropriateness strikes us. We do not find
ourselves hindered from undergoing the keenest sensations of sorrow, pity, or wrath, or of mental or spiritual
elevation, because a short time before we have been
stirred to heartiest laughter. The springs of joy and
grief lie side by side; and it is in the power of the
great orator to cause each to burst forth at pleasure.
He is at liberty to confine himself to but one of many
methods of appeal. He can be serious throughout, he
can be humorous throughout, or he can intermingle the
serious and the humorous. It is by the effect he produces, not by the manner in which it is produced, that
the excellence of his course is to be tested. If he suc-
ceeds through the agency of the one or the other exclusively, no fault can be found with him for so limiting
himself. But equally is it true that no fault can be
found with him if he chooses to call into action both
classes of emotions. All that is required of him is that
what he does must conduce properly to the end he has
in view. This freedom conceded on all sides to the orator belongs by right to the dramatist also. By Shakespeare it was assumed without hesitation and without
apology.

From this bondage of the so-called proprieties, as
from that of the unities, has the mighty dramatist
delivered us. The comedies and tragedies which the

classicists maintained to be the only ones that could be correct, if they hold the mirror up to nature at all, hold it up to a very limited aspect of nature, or to an aspect existing for a very limited period. It can be great work in its domain, but its domain is restricted. It is the enlarged power which Shakespeare gave to dramatic representation, it is his skill in raising it above the restraint of mechanical rules, and embracing in its vision the whole field of human life, which place him in some respects in a higher position than even that which the greatest of his classical predecessors, cramped by the condition of their theatre, were able to attain. The ignorance which once decried his methods is now little heard; or, if heard, not heeded. Against the doctrine of the unities there had been, during the course of the eighteenth century, a good deal of critical protest. But the impropriety of mingling the comic and the tragic in the same piece was conceded on every side. Johnson's was almost the solitary voice raised in its favor; for Walpole's defence of the practice, though containing suggestive observations, is rather an expression of personal opinion than an argument. The established custom was either to inveigh furiously against it or to deprecate it mildly; but in either case to regard it as an indefensible violation of propriety.

What indeed may be considered the official critical view of the eighteenth century on this point was indicated by the somewhat heavy-headed Lord Lyttelton, who brought out his ' Dialogues of the Dead ' about the same time that Johnson and Walpole were putting their opinions upon record. One of these dialogues is rep-

resented as taking place between Pope and Boileau.
Shakespeare is the main subject of discussion. Lyttelton was unconsciously true to nature in representing
the French critic as possessing and expressing very
positive opinions as to the merits of the English author,
though he had never read and could not have read a
line of his works. Pope makes the usual apologies of his
century for the conduct of the dramatist. "The strange
mixture of tragedy, comedy and farce in the same play,
nay sometimes in the same scene," he is reported as saying, "I acknowledge to be quite inexcusable. But this
was the taste of the time when Shakespeare wrote."
Naturally the purified taste which had come to prevail
could not tolerate such impropriety. Here, as elsewhere, critical opinion was far behind popular opinion.
Long after Johnson had raised the standard of revolt,
the former continued to exhibit unflinching firmness in
denouncing the mixture of the serious and the humorous. The reviewers, connected with the periodical
press, kept as sharp an eye out for this violation of
decorum as they did for the disregard of the unities.
Cumberland, for instance, produced in 1783 his tragedy
of 'The Mysterious Husband.' In it he ran counter
to several well-established conventions. The one, however, for which he was taken sharply to task, was the
appearance in his piece of a comic character. This
was a sacrifice, he was told, that the earlier dramatists had been compelled to make to the unpolished
taste of their times. But the cause no longer existed.
There was, accordingly, no excuse for having introduced humor where all should be passion. By so doing

he had arrested the impressions of pity and terror, in order to excite laughter, preferring the approbation of the ignorant to the feelings of the judicious.[1]

This was the established critical view. Men like Congreve, Addison, Young, Thomson, and many others strove to live up to it; but a large number were indifferent. Relying upon Shakespeare's authority, they went to lengths which Shakespeare himself would never have sanctioned. They, in turn, if their works chanced to be popular, were subjected to censure, and in occasional instances, to the correction implied in alteration. Southerne's ' Oronooko ' was frequently attacked, not for the immorality of its comic scenes, but for its having any comic scenes at all. Originally produced in 1696, it remained during the following century a favorite of the theatre-going public. But its mixture of the humorous and the pathetic always offended the advocates of art, and in 1759 Hawkesworth undertook to alter it for the stage in such a way as to remove the reproach. The prologue to this revised version, after praising the author for the tragic portion of his play, went on to add: —

" Yet, slave to custom in a laughing age,
　With ribald mirth he stained the sacred page;
　While virtue's shrine he reared, taught vice to mock,
　And joined, in sport, the buskin and the sock:
　O ! haste to part them ! — burst the opprobrious band !
　Thus Art and Nature with one voice demand."

Nothing indeed shows how much more influential was the popular to what may be called the professional

[1] Critical Review, vol. lv. p. 151.

taste than the fact that from the earliest days of the Restoration period the author, when he set out to write for the stage, was very apt to cast aside the accepted critical view, sometimes even when enunciated by himself, and conform to practices which either his age or he himself condemned. Into the alteration which he made of Shakespeare's 'Richard II,' Tate introduced comedy, for the avowed reason that he judged it necessary so to do, in order "to help off the heaviness of the tale." For that he hoped not only for pardon but for approbation; and further supported his action by the authority of Dryden, who had declared that few tragedies in that age would succeed, unless "lightened with a course of mirth." [1] But the dereliction of Dennis from the right was far worse. He had found great fault with Shakespeare for bringing into the play of 'Coriolanus' the dregs of the populace, and for turning Menenius, as he said, into an errant buffoon, —something which Shakespeare was very far from doing. By this course the dramatist had offended against the dignity of tragedy. Yet in his alteration of the play Dennis added a good deal of low comedy of his own. It was avowedly done for no other purpose than to please the audience. "I desire you," he wrote, "to look upon it as a voluntary fault and as a trespass against conviction." [2]

But however much they have failed when they came to the trial themselves, the critics always held up before others the orthodox view. During the eighteenth century they practically had it all their own way. The

---

[1] Epistle Dedicatory to the Spanish Friar.
[2] Essay on the Genius and Tragedy of Shakespeare, p. 35.

correctness of their theory was hardly questioned publicly, however much it might be disparaged privately, or however frequently it might be disregarded in practice. Belief in the impropriety of introducing the humorous into tragedy, like the belief in witchcraft, was never out-argued; it was simply outgrown. A change in the attitude of the human mind on this point took place during the century, apparently without any appeal to the reason. It was outgrown, because the practice of Shakespeare prevailed by the mere weight of his example. Here, as in other ways, he has been his own best advocate. The steadily increasing appreciation of his superiority, not simply as a poet but as a dramatic artist, is observable in the steadily increasing tendency that went on during the eighteenth century to reject the alterations which had been made in his plays by so-called improvers, and to return to the form in which they had been originally written. Attempts to foist new alterations upon the poet had not ceased, indeed, even when the century was nearing its close. But they were no longer carried out on an extensive scale. They were no longer undertaken with the light heart and easy confidence, which had once prevailed, that the botcher must necessarily be an improver. Above all, they were no longer received with favor, as their perpetrators were speedily given to understand.

Yet in this general stream of tendency there occurred one remarkable eddy. In another chapter it will be necessary to give some account of the havoc which the devotees of art pure and undefiled wrought with

160

the works of the dramatist in order to fit them for the understanding ages which had succeeded the barbarous one in which he flourished. Here, however, is a fitting place to relate the story of one of the latest and most audacious attempts to reform Shakespeare in accordance with the demands of that purified taste which could not away with the introduction of humorous scenes into tragedy. It was made at the time when classicism had entered upon its downward career; when the canons of art it was wont to proclaim arrogantly had begun to be questioned by even the intellectually timid, and to be scouted by bolder spirits. It was furthermore made by a very genuine admirer of Shakespeare. It was made by him professedly to purify the particular drama selected from the debasement which its tragic sternness had incurred by the introduction of comic scenes. The play operated upon was 'Hamlet;' the improver was Garrick. The story of its alteration is worth recording, not merely because it has never been fully told, but because the reception accorded to it brings out prominently the difference between the point of view of the latter parts of the seventeenth and eighteenth centuries. Nothing shows more strikingly the long road which taste and opinion had travelled during the hundred and more years which had followed the Restoration.

The liberties which Garrick had previously taken with several of Shakespeare's plays had been somewhat venturesome. But hitherto he had done no more than tread in the footsteps of those who had preceded him in the same kind of work, or had tried his hand on pieces which were scarcely known to theatrical audiences. But 'Hamlet' was in a different position. It had been and was not only exceedingly popular, but up to this time it, like 'Othello,' had remained untouched by the so-called improver. It came into Garrick's mind that here was an opportunity to remedy the imperfections under which the play labored in consequence of its having been produced in an unpolished age. We find him actually engaged upon the task of altering it in 1771, though we know from his correspondence that he had contemplated the possibility of so doing long before.[1] He seems to have communicated his design to but few. Among them was the future commentator, Steevens, already known for his interest in and knowledge of Shakespeare. From him he received both advice and encouragement. He wrote to Garrick that he expected great pleasure from his altered 'Hamlet.' That play, in his opinion, was a tragi-comedy; and in spite of all that Dr. Johnson had said upon the subject, he should never be reconciled to tragi-comedy. Shakespeare's genius, he declared, had deserted him in the last two acts. Still later in this same letter he advised Garrick to throw what remained of the play after his omissions into a farce, to be produced as an after-piece. This was to be entitled 'The Grave-Diggers, with the Pleasant Humors of Osrick, the Danish Maccaroni.' "No foreigner," he added, "who should happen to be present at the exhibition would ever believe it was formed out of the lappings and excrescences of the tragedy itself." [2]

[1] Garrick Correspondence, vol. i. p. 515.   [2] Ib. p. 451 (1771).

Steevens, as he showed later, was capable at times of expressing literary opinions that are interesting for their very absurdity. Still no one ever charged him with being a fool. Garrick may be pardoned for being misled by his approval. He knew him as the patient and untiring student of the Elizabethan drama. He could not then know him, as we know him, as probably the most unscrupulous as well as one of the very ablest scamps among the commentators of Shakespeare. There was no happiness dearer to his heart than to witness the blunders committed by such as had the misfortune to be what he called his friends. There are those who believe that in his encouragement of this alteration Steevens was, for once in his life, sincere. There can be little question as to the sardonic glee with which he pretended to approve the design and watched the progress of the work. His suggestion of the after-piece was of course not seriously given, nor is there any likelihood that it was so received. But there was a good deal in what he said that ought to have opened Garrick's eyes to the blunder he was committing. "I am talking a kind of heresy," he wrote, after the disparaging opinion of 'Hamlet' just given; "but I am become less afraid of you, since you avowed your present design." [1]

As the work was never printed, it is impossible to tell with certainty either the nature or extent of the alterations. Incidental references, not conveying any specific information, are made to it in contemporary literature; but there are two short accounts of it, one

[1] Garrick Correspondence, vol. i. p. 451.

given by a man who had heard it,[1] and another by a man who saw or thought he saw the manuscript.[2] These two, while agreeing in the main, differ occasionally in details, especially in regard to certain particulars of the catastrophe. In spite of these variations the following account may be trusted as a fairly correct representation, as far as it goes, of the alterations introduced. The acts were divided differently, the changes were few, and those were generally in the form of omission. Garrick himself wrote to Hoadly, his clerical friend, that he had added but twenty-five lines in all to the whole play.[3] But the excisions took place on an extensive scale, especially in the last part. They were directed mainly to the removal of humorous passages. The voyage to England, however, was omitted, as was also the execution of Rosencranz and Guildenstern. The plot arranged between the king and Laertes was also much changed, and the character of the latter was thereby made more estimable. The grave-diggers' scene, that stench in the nostrils of the judicious, was swept away entirely. Osric also disappeared. Ophelia was deprived of her funeral, and passed out of the play with no record of the fate that had befallen her. Hamlet was represented as bursting in upon the court with the resolution to revenge his father. An altercation with the king was followed by a duel in which the king was slain. The miserable queen did not perish in the sight of

---

[1] Davies' Dramatic Miscellanies, vol. iii. p. 151.
[2] Boaden's Life of Kemble, vol. i. p. 110.
[3] Garrick Correspondence, vol. i. p. 515.

the audience from the effects of poison, but after the killing of her husband rushed out of the presence-chamber, became frantic and prepared to die in the most approved French fashion behind the scenes. Hamlet himself, in a duel which took place with Laertes, was mortally wounded. Up to this point the two accounts agree ; at least they do not conflict. But henceforth there is a variation in the details. According to the one account Laertes also fell mortally wounded.[1] According to the other — which is, on the whole, preferable — Laertes was about to meet his death at the hands of Horatio, when the dying Hamlet interfered. He joined the hands of the two, and commended to their united effort the care of the troubled land.[2]

It was probably impossible for Garrick to preserve the unities in his altered version. Perhaps no attempt was made to do so. Yet the changes introduced seem to have had the effect of making their violation comparatively inconspicuous. The worst defiance of them in the original was to all appearances eliminated. It had grieved mightily the soul of Voltaire that at the beginning of the play Fortinbras had been represented as setting out with his army for Poland, and at the very close as having returned from its conquest. In the altered version he plainly did not return, if indeed he went forth. In truth, as far as can be collected from the conflicting accounts of this revision, the subsidiary characters became more subsidiary than ever. In its original form 'Hamlet' is a tragedy in which the actor

[1] By Davies.   [2] By Boaden.

who plays the title-rôle has to divide the honors less with subordinate performers than in any other one of Shakespeare's greater plays. This is a main reason why it is so frequently selected by youthful aspirants for histrionic reputation. It furnishes peculiar opportunities to the actor who is seeking to gain for himself a name. Garrick by his alterations made this characteristic even more pronounced. One result of this procedure — according to his enemies, the object of it — was to reduce the consequence of the other parts and to increase that of the principal one. On this last the omissions tended to concentrate still more the attention of the audience. There was a good deal of justification for the criticism of the version by Steevens's follower, Isaac Reed, that the alterations had been made by Garrick in the true spirit of Bottom, who wished to play not only the part assigned him but all the rest of the piece.[1]

The play thus mutilated was brought out at Drury Lane on the eighteenth of December, 1772.[2] There was evidently anxiety as to the reception it might meet. This seems hardly necessary, for Garrick's wonderful performance would have been enough to insure from hostile treatment a play in which he took so prominent a part, even if it did not meet with positive applause. Still the uneasiness existed. From Hoadly he received soon after an inquiry upon this very point. " How did the galleries behave," he asked, " when they found themselves deprived of their grave-

[1] Biographia Dramatica, under Hamlet, ed. of 1782.
[2] Genest's English Stage, 1660–1830, vol. v. p. 343.

diggers? Or did they not miss them? That would be the greatest applause to your alterations." [1] Whatever might be the feelings of the galleries, it was assumed that the new version would meet with the unqualified approval of the boxes, and of the critics who stationed themselves in the pit. "The judicious," however, had now begun to be a scattered people in England. Furthermore they no longer received that frank acknowledgment of their superiority which had once been conceded to them ungrudgingly. Still the small proportion that had survived from the multitude of former generations were unquestionably pleased. One of these, who has left us a record of his sentiments, was Edward Taylor. The son of a church dignitary, he had spent several years of study and travel abroad, and had come back to England in full possession of the refined taste of the continent. About a year and a half after the production of this altered 'Hamlet' he brought out some 'Cursory Remarks,' as he called them, on tragedy and on Shakespeare. He hailed the abolition of the grave-diggers' scene, so unworthy of the dramatist, as evidence of the approaching triumph of taste. "To the credit of the present times, indeed," he wrote, "these puerilities are now omitted. Let us hope that they will not be the only ones, nor let us be afraid to reject what our ancestors, in conformity to the grosser notions then prevalent, beheld with pleasure and applause." [2]

[1] Garrick Correspondence, vol. i. p. 515.
[2] Page 40. See also an apparent approval of the version in a piece called " Conversation": reproduced in the New Foundling Hospital for Wit, vol. ii. pp. 186–190.

Far more enthusiastic was the reception accorded to this alteration in France by the party there that dreaded the effects of the growing interest in Shakespeare, and the growing admiration of his methods which were beginning to manifest themselves in that country. Marmontel not only welcomed the version with exultation, but he gave an account of its reception by the English public, which if not the product of his own imagination, was communicated to him exclusively. "Every day," he wrote, "the works of Shakespeare are abridged, are corrected. The celebrated Garrick has just cut out upon his stage the gravediggers' scene and almost all the fifth act. Both piece and author have been only the more applauded." This felicitation of his disciple over the triumph which true art had achieved, Voltaire embodied later in his noted 'Letter to the French Academy' which was read at the meeting of August 25, 1776. He was then waging war with Le Tourneur's translation of Shakespeare, and Garrick's action had brought him peculiar gratification. It constituted a reproof to the perverted enthusiasts of his native land who were seeking to fasten upon France the acceptance of those barbarous atrocities which the reviving taste of England was beginning to cast aside.

Neither Taylor's anticipation of future improvements of the same sort, nor Marmontel's belief that England was turning at last to the better way, was destined to be realized. Garrick's extraordinary ability sustained the altered version while he himself was acting. His influence kept it on the Drury Lane stage for some

time after he had retired.   But it is clear that the
changes which he had made met with silent disfavor,
where they did not receive outspoken condemnation.
The time had gone by for any new liberties of this
sort to be taken with approval; it was a good deal,
even, that they could be taken with impunity.   "No
bribe," says Reed, "but his own inimitable performance could have prevailed on an English audience to
sit patiently and behold the martyrdom of their favorite
author." [1]   This statement is not strictly true.   The
version was played by other actors while he was still
manager, and also after he had left the stage.   But
it was never liked.   "The spectators of Hamlet," says
Davies, somewhat sadly, "would not part with their
old friends, the grave-diggers.   The people soon called
for 'Hamlet,' as it had been acted from time immemorial." [2]   What was most painful of all was that the alteration met with but little favor from the judicious who,
it was expected, would welcome with delight the rejection of what Garrick termed the rubbish of the fifth
act.   Walpole communicated the news of what the actor
had done to his correspondent Mason.   "I hope," was
his accompanying sarcastic comment, "he will be rewarded with a place in the French Academy." [3]

It did not, indeed, take Garrick long to become
aware of the peril which he was running.   He had
made arrangements to publish his altered version.   He
speedily abandoned the project.   He gave further evi-

---

[1] In Biographia Dramatica, under Hamlet, ed. of 1782.
[2] Davies' Dramatic Miscellanies, vol. iii. p. 153.
[3] Correspondence of Walpole and Mason, vol. i. p. 48.

dence of the fear which had taken hold of him. Not only was the altered play not printed, but no written copies of it were allowed to get into circulation. The actor, Tate Wilkinson, then patentee of the York and other theatres in the North, applied for one in vain. "It is not in my power to comply with your request to send you the corrections lately made in 'Hamlet,'" wrote in reply Victor, the treasurer of Drury Lane; "but no such favor can be granted to any one, as I presume the play will never be printed so altered, as they are far from being universally approved; nay, in general greatly disliked by the million; — therefore, no doubt, your country 'squires would be for horsewhipping the actor that had struck out that natural scene of the grave-diggers." Victor then went on to point out that Hamlet's consenting to go to England, and being brought back by miracle, is altogether absurd, when his solemn engagement with his father's ghost is duly considered. Then unconsciously he revealed the superiority of the judgment of the masses to his own. "As I have already observed," he concluded, "the million will like, nay understand Shakespeare with all his glorious absurdities, nor suffer a bold intruder to cut them up." [1]

The only consolation that could be received for this attitude of the artistically unregenerate was that they were incapable of reaching the elevated plane which their betters occupied. There were some of Garrick's admirers, however, who stood by him manfully, and without doubt approved in fullest sincerity of his

[1] Wilkinson's Memoirs of his own Life, vol. iv. p. 260.

course. One of them complained that he had not gone far enough. "Twenty-five lines only added," wrote Hoadly, when his friend sent him word to that effect: "I fear too little has been done." [1] This writer, who was a clergyman for livelihood, and would have been a dramatist if he had had sufficient ability, had felt somewhat hurt because he had not been consulted about this revision. It was a matter which he had more than once discussed with the actor. His inborn discernment and educated taste had indicated to him numerous places where Shakespeare's work required improvement. The behavior to each other of Hamlet and Ophelia was in his opinion a part that needed and most admitted great alteration. The conduct of the hero towards the heroine, in particular, had not been sufficiently worked out by the dramatist. No adequate cause had been given to account for the madness and death of the latter. This could and should be remedied; and here was the way in which it was done in one instance. The concluding lines of Hamlet's soliloquy end with his recognition of Ophelia in these words, —

> " Soft you now !
> The fair Ophelia ! "

Then follows the request to be remembered in her prayers. After Hamlet's recognition of her presence, but before he addresses her personally, Hoadly suggested that the following lines should be added to the soliloquy, which would explain to the satisfaction of everybody the prince's subsequent conduct: —

---

[1] Garrick Correspondence, vol. i. p. 515.

> "I have made too free
> With that sweet lady's ear.   My place in Denmark,
> The time's misrule, my heavenly-urged revenge,
> Matters of giant-stature, gorge her love,
> As fish the cormorant. — She drops a tear,
> As from her book she steals her eyes on me.
> My heart !   Could I in my assumed distraction
> (Bred, says the common voice, from love of her)
> Drive her sad mind from all so ill-timed thoughts
> Of me, of mad ambition, and this world !
> Nymph, in thy orisons be my sins remembered." [1]

These priceless lines show us what the eighteenth century could do when it set out seriously to reform Shakespeare, to correct his negligence and refine his ruggedness in accordance with the requirements of taste and art.

The altered 'Hamlet' held the stage at Drury Lane for nearly eight years.   But it was not often played. The audience might put up with the version; but they plainly did not love it.   In this feeling high and low concurred.   Accordingly, on April 21, 1780, little more than a year after Garrick's death, Hamlet was advertised to be acted as Shakespeare wrote it.[2] Contemporary testimony shows that the abandonment of the alteration took place, not under the compulsion of active hostility, manifested according to the then usual custom in the playhouse itself, but simply in consequence of the refusal of people to attend the performance of the piece.   " Since the death of the player," said Reed in 1782, " the public has vindicated the rights of the poet by starving the theatre into compliance with

[1] Garrick Correspondence, vol. i. p. 573.   Letter dated Sept. 30, 1773.
[2] Genest, vol. vi. p. 133.

their wishes to see Hamlet as originally meant for exhibition." [1] Thus early disappeared from the boards the alteration so long desired by a certain class. It was practically the last serious attempt upon Shakespeare which correctness made as a tribute to an assumed higher taste. Some of Kemble's later versions were even viler; but they were not original. That actor only refashioned what others had previously accomplished. Garrick's course in this matter is one of which explanation can be given, but for which defence cannot be made. The student of English constitutional history has frequent occasion to observe how infinitely superior has sometimes been the stupidity of juries to the wisdom of judiciaries. Examples of a similar sort do not so often meet the eye of the student of literary history. Still they are to be found. Among them there is perhaps no more striking illustration than the present, of the superiority of judgment sometimes shown by the great mass of men to that arrogantly boasted of by the select body of self-appointed arbiters of taste and guardians of dramatic propriety.

[1] Biographia Dramatica, ed. of 1782, under Hamlet.

CHAPTER V

THE violation of the unities, the intermixture of comic scenes with tragic were two faults which in the eyes of the classicists placed an ineffaceable stigma upon the romantic drama. About their essential depravity both continental and English critics were agreed. Shakespeare, in consequence of his exemplifying these atrocities, was regularly made the subject of the tale which he was not thought to adorn, and served constantly to point its moral. It is true that he had not acted differently from almost every one of his contemporaries. They were as regardless of these rules as he. But while others had sinned as much against art, he was the only one who had really survived. He was the only one who continued to impress himself upon successive generations. Particular plays of certain of his contemporaries — Fletcher especially, and occasionally Jonson and Massinger — were from time to time refitted for the stage and brought out during the eighteenth century. But they had at best but a partial success; they often met with positive failure. "It may be remembered," said Colman in 1763, "that 'The Spanish Curate,' 'The Little French Lawyer,' and 'Scornful Lady' of our authors," — that is, Beaumont and Fletcher, — "as well as 'The Silent Woman' of Jonson,

174

all favorite entertainments of our predecessors, have within these few years encountered the severity of the pit, and received sentence of condemnation." [1] But of Shakespeare nothing of this sort could be said. His reign had never been disturbed. He had not only kept unbroken possession of the theatre, but was constantly extending his occupancy. It was therefore upon him that the weight of criticism fell.

But a third grand distinction existed between the classical and the romantic drama. The French theatre — and the French theatre for a long time gave the law to continental Europe — had made an advance upon the ancient in the rigidity of its requirements. It restricted the liberty of representation to exceedingly narrow bounds. In particular, it carried, to an extreme, hostility to the introduction of scenes of violence. The audience were to be treated with the tenderest consideration. Nothing was to take place on the stage that could offend the susceptibilities of the most fastidious. No blood was to be shed in the sight of the spectator. There was indeed one singular modification of this restriction. A character in the tragedy could be permitted to kill himself, whether he did it by poison or steel: what he was not suffered to do was to kill some one else. And while nothing was to be shown on the stage which could offend the feelings through the medium of the eyes, equally was nothing to be narrated with the accompaniment of any adjuncts that could possibly arouse disagreeable sensations in the mind. Voltaire tells us how he was stirred in the

[1] Advertisement to the alteration of Philaster, 1763.

English theatre by seeing Brutus harangue the people, while holding in his hand the bloody knife with which he had just stabbed Cæsar. He somewhat regretfully remarked that no such method of representation would have been tolerated on the French stage, any more than would have been an assemblage made up of Roman plebeians and artisans. No bleeding body of the dead dictator could have been exposed in public. He was inclined to think — at least at first — that in this respect the French stage had gone too far. Here were legitimate opportunities for stage effect which it had deliberately abandoned. At other times he was disposed to justify its course. Scenes like these just mentioned, he admitted, were natural; but a French audience expected that nature should always be presented with some strokes of art.

On their stage consequently all deeds of violence had to be narrated. Their actual performance took place behind the scenes. The audience learned of them from the mouth of some eyewitness who came to tell it what had happened. This method might spare the sensibilities of the hearers, but it assuredly did not add to the effectiveness of the play. One finds his admiration of the great French dramatists increasing when he recognizes under what limitations they labored. Nor need we shut our eyes to the fact that the method thus forced upon them had the advantages of its defects. It acted as a spur to the writer. It compelled him, in particular, to pay attention to expression. Conscious that the success of his production would be little aided by attractions which appealed to the eye, but must depend largely upon those which addressed the ear, he made up, so far as in him lay, for failure of action, by interest of narration, by beauty of description, and by all possible charm of verse. Exquisite poetry could undoubtedly add to the interest of dramatic action. The problem which the French author was called upon to solve was the extent to which it could be made to take its place.

At this point the stages of the two nations diverged. During the period of which we are speaking, the English critics had almost universally consented to the exceeding wickedness of the negative sin of disregarding the unities, and to the positive crime of introducing comic matter into tragedy. But here as a body they stopped. They were no more satisfied than were English audiences, with plays in which narration took the place of action. There were those indeed, as we shall have occasion to observe, who sympathized with the French attitude. Some of them too were men of high literary and social position. On these accounts deference was paid to their opinions; but after all it was only in a half-hearted way that their views were supported by those who professed to follow their authority. Hence what is the third great distinction between the classical and the romantic school extended largely to theory as well as practice. The distinction is implied in the following queries: What is permissible to be shown upon the stage? What is forbidden? Or at least what is inexpedient? These are questions that always present themselves to the dramatic author in the construction, and to the dramatic critic in the

consideration, of plays which involve the results of
violence and bloodshed. One business of a tragedy
is to make away with people. How can this best be
done, not effectually as regards the personages of the
play, but effectively as regards the persons present to
see and hear? Will it produce the most gratifying
impression upon the audience to despatch the characters
of the drama before their eyes, or to dispose of them
behind the scenes, and let the knowledge of what has
occurred reach them through the medium of their ears?
The classicists maintained stoutly that acts of violence
should always be narrated and never represented. According to their view that which would be disagreeable
or painful to see in real life should never be brought
before us on the stage. Hence in their drama not even
the quietest and most commonplace of murders could
be perpetrated in the sight of the spectators, for fear
of shocking their feelings.

But the Teutonic nations, at least the English, never
took kindly to expedients of this nature. They wanted
to see the business done themselves, and not get their
knowledge of it from the reports of interested or pre-
judiced observers. At the outset they unquestionably
carried this feeling to an extreme. Our ancestors were
very much like children who never enjoy a story so
much as when it makes them shudder. " I wants to
make your flesh creep," says the fat boy in ' Pickwick '
to Mrs. Wardle; and to have the flesh creep all the
while was an end frequently aimed at in the early
tragedy of England. It was given to the shedding
of blood on a grand scale. At times the boards fairly

swim in gore, as character after character is despatched. There can be no doubt that in the rude beginnings of the stage the audience, made up of all classes in the community, enjoyed this kind of treat. The coarse plenty of the feast was more than a compensation for its lack of flavor and elegance. Provided there was an ample supply of deeds of violence, they were ready to excuse the neglect of providing any motive for the acts, or the neglect of probability throughout the entire action.

There is, however, a medium between the tameness of the classical school and the extravagance of the romantic. The adherents of the former, by the extreme aversion they manifested to the shedding of blood, were as eager to abolish the death penalty on the stage as the most pronounced sentimentalist is now in general legislation. They consequently abandoned opportunities of producing certain perfectly legitimate impressions. Especially did they deprive themselves of the ability to make use of pathetic and telling situations, which add often to the effectiveness of a play, and afford no just reason to suppose that any outrage will be offered to the feelings of the most sensitive. A duel upon the stage, if properly conducted, gives vividness to the action; it never fills us with serious apprehension. We may have the keenest interest aroused in the struggle; but we experience no grief when we see one of the combatants fall. He is simply carrying on the necessary business of the play. His assumed death, accordingly, excites no more painful emotion in our souls than if we had learned that he had just stepped out into the next street. We do not even object to an occasional assassination, provided it be done with decency and discretion. If it is merely a plain businesslike despatching of a character, of whom it is desirable to get rid, its effect upon our sensibilities is far less than if in our daily walk we should chance to come across the actual killing of some dumb animal of even a low grade.

But art which takes pleasure in the pathetic, and does not altogether shrink from the painful, can never well put up with the revolting and merely horrible. In representations of this sort the early English stage went to great lengths. Those plays which furnished the greatest number of scenes of blood were among the more successful, and frequently remained popular for long periods. Even after a purer taste had in large measure supplanted them with the majority, the craving for this particular species of intellectual diet continued to linger with individuals. "He that will swear," says Ben Jonson, in 1614, in the Induction to ' Bartholomew Fair,' "Jeronimo or Andronicus are the best plays yet, shall pass unexcepted here, as a man whose judgment shows it is constant, and hath stood still these five and twenty or thirty years. Though it be an ignorance, it is a virtuous and staid ignorance." These words make clear that more than one theatre-goer of the early time, after wandering about in what seemed to him the later barren wilderness of sentiment, looked back with a sigh to the strong stimulus which pieces of this sort afforded to his jaded nerves. The larger proportion of such early plays have

perished. Still there are a sufficient number of examples extant to reveal the nature of the taste which
caused their creation.

Perhaps no fairer specimen of this kind of drama
exists than the second part of ' Jeronimo,' called ' The
Spanish Tragedy,' which has just been mentioned.
The popularity of this play during the early years of
Shakespeare's professional life is attested by ample evidence. Lines taken from it are constantly bandied
about by the characters in the contemporary or later
drama. Usually, and perhaps invariably, this is done
in sport; but the play would never have been ridiculed,
had not passages in it been made familiar by the frequent representation of the piece on the stage. Furthermore, Ben Jonson's words furnish direct testimony to
the favor with which it had been regarded. The secret
of this favor is not hard to find. Murder goes on in it
at the very liveliest rate. The last act in particular
contributes a quota of six corpses to the grand total
which is heaped upon the stage in the course of the
performance. In truth, the personages of the drama
disappear so rapidly towards the close, that by the time
the play has reached its conclusion, it has to stop
because there is hardly any one left to carry it on.
Women as well as men take part in this war of exter-
mination. Ways of death are various. One of the
characters has the distinction of being killed by a pistol-
shot; but there are three suicides, two hangings, and
three stabbings. All these things take place in full
view of the audience, while the hero, who gives his
name to the piece, contributes an additional attraction

to the general horror by biting off and spitting out his own tongue.

Still the destruction of life in this play is so far from being unexampled that it has sometimes been rivalled, and in one instance at least has been surpassed. This is in the tragedy of 'Soliman and Perseda.' In it are fifteen characters besides the supernumeraries who are not of importance enough to be named. When the end is reached, there remains of this number of fifteen but one solitary survivor, and he a servant. Furthermore, of the miscellaneous crowd four are despatched, — two by the sword and two by being tumbled from the top of a tower. The lack, however, of contemporary allusion shows that this play never had the repute of 'The Spanish Tragedy.' The favor with which the latter was regarded cannot be questioned. No one will pretend it to be a specimen of the fine arts. But a large part of the audience that heard it originally with applause was not made up of persons of refined taste, and had not as yet been taught by great exemplars what it was that a refined taste could accomplish. It therefore suited their humor. They did not object to it because of its excessive bloodshed; they liked it the better on that very account. Even those who did not altogether approve it doubtless felt in a dim way that it possessed certain positive qualities which more than compensated for its literary defects. It meant business from the start. The characters did something; and the Elizabethan play-goer, especially of the earliest period, was very much like some novel-readers of our time, who are not contented unless they have an exciting situation in the first chapter. At any rate, they fully appreciated the fact that the first duty of a play that is to be acted is to have action. Accordingly, a few murders more or less were not worth taking into consideration. Whatever extravagance there may have been at times in its manifestation, it was in the eyes of the most cultivated a sound and healthy instinct which demanded that something should take place in stage representation besides the glittering generalities of rhetorical speeches under the guise of conversation.

It was productions of the kind just mentioned that would present themselves to the young and aspiring dramatist as stamped with the seal of popular approbation. There would be nothing strange, therefore, in the fact that at the outset of his career Shakespeare should have been influenced by the practices of his predecessors, and would be disposed to give his audience the precise sort of food which he knew from both observation and experience would please its palate. Nor would it be remarkable if traces of this truculent style of representation should cling to him through the whole of his career. That such was, to some extent, the case there can be no question. He followed the custom of his time in this as in other matters, though he usually followed it a great way off. In truth, here as elsewhere, his genius generally enabled him to seize what was good in the methods which were in vogue, and to reject what was bad. That he was in full sympathy with the principles of the romantic school in this very particular is evident from his procedure. The destruction of life in full view of the spectators takes place on a grand scale in some of his finest tragedies. At the close of ' Hamlet,' for instance, four of the principal characters of the play perish in swift succession in sight of the audience, and a fifth consents to live only at the dying request of the hero of the piece. Such incidents as these shocked beyond expression the French critics of the eighteenth century and their followers. It was one of the things that led Voltaire to stigmatize this particular play as a coarse and barbarous piece, that would never be tolerated by the lowest of the rabble in France and Italy; and to express surprise that Shakespeare's example should still be followed by a people which possessed so pure and perfect a work of art as the 'Cato' of Addison.

It is the extent to which this indiscriminate bloodshed is carried on in ' Titus Andronicus ' — the other play mentioned by Jonson — which has largely occasioned the controversy about the genuineness of that piece. If it be adjudged a production of Shakespeare's, it must be confessed that he improved upon even ' The Spanish Tragedy ' in the gruesome and the terrible. This particular play is found in the folio of 1623. It forms one of the six tragedies specifically mentioned by Meres, in 1598, as having been written by Shakespeare. Hardly any more convincing external evidence could be given. If testimony about authorship is worth anything at all, not much better can be asked. Yet so different is ' Titus Andronicus ' in style and treatment from the dramatist's other pieces, that many, and perhaps most, critics and commentators have not only been unwilling to concede that it is a production of his early apprenticeship as a dramatist, but that it is even a production of some one else which has undergone his revision sufficiently to be entitled to a place among his works. Such at least is the avowed reason. Largely different is the real one. That is the character of the play itself. An atmosphere of cruelty, lust, adultery, and murder hangs like a pall over the whole piece. It is so repulsive in its savagery, so unsavory in what may fairly be termed its beastliness, that in spite of the strong external evidence in its favor, it is too much for the delicate nerves of most editors to admit even the possibility of its genuineness.

However this may be, the play has an interest of its own as an illustration of what the early English stage could do in the accumulation of abhorrent incidents. Even could he be proved to have had no connection with it, the piece would be worthy of attention as a specimen of the example which Shakespeare had frequently before his eyes. The characters in it, whether designed as good or bad, all display the same propensity to crime. Titus Andronicus, the hero and patriot, kills one of his sons for venturing to remonstrate with him against a peculiarly foolish course of conduct he has determined to adopt. He stabs his daughter, Lavinia, in a fit of tenderness for her reputation. Two brothers are only prevented from slaying each other by the enticing prospect held out to them of having an equal share in crimes of ravishment, mutilation, and murder. The play indeed not only surpasses ' The Spanish Tragedy ' in the coarseness of its horrors, but in the number and variety of deaths that are shown upon the stage. The plot of 'Titus Andronicus' is carried on by fourteen principal characters. There are also eight minor ones that take part in the action, and in most cases appear in but a single scene. Of the fourteen principal characters eleven are successively despatched. The minor ones are somewhat more fortunate: of the eight five escape alive. There is a certain variety in the manner of the deaths inflicted. Seven are stabbed, two have their throats cut, two are officially beheaded, one is hewn in pieces for a sacrifice, and one hanged; and what must have been a bitter disappointment to the audience of that day, the principal villain of all does not meet his fate before their eyes, but is reserved to be set breast deep in earth and there starve to death. The only satisfaction to the reader of this ghastly story is that hardly one of the characters who is poetically condemned to die appears fit to live.

Terrible as this account may seem — and some of the most repulsive features of the work have not been mentioned — there is no question that it was and remained for a considerable period a popular play. It was a popular play for the same reason as was 'The Spanish Tragedy.' Harrowing scenes were what those desired who attended the theatre. In both of these productions they got for the least expenditure of money the amplest supply of horror. Whether Shakespeare wrote this particular piece or not, it can hardly be denied that to a certain extent he was influenced by the taste which begot it and enjoyed it. There are one or two things in his greatest plays which it does not require peculiar delicacy of feeling to regard with a slight

sensation of distaste. The smothering of Desdemona
by Othello in sight of the spectators may perhaps be
endured; but it is, assuredly, not a scene which minds
ordinarily constituted can look upon with unalloyed
pleasure. But it is difficult to find any defence for
the representation in ' Lear ' of the extrusion of Gloucester's eyes. It is horrible even to read of, and
naturally far more horrible to see enacted. Similar
atrocities, it is fair to say, had been exhibited upon the
English stage before. In ' Selimus,' a tragedy now
ascribed to Greene, one of the sultan's advisers, acting
as his messenger, has not only his eyes put out in full
view of the audience, but has his arms cut off also;
and with these latter carefully deposited in his bosom
is sent back to his master. It may be added that the loss
of life which goes on in this last-mentioned play makes
it worthy to take its place by the side of the pieces
already described. There are about two dozen personages who take part in its action. Of this number more
than half — embracing nearly all the important characters — suffer violent deaths. Three are disposed of
by poison; but the favorite method is strangulation,
which carries off six. At the end the author encouraged his hearers by the assurance that if the first part
gave them pleasure he should follow it with a second
part, which would recount even greater murders.

Representations of this sort are not only inartistic,
but in the long run they are ineffective even with the
class which at first takes delight in them. They are
not only repellent to the cultivated; they cease in time
to stimulate the over-jaded appetites of the rude, soon

satiated with horror. In its insistence upon the rejection of revolting details of this character the French theatre was unquestionably right. Nor is there any necessity for their representation in order to produce the desired impression upon the audience. Even deeds of violence, which can be properly acted under certain conditions, can in the hands of the great master be often made to stir the feelings more profoundly by narration than could possibly be done by exhibition. In 'Macbeth' the murder of Duncan affects the hearer far more deeply because it is not seen. The accessories impress us far more than could the actual sight. The marvellous art of the dramatist has here drawn a picture which thrills the soul, but never once offends the susceptibilities. We feel the terrible nature of the deed that has been perpetrated; we are in the fullest sympathy of comprehension with the actors in the work of darkness, which for them will murder sleep forever after; but never once does there pass through the mind a suggestion of that disgust, that shrinking horror which the mere sight of blood often causes, when shed by men acting under the ordinary instincts of self-preservation. In this particular the art of 'Macbeth' is far higher than that exhibited in the corresponding passages of 'Lear' and 'Othello,' to which reference has just been made.

If the English stage had gone to one extreme in the portrayal of scenes of violence, the French had gone to the other in refraining from the slightest exhibition of them, with the one exception of suicide. In this abstention their critics took great pride. In their eyes the shedding of blood, whether of a single individual

or in the shape of wholesale slaughter, was equally unpardonable. It was contrary to decorum, to theatrical
good manners. Naturally the opposite course of proceeding met with their severest condemnation. The
censures of the practice by some of their authors affected to a certain extent English opinion. This is
true at least of the criticism of those of them who were
translated. One of these was the exile, St. Evremond,
who spent in London most of the last forty years of
his long life. Essays of his on the drama were brought
out in 1687 in an English version. They reflected those
critical views prevailing in his native land, which had
become accepted in a small circle in his adopted one.
But the circle was an aristocratic one, and St. Evremond is not to be blamed, therefore, for regarding it
as the exponent of the best taste. Like most French
critics, he did not deem it necessary to know a language in order to pass decisive judgments both upon
the character of the people who spoke it and of the
literature they produced. Though living in England,
he had not thought it worth while to learn the English
tongue. That ignorance, however, did not prevent him
from finding in their drama four or five tragedies which
with proper omissions could be regarded as excellent
plays. Outside of these four and five he saw nothing
but a shapeless and indigested mass, a crowd of con-
fused adventures, without consideration of time or
place, and without any regard to decorum, where eyes
that rejoice in cruel sights may be fed with murders
and with bodies weltering in blood. He was struck by
the delight which the audience took in plays of this

character. To palliate the horror of their scenes by relating instead of performing cruel acts would result, he observed, in depriving the spectators of the sight that pleased them most.

This was the view generally taken by French critics during the whole of the century that followed. Upon the enormity of the English drama in the matter of violence Voltaire, in particular, insisted vehemently. In the dedication of *Zaïre*, published in 1732, to his friend Falkener, he gave a good deal of advice to his friend's countrymen on this point. It was substantially as follows. Your stage, he wrote, is contaminated with horrors, with gibbets, with blood-sheddings. Refine the uncouth action of your savage Melpomenes, and strive for the praise of the best judges of all times and nations. Addison has shown you the way. In spite of particular defects, he is the poet of the wise. Imitate that great man, therefore, though only when he is right. Voltaire recognized later the impossibility of changing the national taste. In his opinion Shakespeare had corrupted it; and against the overpowering influence of that dramatist it was vain to struggle.

For, that the taste for scenes of this sort was bad taste, there was no doubt in the minds of French critics, and of those in England who re-echoed their opinions. St. Evremond tells us that the better-bred objected to these bloody spectacles. But he adds, ancient custom and national preference prevail over the delicacy of private persons. It cannot, however, be denied that this foreign view affected in some measure English opinion, and, during the eighteenth century particularly, English practice. Several of their writers condemned the extent to which representations of these scenes of violence and bloodshed were carried, while not condemning the practice itself. The dreadful butchery which took place upon the English stage was denounced by Addison as the most absurd and barbarous of the methods used to excite pity and terror.[1] It exposed the nation to the contempt and ridicule of its neighbors. Yet even his somewhat timid nature could not approve the conduct of the French in banishing death from representation entirely. Their avoidance of blood had, in his opinion, led them into absurdities as great as those which accompanied its indiscriminate shedding. There were others, however, — they were not numerous, but they existed, — who were willing to go much farther than he in concession to the classicists. A body of men could be found in England who would gladly have shorn the stage of the representation of all acts of violence whatever. They professed to regard them as lacking in art. "Murders," said Roscommon, "cannot be allowed on the stage, let 'em be of what nature soever. None but bad poets, who had not genius enough to move by the narration, have introduced bloody spectacles."[2] Chesterfield, in commenting upon the faults of the theatre of his own country, said that the English ought to give up "all their massacres, racks, dead bodies, and mangled carcasses, which they so frequently exhibit upon the

[1] Spectator, No. 44, April 20, 1711.
[2] Notes on Horace's 'Art of Poetry,' line 185 (1680).

stage." [1]   Arthur Murphy, the dramatist, admitted that
it was a corruption of the liberty enjoyed by the playwright to permit blood to be shed before the audience. [2]
In 1759 Mrs. Lennox, assisted by certain writers, —
among whom was Dr. Johnson, — brought out a translation of Brumoy's *Théâtre des Grecs*. It was preceded
by a preface contributed by the Earl of Orrery, the friend
of Pope and Swift. In it he gave expression to what
had now become in some quarters a regular conventional criticism. "Whatever may have been chosen
for the subject of tragedy," he wrote, "the English
theatre has made itself too long remarkable for cover-
ing the stage with dead bodies, and exhibiting all the
horrors of murder and execution."

But these views, however warmly and frequently expressed, were, after all, confined to a comparatively
limited number. Nor did they exert much influence
over the opinion of the general public. There is no
question that the vast body of frequenters of the
theatre — the common people they may be called, if
one so chooses, though there were among them many
uncommon people — could not endure a tame recital to
the ear of what they felt should be pictured to the eye.
Addison was not alone in thinking the French theatre
had gone too far. Even Chesterfield, who denounced
the English stage for its barbarous ferocity, found fault
with the French for its constant substitution of declamation for action. If those so partial by nature
to restraint upon the liberty of the dramatist could

---

[1] Letter to his son, Jan. 23, 1752.
[2] Gray's Inn Journal, No. 20, Feb. 9, 1754.

express themselves in this way, it was inevitable that the great mass of cultivated men should be much more outspoken. Not only did a large number of the English playwrights refuse to adapt their action to continental ideas of decorum, but the English criticism of that day, ordinarily subservient to the French in questions concerning the drama, revolted in this instance against the imposition of this restriction. Furthermore, it resented the attempt. In answer to the attacks made upon its own theatre, it retorted, with a good deal of justice, that the declamatory speeches in which the French delighted would make an English audience yawn. Even such as were willing to accept the unities as the final deliverance of art could not look with approval upon plays in which there was little but monologue, or orations in the form of dialogue. Their resentment was pictured by Garrick in the epilogue previously quoted, to the tragedy of ' Athelstan,' produced in 1756. That great manager as well as great actor had his eye constantly fixed upon what his audiences would care to see and hear. In the following lines he bore witness not only to the diversities of opinion then prevailing, but clearly indicated, also, how deep was becoming the indignation of his countrymen at the depreciation to which Shakespeare was subjected in this matter at the instance of the idolaters of the French stage: —

" The youths, to whom France gives a new belief,
Who look with horror on a rump of beef ;
On Shakespeare's plays with shrugged-up shoulders stare.
These plays ? They 're bloody murders, — *O barbare.*

And yet the man has merit — *Entre nous,*
He 'd been damned clever, had he read Bossu.
' Shakespeare read French ! ' roars out a surly cit,
When Shakespeare wrote, our valor matched our wit :
Had Britons then been fops, Queen Bess had hanged 'em,
Those days they never read the French, — they banged 'em."

So deeply ingrained, indeed, in the national character was the taste for action as opposed to narration, that it is noticeable that in the alterations of all sorts to which the plays of Shakespeare were subjected to meet the requirements of an assumed higher art, it was rarely the case that his scenes of violence were struck out or even modified. All other kinds of changes could be made and were made. Other agencies demanded by the taste of the age or of the writer were brought into operation, such as the principle of poetic justice, the introduction of the passion of love, the elevation of the character of the hero or heroine. But no inclination was manifested to dispense with acts of bloodshed or with scenes of horror. If such were discarded, it was for some other reason than objection to their nature. It was so little the case that fault was found with representations of this sort by the public or by the majority of the critics, that in the alterations which were made the number of cruel deeds was more often increased than diminished. Tate subjected the tragedy of ' Lear ' to most violent and indefensible changes; yet in his version the extrusion of Gloucester's eyes went on in sight of the audience. He could plead that this was a necessity forced upon him; but no such excuse can be offered for the introduction of a similar scene in the adaptation of ' Cymbeline,' which Durfey produced in

1682 under the title of ' The Injured Princess, or the
Fatal Wager.' In this Cloten is represented as putting out the eyes of one of the characters in full view
of the spectators.

In fact, there was frequently a disposition to revert
to the taste of the pre-Shakespearean period, as if the
age needed a stronger stimulus for enjoyment than
his comparatively bloodless scenes provided. In Colley
Cibber's version of ' Richard III.' a portion of the final
act of the last part of ' Henry VI.' was added. This
had the incidental result of contributing an additional
murder to a play amply stocked with them at the outset. Tate in his alteration of ' Coriolanus ' took pains
to set forth a feast of horrors. Not only does the hero
of the piece meet with a violent death, but also his wife
and his son. He kills Aufidius, by whom he is in turn
mortally wounded; while a new character, Nigridius,
the villain of the play, who has just been boasting that
he has broken the bones of young Marcius, is himself
slain by Volumnia, who has been made raving mad.
As a result, the stage at the end is piled with corpses.
No part of this ridiculous travesty of the terrible was
retained by Dennis in the alteration which he prepared
some thirty years later of this same tragedy. But even
for him there were apparently not deaths enough. His
sense of poetical justice, as we shall see later, over-rode
the requirements of history, lack of conformity to which
he had elsewhere imputed as a fault to Shakespeare.

It is unnecessary to multiply instances; but as regards
this matter, there is one alteration which demands special notice as an example of the taste of the times. The

terrible character of the drama of ' Titus Andronicus ' assuredly stood in no need of being heightened. It might seem impossible to improve upon it in the accumulation of horrors. Yet this was accomplished by Edward Ravenscroft in an adaptation brought out in 1678, and published in 1687. To the emperor and Tamora he served up a banquet surpassing even the Thyestean. No dish is brought in which does not contain some part of the hearts and tongues of the two sons of the queen, no wine is drunk which is not mixed with their blood. Tamora also stabs the infant which she has borne to the Moor. The latter is struck with admiration for the height of iniquity to which his paramour has risen above him; all he can do is to express a desire to eat the slain child. The audience was further gratified by having this most detestable of characters put on the rack, tortured, and finally burned to death. Ravenscroft was impressed with the excellence of his improvements. "Compare the old play with this," he proudly said in his preface; "you'll find that none in all that author's works ever received greater alterations or additions, the language not only refined, but many scenes entirely new, besides most of the principal characters heightened, and the plot much increased." Horrors like these are disagreeable even to read about; to see them enacted with satisfaction requires a stronger stomach than that possessed by the modern man. Yet Ravenscroft tells us that his version was successful on the stage.

Such a play marked the extreme in one direction; it is fair to add that it was an extreme very rarely reached. Still the taste for productions of this sort never ceased to exist. As early as 1667 Dryden had commented on the increasing fondness for carnage on the stage. In the epilogue to his ' Wild Gallant,' revived that year, he told his audience that they were growing savages; that nothing but human flesh could please their palate; that if no blood was drawn, then the play was naught. The extreme in the other direction met with favor from some, but it was not often that it pleased generally. About the middle of the eighteenth century Colley Cibber brought out in an epilogue to a piece, then first acted, the distinction between the feelings of French and English audiences. Of the character of the production in question, which was called ' Eugenia,' he said, —

> " Ours is all sentiment, blank verse, and virtue,
> Distress — but yet no bloodshed to divert ye.
> Such plays in France perhaps may cut a figure;
> But to our critics here they 're mere soup-meagre ;
> Though there they never stain their stage with blood,
> Yet English stomachs love substantial food.
> Give us the lightning's blaze, the thunder's roll !
> The pointed dagger, and the poisoning bowl !
> Let drums' and trumpets' clangor swell the scene,
> Till the gor'd battle bleed in every vein."

The preference of English audiences for scenes of violence to the exhibition of delicate sentiment, as it was called, was a source of perpetual grief to the English admirers of the French stage. Works modelled after those which on that had found favor, with their careful abstention from the flow of blood and their unlimited indulgence in the flow of words, either did not succeed at all, or their success was usually restricted to a single season. The reason of this was clear to the advocates of pure dramatic art. Such productions were too chaste, too elegant to suit the coarse intellectual appetite of the crowd which frequented the English theatre. It was primarily the fault of the race that it could not appreciate their quiet refined beauty. From the very beginning it had been in love with tumult and noise and slaughter. But for the continuous and continued existence of this taste Shakespeare was held responsible. A multitude of witnesses might be summoned to prove the existence of both these beliefs. Here we content ourselves with two verdicts pronounced from different quarters upon two pieces produced at about the same time. These will give a correct conception of the state of mind that was then widely prevalent with a certain class of men.

The first of these pieces is the play of ' Eugenia,' which has just been mentioned. It was the work of the Rev. Philip Francis, better known as a translator of Horace, best known as the father of the man in whose behalf the most persistent claim has been put forth for the authorship of the letters of Junius. It was an imitation of the *Cénie* of Madame de Grafigny, and was brought out at Drury Lane in February, 1752. In successive letters to his son Chesterfield gave an account of its fortunes. He reported its success on the first two nights with pleasure and also with surprise. He had no expectation that it would do so well, considering how long British audiences had been accustomed to murder, rack, and poison in every tragedy.

"But," he added, "it affected the heart so much that it triumphed over habit and prejudice. All the women cried, and all the men were moved." But this agreeable prospect of the triumph of delicacy and refinement did not continue. A few days later he wrote that the play had failed, in spite of the fact that it pleased most people of good taste. "The boxes," he said, "were crowded till the sixth night, when the pit and gallery were totally deserted, and it was dropped. Distress without death was not sufficient to affect a true British audience."[1] The modern reader will find this piece a representative of a numerous class of eighteenth-century plays, in which English dulness has been added to French regularity. It is a tragi-comedy, though styled by its author a tragedy. The plot is a love-story, without reality, without probability, and without interest. Even its villain gains not the slightest share of respect, because he imitates the others in persistently acting like a fool. It is a tribute to Garrick's phenomenal power of representation that the piece was played for more than a single night. Yet there is no doubt that this wretched stuff pleased a certain class of both hearers and readers who affected to admire its peculiar delicacy of sentiment. To her sister Mrs. Delany wrote that it was "much the most pleasing (I won't presume to say best, not being a sufficient judge) of any modern play that has come out these twenty years."[2]

The other one of these two pieces was a tragedy

---

[1] Letters of Feb. 20 and March 2, 1752.
[2] Delany Correspondence, vol. iii. p. 85.

styled ' Boadicia.' It was written by Richard Glover, echoes of whose once much-lauded epic of ' Leonidas ' occasionally fall upon modern ears; it was brought out at Drury Lane in December, 1753. As regards bloodshed, it had followed the most approved French methods. Battles are fought, but no one sees them. Several of the characters are reported as losing their lives, but all of them refrain from shocking the audience by any actual exhibition of death-agony. One of them, indeed — the wife of the Briton leader — perishes in their sight; but she conforms to the proprieties by taking a potion which lulls her to death as gently as if it were a delightful sleep. The play is further written with all the pomp of eighteenth-century poetical diction. Genuine passion expresses itself simply and directly; but nothing of that sort is found here. No stress of approaching danger can restrain the utterance of protracted similes; no excitement of feeling can induce the speaker to use ordinary words. A Roman indignantly reproaching his comrade for effeminacy bids him seek his Campanian garden, and there nurse, not flowers, but "the gaudy-vested progeny of Flora." This play, in which Garrick took a leading part, met with a fair degree of favor. It was acted eight times continuously, and twice more before the season closed. After that it was never heard of again. But the success which it had at the time was felt by the friends of art not to be commensurate with the elegant language employed. "I cannot but remark," said Murphy, "that the applause it met with was scarcely warm enough for such fine writing." He then went on to give the reason of this coolness. It was, as might have been expected, the now conventional one. Shakespeare had made the English all so fond of savage liberty that if plays were written in accordance with the rules and simplicity of the Stagirite, the scenes would not be thought busy enough. Still he was confident that if the judicious Voltaire were to examine this tragedy, he would confess that it was conformable to his own delicacy and good sense, and deserved a place among the best of modern productions.[1]

This piece, in its turn, was a representative of numerous eighteenth-century tragedies. Its heroine, so far from being an impressive character, does nothing but scold. She is really little more than a virago of a low type. Declamatory rant, such as is found in it in profusion, was not likely to wean away an English audience from the love of plays in which there was plenty of action, and frequently of action involving the loss of life by various methods and on a grand scale. In consequence, at least partly in consequence, of their fondness for spectacles of this kind the English came to be considered on the continent as a peculiarly savage and sanguinary people. They were supposed to delight in brutal acts and bloody shows. Their reputation for this was perhaps established before their theatrical exhibitions confirmed and extended it. The French critic, Rapin, for instance, who made no pretence to know anything about English literature, assumed as an indisputable fact the ferocity of the English people. For that reason, as well as on account of the energy of

[1] Gray's Inn Journal, No. 11, Dec. 8, 1753.

their language, he believed the race to be possessed of a genius for tragedy. These islanders, he tells us, are separated from the rest of men. By the nature of their temperament they love blood in their sports, they delight in cruelty. Imputations of this sort led Rapin's translator, the amiable Rymer, to put in a mild protest against such an estimate being taken of "the best-natured nation under the sun." He could only ascribe so gross a misconception to the character of their tragedies. There are probably more murders done on our stage, he said, than upon all the other stages of Europe. Travellers, therefore, who got their conception of the English character from the English theatre might fairly conclude that the English were the cruellest-minded people in Christendom.[1]

This belief continued to prevail on the continent for no short time. Before the end of the seventeenth century reference is made to its existence by several writers. At a later period Addison, in his protest against the undue exhibition of scenes of violence upon the stage, remarked that in consequence of the frequency of their portrayal, foreign critics had taken occasion to describe the English as a people that delight in blood.[2] This view, however widely accepted, could not long endure, as soon as intercourse between nations became closer. When the islanders began to be seen frequently upon the continent, the futility of the opinion was speedily made manifest. It was recognized that the English

---

[1] Preface to Rymer's translation of Rapin's *Réflexions sur la Poétique d'Aristote* (1674).

[2] Spectator, No. 44, April 20, 1711.

were no fonder of blood than their neighbors. Hence it became necessary to devise some other reason to account for the fondness they displayed for spectacles full of terrible scenes. What was it in their nature that led them to see with pleasure such exhibitions? It was a perverted taste, to be sure, but how did the taste come to be perverted? St. Evremond had long before been ready with his answer. "To die is so small a matter to the English," he wrote, "that there is need of images more ghastly than death itself to affect them." A somewhat different theory was put forth later by the actor and author Riccoboni, who in 1738 published a work containing reflections upon the different theatres of Europe. From him it was adopted by LaPlace, who about the middle of the eighteenth century introduced to the knowledge of his countrymen some of the chief works of the English stage. The first of his eight volumes began with a discourse upon the characteristics of the drama he was translating. In it we find the English fondness for the terrible and the horrible philosophically explained.

It was all owing to temperament. The English, we are told, are by nature contemplative, disposed to revery, liable to be absorbed in profound thought. It is for that reason that their writers have treated the most elevated subjects with profundity and success. Consequently, their dramatic authors are compelled to resort to the most violent devices in order to break up this constitutional habit. Unless the matter which the theatre brings before them be presented with striking and terrible accompaniments, their minds will not be stirred nor their attention fixed. Thoughtful persons, furthermore, are by nature melancholy, and are little disposed to give themselves up to the illusions of the theatre. Their constant study of the true renders their hearts unwilling to accept that which merely resembles the true. They want to see things as they are, and not as they are reported. They are averse to being bored by a recital of what they feel they have a right to witness at first hand. Hence the frequent changes of scene, the diverse spectacles represented. It was in this genial way that friendly criticism explained what hostile criticism denounced as nothing but the outcome of a rude and barbarous taste.

It can be conceded that up to a certain point the objection to the introduction of scenes of violence has a foundation in both nature and reason. The sense of sight is no more to be unnecessarily offended than the sense of hearing or the sense of smell. Nothing should be seen on the stage which will arouse disagreeable sensations, nothing heard from it which will call up revolting or disgusting images. The French critics carried their objections to any representations of this sort very far. They did not spare the ancients for failing to conform to French ideas of propriety. They took exception to the way in which Philoctetes speaks of the plasters and rags which he applied to his sores; and equally so to the description which Tiresias gives in the ' Antigone ' of the filth of the ill-omened birds which had fed on the carcass of Polynices. There is always risk in criticism of this sort, directed against details in works known to us only through the medium of translation, whether made by ourselves or others. The words of one language frequently arouse quite different sensations in the mind from those produced by the words of another, which strictly correspond in meaning. The associations that gather about them in two tongues are often essentially unlike. Only in the matter of our own speech can we feel justified in expressing positive opinion. Nothing, for illustration, can be more offensive than Fletcher's representation in ' The Sea-Voyage ' of the suffering that goes on among those who are so reduced by the lack of food that they contemplate killing one of their own number to save themselves from starvation.[1] Of all times, this would seem the last for the display of wit; yet it is the very time he selects. Everything which is said is, in consequence, wholly out of place. Nor is that the worst. We are not only struck by the inappropriateness of the conversation which goes on, we are also disgusted by the nauseousness of its details.

In the matter of tragi-comedy we have seen that it was Shakespeare's practice that had finally justified the romantic drama. Just so did his example justify the artistic liberty of the playwright to deal with representation of scenes of violence, subject not to conventional law, but to the capability he possessed of producing effects at once powerful and pleasing. That in this particular he himself occasionally went to an extreme, may be conceded. Still it is very rarely the case that he pushed the privilege of the stage too far, or put the feelings of the audience to any undue test. On that

[1] Act iii. scene 1.

delicate border line which separates the more from the less, he in general trod not only unhesitatingly but safely. It was his conduct in the revolt that went on from this rule of the classicists, as well as in the deviations previously considered, which secured for the romantic drama, even in foreign lands, first toleration and then approval. For its adherents he vindicated their full right to deal in their own way with the materials upon which they labored. Had it not been for him, there was certainly danger, at one time, that the English race, in spite of its natural distaste for productions in which declamation and narrative usurp the place of action, might have taken up its home for a while within that narrow circle of ideas which looked upon such pieces as the only ones conforming to true art. Efforts were put forth at various periods to banish from the stage painful and cruel scenes. Examples of this disposition can be found in the very time in which Shakespeare flourished. In Daniel's never-acted play of ' Cleopatra ' the death of the heroine was not to be witnessed; instead a messenger announces the circumstances attending it in a speech that takes up more than two hundred and fifty lines. It requires no great stretch of imagination to surmise the sort of reception which a long-winded oration of this sort would have had in the stormy English theatre of the Elizabethan period. The actor who persisted in repeating it would have run the risk of meeting at the hands of an indignant audience the fate he was trying to describe; and few would then have been found to deny that he deserved the death he had been made to suffer.

Attempts of this same general nature met with more favor in the eighteenth century. It seemed for a time, indeed, that the effort to discard from stage representation scenes of violence with the circumstances attending them, might gain a temporary triumph: anything more than temporary it never could have been. The impropriety of such representations was preached from a hundred critical pulpits. Supported, too, as this view was by many who were regarded as authoritative leaders of public opinion, it could not fail to make then a certain number of converts. Writers for the stage were disposed to comply with the requirement. The politer part of the audiences — the occupants of the boxes — frequently felt it their duty to admire works in which restraint of this sort, as well as other kinds of poetical decorum, had been faithfully observed. In their secret hearts they found such plays depressingly dull; but they were prepared to sacrifice their genuine feelings on the altar of art. Their state of mind is depicted in a lively afterpiece of Mrs. Clive's, first brought out in 1750, in which a female author gives her reasons for preparing a burletta for the stage. "My motive for writing," she is represented as saying, "was really compassion: the town has been so overwhelmed with tragedies lately that they are in one entire fit of the vapors. They think they love 'em, but it is no such thing. I was there one night this season at a tragedy, and there was such a universal yawn in the house, that had it not been for a great quantity of drums and trumpets, that most judiciously came in every now and then to their relief, the whole audience would have fallen asleep." [1]

[1] The Rehearsal, or Bays in Petticoats, p. 15.

In a similar strain Bentley's son, the friend of Walpole and Gray, deplored the general decadence which had overtaken creative work in the age which felicitated itself upon its lofty critical standards. In a poetical epistle to Lord Melcombe, he observed, —

> "With Milton epic drew its latest breath,
> Since Shakespeare tragedy puts *us* to death." [1]

It requires now the painful reading of the eighteenth-century classical drama to appreciate the exact justice of these references to its character. Fortunately that portion of the audience which filled the pit and the galleries felt themselves under no obligation to pretend to like what they found unendurably tedious. It was they who all along had instinctively recognized that the course which Shakespeare had taken was the only one which ought to be taken. It can therefore be said justly that to him in this respect, as in others, the deliverance of the drama is due. Furthermore, he not only wrought it solely, he wrought it completely. Criticism, which once found no word too severe to arraign his methods, has at last toiled tardily after him to acknowledge them as being in accordance with the highest art. For Shakespeare himself it has therefore been a personal triumph as well as the triumph of a cause.

[1] St. James's Magazine, vol. ii. p. 5 (1762).

CHAPTER VI

MINOR DRAMATIC CONVENTIONS

THE disregard of the unities, the intermingling of comic and tragic scenes in the same production, the representation of deeds of violence by action instead of narration, — these are the three essential characteristics of the romantic drama as opposed to the classical. Other differences there are; but they are accidental and changing: these are distinctive and permanent. But in addition to them sprang up a body of conventions of another kind. Some of them were accepted only in limited circles, and served little other purpose than to give the critic who looked upon them as infallible an opportunity to chastise the author who failed to observe them. Others there were which for a certain period were very generally accepted. They have furthermore been treated occasionally as distinctions between the two dramatic schools. Such, however, they are not in reality. To a slight extent they became so, owing to the tendency of the one to grant to the writer the fullest liberty of action, and the corresponding tendency of the other to restrict it within the narrowest possible limits. But they pertain rather to the freedom of the stage itself than to the methods of any particular school.

Shakespeare in consequence is only indirectly concerned in the controversies that went on in regard to these conventions. Unlike the doctrine of the unities, many, and perhaps all of them, were not fully formulated till after his time. Unlike, too, the mixture of the tragic and the comic, unlike the shedding of blood on the stage, their rejection or employment does not denote characteristic differences of the theatres of rival nations. They indicate a general trend of belief or action during particular periods, rather than any established principles of dramatic conduct. But as these conventional rules had been uniformly disregarded by Shakespeare, it enabled those who paid no heed to them to use him as an authority for their opinion or practice. Hence in any account of the controversies which went on in regard to his dramatic art, it is necessary to pay them some consideration. They fall into two classes. One concerns the form in which the language of the play is clothed, the other the treatment of the subject.

In regard to form a number of conventional rules came to be widely adopted. One of these was that different kinds of writing should not be employed in the same play. The mixture of prose and verse was as bad as regards manner as was the mixture of the humorous and the pathetic as regards matter. This was a canon so generally accepted and so regularly obeyed that it needs mention rather than exemplification. It was doubtless inevitable that it should undergo extension. This, at any rate, took place. It became the accepted creed that comedy must always be in prose, tragedy in blank verse. During the eighteenth century this rule was so firmly established that the occasional exceptions which occur are so occasional that they serve to emphasize the strictness with which it was enforced. Especially was this true of the introduction into comedy either of blank verse or of ryme. The latter was an offence to which no quarter was shown. Chesterfield founded the reason of the rule upon the very nature of things. Comedy should represent mere common life and nothing beyond. Its characters accordingly should talk upon the stage just as they would in the street or the drawing-room. Hence ryme was inadmissible in it. He would not allow it, unless it was put into the mouth or came out of the mouth of a mad poet.[1] Belief in realism, it will be seen, was just as potent in the eighteenth century as it has ever been since, though it did not clothe itself with that name.

The view taken by Chesterfield was far from being exceptional. It may justly be said to represent not only the general belief but the general practice. Rarely was there any attempt to run counter to it. In 1784 Hayley published three comedies in ryme. This author had somehow stumbled upon one of those incomprehensible reputations which it is the fortune of a few to have for a time, and the despair of future generations to explain how they came to have it. One of these comedies, entitled 'The Two Connoisseurs,' was brought out at the Haymarket the year of its appearance in print. The very nature of the attempt aroused

---

[1] Letter to his son, Jan. 23, 1752.

curiosity. Colman wrote a prologue for it, to be recited by a performer in the character of Bays. In the course of it he was represented as saying that though he had written much, he had

> " Ne'er tried aught so *low*, or so *sublime*,
> As Tragedy in Prose, or Comedy in Ryme."

Hayley was then in the height of his factitious reputation. The novelty of the performance awakened interest, and caused the play to be received with a certain measure of tolerance. But the success was not great enough to justify imitation.

The feeling which sought to confine comedy to prose naturally did not content itself with the rejection of ryme. It frowned equally upon blank verse. In regard to this there was however no such unanimity of opinion; and at a period when the plays of Shakespeare were constantly becoming more familiar to the whole world of readers, an exclusion of this measure could not always hold its ground unchallenged. In truth, what almost might be called an organized movement in its favor broke out among that group of old Westminster fellow-students whose names occur so frequently in the early story of Cowper's life. Three of them, George Colman, Bonnell Thornton, and Robert Lloyd, put themselves in direct opposition to the prevailing sentiment. To the edition of Massinger which was published in 1761, Colman furnished a preface. In it he denounced the use of ryme in comedy. Furthermore, though he did not deny the propriety of prose in works of this sort, he advocated in place of it the adoption of blank verse after the manner of the authors of the older Eng-

lish drama. His argument was based upon the ground
that this measure, while representing with fidelity
the words and acts of every-day life, was capable
of rising easily to heights of expression above the
range of ordinary conversation. It therefore gave
the writer opportunity to exhibit his powers as a
poet as well as a dramatist. He announced that
in accordance with this view he was purposing to bring
out a version of Terence in familiar blank verse. If
he failed, he was confident it would not be due to the
unhappiness of the plan but to the poorness of the
execution. Meanwhile the design had kindled the ambition of his friend Thornton. In 1762 that writer published in the 'St. James's Magazine,' edited by Lloyd,
a specimen of an intended translation of Plautus upon
the same lines.[1] This called forth a whole series of
articles from another scholar, who went farther than
either Colman or Thornton in his defiance of the established opinion. He took the ground that not only
should comedy be written in measure, but that it should
never be written in prose.[2]

There were not many, however, who entertained
these sentiments, still fewer who acted upon them.
Examples of comedy, not written in prose, whether
original or translated, are far from being numerous
in the eighteenth century. Colman's version of Terence was published in 1764. It met with the general
approval of the classical scholars of the time. But
there was occasionally heard a discordant note. It

---

[1] Vol. i. pp. 265–274 (Dec. 1762).
[2] St. James's Magazine, vol. i. pp. 384–392, etc.

had been made in blank verse. It was felt by many that Colman had chosen an inappropriate vehicle for conveying the meaning of his original. More than a dozen years after — in 1777 — a translation of two comedies of this same Latin author was put forth in prose by a writer who signed himself simply a member of the university of Oxford. In his preface he praised Colman's version in many particulars, but took most decided exception to the " unnatural combination," as he termed it, of comedy and blank verse. His further criticism renders noticeable how all-important had become by this time the influence of Shakespeare's example, how profound was the deference paid to his authority. The writer in his contention that blank verse was adapted only to tragedy or to epic poetry, felt compelled to parry the force of the argument that could be drawn from the practice of the great dramatist, or rather to misrepresent it. He maintained that 'The Merchant of Venice' and 'Measure for Measure' were really tragedies. Therefore in them blank verse was allowable. On the other hand 'Much Ado about Nothing' and 'The Merry Wives of Windsor' were pure comedies. Therefore they were almost entirely written in prose. A complete application of this rule would show that Shakespeare wrote hardly anything but tragedies; for in all of his pieces that go under the name of comedies, blank verse prevails to a greater or less extent, and is almost certain to be employed whenever the expression assumes a serious character.

In this he followed the practice of his age. Blank verse, while generally employed in tragedy, had never been limited to it by the Elizabethans. With them it did not reach its position without a struggle. For a long time various sorts of measures were used side by side. Quatrains, seven-line stanzas, eight-line stanzas, couplets of twelve and fourteen syllables are to be found along with the regular heroic verse, whether rymed or unrymed. Some, and even many of them, appear intermingled in the same piece. The 'Promos and Cassandra' of Whetstone is written in rymed couplets of ten, twelve, and fourteen syllables, with occasional use of blank verse. 'Selimus,' while principally in blank verse, has no small number of seven-line and eight-line stanzas. Both the 'Cleopatra' and the 'Philotas' of Daniel are written mainly in quatrains. Traces of several of these measures can be found in the earlier work of Shakespeare. Ryme appears in nearly every one of his plays; and though the use of it he gradually laid aside, he cannot be said to have ever discarded it entirely. The same thing was true of those who were in the strictest sense his contemporaries. The rejection of other measures and the adoption of blank verse was a general movement in which, during the Elizabethan period, all writers for the stage shared to some extent. To employ the terminology of science, it was an evolution which took place and not a catastrophe.

There is sufficient reason for the emergence to supremacy of blank verse from this confusion of measures that for a while prevailed. No other form was found so effective. Its capacity for giving voice, with no sensible impairment of dignity, to the simplest statement of fact or to the easy language of conversation, and of passing at once from either of these, without the slightest perceptible strain, to the sublimest heights of thought or to the utterance of intensest passion, made it an instrument of expression which has never been surpassed for dramatic purposes, if it has ever been equalled. When its capabilities were fully revealed, as they were by Marlowe, its general adoption was inevitable. It was accepted, both then and afterward, as the recognized medium for the expression of all earnest speech. Once only was an attempt made to displace it from the position which it had acquired. It was during the reign of Charles II. that this occurred. Then a determined effort was put forth to substitute for it ryme. The matter became a subject of vehement controversy. The struggle in behalf of ryme was stoutly maintained for a while; but when Dryden, its great champion, capitulated, and wrote ' All for Love' in blank verse, its cause was felt to be lost. Though it did not die out immediately, its doom had been sealed. Henceforward there were few to say a word in its favor, and many to attack it as a gross impropriety.

Unlike its original appearance, this later introduction of ryme had been due to French influence. It was that, too, which for a while maintained it. Later it was conceded, by those opposed to its use in the English drama, that there was justice in Voltaire's contention that in French ryme must be employed. To that language was denied what he at first was willing to call the happy liberty of blank verse. It was a tongue which would not admit of inversions. The lines could not be made to run into one another. A mere cæsura and a fixed number of feet would not be sufficient to distinguish poetry from prose. Therefore in Voltaire's opinion ryme was essential to French tragedy and would be an ornament to French comedy.[1] But no necessity of this sort existed in English; hence the hostility manifested to ryme during the eighteenth century was carried to an extreme. Not even would Shakespeare's practice of intermingling it with blank verse have been tolerated in the work of a professed imitator. He himself was pardoned, because, living in the unrefined age he did, he could not be expected to know better. But no privilege of this kind could be conceded to the writer of the understanding ages which had followed. The union of prose and verse in the same play was as bad as anything could be; but the iniquity of indulgence in such a mixture hardly surpassed that of intermingling different kinds of verse. Addison declared himself to be very much offended when he saw a play in ryme. This he termed a solecism. But he found still more objectionable those plays which had some parts in ryme and some in blank verse. These were really two different languages. He was willing to admit that the speaker at the very end of a scene might be permitted to take his departure with two or three couplets. Beyond that point he was unwilling to go.[2]

Blank verse became therefore sacred to tragedy. Critical opinion assumed that in this species of dra-

---

[1] Letter to Lord Bolingbroke, prefixed to *Brutus*.
[2] Spectator, No. 40, April 11, 1711.

matic composition no other form of versification was permissible. If the employment in it of ryme met with disfavor, we can accordingly conceive something of the state of feeling that would be aroused by the use of prose. "Tragedy," said Chesterfield, "must be something bigger than life, or it would not affect us." In it the violent passions must not only speak, but furthermore they must speak with dignity. Hence the necessity of their being expressed in verse.[1] Colman in the prologue to Hayley's play, besides speaking of comedies in ryme, had also mentioned tragedies in prose. Few experiments of this latter kind were ever attempted; yet it is to be said that in at least two instances, when so written, they achieved notable success. The experiments of this nature belonged, however, to the tragic drama which dealt not with persons of high position, but with characters taken from a comparatively low station in life. It was too venturesome for even the most reckless of playwrights to make a king or hero talk the humble language of prose. But with the personages coming from the middle class this liberty could be taken more safely. In 1731 Lillo brought out his domestic tragedy of 'George Barnwell.' It was in prose, though, it must be admitted, it was a sort of spurious prose. It had a measured movement; it was full of inversions; and a good deal of it could have been turned with little difficulty into passable blank verse. The success it achieved was so great that it continued to be acted for the rest of the century. But however popular with the public, it offended the critical frater-

[1] Letter to his son, Jan. 23, 1752.

nity. This was partly due to its violation of the unities, but mainly to the form in which it had been put. The experiment Lillo never afterward cared, or at least never chose, to repeat, in spite of the success which his first venture had met. In 1740, about a year after his death, his play of 'Elmerick' was produced. These words of its prologue bear witness to the fact that all other qualities of his most popular work had never entirely appeased critical fury : —

> " He knew no art, no rule ; but warmly thought
> From passion's force, and as he felt he wrote.
> His Barnwell once no critic's test could bear,
> Yet from each eye still draws the natural tear."

The next successful piece of this kind was 'The Gamester' of Edward Moore. It was brought out in 1753, and met with the greatest public favor. Though written in prose, there could be no question as to its being a tragedy. To that form of art which excluded the comic entirely its author was unswerving in his allegiance. From beginning to end there is little but misery, unrelieved by a single sally of wit, not even by a single diverting incident. It differed from Lillo's work in the obedience it paid to the unities, with the usual absurdity of crowding into twenty-four hours events which could hardly have taken place in twenty-four days. But this violation of the truth of life did not disturb the critics. It did not even occur to their minds. It was the way in which it was written which they found objectionable. All properly constituted persons of taste, it was asserted, regarded the use of prose as something altogether below the dignity of tragedy.[1] Successful as the piece had been, it was not enough so to encourage imitation. This employment of prose involved therefore an additional risk which no playwright cared to run. Thirty years passed before any one ventured again upon so hazardous an undertaking. In 1783 Cumberland brought out his tragedy of 'The Mysterious Husband.' In it he too made use of the forbidden medium. That the course was felt to be fraught with danger is plain from the words of the prologue : —

> "Sad omen for our poet when he chose
> The narrow grovelling path of humble prose,
> A path indeed which Moore and Lillo trod,
> And reached Parnassus by the bridle road."

Against the deference paid to these conventional rules Shakespeare's practice was a silent but perpetual protest. He had employed ryme and blank verse in his comedies. In so doing he had aggravated the original offence by the further crime of mingling the two in the same production. Into his tragedies he had introduced prose. Sometimes in the very same scene specimens of all these different methods of expression were to be found. The same characters occasionally passed from one to the other without the slightest hesitation. In truth, there was not a dramatic sin of which he had not been guilty. As his plays became more read and studied and acted, the sense of the enormity of these proceedings gradually waxed fainter with familiarity. For a long period, it is true, the opinion

[1] For example, see a long notice of the play in the 'Universal Magazine,' vol. xii. pp. 77–88 (1753).

prevailed, sometimes even with his admirers, that the mixture of these various modes of expression in the same piece was merely another illustration of his wild and irregular genius. But in process of time it dawned upon the minds of men that these conventions concerned only the mechanism of the play; they had little to do with its character as a work of art. This depended upon its effectiveness in producing properly the result at which the writer aimed. If a person reaches at the right moment the place he is seeking, it makes comparatively little difference whether he has travelled on foot, or on horseback, or in a chariot-and-four, or if he has adopted in turn each one of these modes of conveyance. The choice is largely a matter of convenience. Undoubtedly certain mediums of expression are in themselves better suited to one kind of production than to another; but it is the success in any given case that determines whether the particular one resorted to in it has been the best or not. Each can be so used as to cause offence; but that consists in the way it is employed, not in the fact of its employment.

Controversies on points like these are taken up with the nature of the vehicle. There were others which concerned either the material which was sought to be conveyed, or its method of treatment. About these latter a number of conventional rules strove to find acceptance. In certain instances they gained it. They were frequently put forth in conformity to some fanciful theory which might or might not have the least relation to nature or truth. According as the work of the dramatist harmonized or failed to harmonize with the view adopted, it was adjudged right or wrong. One of the most important of these, the doctrine of poetical justice, belongs strictly to the controversy about the morality of the Shakespearean drama. At this place, therefore, it will merely receive mention and not treatment. Furthermore, the variation from the classical precedent which goes under the name of domestic tragedy does not strictly come into any discussion of Shakespeare as a dramatic artist. With this sort of production, not uncommon in his time and perhaps even more common later, he did not concern himself. Though he brings men of low position into these pieces, his heroes are always of exalted station. In most of them they are either royal or connected with royalty. The apparent exceptions are only apparent. Both Romeo and Juliet are representatives of great families whose strife has deluged the streets of an Italian city with blood. Othello is a renowned military leader. Timon, against whom most exception can be taken on this ground, is a man of highest social position, and allied in a way with the great historical personage who appears at the conclusion of the play as the conqueror of Athens. While Shakespeare's tragedies do not therefore always conform to the classical practice of dealing with the fate of kings and the fortune of states, they do concern themselves invariably with persons of lofty station. In general this is also true even of his comedies. 'The Merry Wives of Windsor' and 'The Taming of the Shrew' are the only two of these in which persons of the dignity of rulers do not bear some part.

Yet the belief in the necessity of confining tragedy as far as possible to royalty exercised some influence in the alterations which were made in Shakespeare's plays. But any effect wrought by it was slight in comparison with the extension given to the part love was made to fill. From the beginning this passion had been the staple of comedy. There, it was felt, was its legitimate province. But love with the Elizabethans had also invaded tragedy; in France it subsequently made a complete conquest of it. On that stage no piece could succeed which did not contain it as a leading motive, if not the leading motive. If it were lacking, actors refused to play it, audiences refused to listen to it. From France, as we have seen, the practice was carried to England at the era of the Restoration, and came to occupy a prominent place in the transformations which Shakespeare's dramas were made to undergo. However much men might dislike the idea of thrusting the operation of this passion into every production, whether suitable to it or not, they conformed to the prevailing taste of the age in so doing. It was the general adoption of this practice by the French playwrights which led to love in tragedy being sometimes considered an essential distinction between romanticism and classicism. Such it never really was. It could not be a distinction between the purely classical drama and the romantic; for the ancient tragedy did not deal in love between the sexes at all. It could not be a distinction between the French and the English tragedy; for both dealt in it more or less. There is just this slight foundation for the contention. It is to a certain extent a distinction between the stage of Corneille and Racine and that of Shakespeare, using Shakespeare as the representative of his period. Even there it is not a thorough-going distinction. It is so only to the extent that in the latter love was made the subject of tragedy occasionally; in the former it was made so habitually.

So little, however, was the position given to the subject of love regarded as a real distinction between the classical and the romantic drama that the practice of introducing it on all occasions met with as much disfavor from many adherents of the former as it did from the stoutest upholders of the latter. True, this disfavor was in part due to the belief in certain conventional rules which had no foundation in nature, in reason, or in common sense. With the full operation of these rules love was supposed to interfere. Opposition was therefore sometimes manifested to any introduction of it whatever. In the eyes of René Rapin, who in 1674 published reflections on Aristotle's 'Poetics,' modern tragedy had degenerated on this very account from the standard set by the ancients. Tragedy, he maintained, must always be invested with an heroic air. For that reason love is unsuitable to it. To him it seemed that there could be nothing more senseless and contemptible than for a man to spend his time whining about frivolous kindnesses, when he might be making himself an object of admiration by great and noble thoughts and sublime expressions. It shows, nevertheless, how strong was the sentiment in favor of the course he condemned that Rapin recognized and confessed that his was but a solitary voice which was lifted up against established usage.

But if the practice annoyed Rapin the critic, it irritated Voltaire the dramatist almost beyond endurance. Protests against it abound in the introductions to his tragedies. Our stage is filled with nothing but gallantry and intrigue, he wrote in the preface to his *Rome Sauvée*. Nobody with us enters into conspiracies, but everybody is in love. He reiterated his opinion in the dissertation prefixed to his *Sémiramis*. Love and gallantry have almost ruined the French theatre, was his cry. He had told us previously how great had been his annoyance and indignation, when he offered *Œdipe* to the stage in 1718, to find that he could not get it acted because it contained nothing of that passion. The actresses laughed at him when they discovered there were no scenes of tenderness in which they could display their powers. So he tells us he was compelled to spoil his play by putting in some love-passages in a piece in which they had no business. Rapin's feelings, which differed only in degree from those of Voltaire, were reflected in Rapin's English translator, Rymer. This writer was the most ardent upholder of both the theory and the practice of the ancient drama. It was because love did not appear there that he was led to regard it as unsuitable to the stage. Dennis did not altogether agree with his fellow-critic in his demand for the complete exclusion of this passion. Yet he denounced the introduction

225

of love-scenes in Addison's ' Cato,' partly, to be sure, because of their insipidity, but also because they were utterly foreign to the actual interests of the play.[1] Critical opinion in England pretty generally condemned the practice ; yet it had but little influence upon usage. As late as 1753 Joseph Warton complained that love, by totally engrossing the theatre, had contributed to degrade that noble school into an academy of effeminacy.[2]

The introduction of love into tragedy is important to us, because of the prominence of the part it played in the alterations of Shakespeare. But it cannot fairly be imputed to the classicists, though it had established itself completely upon their stage. It was, however, by those belonging to their school that a number of other doctrines were propounded at the era of the Restoration in order to meet fully the requirements of poetical art. Some of these can hardly be considered anything more than the expression of personal opinion; others there were which had a good deal of vogue, and affected to no small extent the practice of the dramatists of the time. They were, furthermore, made tests to try the merits of Shakespeare. The reader of the critical literature of the period following the Restoration gets tired beyond measure at the constant gabble about the poetic art, — what it demands, what it disallows. He finds wearisome beyond endurance the persistent harping upon Aristotle's assertion that the design of tragedy is to inspire pity or terror; the regular examination of every play in order to ascertain whether or not it

---

[1] Remarks upon Cato.
[2] Adventurer, No. 113, Dec. 4, 1753.

has been successful in exciting one or both of those emotions. In all the controversies about these various points the historiographer, Thomas Rymer, who has already been mentioned, bore a conspicuous part. He was largely responsible for the acceptance of some of the views then promulgated, so far as they were accepted at all. Of one or two he may have been the originator. For these reasons, as well as for his attitude toward Shakespeare, it is necessary to give some account of him as a man and a critic.

Fortunately for his reputation Rymer is now known to us mainly as the compiler of the documents which go under the name of 'Fœdera.' The diligence and zeal he displayed in collecting this mass of historical material has always found its due meed of praise. But to his contemporaries he was known almost wholly as a critic. [1] About his qualifications for exercising the duties of this calling, as well as for the success which he met in its pursuit, widely conflicting opinions have been entertained. The generally received modern view has been expressed by Macaulay with his usual energy, or, as some hold, with his usual over-emphasis. Accord-

[1] A most singular error is found in the memoir of Rymer, which was prefixed by Sir Thomas Duffus Hardy to the Syllabus of the documents contained in the 'Fœdera.' published in 1869. In that an extract, under the title of 'The Garreteer Poet,' was printed as a specimen of the bitter feeling entertained and exhibited towards Rymer personally. The passage in question is an extract from one of the chapters in a novel called 'The History of Pompey the Little,' written by Francis Coventry, and first published in 1751. It is a picture of the misery and squalor in which poor authors lived at that time. The character is designated as "Mr. Rhymer, the poet;" but it has nothing whatever to do with Rymer, the critic, who had been dead about forty years.

ing to him, Rymer was the worst critic that ever lived. Even those who regard him most contemptuously might naturally hesitate to accord to one alone, out of the multitude of aspirants, the right to the occupancy of this particular throne. Still, there is no question that he possessed qualities which afford no small justification for the claim Macaulay set up in his behalf. To incompetency of appreciation he joined peculiar wretchedness of expression. To make use of one of his own phrases, " for tongue and wind "[1] he never had a rival. His methods of criticism were very much of the nature of those with which purists have made us all familiar in judging of the correctness of usage. He first laid down dogmatically certain rules for deciding upon the merits of the work he was considering. Whether these rules were right or wrong was a detail which did not engage his attention. He announced them, he tried everybody by them. According as men conformed to them or failed to conform, they were adjudged innocent or guilty.

To Rymer belonged one characteristic which some seem to regard as the crowning qualification of a critic. He was entirely devoid of literary taste. The danger of having it is patent. Its possessor may be tempted to entertain and even express a high opinion of what the rules he has adopted teach him he ought to disapprove. This was something liable to exert at times a baleful influence over the best-intentioned judges, who had fortified themselves against such misleading admiration by a thorough mastery of the principles of

[1] Tragedies of the Last Age, p. 44.

art. There is a remarkable confession of this sort by Gildon, much learned in the critical jargon of the time. "In spite of his known and visible errors," he said, "when I read Shakespeare, even in some of his most irregular plays, I am surprised into a pleasure so great, that my judgment is no longer free to see the faults, though they are ever so gross and evident. There is such a witchery in him, that all the rules of art which he does not observe, though built on an equally solid and infallible reason, as entirely vanish away in the transports of those that he does observe, as if I had never known anything of the matter." [1]

Rymer never fell a prey to feelings of this nature. From any temptation to swerve from the plain path of critical duty by the operation of literary taste he always remained perfectly free. In the preface to his translation of Rapin he gave an account of English epic poetry. Spenser was the first author considered in connection with it. To him Rymer accorded a qualified praise. He possessed genius for heroic poetry ; unfortunately, he lacked a true idea of it. Hence in his matter he had been misled by following Ariosto as a guide, and in his manner by adopting a stanza which is in no wise proper for our tongue. The only two other examples he found to make the subject of comment were the ' Davideis ' of Cowley and the ' Gondibert ' of D'Avenant. There was not even an allusion to ' Paradise Lost,' though it had already passed into its second edition in the very year in which Rapin's

[1] Essay on the Art, Rise, and Progress of the Stage (1710), in edition of Shakespeare, 1728, vol. x. p. 3.

work appeared in France. Later the increasing vogue
of this epic compelled him to mention it. This he
did at the end of the volume containing a castigation of a few of Beaumont and Fletcher's plays.
There he promised another work which should deal
with certain popular dramas of the previous age. It
was also to contain, he assured his readers, "reflections
on that ' Paradise Lost ' of Milton's which some are
pleased to call a poem." This last promise or threat was
never fulfilled. The loss to criticism can be endured;
the loss to harmless gayety is irreparable. Furthermore, Rymer's want of taste in appreciation had
its complement in an equivalent want of taste in expression. His critical efforts bear throughout the
marks of literary vulgarity. He wrote in a violent style
under the impression that it was vigorous. He constantly indulged in coarse phrases which, because they
were coarse, he deemed idiomatic. It was probably his
only method of saving himself from being tedious. A
noisy drunkard may be disagreeable, but he is not dull.
Specimens of what is really little more than foul-
mouthed railing will force themselves upon the attention in the account, to be given later, of his attack
upon Shakespeare. Yet, as a foretaste of their character, it may be well to cite his description of the
way in which Amintor is described in ' The Maid's
Tragedy.' "All the passions in him," he wrote,
"work so awkwardly, as if he had sucked a sow."[1]

But, however little worth consideration Rymer may
now be conceded to have been in himself, in the history

[1] Tragedies of the Last Age, p. 127.

of critical controversy he has always to be reckoned with for what he was thought to be by others. There can be no denying the influence he wielded in the closing years of the seventeenth century. Undoubtedly there were many of his contemporaries who estimated his views at their real value. But we have to look the fact in the face that his opinions were then usually cited with deference, and that, when controverted, it was done with a certain uneasiness, as if it partook of the nature of a venturesome proceeding. Nor has the regard paid to his authority been limited to the men of his own age. According to Spence, he was declared by Pope to be "on the whole one of the best critics we ever had." He was mentioned with respect by Walter Scott as having been one of those who produced by his writings a more than salutary influence upon the drama.[1] By Hallam he was treated with consideration, though he confessed to having read but one of his works, and that, it is clear, he had read very carelessly.[2] With such credentials as these, the views he expressed must receive a certain amount of consideration from the student of literary history. It is a deplorable necessity. The estimation in which Rymer was held by many during his lifetime, the high or at least respectful opinion expressed of him by eminent men who lived long after his death, tend to make one distrustful of anything and everything which goes under the name of criticism.

There were two things which contributed to Rymer's

[1] Essay on the Drama (1814), in Chandos Classics ed., p. 213.
[2] Literature of Europe, part iv., ch. 7.

repute in his own day. One was his reputation for learning. So far as literature pure and simple is concerned, it was out of all proportion to his real acquirements. In that it was neither varied nor profound. But however limited his knowledge, that of the persons with whom he consorted was much less. He had fallen upon a time in which few of his contemporaries could be accounted scholars in the subjects in which he pronounced his decisions magisterially. Here was a man who could talk familiarly not only about Greek and Latin, but about Old French and Provencal and Italian authors. Those who knew nothing of these latter were not likely to question any misinformation in regard to them which he cared to impart. Upon the men of his time his self-confidence and his dogmatism not unnaturally made a great impression. They honestly looked up to him as an authority. Nor, as an element in his success, can we afford to overlook the effect wrought by the violence and abusiveness with which he delivered his judgments. It is wonderful to observe how often and how well ill-nature will supply the place of brains. Rymer's bad temper brought him a consideration and respect which his unaided intellect could never have secured.

It shows indeed how much the repute of learning can make up for the lack of real insight and all genuine appreciation that Rymer's critical essays, which were only saved from being intolerably dull by their exceeding ferocity, imposed even upon the manly understanding of Dryden. It was partly to the countenance which he received from this author, who as a literary judge was really great, however unequal, that much of the influence which he exerted was due. To a certain extent it was a case of reciprocal flattery. In the preface to his translation of Rapin, Rymer had paid a tribute of adulation to the most eminent man of letters among his contemporaries. He had selected for comparison a description of night taken from the Greek of Apollonius, the Latin of Vergil, the Italian of Tasso and of Marini, the French of Chapelain and of Le Moyne. From Dryden he took a few lines from ' The Conquest of Mexico.' In these Rymer asserted that the English poet had outdone all his rivals. "Here," said he, "is something more fortunate than the boldest fancy has yet reached, and something more just than the severest reason has observed. Here are the flights of Statius and Marino, tempered with a more discerning judgment, and the judgment of Virgil and Tasso animated with a more sprightly wit." This is very silly criticism, for the lines thus exalted, while respectable, are not in the least remarkable. But Dryden would have been more than human, had he not treated with tenderness a writer who had not only gone out of his way to praise him, but had ranked him higher than Vergil and Tasso. Still his respect for the acquirements of his panegyrist was unquestionably genuine. "Judicious" was the term he more than once applied to his observations. To him he was "our learned Mr. Rymer;" and he paid a deference to his opinions which now impairs the deference we pay to his own.

Rymer's critical views upon the drama were first communicated to the world in a treatise, published in

1678, which was entitled ' The Tragedies of the Last Age considered and examined by the practice of the ancients and the common sense of all ages.' He set out in this to devote himself to the six then most applauded productions of the Elizabethan stage. He actually did not get much further than a discussion of the merits of three plays of Beaumont and Fletcher. From the work we can gather, however, a pretty definite conception of the opinions he held. It hardly need to be said that he was an ardent upholder of the rules. It was a matter of course that he should advocate the unities and disapprove of the intermixture of comedy and tragedy and the shedding of blood. But he was far from being satisfied with limitations of this limited nature. He devised a number of other restrictions, or at least brought them to the attention of men, which were designed to add to the decorum of the stage. One, to which reference has already been made, is the doctrine of poetic justice. In regard to this he was particularly emphatic. But there were several other rules for the conduct of the drama upon which he laid stress; and these deserve mention as evidence of the sort of ideas that were prevalent at the time, even when they apparently received the sanction of no one but himself.

Rymer's father had been hanged for treason shortly after the Restoration. The son seems to have felt it incumbent on him to make up for the parental dereliction by the extravagance of the views he took as to what was due to the head of the state. The feelings he expressed may or may not have been exhibited by

him in his personal conduct; but in the theoretical
conduct of the drama he carried loyalty to the highest
pitch of devotion. He insisted upon the applicability
to poetry of the political maxim that the king can do
no wrong. He drew a marked distinction between
monarchs as exhibited by the historian and by the playwright. If such personages were weak and bad in real
life, they must not be so represented in letters. History may know of feeble kings, of vicious kings; but to
such in the drama, Rymer tells us that Aristotle cries
shame.[1] Poetry will allow no such unbecoming treatment of the Lord's anointed. Though it is not necessary that all the heroes of tragedy should be of the class
of rulers, all rulers of tragedy must be heroes. It was
a prerogative inviolably attached to the crown, which
neither a poet nor a parliament of poets had the right
to invade. He carried this doctrine to the farthest
extreme in its applications. A king, so far from being
criminal, cannot be accessary to a crime.[2] Naturally
the Elizabethan dramatists would suffer condemnation
under the working of this principle. For plays so
flagrantly violating it as ' Richard III.' and ' Macbeth,'
it was demanding too much of Rymer to take the
trouble to express the contempt which he unquestionably felt. The tragedies of Beaumont and Fletcher,
directly under his consideration, gave him all the opportunity for censure he needed. In this particular he
contrasted the stage of England under a monarch much
to its disadvantage, with the stage of Athens under a
democratic government. The latter made its kings

---

[1] Tragedies of the Last Age, p. 47.   [2] Ibid. p. 115.

unfortunate and to be pitied; the former made them wicked and to be cursed and abhorred.[1]

It was one of the inferences drawn by Rymer from the respect which must always be paid to theatrical propriety, that according to it no private man, still less a subject, could dramatically kill a king and preserve decorum.[2] To the absolute universality of this rule he allowed two exceptions. A good sound Christian might be permitted without offence to make way with a heathen monarch, who, in truth, by being a heathen, was little better than a dog. Again, a private English hero could be permitted to overcome in combat the king of a rival nation. In both these instances there was sufficient partiality to be presumed in the audience on the ground of religion and patriotism to justify such deviations from the strict principles of poetic propriety. It is right to add that this deference to monarchs was no more than an extension of the general rule that no person could be suffered to deal death to another on the stage, unless the rank of both was such that in real life the laws of the duello would permit them to meet in mortal combat.[3] At least a man could not deal death to one above him; to slay an inferior was at worst a peccadillo. But no servant could slay his master; hence we can see how much more would dramatic propriety be outraged by a subject killing his liege lord. The conduct of Cornwall in ' King Lear ' would be conceded to be revolting, morally; but it could not compare in artistic hideousness with that of his ser-

[1] Tragedies of the Last Age, p. 29.
[2] Ibid. p. 117.   [3] Ibid.

vant, who engages him in combat and wounds him mortally.

Not merely must he be possessed of masculine vanity, but thrice must he be armed with desperate daring, who at the present day should venture to put forth a further amplification of this rule which Rymer then fearlessly enounced. In poetry, he tells us, no woman is to be permitted to kill a man unless her superiority of station is sufficient to counterbalance her inferiority of sex.[1] In truth, the laws of the drama, as set forth by its then leading expounders, were very strict on the subject of female propriety. The distinguishing characteristic of woman, according to Rymer, is modesty; and therefore tragedy cannot properly represent her as being without that quality. Although he maintains an air of reserve as to the truth of the asserted fact, Rymer fortifies the position he takes on this point by a reference to what some writers of natural history have reported, which is that "women when drowned swim with their faces downwards, though men on the contrary."[2] This establishes, beyond question, the principle that modesty must be regarded as an essential characteristic of the female sex. Accordingly, if one of their number has chanced to get "any accidental historic impudence," as Rymer phrases it, she must cease to stalk in tragedy and pack off instead to comedy.[3] In truth, woman had a pretty hard time of it at the hands of the apostles of the pure principles of art. Not merely was her right to be wicked and immodest questioned; her

---

[1] Tragedies of the Last Age, p. 117.
[2] Ibid. p. 113.   [3] Ibid. p. 114.

liberty of action in more decorous ways was restricted. Thus Gildon tells us that in drawing the manners in the drama they ought always to be made agreeable to the character. This requires every member of the female sex to be depicted as destitute of valor: for valor, though a moral virtue, is a masculine one; it does not belong to a woman, who ought neither to be bold nor valiant.[1] Furthermore, she must not be credited with abstruse knowledge, "which the ladies are by no means esteemed capable of."[2]

Much more had Rymer to say of what the poetic art required and what it forbade. All through his work are scattered reflections which are anything but the result of reflection. He invariably laid down the law with an assurance equal to the assurance with which we can reject it. But his views, if not worthy of acceptance, are worthy of mention ; for they are those of a man whom his age regarded as one of the most judicious, if not the greatest of critics. Accordingly here will be given a statement of all of any importance, in addition to those already indicated or described. They are briefly as follows. Tragedy requires not only what is natural, but what is great in nature. Both matter and expression must be in consonance with the thoughts and feelings which high position and court-education might inspire.[3] The malefactors of this species of the drama must be of a better sort than those usually found among the living; for an obdurate, impudent, and impenitent malefactor can neither move pity

---

[1] Complete Art of Poetry, vol. i. p. 247.   [2] Ibid. p. 250.
[3] Tragedies of the Last Age, p. 43.

nor terror.[1] Poetry will allow no provocation in injury
where it allows no revenge. It will permit no affront
where there can be no reparation.[2] When a sword is
once drawn, the scabbard must be thrown away. There
is no abandoning what is once designed until it be thoroughly effected. Tragedy is no place for cowards, nor
for giddy fellows, nor for bullies with their squabbles.[3]
Furthermore, if actions morally unnatural, if strange
events are to be represented as happening, they must be
duly foretold by signs and portents. Heaven and earth
must be in disorder; nature must be troubled; unheard of
prodigies must occur; spirits must rise from the dead and
breathe forth cursing and slaughter.[4] Rules like these
are specimens of the inanities which, according to Scott,
produced a more than salutary influence upon the stage.

In one respect Rymer treated fairly the men he criticised. He set out to illustrate his faith by his works.
His volume commenting upon the tragedies of the last
age bore an advertisement to the effect that shortly
would be published an heroic play of his own under
the title of ' Edgar, or the English Monarch.' In due
time the work appeared. Scott has told us that both
Rymer and Dennis were ill-advised enough to attempt
themselves to write for the stage, and thereby proved
most effectually that it was possible for a drama to be
extremely regular, and at the same time intolerably
dull. The observation leads one to suspect that Scott
had never read the works he compared. The plays of
Dennis, like most of those of his time, may justly

---

[1] Tragedies of the Last Age, p. 36.   [2] Ibid. p. 126.
[3] Ibid. p. 135.   [4] Ibid. p. 22.

enough be termed dull, though two or three of them
met with a fair degree of success. But that adjective
is altogether too respectable an epithet to apply to the
single production which Rymer wrote. Were it merely
dull, it might take its place by the side of hundreds
of pieces produced in strictest conformity to what
was called art. The student of the English drama,
especially from the Restoration onward, has to wade
through a mass of worthless works, but he will find
none poorer in plot and wretcheder in execution than
Rymer's ' Edgar.' It is not mediocre: it is mean. It
is a rymed heroic tragedy, and Dryden had caused this
species of dramatic production to be liked by many and
to be made tolerable to all by the excellence of his
versification. But in ' Edgar ' the meanness of the
matter is only exceeded by the meanness of the manner.
It is a ryming play, and no small proportion of its so-
called rymes cannot properly be said to ryme at all.
It furthermore abounds in rugged and halting lines.
In truth, its sixty-three pages contain more execrable
rymes and splayfoot verse — to use Pope's phrase —
than any similar production in our literature written by
an author of the least pretension whatsoever.

No one has ever been found, so far as I can discover,
to speak a word in commendation of this play, which
no one, furthermore, ever thought it worth while to
bring out on the stage. But the frailty of human
nature is shown in the fact that in writing it Rymer
found himself unable to live up to the rigor of his own
precepts. Into an heroic play he perhaps had to introduce love; this, at all events, he did on a grand scale.

But he certainly sinned against what he deemed light by permitting a woman to perpetrate a murder, even though it was done decorously behind the scenes. But the failure of his work to interest, its inability to excite any other feelings than those of ennui or derision, did not discredit the doctrines of its author with the partisans of his school. Art is true, they would say, however much its champions cast reproach upon it in their efforts to illustrate it. The doctrine, in particular, that the hero of a tragedy must never be portrayed as a feather-head or a reprobate, especially when that hero is a monarch, found ready acceptance in days when the duty of passive obedience was preached from every loyal pulpit. It received on more than one occasion the sanction of Dryden. The effect of this belief can be traced not only in original pieces, but in the alterations that were made of Shakespeare's plays. Tate, in his version of ' Richard II.,' informs us in his dedicatory epistle that he has modified the action of the monarch, as depicted in the earlier work, in order to make it conform to Mr. Rymer's theory that kings are always to be presumed heroes.

We do not need to be told now that all such rules, propounded for the enforcement of dramatic propriety, when not merely personal conceits, are nothing but artificial conventions. In devising them there was no thought of attempting to bring about a genuine portrayal of life. Their inception was due in the first instance to French influence; though the English writers, following the manner of all imitators, were constantly disposed to better the instructions of their masters. There is, however, another movement to be considered, which owed its origin largely to the admiration felt for the ancient Greek drama. The modern stage, even when it was most regardful of the rules, had fallen into decay, it was said, in consequence of its being given up to gallantry and intrigue in its matter, with the artificial and complicated situations thereby caused. There was one way to restore it to its ancient simplicity and purity and pathos. This was to revive the chorus. It was the chorus in its genuine Greek sense that was contemplated, — that is, a body of persons who actually take part in the play, commenting upon what is passing before their eyes, expressing opinion and giving advice. This is something altogether distinct from the character who assumes that title in the Elizabethan drama. There it is a personage like Time in ' The Winter's Tale ' or Gower in ' Pericles,' who comes forward to announce to the audience what they may expect to hear and behold in the scenes about to be played. That duty done, he retires and takes no further share in the action. Even in the tragedies formed upon the Senecan model, the chorus is no chorus in the Greek sense. While it adopts the lyric form for its utterance, it plays no necessary part in the drama, and confines itself to the utterance of instructive moral reflections between the acts. It is this limitation which kept Jonson from making any attempt to introduce it into his ' Sejanus.' No one, he said, — not even those who had most affected laws, — had reproduced it in reality. This opinion, however, did not prevent him from adopting it later in his ' Catiline.'

Every one, indeed, who was free from the glamour wrought by classical antiquity saw the uselessness of the attempt to give a second life to what was so thoroughly dead. But in the learned, as opposed to what may be called the lay world, there was always a longing to restore this characteristic of the Greek drama. Its revival was a dream constantly cherished. Milton carried the dream into realization. But his 'Samson Agonistes' was avowedly never intended for the stage, and its form and spirit are too alien to modern tastes to permit it to meet there with genuine success. Still scholars continued to cling to the Greek drama and to hold up its methods as the ideal to be kept in view. They were not disposed to take account of differences wrought by time, by custom, by taste. Roscommon complained that since dramatic poetry had lost its chorus it had lost at least half of its verisimility and greatest ornament, rendering modern tragedy no more than the shadow of the ancient.[1] This same belief gained about the same time a certain sway in France, and to some extent affected the action of its then greatest living dramatist. In his *Esther* and *Athalie* Racine introduced the chorus. His action in so doing was hailed in England as the dawn of a better day. Rymer expressed himself rapturously over the results that would follow from the general adoption of the practice. What reformation, he exclaimed, might not be expected, now that the most necessary part of tragedy has resumed its rightful place. Time and place shall no longer be juggled with, he added; and as the

[1] Note on line 193 of Horace's 'Art of Poetry' (1681).

chorus itself constitutes a goodly·show, there will be no need of running after toys and hobby horses foreign to the subject in order to humor the multitude.[1]

But on this point Rymer's views encountered opposition. His fellow-critic, Dennis, at once attacked his position, not only with vigor, but with a line of reasoning which was not easy to meet successfully.[2] In his opinion not only was the chorus unnecessary to the modern stage, it was improper. If the Greek method and the Greek tragedy were to be set up in England, it would be requisite to introduce not only their religion and their polity but also their climate. To a modern audience the spectacle of a chorus singing and dancing upon every terrible and moving event would not only seem unnatural, but would be actually ridiculous. Dennis went farther. He attacked the ancient drama itself for the existence in it of that very body of performers which it was pretended would add to the perfection of the modern drama. He specifically censured the absurdity which its presence had imparted to the ' Electra ' of Sophocles. In the fourth act of that tragedy Orestes discovers himself and his design to his sister in the sight and hearing of the chorus. Accordingly he intrusts a secret, upon which his rule and life depend, to the faith of sixteen women. It was not the only criticism of this kind which was brought against masterpieces of the Greek stage. Roscommon, for instance, had previously found fault with two plays of Euripides for precisely the same rea-

[1] Short View of Tragedy, p. 1.
[2] In 'The Impartial Critick' (1693).

son.[1] About a century after we find Walpole repeating
the objection. "This mob of confidents," said he, "are
the unnatural excrescences of a drama whose faults are
admired as much as its excellences. With all the
difference of Grecian and French and English manners,
it is impossible to conceive that Phædra trusted her
incestuous passion and Medea her murderous revenge
to a whole troop of attendants."

Objections of this sort produced no effect upon classical scholars. Dr. Francklin, in his 'Dissertation on
Ancient Tragedy,' a sort of supplement to his translation of Sophocles, advocated the restoration of the
chorus. So did Hurd in the notes to his edition of
the *Ars Poetica* of Horace. Still these were purely
academic opinions. No one thought of carrying them
into practice. At least, if any one did, his enthusiasm
was speedily cooled by the chilling reception the proposal met from those who cared more for the taste of
the public than for the prejudices of classical scholars.
If an author did not have the sense to see that it was
about as feasible to revive the old Greeks themselves
as the form of their tragedy, he could rely upon having
his eyes opened by the men who would have to
bear the cost of this artificial product. In 1734
'Junius Brutus,' a play taken by William Duncombe
from the *Brutus* of Voltaire, was brought out at Drury
Lane. In the preface to the piece, as printed, its
adapter told us that he had, at the instance of some
learned friends, purposed choruses for the play, after
the manner of the ancients. But he found no disposi-

---

[1] Note to line 200 of Horace's 'Art of Poetry.'

tion in the managers of the theatre to go to the expense of such an undertaking. Accordingly he had been obliged to drop the design. Few there were, however, who entertained any thought of thus appealing to the public. On the contrary, those who wrote plays after the Greek fashion professed, like Milton, that they never intended them for stage representation.

This was true of the most noted attempt of the kind made in the eighteenth century.[1] It was the work of Mason. The reputation which this writer enjoyed after the death of Gray is almost as inexplicable as that acquired by Hayley, who was his fervent admirer. There was little limit to the praise showered upon him by the leading critical periodicals of his day. Dissenters there were, it is true; but their voice was scarcely heard in the chorus of applause with which his efforts were generally greeted. He was constantly called a great poet. He was not unfrequently mentioned in terms which would not have been inapplicable to Vergil. After his two dramas appeared he was more specifically styled Britain's Sophocles. Not a work he produced, no matter how dull, — and in the production of dull works he achieved some most notable successes, — but was spoken of with respect by almost everybody, and in some quarters was welcomed with acclamation. The classical scholar, Glasse, translated into Greek his 'Caractacus.' For his presumption in so doing he suffered a merited rebuke. "How can any additional embellish-

---

[1] The only other play of this period, aiming to reproduce anything of the form and manner of Greek tragedy, which I have chanced to meet any account of, is a dramatic poem by John Sargent, published in 1785, and entitled 'The Mine.'

ments," wrote the indignant reviewer, "be expected to heighten the beauties of a performance, where strength of reason unites with the boldest flights of imagination; where elevation of sentiment and brilliancy of expression are conspicuous in the most eminent degree, and reflect a mutual light to adorn each other?"[1] Similar outbursts of admiration for the felicity and splendor which characterized this chaste and noble model, as it was declared to be, of the Greek drama, can be found in profusion. It is not the only time in the history of letters that the whistle of a tin-trumpet has been mistaken for the blast of a clarion. It was a saying of Aristotle that the mass of men are better judges of music and poetry than a small number of them, however eminent. Mason's fortunes furnish an additional proof to the many that exist of the justice of this dictum, rightly understood. All the glorification of his poetry by the select few could never make him really popular. He had a thin vein of satire which brought him for a time some genuine success. Even that was a soil which was speedily exhausted; while the false glitter of his other verse, which won him reputation with the critics, never imposed upon the reading multitude. The public that admired Gray could never be induced to accept Gray's imitator.

It was about the middle of the eighteenth century that Mason brought out one of those inane imitations of the Greek drama, which men at times painfully persuade themselves that they admire. Compared with the glowing original, they have the pallor, the smileless-

[1] Critical Review, vol. lvii. p. 1, Jan. 1784.

ness of a corpse, and give the general impression of possessing about the same amount of vitality. This particular one Mason called ' Elfrida.' He not only took care that it should not infringe upon the most unimportant of the proprieties of the classical drama, but he furnished it also with a chorus of the most approved pattern. It was published in 1752. To it he prefixed a series of letters to an unnamed and doubtless imaginary correspondent. Him he raised up for the sake of putting into his mouth objections to the course he had taken, in order to provide them with a reply. In these letters all the ineptitudes of the classicists were repeated, and sometimes in a peculiarly offensive way. What Mason told us of the views of others is, however, much more important than any of his own which he took occasion to express. According to him, it was the common opinion of his day that adherence to the unities restrained the genius of the poet. This, be it remembered, was said at a time when English writers for the stage almost universally felt bound to observe them strictly, and did so observe them. He went on to remark that this false notion was due to the universal veneration paid to Shakespeare. The disregard which he, in compliance with the taste of his age, had shown to all the necessary rules of the drama, had been considered as a characteristic of his vast and original genius. Consequently it had been set up as a model for succeeding writers, and had exercised a baleful influence upon the development of the dramatic art. As a further confirmation of his view he quoted with approval the assertion of Voltaire made about a score of years previously, that the merit of Shakespeare had been the ruin of the English stage.

It is evidence of the great dramatist's influence that this low superstition, as Mason termed it, was, in spite of its absurdity, so popular that he feared it would never be discarded. The only hope he saw for rescuing the stage from the degradation into which it had fallen was to return to the chaste purity of the ancient time and restore the chorus. But this could only come about when a great poet should have arisen who would possess the genius and elevation of Shakespeare and the sober and chastened judgment of Racine. There was not much hope, however, for the speedy appearance of this prodigy. Accordingly he himself, though having, as he humbly expressed it, but common talents, had set out to produce a drama in which the best models of antiquity should be taken for a guide. It was his design, he asserted, to pursue the ancient method so far as it was probable a Greek would do, were he alive, in order to adapt himself to the genius of the times and the character of modern tragedy. Nature and Aristotle were regarded by Mason as equivalent terms; but everything they could dispense with was to be let go in order to accommodate the play to the present taste. The rigor of the classic drama was therefore to be softened by having the action turn on the passion of love. It was private distress, and not the sorrows of royalty and the fate of kingdoms that was to be used to excite the sympathy of the reader.

Such was the nature of the concession made to modern feelings. On the other hand, nothing was to be admitted or omitted at which the Greek judgment could take offence. The things upon which nature and Aristotle insisted were strict adherence to the unities and the retention of the chorus; in fact, the former was a consequent of the latter. In restoring this, and thereby returning to the practice of the ancients, lay the only hope of rescuing the modern stage from the decay which had overtaken it. For the chorus Mason had, as he tells us, early acquired veneration. He was disposed to regard it as essential to the tragic drama. It put necessary restraints of all sorts upon the poet. Its presence involved the unity of place, for its members were too numerous to be following the characters about. As it also bore a part in the play itself, the time of action was necessarily no longer than that of representation. Thus these two unities, whose observance both common sense and antiquity had prescribed, would be restored to the rights they once enjoyed and still claimed by the Magna Charta of Aristotle. The chorus, besides, added superior pomp and majesty to the drama. It brought an agreeable variety into the versification and metre. Above all, it furnished a vehicle for the communication of moral sentiments. Its animadversions instructed the spectator how to be affected properly by the words and acts of the characters. It kept him from being misled by their ill example, and enabled him to profit by whatever good example they furnished.

These are Mason's arguments for the chorus, set forth, whenever possible, in his very words. Yet he admitted that no popular success could attend representations of any such sort of tragic drama. It was therefore the reader to whom he addressed himself. He repelled the ignoble motive of seeking the applause of an unrefined and boisterous English audience, which could not be expected to appreciate the quiet beauties belonging to the chaste and noble style he had adopted, but would require instead action and business and bloodshed in open sight. So, like Milton before him, and Byron after him, he professed not to have in view any performance of his tragedy; though the writing of a play which is not designed to be acted seems very much like training a body of soldiers whose business shall be under no pretext to fight, Still it was felt that pieces of this delicate and lofty character could not safely be exposed to the rude breath of public assemblies. Their beauties would be of the kind that the common class of hearers could neither understand nor feel. The fate which had befallen Racine's work, Mason told us, furnished ample warning of the disaster which would happen to him who attempted to repeat upon the English stage the experiment of that author. The French people were far superior to his own countrymen in the taste for probability and decorum in theatrical diversion. Yet they had not continued willing to put up with the choruses introduced into the two great masterpieces, *Athalie* and *Esther*. These were no longer retained in the representation of the tragedies. What hope, therefore, could there be for pieces of this nature before the kind of audience that filled the pit of an English theatre!

Voltaire with his usual clearness of vision, whenever

preconceived prejudices did not interfere, had recognized the absurdity of attempting to return to this practice of the ancient drama. He tells us that in preparing *Œdipe* for the stage he consulted M. Dacier as to the methods he should follow. That scholar recommended him to put a chorus in every scene, after the manner of the ancients. He might have as well advised me, said the poet dryly, to walk about the streets of Paris wearing Plato's gown. Yet unquestionably there would be at times opportunities for experiments of this sort which, by gratifying curiosity and appealing to attractions other than the purely dramatic, might meet with temporary favor. The venture in which Mason felt that it was impossible to achieve success was undertaken by another. In 1772 Colman, who was at that time managing the Covent Garden Theatre, brought out ' Elfrida.' It ran for the number of twenty-seven nights,[1] though this was largely due to the spectacular character given it, and to the music of Arne. Mason was very indignant at this proceeding of Colman, who had made use of his production without taking the trouble to ask his consent; but the success which the attempt had met led him in 1776 to alter for the stage his second play of the same kind. This was the one entitled ' Caractacus,' which had been published in 1759. In 1779 he further altered ' Elfrida ' with the same intent. Both these were produced at Covent Garden, and the first met with a fair degree of success.[2] But the novelty had worn off, and there was

[1] Genest, vol. v. p. 361.

[2] It was acted fourteen times, according to Genest, vol. v. p. 563. 'Elfrida,' in Mason's later version, was acted five times, vol. vi. p. 95.

a steady decline in interest in these productions from the time of Colman's first undertaking. It was only at rare intervals that they were ever brought out again, and then only for one or two nights; and after the close of the eighteenth century they were never put upon the stage. Colman indeed clearly believed that whatever success they had met with was due to other causes than the interest which the plays themselves had inspired. In truth, in his translation of Horace's *Ars Poetica*, published in 1783, he pointed out the inexpediency and uselessness of the attempts to restore the chorus to the modern stage. Furthermore, he took the ground that if it were revived, the other parts of the ancient drama — music and dancing — ought to be revived with it.[1]

Mason's opinions have been given here in full, not because they are important now or were influential then; but mainly because they show that the classicists plainly recognized what was the influence that was overthrowing their doctrines. They are furthermore worth recording because Mason's friend, whose superiority to him in scholarship was as great as it was in poetry, was thereby enabled to administer to him some wholesome advice, and to lay down the true doctrine in an age which admired the practice of Shakespeare without daring to follow it, and frequently felt under obligation to apologize for admiring it. Gray saw what Mason could not comprehend, that the revival of classic memories is something altogether distinct from the revival of the classic imagination. We know that he thought none

[1] Note to line 288 of Colman's translation of Horace's *Ars Poetica*.

too highly of ' Elfrida; ' but he thought far less of the views which had been expressed in the letters with which it had been introduced. He assured Mason that the reasons advanced by him were all wrong. He declared that the ancients were perpetually confined and hampered by the necessity of using the chorus, and that its abolition had given greater liberty both in the choice of the fable and in the conduct of it. "Love and tenderness," he wrote to his friend, "delight in privacy. The soft effusions of the soul, Mr. Mason, will not bear the presence of a gaping, singing, moralizing, uninteresting crowd. And not love alone, but every passion, is checked and cooled by this fiddling crew. How could Macbeth and his wife have laid the design for Duncan's murder? What could they have said to each other in the hall at midnight, not only if a chorus, but if a single mouse, had been stirring there? Could Hamlet have met the ghost, or taken his mother to task in their company? If Othello had said a harsh word to his wife before them, would they not have danced to the window and called the watch?"[1]

If Gray failed him, Mason had a certain consolation in knowing that his opinions met the approval of Hurd. This writer was in prose very much what he himself was in poetry. He was one of those who have regularly applied to them the epithet of elegant, for no other apparent reason than that they conspicuously lack force. From the first Hurd had been a warm advocate of the restoration of the chorus to the modern drama. In one of the notes in his edition of Horace's ' Art of Poetry, '

[1] Works of Gray, vol. iv. p. 2 (Mitford's edition).

he argued strongly for this course, — that is, strongly in
the sense of earnestly, not in that of effectively. In a
later reprint of this work he brought forward as a sufficient proof of the desirability and possibility of its
restoration the recent tragedies of ' Elfrida ' and ' Caractacus,' "which," he added, "do honor to modern
poetry, and are a better apology than any I could make
for the ancient chorus."[1] Such praise did not too
much elate the author. Even upon his natural self-sat-
isfaction the consciousness of the superiority of the elder
dramatist came down with crushing force, as it has
upon many far greater men. In the dedicatory poem to
Hurd, with which the later editions of ' Caractacus '
were accompanied, Mason told of the desire he had
felt to bring to Britain the choral song, and to mingle
Attic art with Shakespeare's fire. But the muse had
rebuked his presumption. The one he might succeed in attaining; the other was beyond his reach.
All that Parnassus could bestow had been exhausted
to light the flame in Shakespeare's breast. There
was no hope of rivalling him. One consolation indeed there was. Fire might be lacking; but art
remained. It is very plain, however, from his words
that it was not much of a consolation.

In the preceding pages have been given the various
conventional views which have in a measure swayed at
times the theatre, and affected the conduct and treatment of the works produced for it; as also by implication the estimate in which Shakespeare has been held
in consequence of his ignorance or disregard of these

---

[1] Note to line 193 of the *Ars Poetica.*

restrictions. There are others about which less interest and less discussion prevailed in England than in other lands. One of these is the interlocking of the scenes so that the stage shall never be left empty. This is something which Ben Jonson kept in view to a certain extent. By the French critics it came to be considered among the greatest of dramatic beauties. Special stress was laid by them upon it. It was one of the points for which Voltaire claimed superiority for the stage of his own country over that of antiquity. Still it never gained much consideration in England even when French influence was most predominant. That it was not art, but artifice, never occurred to any of its advocates. It may be called artifice of a high order, if one so chooses; but it is none the less artifice. As it was with most of the other conventions, the men who sought to secure it always ran the risk of sacrificing to its acquisition natural beauties far greater. The same thing has been true of all the rules and practices which have been described in the present chapter. It was because the English race had in Shakespeare an example of conformity to nature, to truth, and to life, that it was saved from immolating these upon the conventional altar which the classicists endeavored to set up.

CHAPTER VII

LATE SEVENTEENTH-CENTURY CONTROVERSIES ABOUT SHAKESPEARE

THE gulf which separated the England of the Restoration from the England that preceded the Commonwealth was much deeper and broader than would naturally be indicated by the length of time which intervened. It was a world of different feelings and of different ideas that came in with Charles II. In politics the same formulas continued to be repeated; but the meaning they had assumed was totally unlike that which they had once conveyed. In literature new standards of criticism were set up, new modes of writing came into fashion, new species of productions attracted the popular regard. The drama was quick to respond to the change in the national feeling. As from its very nature it reflects the life of the times, it soon began to show signs of that altered moral tone which was rapidly permeating all classes of society. It is the wholesale revolution of manners, the complete reversal of the attitude previously assumed towards conduct, which is the earliest as well as the most significant characteristic that the Restoration brings to our notice.

Yet though earliest, it must not be imagined that this change took place on the spur of the moment. Men do not throw off in a day the restraints even of

hypocrisy, still less those of virtue. The current began running immediately, it is true, and it soon came
to run very rapidly; but at first it moved so slowly
that for the moment one might deem it was not moving
at all. But when once under full headway it made the
most impressive of manifestations of itself in the reckless, shameless life that was then lived, which was soon
to find its fullest representation in the witty but shameless comedy that was evolved. For the comic drama
of the forty years which followed the Restoration mir-
rors the beliefs and sentiments of its fashionable society
as does no other form of its literature, and perhaps as
does the literature of no other period. The rapid de-
clension of character was at the time a matter of comment and almost of boasting. Dryden's first play, 'The
Wild Gallant,' had been brought out in 1663, and had
proved a failure. Considerably altered for the worse
morally, it was revived with more success in 1667.
In the prologue the author informed the audience that
he himself had once thought his hero monstrous lewd,
but since his knowledge of the town had increased,
he was ashamed to find him a very civil sort of personage. Accordingly he had made him lewder. Yet
he felt that he had not reached the ideal demanded.
" Pray pardon him his want of wickedness," he added.
Still the most repulsive impression produced by the
comic drama of the age is not its licentiousness, gross
as that is, but its selfishness and hardness. Its fine
ladies and gentlemen lack the ordinary feelings of
humanity. They have none of those redeeming traits
of occasional kindliness and of generous impulse which

are frequently found in men who to a great extent spend their lives in frivolous or vicious pursuits. They are cruel, savages at heart, though dressed in the height of the mode and gilded over with a gloss of good manners.

But the most curious spectacle the members of this society present, as they appear in the drama of the period, is their utter ignorance of anything in the shape of a moral code, their manifest unconsciousness of the desirability of refraining from any line of conduct that would conduce to their own pleasure or advantage, merely on the ground that it was improper or wicked. The possessor of morals they seem to have looked upon with the same inquiring gaze of wonder which fills the eye of the ordinary man when he sees some one paying enormous prices for first editions of books. Morality, in fact, was something so entirely outside of their consideration and conduct that they could hardly even comprehend the interest that others appeared to take in it. The most they could do was to recognize it as a factor which had to be reckoned with, because there were cases in which, through the agency of persons with whom they came in contact, it had an indirect connection with themselves. In the eyes of such a body of men neither good behavior nor good character was a necessity. Both, in truth, were looked upon in the light of personal luxuries, indulgence in which partook somewhat of the discreditable, as being of the nature of an unmanly pandering to the prejudices of fanatics. This is the testimony of the comic drama; it is also the testimony of records of the time outside of the drama.

To persons of this class the matter of Shakespeare's plays would generally be of little interest, even if no fault were to be found with their manner. It is obvious at the outset that no writer of the Elizabethan period would in any case have the aids to popularity which belonged to him before the great civil convulsion. Whatever hold upon the public the dramatist had once had from the impression wrought by his own personality, had now disappeared entirely. The men who could remember him or remember his triumphs had passed away. A new generation had arisen which knew him not. It was a generation, in fact, which had largely been taught to avoid him and his kind. We have to keep in mind that for almost twenty years preceding the Restoration the theatres had been closed. Consequently, when Charles II. ascended the throne, a generation had grown up which had never had the opportunity, even if it had had the desire, to witness a stage representation. Furthermore, the iniquity of it had been sedulously preached. It was wicked to act plays; it was wicked to see them acted. No matter how much the reason might reject such views as the outcome of a narrow and ignorant bigotry, the impressions of years were not to be effaced in a moment. To the men of the Restoration period the theatre had not only the allurement of a pleasure from which they had been long debarred; to enhance the keenness of its attractions was also a latent sense that there was something wicked in the enjoyment they felt.

The immortal diarist, Pepys, has here let us into the workings of many minds by revealing his own. He was extravagantly fond of the theatre, and spent no small share of his time in forming resolutions not to go to it so frequently, and in reproaching himself for having broken his resolutions and gone. Part of his remorse was undoubtedly due to the neglect of business such conduct entailed. But it is likewise easy to see that in frequenting plays he was at first snatching also that fearful joy which comes from pursuing a pleasure in which there is an uneasy consciousness that we ought not to indulge. From the point of view of the student of the stage it may be proper to express regret for the wearing away of this particular incentive to theatre-going in the general loosening of ancient beliefs which came to prevail. As the flavor of iniquity, which gave a zest of its own to the attractions of the playhouse, was gradually lost, the temptations that beset him to haunt it were more and more overcome by his business habits. In 1661 he had manifested a noble disregard of his duties, and repaired to the theatre on every imaginable pretext. The record of seventy-four performances which he witnessed that year he never afterward equalled. In 1662 began his downward career as a contributor to our knowledge of the drama. No better example can be cited of the injurious consequences that are liable to result from too earnest and unflinching devotion to one's duty. No doubt Pepys improved his pecuniary situation and prospects by refraining from following his inclinations, and staying instead at his office and looking after matters to which none of the officials attended but himself. But in so doing he sacrificed the future to the present. He deprived posterity of much knowledge which he alone would have given; and in addition, he permanently injured his own eyesight.

As a consequence of the long closing of the theatres, the acting of the plays of the earlier drama was at first a matter of necessity rather than of choice. For a score of years there had been little inducement for those seeking either literary distinction or personal profit to write for the stage. Dramatic production had therefore practically ceased. When the theatre was re-opened at the Restoration, with the exception of D'Avenant and Shirley, — both then nearing the grave, — the prominent members of the older generation of playwrights had gone. None had come forward to take their places. The actors, accordingly, were compelled to resort to the pieces which had been produced before the civil war. Of the writers of these, three still retained the prominence which they had enjoyed from the first. They were Shakespeare, Jonson, and Fletcher. But in the change of taste which was going on, no reputation that came down from the past would avail the dramatist much, or avail him long. Every generation has a thoroughgoing contempt for the critical estimate of the generation which precedes it. It is always disposed to congratulate itself most complacently on the undoubted fact that it itself has reached that summit of perfect taste from which it can look with mingled amusement and contempt upon most of the wretched stuff that pleased the men of the former age. The names they held in highest honor it judges with calm but judicial severity, and assigns them the precise position to which

262

they are entitled. Naturally, this was what the critics of the Restoration period did to the representative playwrights of the Elizabethan era.

The opinion entertained about Shakespeare is the only one that concerns us especially. Here, as elsewhere, Pepys introduces us to the knowledge of the inner belief and feelings of the time. He is by no means our only authority, but he is our best, at least our most delightful one. Nothing can be more entertaining than his delicious bits of criticism, whose impudent inappreciativeness later writers have occasionally equalled, but whose charm they have never been able even remotely to rival. His good opinion of ' Henry IV; '[1] his frequent guarded approval of ' Hamlet ' and ' Macbeth;' his characterization of ' Twelfth Night ' and ' The Taming of the Shrew ' as silly plays;[2] his perusal of ' The Adventures of Five Hours,' which made ' Othello,' which he had previously thought a mighty good play, seem by comparison a mean thing;[3] his feminine addiction to superlatives, which led him to describe ' Romeo and Juliet ' as the worst play he had ever heard in his life,[4] and ' The Midsummer Night's Dream ' as the most insipid ridiculous play he had ever seen in his life,[5] — these choice critical comments cause the most energetic modern censure, dealing, as it does, in insinuation rather than direct assertion, to seem peculiarly tame and pointless. It is not that there are no men now who do not think as he did then; but they

---

[1] Diary, June 4, 1661. [2] Ibid. Jan. 6, 1663, and Nov. 1, 1667.
[3] Ibid. Aug. 20, 1666. [4] Ibid. March 1, 1662.
[5] Ibid. Sept. 29, 1662.

no longer have the courage of their convictions, they dare not commit their real feelings even to their diaries. However strange these comments of Pepys may seem to us, we are not to forget that their writer was an educated man, a graduate of Cambridge University, and possessed of scholarly, or, at any rate, of antiquarian tastes. In this matter he was no more than a representative of feelings widely prevalent among the members of a certain class in his age. The opinions he committed to paper others publicly expressed. For instance, Shirley's earliest written play, ' The School of Compliment,' was brought out in a revised form in 1667, the year after his death. The prologue written for the occasion announces that the change of taste long before presaged had now come to prevail. In it we are told, —

> " In our old plays, the humor, love and passion,
>   Like doublet, hose and cloak, are out of fashion;
>   That which the world called wit in Shakespeare's age,
>   Is laughed at as improper for our stage."

With this altered attitude on the part of the public, there is nothing surprising in the fact that during the score of years immediately following the Restoration the reputation of Shakespeare was lower than it has been at any period before or since. One must guard against the impression that it was a low one in itself. There were then, unquestionably, some who stood ready to deny him a lofty position. But they were comparatively few in number. It was his supreme position only which was not conceded by many. The superiority of Ben Jonson was strongly maintained by a certain class. It was not a large one; but it was made up largely of influential persons. A belief of this nature existed, to some extent, before the civil war, more especially in what may be called the scholastic section of the general body of educated men. Later it increased for a while rather than diminished. For no inconsiderable period after the Restoration, it was no infrequent thing to find Jonson spoken of as surpassing in comedy all writers, whether ancient or modern. Shakespeare's greatness in that field was recognized only occasionally; it was not until the middle of the following century that men began to open their eyes to his superiority. Down to that time it was to tragedy that his reputation was principally confined. But while Jonson was held up as the greatest of English dramatists by a select circle, which arrogated to itself special culture, Fletcher was in the early days of the restored stage the favorite of the theatre-going public. There are plenty of contemporary statements which imply this fact; there is a well-known one which establishes it beyond question. We find it in Dryden's ' Essay of Dramatic Poesy,' which was published in 1668, but was written, as he tells us, in 1665. It bore emphatic witness to the then greater popularity of the plays of Beaumont and Fletcher, though it made no attempt to put them on an equality with Shakespeare's or Jonson's, far less to accord them actual superiority. "Their plays," Dryden wrote, "are now the most pleasant and frequent entertainments of the stage; two of theirs being acted through the year for one of Shakespeare's or of Jonson's."

The preference for Fletcher at that time is perhaps not hard to explain. He is remarkable for the easiness and agreeableness of his dialogue, which furthermore makes far less demand than Shakespeare's either upon the ability of the actor or the attention of the spectator. But the crowning reason for the preference then exhibited is something entirely different. Fletcher's comedies are upon a distinctly inferior plane of morality. The conversation is often coarse, and at times actually offensive. The licentiousness characterizing it, which has largely contributed to drive these plays from the modern stage, undoubtedly added to their attraction at the period of the Restoration. It is probably the fact that in every generation there are people who are as much irritated by the absence of indecency in a dramatic performance as others are by its presence. Such persons, who, it is to be hoped, are exceptional now, seem to have frequently constituted the majority of the audience in the half century that followed the Restoration. This would be a sufficient reason of itself why the comedies of Fletcher should appeal especially to the reigning taste.

In the matter of morality Shakespeare stands on an inconceivably higher level than his then more popular contemporary. Contrast, for illustration, ' The Taming of the Shrew ' with Fletcher's comedy of ' The Woman's Prize, or the Tamer Tamed.' The latter was written as a second part to the former. The moral superiority of the greater dramatist is exhibited on almost every page. ' The Taming of the Shrew ' is by no means one of Shakespeare's best comedies. But whatever its deficiencies as compared with others of his works, there is scarcely a line in it to offend not simply the moral sense, but what may be called the moral taste. It could be acted and has been acted before a modern audience with the slightest possible excision or alteration. But Fletcher's sequel is fairly gross in the indelicacy and even vulgarity of its expression. Speeches of this sort, moreover, are constantly put in the mouths of the female characters. The purely sensual side of the marriage relation is more than brought to the attention; it is forced upon it unremittingly. Yet this play, which no audience of the present time would tolerate, was especially liked in court circles before the civil war, was one of the pieces revived immediately after the Restoration, and was, withal, one of the most popular.

But though Fletcher remained for a time the favorite of the public, his pre-eminence did not continue long. In the race that went on for the position of acknowledged superiority Shakespeare gradually passed not only his rival contemporaries but the whole body of his successors. His rise in estimation was the work of no party. He made his way against a determined disposition in certain quarters to decry his merits. By some his claims to recognition were entirely ignored. The French exile, St. Evremond, informs us that in order to do Ben Jonson honor men called him the Corneille of England; but the people with whom he associated, and from whom he learned all the little he knew of the English drama, apparently thought it hardly worth while to mention to him the name of Shakespeare. Yet amid all this conflict of opinion the steadily growing

267

conviction of his immense superiority is revealed unmistakably in the critical literature of the half century
following the accession of Charles II. The varying
feelings of the times about the great dramatist are best
reflected in the pages of Dryden, its foremost man of
letters. Necessarily, in the special literary estimate
entertained at a particular period about a particular
writer, we must take into account the ideas then dominant. In the judgment expressed in regard to an
author in any epoch there is always manifest the effect
of that general stream of tendency against which men
struggle with difficulty, and with which they are usually contented to drift. The critical standard which is
erected by the age is as much to be considered as the
personal equation of the individual.

It is this which makes the varying views of Dryden
interesting and important. He was a man of broad
sympathies as well as keen insight. There was, in
consequence, going on in his mind a constant struggle
between opinions which reflect the predominant temper
of the times and opinions which are the outgrowth of
his personal taste and judgment, and sometimes are
little more than a reflection of his personal interests.
This explains largely his conflicting utterances. Under
the influence of the doctrines accepted in his age he
was determined to believe in the inferiority of the
Elizabethan dramatists, at least in the matter of art.
They were vigorous, but they were unpolished and
rude. In this particular Dryden made as much as he
could of the superiority of his contemporaries. Yet it
is clear from many of his remarks that there was in his

own mind indecision and uncertainty, even when he most loudly proclaimed his confidence. We recognize in his most positive claims something of that uneasy feeling which characterizes pretenders, who are never quite sure that they have a legitimate title to the possessions which they loudly demand as their right. Dryden might profess to think that the dramatists who flourished before the civil war were ignorant of art; but he could not long hide from himself the conviction of their general superiority to the men of his own time. However lacking they might be in what was called regularity, there was something higher and nobler in which they excelled.

> " Time, place, and action may with pains be wrought,
> But genius must be born, and never can be taught,"

is the exclamation, almost despairing, which he makes in the remarkable epistle to Congreve, upon the difficulties with which the dramatic writers of his time had to contend in order to stand upon a level with the men who had gone before. " Theirs was the giant race before the flood," he declared. True, with the return of Charles the roughness of the early time had been polished, its boisterousness had been subdued; but he added mournfully, —

> " Our age was cultivated thus at length,
> But what we gained in skill we lost in strength.
> Our builders were with want of genius cursed;
> The second temple was not like the first."

It is clear from the various utterances of Dryden that the longer he lived the superiority of Shakespeare grew upon him. In this particular also he reflected the feel-

ings of his age as well as his own individual impressions. That the reputation of the great Elizabethan
continued steadily to increase, instead of diminishing,
disturbed a good deal the classicists of the time. He
had violated every one of the rules upon which they insisted; for it nobody seemed to hold him in less honor.
Much of the learned criticism to which he was subjected was not hostile in spirit. Indeed in its way it
was often inclined to be friendly. What irritated it
was the disposition exhibited by men to doubt the in-
fallibility of the utterances it oracularly pronounced;
further, to deny that the defects which it imputed to
Shakespeare were really defects. As time went on, it
came increasingly into conflict with a belief in his
surpassing excellence which in its eyes was nothing
but bigotry; but it was a bigotry which not only resisted the well-meant attempts to enlighten it, but
resented any disposition manifested to depreciate its
idol. In 1710 Gildon, at the conclusion of his ' Remarks
on the Plays of Shakespeare,' [1] declared that to oppose
the admirers of the dramatist was counted as little less
than heresy in poetry; and that these insisted that he
was the greatest genius of modern times. He could
not speak much, he said, in praise of ' Macbeth;' yet he
did not dare to censure. "It has obtained," he wrote,
"and is in too much esteem with the million, for any
man to say yet much against it." Like many of the
critics after him, his words show that he looked for the
revival of a purer taste; but its expected appearance
kept receding farther and farther in the distance as

[1] In Supplementary Volume (1710) to Rowe's Shakespeare of 1709.

time went on. Yet no one seemed to heed the lesson this steady growth of reputation taught. It took more than a century for men to draw from this continuous and increasing popularity the seemingly unavoidable inference that what Shakespeare did was artistically great, and possessed therefore that enduring vitality which belongs to everything that is so created.

No account of the controversies about Shakespeare's art during the eighteenth century can neglect the consideration of the views about it, put forth by those who, whether little or well known now, made themselves then prominent in the discussion. During the half-century that followed the Restoration there were but three authors who dealt directly in Shakespearean criticism; for Dryden's observations, though frequent and important, were brought in only incidentally. These three were Rymer, — of whom some account has already been given, — John Dennis, and Charles Gildon. In some ways they were men very much alike. They possessed about the same mental characteristics. To a certain extent they encountered similar fortunes. All three fell under the lash of Pope; though Rymer, having died before he had had the opportunity to give the poet any real cause of offence, escaped with slight censure, and, if Spence can be trusted, received from him praise out of all proportion to his desert. Of the other two the modern estimate is largely based not upon what they were, but upon what Pope said they were. All three had then the repute of possessing great erudition. The reader of their writings now is struck much more by the exhibition they make at times of the most in-

sufferable self-conceit and arrogance. All three were
devoted to what they called the poetic art. They all
wrote regular plays in conformity with its requirements; and while neither those of Dennis nor of Gildon
approached anywhere near the unrivalled wretchedness
of Rymer's single attempt, their productions were not
of sufficient merit to commend the practice of the doctrines they preached. All three looked at Shakespeare
from essentially the same point of view. They all
agreed as to his deplorable lack of art. The first
reviled him for it; the other two grieved over it. But
while these last appeared as his apologists and de-
fenders, they did what they could to injure his reputation by bringing out abominable alterations of his plays.

Of these three writers Dennis was much the ablest
man as well as the best critic. His understanding was
in many ways acute, and his appreciation of poetry
keen. Long before Addison's far better known essays
appeared, Dennis had made Milton's epic the subject
of frequent extract and eulogistic comment. In the
preface to his tragedy of ' Iphigenia,' which appeared in
1700, he had spoken of the poet himself as "perhaps
the greatest genius that has appeared in the world these
seventeen hundred years." In a later work he declared
' Paradise Lost' to be "the greatest poem that ever was
written by man."[1] A passage in the fifth book would
always stand alone as the phœnix of lofty hymns. No
equal of it, no second to it could be produced from
the Greek writers of such productions.[2] At that early

[1] Dennis's ' Grounds of Criticism in Poetry ' (1704), p. 54.
[2] Ibid. p. 56.

period Dennis's writings are free from the characteristics by which they were afterward too much distinguished. In truth, the intimate relations in which he stood with many of the most eminent men of the latter part of the seventeenth century furnish convincing evidence of the high opinion which was then entertained of his ability and acquirements. Not to speak of others, he was the friend and correspondent of Dryden and Wycherley. To him Congreve addressed in the form of a letter his well-known essay on humor in comedy. There was a general respect felt for him as a critic by men whose opinions were worthy of respect. To some extent it was justified. But he encountered the fate of those who fall into the error of mistaking temporary conventions for eternal verities. In the treatise on the genius and writings of Shakespeare, which appeared in 1712, he was seen at his worst. Positions taken in it were indefensible, and throughout it was deformed by wearisome twaddle about the poetic art and regret for the ignorance of it exhibited by the dramatist. For all that, his praise of the poet was enthusiastic. His taste was always struggling with his theories, and sense or nonsense followed according as the one or the other prevailed.

As time went by, Dennis found himself passed in the race by younger and abler men. His plays achieved but a moderate success on the stage, and some of them no success at all. This was to him undeniable proof of the poor taste of the age. He purposed the publication of a complete body of criticism in poetry; but as he secured less than eighty guineas subscription, the project had to be abandoned.[1] His ill-fortune soured a temper not originally remarkable for meekness and amiability. He began to assume a hostile attitude towards his generation. He became a professed enemy to all who succeeded. He was undoubtedly sincere in his assertion that he never criticised any one who was not exalted by the public largely above his deserts.[2] But there speedily comes to be a fascination in procedure of this kind which perverts the judgment. That men speak highly of any production is regarded as presumptive proof that it is poor; and the greater the praise they give it, the fiercer is the depreciation. The tendency to dwell on faults exclusively, whether in a work of literature or in the body politic, increases with indulgence. It ends at last in destroying the ability to see things in their true light and estimate their relative importance. Dennis went through the usual experience. He lost all sense of perspective. In addition, his criticism became more and more of an abusive character. He worked himself into mighty passions over the pettiest matters, and along with it indulged in gross personalities. He came, in consequence, into unfriendly relations with the two most eminent men of letters of the time, who belonged themselves to different, if not to hostile parties; though in the case of one of them he seems not to have been the aggressor. Still in both instances it was he who in the long run suffered by it, not they. The adherents of Addison bore him no good-

---

[1] Preface to 'Grounds of Criticism in Poetry;' also Gildon's 'Complete Art of Poetry,' vol. i. p. 185.

[2] Preface to 'Remarks upon Pope's Translation of Homer' (1717).

will, and he will never recover from the representations and misrepresentations of his character which Pope has transmitted.

Gildon, the third of these, wrote much more about Shakespeare than the two others, but is now known the least. Superior himself to Rymer, he looked upon Dennis as his master, and on more than one occasion celebrated him as the most consummate critic of the age.[1] He experienced the same unhappy fate as his leader. He incurred the enmity of Pope, which, like the wrath of Achilles, sent to untimely graves the reputations of scores of writers of more or less ability. Gildon lived until 1724, but it was not till near his death that the hostility of the poet, which had been previously exhibited in prose, embalmed itself in verse. In a fragment published the previous year the epithet of "mean" was attached to his pen; for it, later, was substituted "venal." With Dennis he had his place in the 'Dunciad.' Pope's pretext was a pretended perpetration of acts against himself personally. These, it is almost needless to say, Gildon never committed. His real offence was his friendship with Dennis, and his agreement with that critic in his low estimate of Pope's productions.

Gildon put the climax on one or two previous attacks by the references he both made and failed to make in a work entitled 'The Complete Art of Poetry.' This appeared in 1718. In the introduction to it he discussed the two versions of the 'Iliad,' so far as they were then before the public. He represented Will's

[1] For example, see 'Complete Art of Poetry,' vol. i. p. 185.

coffee-house as favoring Pope's translation, and But-
ton's as favoring Tickell's. For himself, as an indifferent and impartial person, he considered that the latter
author had entered more into the soul of Homer and
had better exhibited his masculine strength and native
simplicity; while the former had embellished his version
with softness and harmony.[1] But in the body of the
work he called it "an abominable translation."[2] He
did even worse than this. In the discussion of pastoral
poetry he wounded Pope in a most sensitive part by
not making even a reference to that which he had
written. As if this were not enough, he exalted Ambrose Philips above all authors of this kind which
later times had produced. He was, indeed, the only
one who could be put alongside of Theocritus and
Vergil. All tolerable judges, said Gildon, gave him
the first place among the moderns. Then came an
allusion to Pope's ironical criticism in ' The Guardian '
of his rival's pastoral poetry. "There have been,"
he wrote, "poor and malicious endeavors made use of
to ridicule that of Mr. Philips; but the effect was so
wretched and the malice so visible, that they are already
dead and therefore not worth our notice."[3] No student
of Pope's life and writings needs to be told that these
are words which would never cease to rankle in the
poet's mind.

The first of these three writers to take the field was
Rymer. He had no special spite against Shakespeare;
no more against him at least than he had against his

[1] Complete Art of Poetry, vol. i. p. xii.   [2] Ibid. p. 185.
[3] Ibid. pp. 157 and 161.

contemporaries. The censure in his volume upon the tragedies of the previous age had fallen almost exclusively upon works of Beaumont and Fletcher. He had spent so much time in demolishing these that he had left himself no space for other authors. He therefore deferred to a future day the remarks on ' Othello ' which he had been intending to make. Years passed, but the promised criticism did not appear. In the mean time the reputation of Fletcher was waning, while that of Shakespeare was waxing. At last Rymer broke his long silence. It may be that he fancied that the fading attractions of the two brother dramatists was due to his efforts in expounding the principles of true art, and that the further duty now devolved upon him to crush the pretensions of the worthless playwright whose repute was steadily rising. At any rate, at the end of 1692, — about fourteen years after the appearance of the previous work, — he came out with a treatise on tragedy, containing reflections upon Shakespeare and other practitioners for the stage. It was preceded by so-called second editions of his first essay and of his ' Edgar.' These consisted in both cases of unsold copies, to which new title-pages had been prefixed. Much of the new work was given up to comment and information which had no real connection with the subject. It was lugged in to exhibit Rymer's learning, and not unfrequently exhibits his lack of it. But when he settles down to his proper business, his treatise has a good deal of that sort of interest which the exertions of a venomous and vigorous mediocrity are often capable of imparting. If Beaumont and Fletcher had not

previously fared well at his hands, Shakespeare was a
still greater sufferer. If any one has become surfeited
with the prevalent praise of the great dramatist, he can
experience a delightful satisfaction in reading the genial
views expressed about him by a writer regarded by
many in his own time as one of its foremost critics.

To two plays, both then exceedingly popular, and
both left unaltered, Rymer devoted himself in particular. These were ' Othello ' and ' Julius Cæsar.' What
is said of them may be summed up briefly. The fable
of the former, we are told, is improbable and absurd,
the characters are unnatural and improper, the thoughts
and their expression are of a piece with the characters.[1] "In the neighing of an horse, or in the growling
of a mastiff," he remarks, "there is a meaning, there
is as lively expression, and, may I say, more humanity,
than many times in the tragical flights of Shakespeare."[2] In another place he speaks of "a long rabble
of Jack-pudden farce betwixt Iago and Desdemona,
that runs on with all the little plays, jingle and trash
below the patience of any country kitchen-maid with
her sweet-heart."[3] This heroine does not, indeed, meet
with much favor at the critic's hands. "No woman,"
he says, "bred out of a pig-sty, could talk so meanly."[4]
He indeed concedes that in the play there is "some
burlesque, some humor and ramble of comical wit, some
shew and some mimicry to divert the spectators; but the
tragical part is plainly none other than a bloody farce
without salt or savor." Naturally he was pained at

[1] Short View of Tragedy, p. 92.   [2] Ibid. p. 96.
[3] Ibid. p. 110.   [4] Ibid. p. 131.

the corrupting effect of such performances upon both taste and manners. "What can remain with the audience," he says, "to carry home with them from this sort of poetry for their use and edification? How can it work unless (instead of settling the mind and purging our passions) to delude our senses, disorder our thoughts, addle our brain, pervert our affections, hare our imaginations, corrupt our appetite, and fill our head with vanity, confusion, Tintamarre and jingle-jangle beyond what all the parish clerks of London, with their Old Testament farces and interludes in Richard the Second's time, could ever pretend to?"[1]

So much for ' Othello.' ' Julius Cæsar ' came off no better. Shakespeare, we are told, had no business to deal with real events. His head "was full of villainous unnatural images, and history has only furnished him with great names, thereby to recommend them to the world."[2] "Never any poet," he says elsewhere, "so boldly and so bare-faced flounced along from contradiction to contradiction."[3] Naturally his disregard of what Rymer deemed decorum was unpardonable. "One would not talk of rules," he remarks, "or what is regular with Shakespeare or any followers in the gang of the strolling fraternity."[4] He does not therefore wonder that the theatre grows corrupt and scandalous, or that poetry is sunk from its ancient reputation and dignity to the utmost contempt and derision "when some senseless trifling tale as that of ' Othello,' or some mangled, abused, undigested, interlarded history " — by

[1] Short View of Tragedy, p. 146.
[2] Ibid. p. 148.
[3] Ibid. p. 151.
[4] Ibid. p. 161.

which he means ' Julius Cæsar ' — "on our stage impiously assumes the sacred name of tragedy."[1] We are indeed assured by Rymer that Shakespeare's genius lay in comedy and humor alone. "In tragedy," it is added, "he appears quite out of his element. His brains are turned, he raves and rambles without any coherence, any spark of reason, or any rule to control him or set bounds to his frenzy."[2] This last sentence is so true a picture of Rymer himself that it would have been an injustice to him personally not to have quoted it in its entirety; but to appreciate fully how thoroughly descriptive it is of the man, one must read the whole book.

One further sentence in this work is worth reproducing, not so much as an exhibition of its author's spirit and critical acumen as for the infinite satisfaction it was later to afford Voltaire. Rymer, who seemed to have as much anxiety to display his incapacity as others have to hide theirs, had commented upon some extracts he had made from ' Othello,' for no other purpose, apparently, than to furnish convincing evidence of his utter lack of literary appreciation. To one passage he appended a remark upon its author. "There is not a monkey," it ran, "but understands nature better; not a pug in Barbary that has not a truer taste of things."[3] All this is entertaining; but one would gain a most erroneous impression of the facts, were he to take the sentences which have been cited as the general, or even a general, opinion prevailing among critics at the time

[1] Short View of Tragedy, p. 164.
[2] Ibid. p. 156.
[3] Ibid. p. 124.

they appeared. The truth is that these tirades, so far
from representing the sentiments of any party, even the
very smallest, are nothing but the views of scattered individuals; and it is not impossible that as large a number of those holding not unlike opinions exist now as
did then. The bitterness Rymer displayed was mainly
due to the exceeding popularity of the poet he affected
to despise. The censurer was stung by the general preference. In one place he refers sarcastically to the
"unimitable" Shakespeare, just as Voltaire subsequently delighted to call him the "divine;" both adjectives being epithets even then constantly applied to
the dramatist. The chapter on 'Othello' bears unwilling witness to the favor with which that play was
regarded. "From all the tragedies acted on our English stage," it begins, "'Othello' is said to bear the
bell away."[1] While criticising ferociously the interview between Iago and Othello, in which the former
by shrugs and suggestions and insinuations arouses the
jealous feelings of the latter, Rymer is compelled to describe it as being in common opinion "the top scene,
the scene that raises Othello above all other tragedies
on our theatres."[2] These are testimonies of an enemy
which cannot be gainsaid.

Rymer had had no occasion to felicitate himself upon
the success which had attended his remarks on Beaumont and Fletcher. This treatise, from its unsold
copies appearing fourteen years later as a second edition, had plainly met with but a small sale. His own
words further imply that his views had encountered a

[1] Short View of Tragedy, p. 86.   [2] Ibid. p. 118.

good deal of censure. In the epistle dedicating his second volume to the Earl of Dorset, he tells us that when years before he had tried the public with observations concerning the stage, it was principally the countenance of that nobleman which had buoyed him up and supported a righteous cause against the prejudice and corruption then reigning. It was in behalf of the sacred principles of the pure doctrine of poetry established by the primitive fathers, such as Aristotle and Horace, that he once again took the field and sallied forth to expose the wretchedness of Shakespeare's work. Such was his repute for learning with all, and for critical sagacity with some, that the announcement of his intention awakened considerable interest. To use the language of the age, his volume was awaited by the ingenious with much impatience.

To the existence of this expectation we have direct contemporary evidence. The French refugee, Motteux, now best known to us by his translations of Rabelais and Cervantes, had a short time before started a monthly miscellany, somewhat of the modern magazine nature, under the title of ' The Gentleman's Journal.' It was the first work of its particular kind in our tongue. Along with its other contents in verse and prose, it furnished a certain amount of literary gossip in regard to books soon to be published and plays soon to be produced. In the number for October, 1692, it announced that Mr. Rhymer — so the name was spelled — "will shortly oblige the world with some more of his nice and judicious criticism on some of our dramatic writings." In the number for the following December he recorded its appearance. Motteux, unlike St. Evremond, had mastered the English language. He had come to know and to admire Shakespeare. Rymer's criticism did not therefore strike him as being so nice and judicious as he had anticipated, though he took care to express his opinion in very guarded terms. "The ingenious," he wrote of the work, "are somewhat divided about some remarks in it, though they concur with Mr. Rhymer in many things, and generally acknowledge that he discovers a great deal of learning." For this reason he refrained from saying anything more of the volume. He concluded his observations, however, with a suggestive quotation from Quintilian about the necessity of using modesty and circumspection in the judgment of great authors, lest that accident which happens to so many should befall the critic of condemning what he fails to understand. This was delightfully and doubtless intentionally vague. It could refer to any criticism Motteux might pass upon Rymer; it was meant to refer to Rymer's criticism of Shakespeare.

Limited as are our means of ascertaining the general critical opinion of the seventeenth century, thereby often giving undue weight to what little accidentally reaches us, sufficient evidence exists to make it certain that whatever opposition Rymer's first volume had encountered was far exceeded by that which waited upon the second. Dryden, whom in it he had once more flattered, expressed his dissent and, indeed, his disgust. These feelings appear in an undated letter written by him to Dennis, which was published by his correspondent — evidently with his own consent — in

1696. His words are an early exemplification of the attitude which we shall see came to be taken in regard to Shakespeare by large numbers throughout the whole of the eighteenth century. They are further interesting for the deference which he continued to pay to Rymer himself and to his pedantic advocacy of the principles of art. In this place, however, they are of importance mainly because of the evidence they furnish as to the ill fortune which had waited upon this venture. "We know," wrote Dryden, "in spite of Mr. Rymer, that genius alone is a greater virtue (if I may so call it) than all other qualifications put together. You see what success this learned critic has found in the world after his blaspheming Shakespeare. Almost all the faults which he has discovered are truly there; yet who will read Mr. Rymer, or not read Shakespeare? For my own part, I reverence Mr. Rymer's learning, but I detest his ill-nature and his arrogance. I indeed, and such as I, have reason to be afraid of him, but Shakespeare has not."

It is clear, indeed, that Rymer's attack met with but little favor. It naturally did Shakespeare no harm; it did its author a good deal. Replies to it came forth at once; and replies, too, from men who in a measure sympathized with its views. Dennis intended to answer all its points; but he never went farther than a treatise, published soon after, entitled ' The Impartial Critic.' This dealt, however, only with certain opinions of Rymer about the drama, — especially about the chorus, — and did not concern itself with those he had expressed about the dramatist. But while controvert-

ing the views of his opponent, he spoke of him respect-
fully. Not so Gildon, who was the next to take up
the discussion. In this same year he published what he
called a vindication of Shakespeare in a letter addressed
to Dryden. He set out with the avowed intention of
treating Rymer as Rymer had treated Shakespeare. He
pretty faithfully kept his word. He accused him of
plagiarism, dulness, conceit, affectation of learning,
and all the other impolite phrases which usually distinguish the controversies of what is termed polite
literature, — not forgetting, among other things, to
bring in the comparison to a pug of Barbary. He
made merry, in particular, with the scheme of a play
suggested by the ' Persæ ' of Æschylus, which the assail-
ant of Shakespeare had drawn up in full and published
in his volume. It was to be entitled ' The Invincible
Armado.' The subject outlined was one which Rymer
expressed a desire that Dryden would try to fill up. If
that poet did so, he was confident that the imitation of
Æschylus, thus produced, would, to use his own peculiar language, "pit, box, and gallery, far beyond anything now in possession of the stage, however wrought
up by the unimitable Shakespeare." It was easy to
turn this whole project into ridicule; for the plot Rymer
had sketched furnished as convincing proof of his inability to plan a play as his ' Edgar ' had furnished of
his inability to write one.

But in this case both the criticiser and the man criticised were too alike in their nature to be kept permanently apart. There are few closer ties which bind
men to each other than the possession of a common

pedantry. In 1710 Gildon contributed two essays to a volume containing the poems of Shakespeare which Curll had published as a supplement to Rowe's edition of the previous year. In the one upon the art, rise, and progress of the stage, he set out to lay down for the reader such principles as would enable him to distinguish the errors of the dramatist from his beauties. These, he tells us, were too much and too unjustly confounded by the foolish bigotry of his blind and partial adorers. Like Dennis, he was anxious that readers should not be so captivated by the author that they should admire what they ought to condemn. So he kindly undertook to open their eyes. They were in the habit of setting Shakespeare above the ancients. A heresy of this sort Gildon, a devout worshipper of Sophocles and Euripides, could by no means suffer to go unrebuked. As a friend of the modern dramatist he pointed out the extreme danger of his being in future unjustly decried as a result of the reaction from this undue exaltation. He was led, in consequence, to explain and apologize for that attack to which he had himself virulently replied. "This unaccountable bigotry of the town to the very errors of Shakespeare," he wrote, "was the occasion of Mr. Rymer's criticisms, and drove him as far into the contrary extreme." Later he paid another and higher tribute to the merits of the man he had once assailed.

The views of men like these are of no special value in themselves. They are, however, of a good deal of importance in the history of opinion. As testimony wrung from witnesses, in no instance partial, in one actively hostile, they furnish evidence, that cannot be impeached, of the hold which Shakespeare had at that time gained over the great body of his countrymen. The dissent that undoubtedly existed did not dare to be too outspoken. The passages which have been cited show that the expression of disparaging judgments about the dramatist himself or about his work was held in check by a general belief in his greatness, too firmly rooted to be unsettled and too powerful to be defied. It was this widespread and increasing admiration that prompted the special study of his writings which then began to be undertaken. The second essay of Gildon in this supplemental volume to Rowe's edition consisted of critical remarks on the various plays. It is the first of a long line of comments and commentaries of the same general character, and is therefore of a certain historic interest. They are what might be expected from a man whose acquisition of what is called liberal education has had the not unexampled result of making him illiberal in his opinions. Yet it is right to say of them that if we are frequently entertained by the absurdity of his views, we are also occasionally struck by their good sense. He condemned most of the alterations to which Shakespeare's plays had been then subjected. He criticised in particular at some length and with just severity D'Avenant's and Dryden's version of ' The Tempest,' which at this time had supplanted the original.

Gildon is very far, indeed, from being an illuminating guide; but he is no such contemptible character as Pope's references to him would lead us to suppose, and as, it must be added, his own utterances sometimes impel one to infer. His occasional pretentiousness makes him peculiarly offensive; his seeming assumption that when he has pronounced an opinion, the last conclusions of the human intellect have been reached. He further exemplified too constantly what he condemned. An abuser of poetasters, he was not only one himself, but he reserved his praise for writers not much above their grade. Not satisfied with regarding Dennis as a great critic, he made him out also "a poet of the first magnitude."[1] His works abound with fulsome laudations of the writings of the Duke of Buckinghamshire, especially of his ' Essay on Poetry.' This very respectable but long-forgotten production he quoted constantly and as reverently as if it were divinely inspired. A censurer of other alterers of Shakespeare, he perpetrated a peculiarly wretched one himself, — a version of ' Measure for Measure,' which was brought out in 1700. This last statement goes on the supposition that he wrote the pieces universally attributed to him; for his name does not appear on the title-page of a single one of the five plays of which he is the reputed author.

Attacks on Shakespeare of the coarse nature which Rymer's treatise exhibits were never made again. There is, indeed, so far as I know, but a single repetition of this style of wholesale and elaborate depreciation to be found in the whole of the century which followed. Yet, as it was the work of a woman, and furthermore of a woman born in America, it may be appropriate to give here a short account of the critic and her criticism. She was the daughter of Col. James

[1] Complete Art of Poetry, vol. i. p. 185.

Ramsay, lieutenant-governor of New York, and was born in 1720. In America she remained until 1735, when she went to London. There, owing to circumstances, she was soon under the necessity of maintaining herself by her own exertions. In the course of events she married a gentleman named Lennox. This ought to have transferred from her own shoulders the burden of support. Apparently it did not. Mr. Lennox seems to have been an inoffensive man, and may have been a particularly worthy one; but history has condescended to record of him no other achievement than his becoming the husband of Margaret Ramsay. She herself was a very miscellaneous writer. She produced poems, plays, and pastorals, executed numberless translations from the French, edited a magazine, and was the author of several long-forgotten novels; though it is perhaps an abuse of language to speak of that as having been forgotten which was never much remembered. To this last statement there is a single exception. In 1752 she published a story, in imitation of the great work of Cervantes, entitled ' The Female Quixote, or the Adventures of Arabella.' It was a satire upon the interminable romances which had been the favorite literature of the two or three generations preceding. This production, which no one would read now save from a sense of duty, was fairly successful then. After a fashion it has preserved her name in literary history. Occasionally it is spoken of even now as a work of genius by those who have not read it.

It was during the years 1753 and 1754 that Mrs. Lennox brought out a work of a new kind entitled

' Shakespeare Illustrated, or the Novels and Histories, on which the Plays of Shakespeare are Founded, collected and translated from the Original Authors with Critical Remarks.' It consisted of three volumes and was dedicated to the Earl of Orrery. This dedication was written by her personal friend, Dr. Johnson, who has in fact been accused of responsibility for some of the criticism. The collection she made of sources is the first of a number of similar ones, which owe their existence purely to the interest inspired by the writings of the dramatist. It therefore serves the double purpose of exemplifying the growth of the poet's reputation and the way in which it was occasionally assailed. The information it furnished, though far from complete and long since superseded, was in general sufficiently satisfactory so far as it went. It was the critical observations with which the work was supplied, that have given it whatever interest or distinction it now possesses. Rymer had led the way for them by asserting that 'Othello' had been altered from the original of Cinthio in several particulars, but always for the worse.[1] In this style of criticism Mrs. Lennox left her predecessor far behind. She made it clear that in his adaptations from previous writers Shakespeare almost invariably fell below them. Whatever he touched he deformed. Anything that was particularly good in what he borrowed he contrived to make bad; everything that was bad he changed to worse. He added to the events in the stories, upon which he founded his plays, useless incidents, unnecessary characters, and absurd and improbable intrigues.

[1] Short View of Tragedy, p. 87.

Even when we admire the beauty of any new passage he introduced, we are usually struck by its inappropriateness. Occasionally she relented; the tenderness of the woman prevailed over the severity of the judge. In a few instances guarded praise was given the dramatist for improvement in certain details. Still, as a general rule, the epithets most frequently employed to describe the variations made by him from his originals were the adjectives "absurd" and "ridiculous."

The work was one of which a good deal of the contemporary periodical criticism spoke highly, — especially in the ' Gentleman's Magazine,' where Johnson possessed influence. It enabled the reader, he was told, to make a just estimate of Shakespeare's merit, to comprehend his resources and detect his faults. Above all, it showed clearly that he did not deserve the veneration with which he had been and still continued to be regarded. The many beauties of which he had been supposed to be the originator had been restored by the authoress to those from whom they had been borrowed. The plagiarist stood exposed.[1] But outside of periodical criticism, the attitude taken and the views expressed in the work met with but scant favor. It reacted, indeed, injuriously at a later period upon Mrs. Lennox's own literary undertakings. The ill-success of her play of 'The Sister,' which was brought out at Covent Garden in February, 1770, but withdrawn after the first night, was attributed by some to the indignation and resentment which her remarks upon Shakespeare had

[1] Gentleman's Magazine, vol. xxiii., June, 1753. See also vol. xxiv. pp. 233, 311.

aroused. Whether this be true or not, the publication of her work furnishes another exemplification of a melancholy fact which, the longer we live, forces itself more persistently upon our observation. There is nothing more to be deplored in the fortunes of individuals than the hard lot that befalls some in having been born at the wrong time or in the wrong country. People are constantly met with now who really belong to the tenth century, and would have made a fitting and delightful acquisition to the society of that epoch. Its prevailing ideas would have been their ideas. Its way of looking at things would have been their way. Its partialities and prejudices, its particular likes and dislikes would have been theirs also. They are simply unfortunate in having been misplaced into a wholly unsuitable time. Such was the unhappy fate of Mrs. Lennox in regard to Shakespeare. She missed her century. Had she flourished in the period immediately following the Restoration, she would have found herself in a far more congenial atmosphere. She would have been enrolled as a distinguished figure in a set which would have sympathized with her opinions and exalted her uncommon learning and critical acumen. Had she in addition become Mrs. Rymer, the conjunction of these two stars, shooting madly from their spheres in the Shakespearean firmament, would have attracted the attention of observers for all time.

CHAPTER VIII

ALTERATIONS OF SHAKESPEARE'S PLAYS

THERE is a well-known remark of Evelyn in his diary under the date of November 26, 1661. He had just attended a performance of ' Hamlet.' "But now," was his comment, "the old plays begin [1] to disgust this refined age, since his majesty's being so long abroad." These words mark the opening of the more than hundred years' war which Shakespeare was to carry on with the French theatre. At this early period the torrent of lewdness and profligacy, which Evelyn was later to deplore so frequently, had not yet burst forth with any violence. Decency was on the point of departing from the stage, but so far had not taken her flight. It was not, therefore, the spirit of the Elizabethan drama, alien as it was to that of the Restoration epoch, which was beginning to make its plays seem distasteful. It was because of their supposed deficiencies in those characteristics which constitute true art.

Of these a full account has been given in the preceding pages. We have seen that a number of rules were laid down for the conduct of the playwright, based not upon how men really thought and felt and acted, but

---

[1] *Began* in printed text. If written by Evelyn at the time, he must have intended *begin ;* if *began* was his word, the remark must have been a later addition to the diary.

how they ought to think and feel and act, in order to preserve poetic decorum. The stage was to anticipate Mr. Turveydrop and become a model of deportment. The vogue of these rules became increasingly prevalent after the eighteenth century had opened. The tendency constantly manifested itself then to strengthen the rigor of the laws which regulated dramatic composition. Naturally eighteenth-century plays conformed to the canons proclaimed by eighteenth-century critics. A large proportion of the tragedies of that time were absolutely faultless from the point of view of the classical school. They were what was called regular. They observed the unities. They never outraged the feelings by pandering to that depraved taste which longed for occasional flashes of enjoyment to light up the atmosphere of gloom in which they were enveloped. In many instances they carefully despatched the destined victims behind the scenes. Some of these productions were the work of able men, a very few of them of men possessed of no slight share of poetic if not of dramatic genius. Nothing, therefore, is so conspicuous about the cleverness of these playwrights as the almost invariable success with which it enabled them to fail. Stately characters were brought by them upon the scene whose speeches were often characterized by elaborate and imposing versification; but somehow they seemed to lack vitality. It was the form of tragedy they possessed without its spirit. The events were few; the words describing them were many. The best that could be said of the best of them was that they avoided gross faults. If they did not stir the heart of the spectator, they did not excite his laughter; and in no case could fault be found with them for the violation of a single one of those rules which by the common consent of critics were deemed essential to dramatic propriety.

It was this last characteristic which constituted their great recommendation in the eyes of the followers of this school. Negative virtues were raised to the dignity of positive ones; if not so in theory, they were in fact. To be free from faults was of more account than to be possessed of merits; and instead of seeking for the latter, writers for the stage were sedulously striving to guard against the former. Nothing of permanent value is ever produced by such methods; no interest long attaches to any work of any sort thus brought into being. A brake on a wheel is often a useful article; but it overrates a great deal its own importance when it fancies itself the wheel that runs the vehicle, still more when it fancies itself the motive power that runs the wheel. It was the concentration of the care and thought of the playwrights upon the observance of these conventional rules which more than any other one thing contributed to render their productions tame and lifeless. Tragedy was the main sufferer by this practice: comedy got along better. Some of the works belonging to the former chanced occasionally to receive for a time an artificial life from the excellence of the acting; but they were rarely heard of later, even when apparent success had crowned their original representation. This was their usual fate; it is not too much to assert that it was usually their merited fate. Even the best of them can hardly be spoken of as any longer really known. To most men of the present day the tragic stage of the eighteenth century is an undiscovered country; and in general it may be said that the unwary traveller who by any chance is led to visit its confines takes precious good care never to return to them again, if that journey can possibly be avoided.

To the men of that age, however, there always remained one consolation. The result of their efforts might be dreadful; but still it was art. Upon that fact they perpetually felicitated themselves. To us the artificial beauties, if they can be termed beauties, which were secured by their methods, seem very much like the rings which men and women of savage nations thrust through their lips and noses. They are inconvenient to the owner to wear; to admire them requires a perverted taste in the beholder. But not so felt those who at the beginning of the Restoration epoch announced that at last the reign of taste had arrived. To some of them Shakespeare was peculiarly offensive. Certain of them were so repelled by his assumed lawlessness that they were hardly disposed to regard him as worthy of consideration at all. This was particularly true of the school which celebrated Ben Jonson as the greatest writer of the preceding age and the greatest comic writer of all time. It was not large in numbers, but it was somewhat vociferous; and as there belonged to it several persons of social and literary position, it exerted for a time considerable influence. It existed, indeed, long before the Restoration. It is manifest, also, that Jonson himself, with all his undoubted admiration for the genius of his friend, was not entirely exempt from emotions of envy at the high estimate in which he was held, and did not refrain from exhibiting what he doubtless deemed righteous indignation at the undeserved praise which was bestowed upon Shakespeare for what were in his eyes manifest defects. It was inevitable that sentiments of this sort should be echoed more or less; and usually more, by that never very limited body of judges who, without any definite views of their own, have to an almost heroic extent the courage of other people's convictions.

Unquestionably there were even at this early period dissenters from the general tribute of admiration which from the first was paid to Shakespeare, though comparatively few evidences of the fact have come down to our time. We can find the feeling indicated, however, in the words of a writer like William Cartwright of Oxford University, who died in 1643, at the age of thirty-two. For reasons which men of the present day find it difficult to comprehend, he was regarded and celebrated by his contemporaries as a person of extraordinary abilities. The view is certainly not borne out by the very respectable plays he left behind; for he was a dramatist before he became a divine. Besides these he wrote a number of poems in which he was usually successful in combining brevity with tediousness. Two of them were upon Fletcher. Cartwright was one of the class of men who cannot exalt one person without disparaging another. He accordingly went out of his way to give us a specimen of his critical judgment in the following lines: —

297

" Shakespeare to thee was dull, whose best jest lies
  In the ladies' questions and the fool's replies ;
  Old-fashioned wit which walked from town to town
  In turned hose, which our fathers called the clown ;
  Whose wit our nice times would obsceneness call,
  And which made bawdry pass for comical :
  Nature was all his art, thy vein was free
  As his, but without his scurrility."

But though feelings of this kind existed both before
and after the Restoration, we should be led into a gross
error if we supposed that they existed on a large scale.
That small number who, because their taste differs
from that of the majority, enjoy the pleasing consolation of believing that it is much better than that of the
majority, may have studiously depreciated Shakespeare;
but they never seriously affected the general estimate
of his reputation. Much more numerous and much
more influential was the body of those who attributed
to him the possession of great excellences mingled with
great defects. Theirs was an attitude, according to
their own opinion, of absolute impartiality. They consequently spoke of him in a tone of mingled pity and
patronage. It could not be denied that he was a man
of vast genius. It was nevertheless a painful fact that
the barbarism of his time had prevented him from attaining to those heights of taste upon which they themselves
were complacently perched. They pardoned, though
they could not approve. This was the prevalent utterance of the years that followed immediately upon the
return of Charles. It is sometimes expressed kindly,
sometimes contemptuously. But whether well or ill
disposed, it never neglected the duty of pointing out

the faults of the dramatist and of holding up to scorn those who denied their existence. It is one of the revenges produced by the whirligig of time that the Restoration period is now regarded as having degenerate taste, because it held that the taste which expressed unbounded admiration of Shakespeare was degenerate.

It was their recognition of his excellences in various ways, combined with their perception of his deficiences, which led men to set about those alterations of his works which went on for a good deal more than a hundred years after the Restoration. It is needless to add that these were undertaken ostensibly in the interests of art. To a certain extent the pretence was justified by the changes made. Efforts were put forth to bring the plays as far as possible under the law of the unities. The comic parts were usually cut out of the serious pieces. Low characters were dropped. To this æsthetic motive was frequently added, according to the professions of those engaged in this work, reverence for Shakespeare himself. It was their regard for him, it was their appreciation of his surpassing merits, which had induced them to enter upon the task of revealing his greatness to an incredulous world. Not a single one of these adapters, even the very wretchedest of them, doubted for a moment that his work was a decided improvement upon the original. No self-effacing modesty caused them to hide their consciousness of the credit to which they were entitled for having conferred upon Shakespeare the benefit of their alterations. This feeling of benevolent superiority they extended to the great French authors, whether writers of tragedy or comedy, whom they plundered. Mrs. Centlivre — to select one instance out of many — admits that her play of ' Love's Contrivance ' is partly taken from Molière; but she is bold enough to affirm, she assures us, that it has not suffered in the translation. Indeed she remarks that whenever she found the style of the original too poor, she "endeavored to give it a turn." If during the reign of French taste and deference to French dramatists men could fancy that they had improved upon Molière, Corneille, and Racine, it is little wonder that they should think they had improved upon Shakespeare. His works, they conceded, abounded in master-strokes of genius; but they lacked more or less of that happy art which it became the pleasing duty of the adapter to supply. It was not unusual for them to talk the language of discoverers. They had stumbled, as it were, upon a mine of gold. It was encumbered with dross, it was mixed with impurities; from these it was their business to set it free, to refine it, so that it should shine in its native lustre.

All these states of mind we know positively, because the authors of these adaptations disclose them. I have already given the self-satisfied comments with which Ravenscroft introduced his horrible additions to a horrible play.[1] Tate, in the dedication of his version of ' Lear,' informed the friend to whom it was addressed, that the original was a heap of jewels, unstrung and unpolished, and yet so dazzling in their disorder that he soon perceived he had got hold of a treasure. Again, in the prologue to his alteration of ' Coriolanus ' he

1 See p. 196.

expressed a feeling of confidence in the success of his play because it was based upon the previous work of Shakespeare. His business it had been to build upon the massive foundation of his predecessor the artfully contrived superstructure which should remove or hide its manifest deformities. As he tells us himself,

> "He only ventures to make gold from ore,
> And turn to money what lay dead before."

In the preface to his alteration of 'Troilus and Cressida,' which he mistakenly fancied an early play, Dryden observed that since there appeared in some places of this tragedy the admirable genius of the author, he had undertaken to remove the rubbish under which many excellent thoughts lay wholly buried. We shall have occasion to notice other manifestations of this same serene satisfaction. Occasionally a fear was expressed that there was danger of going too far. Dennis, who was at heart a most genuine admirer of Shakespeare, exhibited this feeling in the alteration he made of 'Coriolanus.' He tells us in his prologue that his production is a mere grafting upon the work of the great dramatist,

> "In whose original we may descry,
> Where master-strokes in wild confusion lie,
> Here brought to as much order as we can
> Reduce those beauties upon Shakespeare's plan;
> And from his plan we dar'd not to depart,
> Lest nature should be lost in quest of art:
> And art had been attained with too much cost,
> Had Shakespeare's beauties in the search been lost."

But usually no dread of this sort disturbed the heart of the adapter. So between devotion to art and regard for the memory of the poet, the magnificent structures which Shakespeare had reared furnished for more than a century employment to a host of dramatic carpenters, masons, hodcarriers, and other literary mechanics, not to repair them indeed, but to repair their conceptions of them.

During the fifty years which followed the Restoration twenty-one of Shakespeare's plays appeared in some sort of altered form.[1] Five of them were during the time

---

[1] The following is a list of the plays altered or adapted from Shakespeare during the fifty years following the Restoration. They are given according to the date of their publication. This in the case of several, especially the earlier ones, is sometimes quite different from the date of their production : —

1. The Tempest; or the Enchanted Island, by Dryden and D'Avenant, 1670.
2. The Law against Lovers (Measure for Measure), by D'Avenant, 1673.
3. Macbeth, 1673.
4. The Tempest, made into an opera, by Shadwell, 1673.
5. Macbeth, 1674.
6. The Mock-Tempest; or the Enchanted Castle, by Duffett, 1675. For 'The Mock-Tempest' of the title-page, the heading of the play itself is 'The New Tempest.'
7. Timon of Athens, by Shadwell, 1678.
8. Troilus and Cressida, or Truth Found too Late, by Dryden, 1679.
9. History and Fall of Caius Marius (Romeo and Juliet), by Otway, 1680.
10. King Lear, by Tate, 1681.
11. The History of King Richard the Second (acted at the Theatre Royal, under the name of 'The Sicilian Usurper'), by Tate, 1681.
12. Henry VI., The First Part; with the Murder of Humphrey, Duke of Gloucester (Henry VI., Part II.), by Crowne, 1681.
13. Henry VI., The Second Part; or the Miseries of Civil War (Henry VI., Parts II. and III.), by Crowne, 1680.
14. The Ingratitude of a Commonwealth (Coriolanus), by Tate, 1682.
15. The Injured Princess, or the Fatal Wager (Cymbeline), by Durfey, 1682.
16. Titus Andronicus, or the Rape of Lavinia, by Ravenscroft, 1687.
17. The Fairy Queen, an opera (Midsummer Night Dream), 1692.
18. Sawney, the Scott (Taming of the Shrew), by Lacey, 1698.
19. King Henry IV., Part I., by Betterton, 1700.
20. King Henry IV., Part II., by Betterton (not published till 1719).
21. King Richard III., by Colley Cibber, 1700.

subjected more than once to this transmogrifying process — for transforming is too respectable a word to apply to the operation that took place. Before the end of the eighteenth century about fifty other alterations were added to the number. It does not fall within the province of this work to give any account of these versions, save as they illustrate the influences which operated to produce them. For while the plea set up in justification of the changes effected was the desire to make the plays conform to what was then called the purer taste of the age, or what we should call its want of taste, this was by no means the sole motive that led to their alteration. One was an agency which naturally never ceased to act, so long as work of this character could be expected to meet with favor. The dramatic author was always intent upon the production of a new play. Necessarily he was often hard put to it for matter and subject. By him the dramas of the Elizabethan period were looked upon as a sort of quarry, to which in case of need or hurry he could turn for raw material to work up into pieces which would have the charm of novelty. What he could borrow saved him so much

---

22. Measure for Measure, or Beauty the Best Advocate, by Gildon, 1700.
23. The Jew of Venice (The Merchant of Venice) by George Granville (Lord Lansdowne), 1701.
24. The Comical Gallant; or the Amours of Sir John Falstaff (Merry Wives of Windsor), by Dennis, 1702.
25. Love Betrayed, or the Agreeable Disappointment (Twelfth Night), by Burnaby, 1703.

In addition, in 1662, 'Romeo and Juliet' was altered into a tragicomedy by James Howard. It was never printed. The alteration of 'Macbeth'—one of 1673, and on a larger scale in 1674 — is attributed by Downes, in his 'Roscius Anglicanus,' to D'Avenant.

labor. Of the dramatists of this earlier age Shakespeare was by no means the only sufferer; but he was much the greatest.

Pressure of this sort seems to have been the principal motive which led men to add new scenes and characters to certain of Shakespeare's plays, or to piece out from his independent compositions of their own. In one of the first of these alterations this process was carried to an extreme. This was D'Avenant's 'Law against Lovers,' produced as early as February, 1662. Into it he melted the two plays of 'Measure for Measure' and 'Much Ado about Nothing,' with numerous additions of his own; or perhaps it would be more correct to say, that the episode of Benedict and Beatrice was extracted from the latter and inserted with great variations into the former. How violent was the change, and how inferior the plot, can be guessed from the fact that the character of Mariana was discarded entirely, and that Isabella, after refusing to yield to Angelo's attempt upon her virtue is married to him at the conclusion by the order of the duke. There was also a great deal of modification of the language of Shakespeare even where it purported to be retained. The result of this combination is that all the pathos of the one play vanishes and all the wit of the other, while the whole is written in the most villanous blank verse that ever tried to palm itself off as poetry instead of prose. Perhaps even a more extraordinary performance of this nature were the scenes taken from 'Romeo and Juliet,' which Otway introduced into his play entitled 'The History and Fall of Caius Marius,' brought out in 1680. Never was there a more incompatible mixture of blood-letting and love-making. Into the stormy strife of the Roman civil war, with its proscriptions and massacres, was intruded the story of love and hate which in Shakespeare's hands had become the purest embodiment of the fusion of passion and poetry. The incongruity takes on the air of the grotesque, when we find the son of Caius Marius in the place of Romeo, and Sulla in that of the Count Paris who is the destined husband of Juliet.

But the most offensive, as it was the most famous of the alterations which were made for the sake of bringing out a novelty rather than of repairing any supposed artistic imperfections in the original, was that wrought by D'Avenant and Dryden upon ' The Tempest.' This play is one of the most delightful of Shakespeare's creations. To the audiences of his own time it must have had a charm which we may comprehend but can imperfectly appreciate. The romance of worlds as yet unexplored was suggested by it, the imagination was captivated by the portrayal of sights and sounds which men hesitated to believe and yet did not venture wholly to deny. No impressions of this nature will be conveyed even remotely by the adaptation. It excites alternate feelings of amusement and irritation. The former state of mind is largely due to what Dryden termed D'Avenant's "excellent contrivance" of doubling the personages of the play. Miranda has a sister called Dorinda. Caliban too has a sister called Sycorax. Ariel is likewise furnished with "a gentle spirit," as he describes her, who goes under the name of Milcha, and who with fine feminine devotion has been waiting fourteen years for the day of his deliverance. As if these additions were not enough, there was supplied as a counterpart to the daughters of Prospero a young man who had never seen a woman, though he had lived on the same island with two of them until he had reached manhood. All this appears much more ridiculous in the play than in any account which can be given of it; but there is also contained in it a good deal to arouse indignation. The instinctive delicacy, the inborn purity of Miranda, as depicted in the original, utterly disappears in the part she is made to assume in the alteration. Her conversation with her sister Dorinda is of the kind that might have gone on between two maids of honor of the court of Charles II.; but however true to the life then lived, it was certainly not true to any life worth living. The alteration is really little better than a travesty. A lower deep was reached when it in turn was travestied in a play in which Prospero was made keeper of the Bridewell prison, and much of Shakespeare's language converted to vilest use.

Another agency at work in bringing about these alterations was the desire to gratify that fondness for spectacular entertainment which has always existed in the heart of man, and it may safely be predicted will always continue to exist. There was nothing new about it at the era of the Restoration. Complaint on this very score can be found in that earlier period in which we now regard the theatre as being in its highest glory. But it received a powerful impetus after the return of

Charles, in consequence of the introduction of movable scenery. This afforded additional facilities for the production of spectacular effect. Its attractions were further increased by the addition of song and dance, especially as the accompaniment of an inserted masque. The desire of seeing shows of this sort is so inherent in human nature that it is useless to rail against its manifestation. But what astounds the modern reader, and occasionally calls forth his indignation, is the dreadful inappropriateness of introducing these spectacles into the sort of plays in which they frequently occur. The attempt to interrupt the action of a well-constructed comedy with impertinent matter of this kind is bad enough; but to arrest the progress of a tragedy in such a way is little short of a literary crime. Yet this was not unfrequently done by the very men who posed as the champions of art; by some indeed who professed themselves shocked at the introduction into serious pieces of comic scenes and low personages.

Elaborate entertainments of this sort were brought into D'Avenant's 'Law of Love' just described, and one female character was added for little other purpose than to give occasion for singing and dancing. These exhibitions were carried out on a much grander scale in the alteration of 'Measure for Measure' by Gildon, which appeared in 1700. The practice had its worst, because its most inappropriate, exemplification in D'Avenant's version of 'Macbeth.' Into this sternest of tragedies were introduced music and dancing. Yet there can be no question that these additions were received favorably. Pepys, who saw the piece acted several times, was impressed by their appropriateness. He tells us that ' Macbeth ' "appears a most excellent play in all respects, but especially in divertisement, though it be a deep tragedy; which is a strange perfection in a tragedy, it being most proper here and suitable."[1] This change of its character affected directly or indirectly the manner in which the play was represented for a long period following. It was not indeed until the middle of the last century that its baleful influence was shaken off altogether. In 1847, at the Sadler's Wells Theatre, then under the management of the actor Samuel Phelps, the witches were made, for the first time in nearly two centuries, to appear in their true character as hags, instead of good-looking singers.

To this same desire for spectacular exhibitions we owe the transformation of several of Shakespeare's plays into operas, which at that time meant dramas in which singing, dancing, and recitative were the main features. It was a practice which was kept up during a good part of the eighteenth century. But there was another agency of quite different character at work in producing these alterations. This was the aversion to the tragical conclusion of tragedy. Sometimes taking the name of poetic justice, it assumed that it was the representative of a much higher art. In reality it was based upon that characteristic of human nature which prefers a fortunate ending of any story said or sung to a sad one, and which at the present day leads many to object to a novel ending unhappily. The feeling showed itself early. One of the very first alterations of Shakespeare was made in

---

[1] Pepys's Diary, Jan. 7, 1667.

accordance with its demands. 'Romeo and Juliet' was transformed into a tragi-comedy in which the lives of the hero and heroine were preserved. This version — which has not come down — was the work of the Honorable James Howard, one of Dryden's numerous brothers-in-law. The conflicting claims of the partisans of weal and woe were satisfied at the time by the management of the theatre. The drama was acted for a while,— one day with its original tragical ending, the day following with the new and happy one.[1] This same aversion to a sorrowful conclusion was one of the agencies which contributed to maintain the hold of Tate's version of 'King Lear' upon the stage. Even Colman, when he rejected in his own alteration the love-scenes, did not venture to restore the tragic ending. That was not done until 1823, when the fifth act was played by Kean as it was written by Shakespeare.

A more important agency than any yet mentioned has just been indicated. It was the desire to introduce a story of love. Both during the Restoration period and later it played a prominent part in the alterations which were made of Shakespeare's plays. If in them there were no love scenes, they were supplied; if there were love scenes already, they were supplied with more. This was a practice which began early and continued late. It was a peculiarly incongruous mixture that was produced when this passion was made to operate in the Histories. Crowne, who unblushingly stole no small portion of his second part of 'Henry VI.' from "the divine Shakespeare," as he termed him, and

[1] Downes's Roscius Anglicanus, p. 16 (Knight's reprint, 1886).

then did not blush to deny that he stole anything,[1] introduced into his alteration a good deal of love-making, in which Warwick, the king-maker, Edward Plantagenet, his future queen, Lady Grey, and a new character, Lady Eleanor Butler, all have a share. It is as needless as it is gratifying to observe that not a hint for these scenes can be found in the original. The demand for this sort of emotional stimulant seems to have been urgent and continuous. It can be found generally in the alterations made in the eighteenth century. Even Sheffield, Duke of Buckinghamshire, when he divided ' Julius Cæsar ' into two plays in order to preserve his darling unities — and even then succeeded but imperfectly — could not resist the temptation to intersperse some love dialogue in the midst of the political action which was going on.

Such practices were due largely, as we have seen, to the example set by the French stage. Under its influence love had come to be considered essential to tragedy. Indeed the introduction of this passion seems to have been the main reason why Shadwell felt himself justified in boasting that he had made ' Timon ' into a play. In Shakespeare the only female characters in that drama are the two mistresses of Alcibiades. They too are brought in for no other purpose than to give additional vigor and extension to the curses of the misanthrope. There is no suggestion of any love on their part except the love of money; and they come and go in a single

[1] "For by his feeble skill 't is built alone,
   The divine Shakespeare did not lay one stone."
   Prologue to Crowne's ' Miseries of Civil War.'

scene.   No wonder that Shadwell did not consider such a production a play.   He would have been unfaithful to the Restoration ideal, had he treated the passion so disdainfully.   Accordingly he endowed the piece with two female characters, — one a discarded mistress who remains faithful to Timon throughout; the other an expectant bride who deserts him the moment when calamity comes.   Little more than a hundred years afterward Cumberland improved upon this example. In his version of the tragedy, which was brought out in 1771, he furnished Timon with a daughter, with whom Alcibiades is in love, while a more wealthy personage appears also as a suitor for her hand.

There can be no doubt that the introduction of these love scenes contributed a good deal to the success, at least to the temporary success, of some of these alterations.   The most marked illustration of the benefit of this kind derived from them is seen, as has already been pointed out, in the remodelling which ' Lear ' underwent at the hand of Tate.   By that author himself it was regarded as a master stroke.   Tate particularly prided himself upon having had the good fortune to light upon an expedient which was to rectify what was wanting in the regularity and probability of the play, as Shakespeare wrote it.   This was to run through the whole a series of love scenes between Edgar and Cordelia, who never exchanged word in the original. Them accordingly he made attached to each other from the outset.   The advantages of this course, he himself assures us, were obvious.   It gave an air of probability to Cordelia's indifference and Lear's answer.   It further supplied a generous motive for Edgar's disguise. In Shakespeare it was nothing but a poor pitiful shift to save his own life, — an object simply unnatural and contemptible to be kept in view by the hero of a tragedy. In Tate's version it was elevated to a noble design to be of service to Cordelia.

Deride it and despise it as we justly may, the introduction of love into this tragedy found favor, as a general rule, with both the public and the critics of the eighteenth century. To it more than to any one cause was due the permanence of the hold which this alteration kept upon the stage. Garrick, who revived the play in 1756, restored a good deal of the language of the original; for some of its finest passages had been botched by Tate most scandalously. But he retained much which might better have been left out. Nor, in particular, did he venture to discard the love-scenes. He hesitated, but finally decided that the risk was too great to run.[1] Davies indeed tells us that though he had witnessed the representation of the play twenty or thirty times, he had never seen Edgar and Cordelia leave the stage after their unexpected interview — as exhibited in the third act of Tate's version — without the accompaniment of rapturous applause from the spectators.[2] Garrick might possibly have succeeded in restoring the original; but what he failed to do it was not in the power of an inferior man to accomplish. This was shown by the fate of Colman's version, which was produced in February, 1768. In it he threw out the whole episode of love. " ' Romeo,' ' Cymbeline,'

---

[1] Davies, Dramatic Miscellanies, vol. ii. p. 264.　　　[2] Ibid.

'Every Man in his Humor,'" he wrote, "have long been refined from the dross that hindered them from being current with the public; and I have now endeavored to purge the tragedy of 'Lear' of the alloy of Tate which has so long been suffered to debase it." But his alteration never superseded the one which had held the stage for nearly a hundred years. It met with moderate success at its first appearance, and after Colman left the management of Covent Garden Theatre in 1774, it seems to have been dropped entirely.

These were the main motives which under the guise of devotion to art led to the changes which were made in Shakespeare's plays. It shows the growth both of knowledge and of appreciation of his works that with the progress of time these attempts became more and more distasteful to the public. Custom had caused certain of the old alterations to be accepted with equanimity, and in some instances with favor; but new experiments upon the integrity of his writings came to be regarded almost invariably with dislike. If any one of them secured success at all, it was owing to its having been brought out under exceptional conditions. Garrick was indeed the only writer who could venture to make changes with much hope of approval; and that was not really due to the changes, but to his own wonderful acting. The aversion felt to these proceedings was not due, as the classicists tried to persuade themselves, to blind unreasoning devotion, but to a steadily increasing perception of the fact that Shakespeare was not only a great poet but also a great artist; and that these tamperings with his text, which had once been

so common, were of the nature of efforts to improve
the purity of gold by mixing with it a due quantity of
brass. As we have seen, not all the influence of Garrick nor the magnetic charm of his acting could reconcile the public to his alteration of 'Hamlet.' If it
would not accept his essay, naturally inferior men fared
worse. Their versions were often not acted, or, if acted,
met usually with disfavor. If they succeeded at all, it
was owing to circumstances entirely independent of any
approval by the public of the changes which had been
made.

Colley Cibber, tempted by the success of his alteration of 'Richard III,' set out many years after upon
the task of remodelling 'King John.' The revision was
offered to the manager of Drury Lane in 1735. But
times had changed. The criticism which the project
called forth irritated the actor, and led him to withdraw
the piece from consideration. This version was not
published until 1745; yet something of its character
must have become known at the very time in which it
was written. Two years later Fielding made both
Cibber and his proposed action the subject of satire in
his piece entitled 'The Historical Register for the Year
1736.' In this play he brought in the adapter under
the name of Ground Ivy, and represented him as declaring that it was a maxim of his, while he was at the head
of theatrical affairs, that no play, though ever so good,
could do without alteration. Shakespeare was a very
pretty fellow, he was represented as remarking, and
had said some things which only wanted a little of his
licking into shape to do well enough. "For instance,"

he continued, "in the play before us" — which was 'King John' — "the bastard Faulconbridge is a most effeminate character, for which reason I would cut him out, and put all his sentiments in the mouth of Constance, who is so much properer to speak them." When the play was published later, it turned out that this was a change which had actually been carried into effect. It was impossible for even the imagination of Fielding to have foreseen that anything so preposterous could ever have occurred to a rational human being; he must have known it at the time as an actual fact.

Furthermore, in the play just mentioned, Fielding incidentally gave the opinion of alterations, which was beginning to be widely entertained by the men who were not dominated by the views that prevailed among the classicists. It is expressed by the supposed author of the piece, who is one of the characters taking part in the action. "As Shakespeare," says he, "is already good enough for people of taste, he must be altered to the palates of those who have none." Later, when the same character is asked if he intended to burlesque the poet, he replies in a way that conveys clearly Fielding's contempt for the changes which had been made in the past. "I have too great an honor for Shakespeare," he says, "to think of burlesquing him, and to be sure of not burlesquing him, I will never attempt to alter him for fear of burlesquing him by accident, as perhaps some others have done." Again, in this play Fielding put in the mouth of Theophilus Cibber — who appears under the name of Pistol — another satirical reference to his father's adaptation which has just been mentioned, and the fate which would have befallen it, had it actually been brought upon the stage. "Such was the hiss in which great John should have expired," Pistol is represented as exclaiming. Pope borrowed the idea, and in his revised ' Dunciad ' of 1743 commented upon the withdrawal of the piece in the following line : —

"King John in silence modestly expires." [1]

In spite of all this Cibber found his opportunity at last. Early in 1745 the country was going through one of those periodical outbreaks against Roman Catholicism to which Protestant England has always been subject. It had assumed just then an aggravated form in consequence of the threatened invasion of the kingdom by the Young Pretender, and the dreaded return to the throne of the Stuart line. Taking advantage of the occasion, Cibber brought out at Covent Garden his alteration under the title of ' Papal Tyranny in the Reign of King John.' It is a pretty difficult achievement to convert that monarch into a hero, still more difficult to convert him into a Christian hero ; but patriotism has been successful in accomplishing even more formidable tasks. At this time, too, it was assisted by the feeling certain to be prevalent in an English audience that the Pope should be thoroughly and insultingly defied. Cibber fulfilled the requirement nobly, and received his reward. Popular excitement gave the play the then respectable run of ten nights ; just as later in the year when the threatened invasion had become a reality, it caused the revival of ' The Non-juror ' in both

[1] Dunciad, book i. line 252.

houses. Cibber however attributed his success to no adventitious circumstances, but to the inherent merit of the changes he had introduced into the performance. In his dedication of the play to Lord Chesterfield he rivalled the modesty of the earlier adapters by asserting that he had made it more like a play than when he found it in Shakespeare. When the cause of the popularity of the piece passed away, the effect disappeared also. It seems never to have been heard of again.

It would be a mistake to assume that attempts of this nature had generally ceased by the middle of the eighteenth century. On the contrary they continued to be common. Still the hesitation with which projects of this kind were put forth becomes noticeable, as well as the apologetic attitude with which the slightest thought of reflecting upon the poet is disclaimed. Hawkins, for instance, one of the most unpoetical of the professors of poetry at Oxford, produced an alteration of 'Cymbeline.' In his preface he professed that he felt it an honor to tread in the steps of Shakespeare and to imitate his style with the reverence and humility of a son. This particular play, he told us, was one of the most irregular written by the dramatist. Still its defects, or rather its superfluities, were more than equalled by beauties and excellences of various kinds. All he therefore aimed to do was to reduce it as far as possible to the laws of the unities. In his additions he assured us he sought to copy the vigor, the diction, the glowing vein of the mighty mind which had produced the original; but likewise he had

317

presumed to regulate and modernize the plot of the play. As he tells us in the prologue,

> " For other points our new adventurer tries
> The bard's luxuriant plan to modernize :
> And by the rules of ancient art refine
> The same eventful pleasing bold design."

This alteration was brought out at Covent Garden in February, 1759. It met with no success. The spectators had ceased to desire Shakespeare's work to be refined by the rules of ancient art. The version "after freezing one or two thin audiences sunk into oblivion."[1] The classicists themselves came at last to recognize that this sort of work would no longer do. Cumberland's alteration of 'Timon,' which appeared in 1771, pleased the critics, at least some of them. They praised him for retrenching the extravagances and lopping off the excrescences which had disfigured the original. But though it pleased them, it did not please the audience. Garrick confessed to one of his correspondents that it had not succeeded to his wish.[2] It ran counter to the prejudices of the public, or, as one of the reviewers was sorrowfully constrained to admit, to "the *devout* reverence in which even the faults of Shakespeare are generally held."[3]

We have now reached a point where it is necessary to consider these alterations not merely with reference to the agencies which brought them into being, but to their merit as works of art contrasted with their

---

[1] European Magazine, vol. i. p. 358.
[2] Garrick Correspondence, vol. i. p. 448.
[3] Monthly Review, vol. xlv. p. 507, December, 1771.

originals. Volumes could be filled with exemplifications of their absurdities. A few can only be mentioned here, taken mainly from those plays which longest held possession of the stage. Three of these in particular met with special success, and their later fortunes therefore deserve mention. They are Colley Cibber's version of ' Richard III,' which was brought out in 1700 ; Nahum Tate's version of ' Lear,' which was brought out in 1681 ; and Lord Lansdowne's version of the 'Merchant of Venice,' which was brought out in 1701. This last was the shortest-lived of the three. It kept exclusive possession of the stage until 1741, when on the 14th of February Macklin's celebrated revival of the original took place at Drury Lane. It is a common statement that the alteration then disappeared forever. Genest, the annalist of the later drama, whose accuracy can almost invariably be trusted as safely as his critical comments can frequently be disregarded, declares that " from this time Lansdowne's Jew of Venice has been consigned to oblivion." [1] Yet the remarks made upon it in Baker's ' Companion to the Stage,' published in 1764, certainly give the impression that it was then holding its own with the original.[2]

On the other hand Cibber's version of 'Richard III.' was the longest-lived. In March, 1821, Macready made an attempt to have the play, as Shakespeare wrote it, revived at the Covent Garden Theatre ; but the undertaking was ill-managed, and the experiment was a

[1] Genest, vol. iii. p. 629.

[2] The second edition of this work, which appeared in 1782 under the title of 'Biographia Dramatica,' was largely rewritten by Isaac Reed, but it made no change in this statement.

failure. It was acted but two nights. Macready tells us in his diary that later he would have presented it in its purity, had his management of Covent Garden Theatre — which extended from 1837 to 1839 — been continued.[1] The task he did not attempt was undertaken by Phelps at the Sadler's Wells Theatre in 1845. During the first season of his management he played the piece with certain condensations as it was originally written. Its revival took place on the 20th of February of that year. Before the season closed it had been performed at least twenty-one times.[2]

The memory of this attempt had died away, when in January, 1877, 'Richard III.' was revived for a second time by Henry Irving, and, as it is claimed, with stricter adherence to the original text than when it was played by Phelps. On January 29 of the year just mentioned it was put on the stage of the Lyceum Theatre. It is spoken of as having been highly successful; it certainly ran until May 12, when it gave way to 'The Lyons Mail,' adapted by Charles Reade from the French. During that period it had been acted in all eighty-four times. A similar course was taken a year later in America. On the 6th of January, 1878, Edwin Booth opened a six weeks' engagement at the Fifth Avenue Theatre, New York, with the performance of this tragedy, as written by Shakespeare. Before he had finished, he had played it a dozen times. At the close of this same year he repeated the same

[1] Macready, Diary, p. 170 (American edition).

[2] 'The Life and Life-Work of Samuel Phelps' (p. 69) says "twenty-four times," and it is very likely right; but I find the piece advertised for only twenty-one nights.

performance during a short engagement at the Winter Garden Theatre.[1]

Of the original text of 'Lear,' there had been, as we have seen, spasmodic partial revivals. It was not until January 25, 1838, that Macready brought it out in its entirety at the Covent Garden Theatre. He hesitated for a while about restoring the fool, not on any ground of its failure in art, but from the fear that the terrible contrast of the characters would destroy instead of enhancing the effect in acting representation. Both Garrick and Colman had considered the advisability of reviving this part.[2] Macready's 'Lear' seems to have achieved a respectable, but only respectable, success. It was played eleven times before the season closed on the sixth of July. It was subsequently produced from the original of Shakespeare by Phelps in November, 1845, at the Sadler's Wells Theatre.

So much for the later fortunes of these plays, remodellings of which were the last survivals of practices that had once been common. Our wonder at the audacity, not to call it impudence of these alterations, is increased — if increase be possible — when we come to consider that Shakespeare was not only a born dramatist with an eye constantly fixed upon stage effect, but that he was in addition a born poet, who was able to give to the interest of impressive or startling situations the further charm of beautiful imagery and exquisite verse. The ability to accomplish the

---

[1] New York Tribune, Jan. 8, 1878, and Dec. 5, 1878, p. 5 and col. 2 of both issues.

[2] Davies, Dramatic Miscellanies, vol. ii. p. 267.

latter, it is needless to say, is not only of a far higher kind than that of producing the former, but it is something rarely found in conjunction with it. One would therefore fancy when the two qualities happened to meet in any particular work, the parts exhibiting this union in its most perfect form would be carefully retained, no matter what disposition might be made for stage purposes of the rest of the play. This not unreasonable anticipation is doomed to disappointment. The large majority of the men who meddled with Shakespeare's dramas were not only incapable of doing a good thing themselves, they did not appear to know it when they saw it done by somebody else. One of the most singular things connected with these alterations is that in many cases where the stage situation is retained, that which gives the part its greatest distinction as literature is carelessly allowed or carefully made to disappear. Sometimes it is omitted altogether; sometimes it is subjected to modification just sufficient to turn highly poetical poetry into very prosaic prose. Worse than all, there is occasionally matter added to it which causes to the sensitive soul almost a thrill of pain that stuff so abominable should have ever by any chance come to be associated with the name of Shakespeare.

Omission indeed, the most numerous perhaps of all these changes, can up to a certain point plead in its defence that things were left out, not because there was lack of appreciation of the poetry, but because there is a limit to the time of the representation of a play. This affords, of course, no excuse when matter from outside sources has been brought in, thereby necessitating the rejection of much of the original. In Cibber's version of ' Richard III.' not only were entire scenes discarded — such for instance as the one containing the dream of Clarence — but with them disappeared any number of short passages, which are as beautiful on the poetic side as they are effective on the dramatic. Take for illustration the sense of security arising from high birth and family connections which Gloucester, when warned to beware of falling, depicts in these two lines, —

> "Our aery buildeth in the cedar's top,
> And dallies with the wind and scorns the sun."

It is fair to say for Cibber that the very plan of his stagey version rendered the rejection of scenes containing such passages almost a necessity. He tried to make up for their disappearance by introducing extracts taken from other plays. Thus the announcement to Henry VI., while in the Tower, of the death of his son, is borrowed from the announcement in ' Henry IV.' of the death of Hotspur to Northumberland. Conveyances of this sort appear only as patches in the piece in which they are inserted. Dramatically the fine speeches found in Shakespeare can never be safely wrenched from the characters who utter them. They are flowers which lose their freshness when torn from the branch to which they belong; they live only an artificial life when transplanted to another soil than that which has given them birth.

It is not omission, however, with which most fault is to be found. Rejection, indeed, on the most extensive scale can be regarded with actual approval, when once we contrast it with the havoc which was made with both sentiment and verse in the cases where the original was supposed to be retained. It is not, for illustration, within the power of hyperbole to characterize adequately the changes which Otway made in transplanting the balcony scene from 'Romeo and Juliet' into his play of 'Caius Marius.' As one specimen, here is the way in which the approach of dawn is described. Romeo, it is to be borne in mind, has been exiled, and death is his portion if he be found within Verona's walls. Juliet, in the parting scene, in urging him to remain still longer, declares that day is not near at hand, and that it is the song of no bird of early morn which has aroused his apprehensions but that of the nightingale. In his answer expressing the contrary view, we have the picture of the rising sun first gilding with its rays the mountain tops, and scattering the clouds with its shafts of light, before driving the darkness from the plains below. The same passage occurs in Otway, but not the same. The day is no longer pictured standing tiptoe on the mountain tops for a brief moment before descending into the valleys. On the contrary, after having put on gay attire, it apparently leaves the valleys to take care of themselves, and continues to stay on these same mountain tops long enough to hold a morning reception, at which of all places in the world the birds are represented as appearing. Here are the lines as they are found in Otway, —

> " Oh! 't was the lark, the herald of the morn,
> No nightingale: Look, love, what envious streaks
> Of light embroider all the cloudy east.

> Night's candles are burnt out, and jocund day
> Upon the mountain tops sits gaily drest,
> Whilst all the birds bring music to his levee.
> I must be gone and live or stay and die." [1]

All that is good in this passage is the work of Shakespeare; all that is bad is the work of Otway. Yet the spoliation which he accomplished practically excluded the original from the stage till about the middle of the eighteenth century.

Despicable as such alterations are — and many as bad could be cited — they are on the whole surpassed by passages in the revised 'Lear,' in which the majestic lines of Shakespeare are joined with the inanities of Tate. There has been frequent occasion to speak of this version and of its concocter. Tate indeed has been somewhat concisely and comprehensively described as "the author of the worst alterations of Shakespeare, the worst version of the Psalms, and the worst continuation of a great poem extant." [2] This is doing him altogether too high honor. None of these things are true. Tate would be a much more interesting man if a single one of them were true. It is the dead level of his mediocrity which makes misplaced any application to his

---

[1] For the sake of easy comparison the passage, as found in Shakespeare, is subjoined: —

> "It was the lark, the herald of the morn,
> No nightingale: look, love, what envious streaks
> Do lace the severing clouds in yonder east.
> Night's candles are burnt out, and jocund day
> Stands tiptoe on the misty mountain tops:
> I must be gone and live or stay and die."

[2] By Craik in his 'History of English Literature,' vol. ii. p. 121 (American edition).

attempts of the superlative employed. Yet the description is so far justified that of all the alterations of Shakespeare, his of ' Lear ' is on the whole the most pretentious and the most feeble; yet owing to the agencies which have been mentioned it was and long continued to be the most successful with the public. It is its popularity, indeed, which has made his version exasperating; for every change in it is a change for the worse. This is true both of the characters and of the way in which they express themselves. To exemplify the former, Edmund is one who will serve as an illustration for all. In Shakespeare he is pictured as a bold, unscrupulous, intellectual, and able villain: Tate thought fit to endow him further with the vulgar brutality of a ruffian and a ravisher.

It is, however, in the forcible-feeble way in which he endeavored to add to the power of passages in his original that Tate shines. One or two extracts will give some slight conception of the improvements which certain of our fathers regarded as constituting this alteration a work of higher art than Shakespeare, owing to his ignorance, was able to accomplish. In one place in the original Edmund, the natural son of Gloucester, is represented as imposing upon his father's credulity by a forged letter which he pretends to have received from Edgar, the legitimate son. In it the writer appears anxious for the death of his parent that he may the sooner succeed to his inheritance. When Gloucester reads the letter he is utterly confounded by its contents. What can it mean? He is willing to give up rank and estate to be fully satisfied, and asks

Edmund to ascertain the exact truth. "To his father
that so tenderly and entirely loves him," is his startled
comment. "Heaven and earth! Edmund, seek him
out; wind me into him, I pray you; frame the business
after your own wisdom. I would unstate myself to be
in a due resolution." In Tate's version this natural
expression of troubled doubt, anxiety, surprise, and
sorrow gives way to this extraordinary manifestation
of parental wrath: —

> " Edgar to write this
> 'Gainst his indulgent father ! Death and hell !
> Fly, Edmund, seek him out, wind me into him,
> That I may bite the traitor's heart, and fold
> His bleeding entrails on my vengeful arm."

This cannot be surpassed, but it is approached by the
exclamatory utterances with which Lear himself greets
the proposal of his daughters that his retinue shall be
dismissed, and that he shall henceforth receive only the
attendance of their servants. It is in these words that
he gives vent to his feelings: —

> " Blood ! fire ! here — leprosies and bluest plagues !
> Room, room for hell to belch her horrors up
> And drench the Circes in a stream of fire ;
> Hark, how the infernals echo to my rage
> Their whips and snakes."

After this we need no commentary to understand what
Shakespeare meant when he spoke of " 'Ercles' vein,"
"a tyrant's vein," or "a part to tear a cat in, to make
all split."

In this version the scene of the extrusion of the eyes
is retained. It is unquestionably terrible; still it is so
wrought into the texture of the play that it would

require a genius almost equal to Shakespeare's to remove it and yet produce the required effect. But Tate felt it incumbent to add irony to the horror. Regan, after revealing to Gloucester how he had been betrayed by his son, draws forth the papers which contain what she calls his treason. She asks the blinded man to read them, and tauntingly adds, —

"If thy eyes fail thee, call for spectacles."

Gloucester in turn does not suffer himself to be outdone in these exhibitions. Delightful in quite another way are the concluding lines of his soliloquy in which he pictures how in the future life his loss of sight will be recompensed a thousandfold. After announcing his intention — which in Shakespeare though implied is never asserted — of throwing himself from the summit of some precipice and dashing out his life on the ragged flint beneath, he adds, —

" Whence my freed soul to her bright sphere shall fly,
Through boundless orbs eternal regions spy,
And like the sun be all one glorious eye."

After familiarizing ourselves with extracts, such as these which have been quoted, we feel that Tate has claims upon us. Things so atrociously bad arouse feelings quite different from that depressing ennui which attends the re-reading of nearly all other Shakespearean alterations.

It is, however, the remodelling of ' The Merchant of Venice ' which will best exemplify the nature of the changes that were made in these adaptations, and will furnish the best means of contrasting the art of Shake-

speare with the art of the men who regarded him as
merely a barbarian of genius. A detailed description
of certain features of this one piece will therefore give
a fairly reasonable conception of the characteristics of
all. It was the work of Lord Lansdowne, or, as his
name was at the time of the production of the play,
George Granville. His version, under the title of ' The
Jew of Venice,' though not often played, met with
general favor. It not merely long held the stage to the
exclusion of the original, but it was spoken of in high
terms by those who assumed to lay down the laws of
taste. Something of this may have been due to the
social position of the adapter; but, after all, the views
expressed must have had behind them a very genuine
belief. Gildon tells us that Shakespeare's play had
received considerable advantage from the pen of Granville. Dennis, in dedicating to him his ' Essay on the
Genius and Writings of Shakespeare,' said that such
a treatise could not be so properly addressed as to the
man who best understood Shakespeare and who had
most improved him. This was certainly a general sentiment, if not the general sentiment; and from its existence we can get a pretty just conception of the value
of much of the criticism which was then applied to the
works of Shakespeare.

Lansdowne's version was published in 1701, the year
of its production on the stage. His advertisement to
the reader was in the happiest and most suggestive
style of the criticism which was in vogue during the
half-century following the Restoration. The writer
started out with the statement that, as the foundations

of the comedy were liable to some objections, it might be a matter of wonder that any one should make choice of it in order to bestow upon it the labor which had been expended. The judicious reader, however, would not be misled by these specious appearances. He would find in this old play so many manly and moral graces in the characters and sentiments that he would excuse the story for the sake of the ornamental parts. Lansdowne then went on to justify the task of altering, which he had undertaken, by the examples of the great men who had made attempts of this same kind. These great men were Waller, the Earl of Rochester, the Duke of Buckingham, Dryden, D'Avenant, and the two laureates — Shadwell and Tate — who had succeeded Dryden. With the exception of the last-mentioned, it was a pretty sorry list of authors to bring forward in defence of the practice of remodelling, or, as it was then called, of restoring old plays. He further professed to be anxious that nothing should be imputed to Shakespeare that was unworthy of him. Accordingly he put between inverted commas the lines which were purely of his own composition, though he observed that in these additions he had taken care to imitate the same fashion of period and turn of style which the original possessed. The fact it was well to state; if unmentioned, it would have pretty surely escaped attention. "She robs her father with a Christian grace," is a remark about Jessica which he puts in the mouth of Gratiano. It is the only line of his additions which is worth quoting, and it conveys a very untrue impression of his own thefts.

The prologue to this adaptation was written by Bevil Higgons, a poet of about the same grade as Lansdowne, of whom he was a kinsman. It was of the nature of a dialogue between the ghosts of Shakespeare and Dryden, both of whom rise crowned with laurel. They indulge in elaborate compliments to each other, but it is not till he comes to speak of his adapter that the former, most complaisant of spirits, rises to eulogy. It is in this way he comments upon the work which has been done upon his play: —

> " These scenes in their rough native dress were mine,
> But now improved with nobler lustre shine;
> The first rude sketches Shakespeare's pencil drew,
> But all the shining master strokes are new.
> This play, ye critics, shall your fury stand,
> Adorned and rescued by a faultless hand."

It is evident from the lines given to him, in which he specifically mentions himself, that for the moment Shakespeare had lost the sense of his art, and spoke the sentiments of Higgons, and not his own. It would seem as if it must have required a good deal of courage on the part of the adapter to permit a prologue to be recited or printed, containing adulation so gross. Every one indeed can understand that the play of ' The Merchant of Venice ' is based upon two improbable or rather impossible stories — at least impossible in any world with which the modern man is acquainted. The distinguishing characteristic of this alteration was to retain of the original all that could offend the mere understanding, and either leave out or deform a large part of it that appealed to the feelings. The plot as retold continued to be as improbable, but ceased to be exciting.

The changes that were made in the alteration were on a very extensive scale. Lines are taken from their proper place or proper speaker and put in the mouth of some other character. The masque, which Shakespeare contemplated but left out, was supplied. It was entitled ' Peleus and Thetis,' and in it the lover in the true style of the heroic plays of a somewhat earlier period defies Jupiter himself, and with the aid of Prometheus fairly bullies the god of thunder into abandoning his designs upon the bride. One would be glad to have had Shylock's opinion of this entertainment, at which he is represented as being present, if Shakespeare could only have returned to earth long enough to have given it just expression. This is the only addition of much length to the play. Omissions, as might be expected, are numerous. Not only are speeches rejected or cut down, but a large number of the characters are dropped. Naturally the Gobbos, father and son, would disappear according to the approved canons of taste then in vogue. These could not be expected to tolerate personages of so low a position in a scene generally so stately. The other extreme is also discarded. Neither the prince of Morocco nor the prince of Aragon is retained. There are, besides, alterations peculiarly absurd in the speeches, sometimes due to the adapter's lack of taste, sometimes to his lack of knowledge. As an illustration of the latter, Granville changed the words in the trial scene with which in Shakespeare Shylock apostrophizes Portia: —

> " A Daniel come to judgment ! yea, a Daniel !
> O wise young judge, how do I honor thee ! "

Here the reference is to the story of Susanna and the elders, as told in the apocryphal scriptures of the Old Testament. In them Daniel, described as "a young youth," is called to a seat on the tribunal, there examines the elders, convicts them of false witness, and saves the innocent. It is accordingly a peculiarly appropriate designation to apply to the disguised Portia; for it is the youthful appearance of the judge that suggests the comparison to Shylock. In Granville's version it reads as follows:—

> " A Daniel, a Daniel : so ripe in wisdom,
> And so young in years! A second Solomon."

These words, with the addition of the reference to Solomon, show that Granville had no conception of what was in Shakespeare's mind when he applied to the youthful judge, who was determining the case, the name of Daniel. He is perhaps not so much to blame; it is an ignorance which he has shared with many of the commentators.

All this mutilation would not have been so bad, had there been any adherence to Shakespeare's art in what was preserved from the wreck. For in many ways ' The Merchant of Venice ' is worked up with a care that will escape the attention of every one who does not subject its details to close scrutiny, no matter how much he may be impressed with its general effect. The keynote of the story is contained in the opening lines. It is the presentiment of approaching disaster, haunting the heart of Antonio, that foreshadows the tragical situation about which the interest of the play is to revolve. In the very first words of the first scene he sounds the ominous note of impending evil: —

> " In sooth I know not why I am so sad:
> It wearies me; you say it wearies you;
> But how I caught it, found it, or came by it,
> What stuff 't is made of, whereof it is born,
> I am to learn;
> And such a want-wit sadness makes of me,
> That I have much ado to know myself."

At the very outset therefore we meet with the merchant prince's anticipation of calamity, coming from a quarter he cannot tell where, presenting itself in a form he cannot imagine what; but, however vague in shape or misty in outline, it has already been sufficient to cast a shadow over his life. It is the artist-like care with which Shakespeare, in the midst of the gayety of the opening scenes, prepares us for the horrible reality that is speedily to confront the chief actors in the drama, which removes the improbability of the story as a story entirely out of our thoughts, and fixes them with almost painful absorption upon the incidents that occur, with the fullest belief on our part in their consonancy with the truth of life. All this skilfully wrought foretokening of what is to follow is discarded in the adaptation. It was not understood, and therefore it was deemed unnecessary or inappropriate.

Still the utter lack of comprehension of the requirements of the highest art is most conspicuous in the changes which were made in the judicial scene in the fourth act. With this part most of us have become so well acquainted, at an age when we feel rather than reflect, that the very familiarity blunts our perception of the extraordinary skill which has been displayed in the whole conduct of the trial, the almost impossibility of altering a word or of adding or omitting a line without impairing the flawlessness of the perfect whole. For the task set before the poet was one of peculiar difficulty; it is his triumph that neither reader nor hearer observes how great a difficulty it is. For in spite of the evil repute in which the Jewish race had been held for centuries, Shakespeare could not but have felt that in following the story out to its conclusion — a conclusion which was probably as well known to the audience as to himself — he could hardly fail to outrage to a certain extent our latent natural sense of justice by a result which purports to be in strictest accordance with justice. Whatever may have been the guilt and bloodthirstiness of Shylock, one cannot get entirely over the impression that he is a hardly used man. In the matter of deriving profit from money lent, he is a long way ahead of Antonio, who is nothing more than the ignorant upholder of a sentimental notion about the taking of interest, the prevalence of which produces the very evils it ostentatiously professes to deplore; and it must be remembered that the taking of one per cent would have been then reckoned an offence against the moral law as well as the taking of a hundred. In the pursuance of his philanthropic zeal against usury he has accordingly treated the Jew as a dog, as a cur of the meanest kind; he has in particular endeavored to convince him of the error of his ways in the usual manner then adopted by Christians with the chosen people, that is, by spitting upon him, buffeting him, and kicking him.

That a man subjected for years to treatment of this sort should be ready at the proper moment to make a lively exhibition of the Christian graces seems to have occurred only to critics of Shakespeare; it assuredly never occurred to Shakespeare himself. It was, therefore, all-important, from the point of view of art, that the malevolence of the Jew should be brought out in this trial scene in as impressive a manner as possible. To the production of this effect the poet paid special heed. Again and again is Shylock entreated to accept the money due him. Not the mere amount only, but three times the amount; not only three times, but practically any amount he chooses to demand. Again and again does Portia press upon him the cancellation of the bond. Again and again she brings up the question of releasing the merchant now in his power. By fine but steadily increasing gradations the refusal in each case is made more emphatic. Appeals to his clemency, appeals to his avarice are alike in vain. It is by these repeated offers and repeated denials that the malignity of Shylock forces itself upon the apprehension of the dullest of us all. It is our consciousness of this which alone reconciles us to the result of the trial, which in one sense is an utter travesty of justice.

No feeling of this sort will be awakened by Lansdowne's version. It has in one way an interest of its own, because it enables us to see how slight are the changes, how few are the omissions which are required to convert a high-wrought scene into commonplace, which is always crude and sometimes offensive. The apparent leaning of the tribunal at the outset to the justice of Shylock's plea, heightening by contrast the dramatic effect of the subsequent action, is sensibly lessened in this alteration. To compensate for this abatement, Portia, at the end, casts off the judicial dignity, which in the original she never for a moment lays aside, and hastens to exhibit the feelings of a partisan and to proclaim herself such openly and even offensively. The railing invectives of Gratiano, thoroughly in keeping with the character, are transferred to Bassanio, in whose mouth they are inappropriate and unbecoming; while the dignity of the whole scene is impaired and indeed almost destroyed by the cheap expedients of the latter in seeking to interfere with the processes of the court, by making offers of self-sacrifice, which he must know cannot be accepted, and by attempting acts of violence which he must know equally well cannot prevail. Very little, in truth, of the skilful art of the original has been preserved in the version of the trial scene which Lansdowne perpetrated. It is throughout hurried and crude. The almost agonizing intensity of feeling, which slowly but steadily deepens and broadens on both sides, is no longer seen or felt. The repeated offers and repeated refusals to accept anything that will stand in the way of the accomplishment of revenge no longer force themselves upon the attention. These variations would of themselves settle the question of art, if there were a question in regard to it, independent of the genius of the writers.

But even more pronounced is the difference of light in which the Jew appears in the two productions. In the Shylock of Shakespeare is concentrated the wrath of a race turning upon its oppressors, — a race conscious of the importance of the part it has played in the past, with its long line of lawgivers and prophets to which all nations turn, equally conscious of the misery it has endured and is continuing to endure in the present. As it has been great in suffering, so will it be great in vengeance. Entreaties are useless; threats are mere empty breath. Pity will not soften the heart nor obloquy cause it to yield. In Lansdowne, on the contrary, Shylock is no longer exalted by wrath. He is not indeed a comic character, as has been so persistently asserted; but he is essentially a vulgar one. He exhibits nothing of that sublimity of hate which awes us by its intensity, and gives to malignity a character almost of grandeur. Though he feels antipathy, his antipathy is purely of the nature of a business investment. He is willing to sacrifice the wealth he holds dear in order to free himself from the further interposition of a man who has hindered him in his gains, thwarted him in his bargains, and laughed at his losses. He is not, as in Shakespeare, the representative of the long martyrdom of a race. He is nothing but the Jew of the huckster's stall, of the old-clothes' shop, whose ideal in life is a profit of at least two hundred per cent, and whose Messiah is desired to come, not to effect the conquest of the world, but to give his people the possession of its traffic.

CHAPTER IX

CONFLICTING EIGHTEENTH-CENTURY VIEWS
ABOUT SHAKESPEARE

To the men of modern times there is something very amusing, when it is not exasperating, in the attitude exhibited by the eighteenth century towards the Elizabethan age. There was, to be sure, nothing new about it then; it had begun to be displayed with the beginning of the Restoration period. Strength and force, it was always confessed, had been shown by the writers of the past; but it was Charles who, on his return from exile, had brought with him correctness and grace and refinement. To use the language of Dryden, he had cured the rankness of the soil with the rules of husbandry; he had tamed the rudeness of the stage, and had imparted to it manners and decorum; he had, in fine, endowed boisterous English wit with art.[1] But it was not until the so-called Augustan age was in full bloom that men rose to the full consciousness of their superiority to their fathers. The audience which Shakespeare addressed, it was then held, was the most incapable of judgment of any that ever existed. It was made up of the lowest and the meanest of the populace. It was the tastes and the wishes of this class which the

[1] Epistle to Congreve.

dramatic writer was compelled to consult. This is the view regularly expressed during the whole of the eighteenth century. It is what Gildon tells us in the early part of it.[1] In the latter part of it we find the same assertions made by Mrs. Montagu, who had put herself forward as the champion of Shakespeare against Voltaire.

The absurdity of this self-satisfied complacency of the eighteenth century comes home to us with peculiar force the moment we stop to contrast the men who stand out as the conspicuous representatives of its political and intellectual life with the corresponding characters of the period to which it felt and expressed superiority. It approaches the comic to find the petty writers of an inferior time gravely commenting upon the barbarism of an age in which had flourished Raleigh, Sidney, Spenser, Bacon, Jonson, Shakespeare,— to name some of the greatest,— beside a whole host of writers who, while falling below the grade of the highest, were nevertheless distinctively men of genius. Yet this attitude of condescension was taken in all sincerity and seriousness. The men who assumed it had of course no knowledge of the period they were criticising. There was accordingly displayed by them a total ignorance of the predecessors of Shakespeare. He was represented as having been the one to create the stage, and his advocates constantly dwelt upon the barbarism of his times as a palliation, if not a complete excuse for his conceded faults. The prologue to Dryden's alteration of 'Troilus and Cressida' is

[1] The Complete Art of Poetry, vol. i. p. 64.

supposed to be spoken by the ghost of the great dramatist. It is in these lines that he delivers a common opinion then entertained about himself, —

> " Untaught, unpractised, in a barbarous age,
> I found not, but created first the stage.
> And if I drained no Greek or Latin store,
> 'T was that my own abundance gave me more.
> On foreign trade I needed not rely,
> Like fruitful Britain, rich without supply."

It was this belief in the rudeness of Shakespeare's age and the inevitable resulting rudeness of himself, which had brought about the mangling of his plays under the honest conviction that the alterations to which they were subjected were improvements. This same belief led in time to the development among those holding it of divergent opinions in regard to his art. By the close of the seventeenth century we become aware of the prevalence of two estimates of Shakespeare, which though not diametrically opposite are yet far from being in harmony. The modern view which regards him as an exponent of true art was evidently even then in being; but it had nowhere any authoritative expression. So far as literature was concerned, it lurked unseen and unheard. None the less was it potential with that mass of men who knew nothing about the rules then so much insisted upon, and cared less. They remained faithful to the poet during all variations of taste, and amid the changing fortunes of critical controversy. Through them he steadily passed all competitors in the race for popularity. Though they left no record of their opinions in poem

341

or pamphlet or book, they were so numerous that deference had to be paid to their feelings, even when contempt was expressed for their judgment.

The contrasted attitude of mind of what may be called the more or less educated laity and the critical clergy is unconsciously exemplified in the different views recorded by Edward Phillips, the nephew of Milton, in his volume, published in 1675, dealing with poets and poetry. In the body of the work Shakespeare is spoken of as "the glory of the English stage." Others might pretend to a more exact decorum and economy, never any one expressed a more lofty and tragic height; never any one represented nature more purely to the life. Even when the polishments of art are wanting, he was declared to please with a certain wild and native elegance.[1] It has been common to hold Milton responsible for the appearance in the work of these opinions. There is as little ground for such a contention as there is evidence. The sentiments here expressed were by no means unusual. They were those of the men who at that time paid little or no heed to the observance of dramatic rules. We are apt to get a wrong estimate of the number of these, because the many never troubled themselves to record their faith, while the few were generally careful to express their dissent; and it is the views alone of these latter, consequently, that reach us. In this instance they are distinctly conveyed in the preface to the work. There we are informed that the unfiled expression of the dramatist and his rambling and indigested fancies are the laughter of the critical.

[1] Theatrum Poetarum (1675), p. 194.

It cannot be repeated too often that there is no support for the assumption that such wholesale denunciation of Shakespeare as occurs in Rymer ever represented the sentiments of either a large or an influential body of men. It was at best nothing but the expression of the prejudice and incapacity of a few individuals. It never exerted any appreciable influence upon the estimate taken of the dramatist. But in the history of critical controversy as distinguished from that of popular opinion, the existence of two classes holding divergent opinions about his dramatic art is distinctly recognizable at the end of the seventeenth century. During the whole of the century following they are both constantly in evidence and often in collision. To some extent too they acted and reacted upon each other. The one of these which is first to be considered, was the one which was most prominent at the outset. In the world of purely professional criticism it may be said to have had then nearly absolute sway. It did not — at least in its own opinion — disparage Shakespeare. It took of him what may be termed the inspired-barbarian view. It went upon the assumption that while his genius was vast, it worked independently of the rules of the highest art. Accordingly its manifestations were never kept under the restraints of that chastened propriety of sentiment and diction which by common consent of eighteenth-century writers had become the distinguishing trait of the productions of their own age. In consequence the judicious reader was alternately delighted and disgusted with what he met in the poet. This estimate, widely held and long accepted as indisputably true by many critics, and at one period perhaps by the majority of them, is best summed up in an epigram which appeared in a magazine of 1745. The couplet, which bore as its title the simple heading "On Shakespeare," runs as follows : —

> "His faults, or virtues who could justly tell?
> No mortal higher soared, nor lower fell."[1]

Opinions of this sort can be found in abundance during the one hundred and fifty years which followed the Restoration. It is the view taken by Dryden in his earlier criticism, in which, while conceding the genius of Shakespeare, he was more disposed than he was at a later period to lay stress upon his imputed faults. In the epilogue to the second part of 'The Conquest of Granada,' brought out in 1670, he had maintained that wit had reached a higher degree of refinement than in the previous age, that the humor of the Elizabethan drama was mechanic, its conversation was low, and its love was mean; that the writers of that period had got their fame by being first-comers and had kept it since by being dead. The criticism was directed mainly against Jonson, but it stirred up all the believers in the earlier stage. Dryden defended himself in a prose pamphlet, in the course of which he had this to say about the greatest of the Elizabethans. "Shakespeare," he observed, "who many times has written better than any poet in any language, is yet so far from writing wit always, or expressing that wit according to the dignity of the subject, that he writes in many places below the

[1] Gentleman's Magazine, vol. xv. p. 213, April, 1745.

dullest writer of ours or any precedent age. Never did any author precipitate himself from such heights of thought to such low expressions as he often does. He is the very Janus of poets: he wears almost everywhere two faces; and you have scarce begun to admire the one ere you despise the other."[1] To the same effect spoke Crowne, a few years later, in dedicating to Sir Charles Sedley his adaptation of 'Henry VI.' "Though Shakespeare," he wrote, "be generally very delightful, he is not so always. His volume is all uphill and down. Paradise was never more pleasant than some parts of it, nor Ireland and Greenland colder and more uninhabitable than others."

Criticism of this sort we have had occasion to see constantly expressed or implied in the writings of Dennis and Gildon. The latter assures us that when Shakespeare does not follow the rules, he falls into such monstrous absurdities that nothing but his uncommon excellences in other parts could prevail with men of judgment and good sense to endure his works.[2] This is a view which finds frequent expression through the whole of the eighteenth century. Bolingbroke told Voltaire that the English had not one good tragedy as a whole; the merit of the best of them lay in detached scenes. Chesterfield held an opinion not essentially different. Joseph Warton opens some observations on 'The Tempest' with the remark that Shakespeare exhibited more numerous examples of excellences and faults of every kind than can perhaps be

---

[1] Defence of the Epilogue to the Conquest of Granada.
[2] Complete Art of Poetry, vol. i. p. 99.

discovered in any other author.[1] Later he observed
that Shakespeare, Corneille, and Racine are the only
modern writers of tragedy that could be opposed to
Æschylus, Sophocles, and Euripides; but he added that
the first was an author so uncommon and so eccentric
that he can scarcely be tried by dramatic rules.[2] Years
afterward Cumberland repeated the same old story.
According to him, Shakespeare was an author whose
excellences are beyond comparison and whose errors are
beyond number.[3]

This view had supporters down to the very close of
the eighteenth century. It was perhaps most violent
in its utterances at the very time it was on the point of
falling into disrepute. The opinions expressed by those
who held it ran naturally to extremes, and were favorable or unfavorable according as the critic was shocked
most by the absurdities of Shakespeare or impressed by
his counterbalancing merits. His steadily increasing
popularity during the century, shown by the increasing
number of revivals of his plays, was very distressing to
many members of this class. Their feelings are fully
portrayed in the invective against Garrick and the
stage which Goldsmith introduced into his 'Inquiry
into the Present State of Polite Learning in Europe.'
These revived plays are there termed hashes of absurdity which disgusted our ancestors even in an age of
ignorance. They were full of forced humor, far-fetched
conceit, and unnatural hyperbole. Goldsmith was good
enough to say that he admired the beauties of the great

---

[1] Adventurer, No. 93, Sept. 25, 1753. [2] Ibid., No. 127, Jan. 22, 1754.
[3] Observer, No. 75 (1785).

father of the English stage as much as they deserved; but he could wish for both the honor of the country and of the author himself that many of his scenes should be forgotten.[1] This reminds one of Charles James Fox's remark that he thought Shakespeare's credit would have stood higher if he had never written 'Hamlet.'[2] Goldsmith further brought forward the observation, which turns up with unvarying regularity in every generation, that the success of the great dramatist was not really due to himself, but to prescription. "Let the spectator," said he, "who assists at any of these newly revived pieces only ask himself whether he would approve such a performance if written by a modern poet. I fear he will find that much of his applause proceeds merely from the sound of a name and an empty veneration for antiquity."

Goldsmith's knowledge of any subject he treated was always in an inverse ratio to the charm of his style; and this is not the only place where he made it manifest that his critical judgment was on a par with his knowledge. The view he expressed in this work published in 1759 he reiterated in 'The Vicar of Wakefield' which came out a few years later. In it Dr. Primrose is represented as asking the strolling player whom he has met who are the present theatrical writers in vogue; who the Drydens and Otways of the day. The clergyman is astonished and disgusted when told that these writers are quite out of fashion; that the taste had gone

---

[1] Chapter xi.
[2] Northcote, Life of Sir Joshua Reynolds, vol. ii. p. 234 (ed. of 1818).

back a whole century; that Fletcher, Ben Jonson, and all the plays of Shakespeare are the only things that go down. Here is his comment upon this information. "'How,' cried I, 'is it possible the present age can be pleased with that antiquated dialect, that obsolete humor, those overcharged characters, which abound in the works you mention?'"[1] The words are the words of the vicar; the sentiments are the sentiments of Goldsmith.

But the feeling here depicted was by no means confined to fiction; it is exhibited and exemplified in works dealing with the dullest fact. The worthy Blair, who set out to correct the bad English of others in pretty bad English of his own, had a good deal to say in his treatise on rhetoric about the failure of the dramatist to come up to the severe standard he had himself in mind. On the whole, he may be considered as not having been actually unkind to Shakespeare. He doubtless pitied him more than he admired; but considering who he was himself, and how lofty were his ideals, it was a good deal to his credit that he refrained from expressing unbounded contempt. Shakespeare had genius, he conceded; "but at the same time it is genius shooting wild; deficient in just taste, and altogether unassisted by knowledge and art." Accordingly he was in doubt whether the beauties or the faults of the dramatist were greater. He naturally expressed himself as shocked by his extreme irregularities in the conduct of the plot, and at the grotesque mixture of the serious and the comic in one piece. "There is hardly any one of his plays," he concluded,

[1] Chapter xviii.

" which can be called altogether a good one, and which can be read with uninterrupted pleasure from beginning to end." [1] These words, it is to be remembered, come from the lips of a man who is nominally reckoned among the editors of Shakespeare.

The standard of taste of the kind here indicated was in truth so high in Scotland during the eighteenth century that the imperfections of Shakespeare lay heavy on the heart of several of its men of letters. It was felt that something should be done to redeem the English theatre from the barbarism with which that dramatist had infected it. Hopes were at times entertained that North Britain might come to the relief of the suffering stage. In a letter written in 1754 to Spence, Hume communicated to his correspondent something which he observed was an agreeable piece of news. At last we might expect to see good tragedies in the English language. A namesake of his own had discovered a very fine genius for that species of composition. Years before he had written a play called ' Agis ; ' but this, though approved by some of the best judges, had not been altogether satisfactory to Hume himself. The author had corrupted his taste by imitating Shakespeare, whom he ought to have contented himself with simply admiring. But from this clearly debasing influence his namesake had now freed himself. He had composed a new tragedy in which he had shown himself the true disciple of Sophocles and Racine. " I hope in time," continued Hume, " he will vindicate the English stage from the reproach of barbarism." [2]

---

[1] Lectures on Rhetoric, Lecture xlvi.
[2] Burton's Hume, vol. i. p. 392. Letter of Oct. 15, 1754.

This tragedy which was to usher in the English dramatic golden age was the 'Douglas' of John Home. It is a very good specimen of a very poor kind. First acted in 1756 at Edinburgh, it was brought out with great success in 1757 at Covent Garden, and during the rest of the century kept possession of the stage. The feeling existed among many Scotchmen that Shakespeare had been outdone. Here was a writer who had rivalled, if not surpassed, him in his excellences, while he was free from his gross faults. He had fulfilled all the conditions required by the dramatic art. Time and place had been faithfully observed. Decorum had been maintained throughout. Acts of violence occur; but they are properly kept out of sight. To adopt the language of Hume, the author had exhibited "the true theatric genius of Shakespeare and Otway, refined from the unhappy barbarism of the one and the licentiousness of the other." Scotchmen indeed took the matter very seriously. Hannah More tells us of the quarrel she had on this subject in the year 1786 with Lord Monboddo. It amused the English who were bystanders, though she complained that none of them would come to her help. They naturally had too much enjoyment of the exhibition to desire its discontinuance. Monboddo asserted, in all the sincerity of anger, that 'Douglas' was a better play than Shakespeare could have written.[1] Yet what he said in his wrath Hume had more than once said before in all coolness. "I am persuaded," he wrote of the play to Adam Smith, "it will be esteemed the best, and by French critics the only, tragedy of our lan-

[1] Hannah More, Life and Correspondence, vol. ii. p. 22 (1834).

guage." [1] To the author himself he said that it was reserved for him, and for him alone, "to redeem our stage from the reproach of barbarism." [2]

Ridiculous as this may seem now, it did not seem to many ridiculous then. It only reflected the extreme form of a view which, as we have seen, was generally entertained by critics of this first class of which we have been speaking. Early in the century it was the prevailing judgment; towards its close it was still prevalent. In fact, for a time the influence of Voltaire gave it renewed vigor and vogue. Furthermore, it must be understood that whatever we think of it, the eighteenth century had no poor opinion of itself. In its own eyes it had reached a height of literary judgment above which it was impossible for the human mind to ascend. At last the unadulterated article of perfect taste had been secured, stripped of the meretricious attractions which had sullied its chastity in the past, and like refined gold purified in the fierce fire of critical assaying from incrustations which had deformed it, and from baser matter which had been mingled with it. There was no hesitation expressed on this point, for there was none entertained. Shakespeare in consequence was exalted or condemned according as he conformed or failed to conform to the standard the individual critic set up. To ascertain the particular place that was to be assigned him by the severer judges of this class, we must go back to Hume. It is found in the celebrated passage which he inserted in the appendix to his account of the reign of James I.

[1] Burton's Hume, vol. ii. p. 17.   [2] Ibid., vol. i. p. 419.

Hume's theory was that the English writers were possessed of great genius before they were endowed with any degree of taste. Hence we admire their imagination while blaming their judgment. It is in the following words that he made a particular application of his general view. "If Shakespeare," he wrote, "be considered as a *man,* born in a rude age, and educated in the lowest manner, without any instruction either from the world or from books, he may be regarded as a prodigy; if represented as a *poet,* capable of furnishing a proper entertainment to a refined or intelligent audience, we must abate much of this eulogy. In his compositions we regret that many irregularities, and even absurdities, should so frequently disfigure the animated and passionate scenes intermixed with them; and at the same time we perhaps admire the more those beauties on account of their being surrounded with such deformities. A striking peculiarity of sentiment, adapted to a singular character he frequently hits, as it were, by inspiration; but a reasonable propriety of thought he cannot for any time uphold. Nervous and picturesque expressions, as well as descriptions, abound in him; but it is in vain we look either for purity or simplicity of diction. His total ignorance of all theatrical art and conduct, however material a defect, yet as it affects the spectator rather than the reader, we can more easily excuse than that want of taste which often prevails in his productions, and which gives way only by intervals to the irradiations of genius. A great and fertile genius he certainly possessed, and one enriched equally with a tragic and comic vein; but he ought to be cited as a proof, how dangerous it is to rely on these advantages alone for attaining an excellence in the finer arts. And there may even remain a suspicion that we overrate, if possible, the greatness of his genius; in the same manner as bodies often appear more gigantic, on account of their being disproportioned and misshapen."

The passage is a familiar one; but no frequency of repetition can destroy the charm of its delightfulness. To have the greatest dramatist of our race, if not of all time, spoken of in a matter-of-course way as totally ignorant of all theatrical art and conduct is a touch to which men of our age with similar beliefs on this or other subjects would never dare to give expression. Elsewhere Hume speaks in the most assured manner of both Shakespeare and Ben Jonson as being equally deficient in taste and elegance, in harmony and correctness. The rude genius of the former, we are told, had prevailed over the rude art of the latter. In consequence the English theatre has ever since taken a strong tincture of Shakespeare's spirit and character. The results had been in one way deplorable. Its valuable productions in other parts of learning had not been able to save the nation from incurring from all its neighbors the reproach of barbarism.

Speaking merely for myself, I confess I like this critical confidence of the eighteenth century, little as I believe in its criticism. There was an open magnificent sort of way in which it looked upon itself as omniscient, which contrasts, a good deal to its credit, with the hesitating, one might almost say sneaking, manner in which we occasionally try to imply the same thing, not daring boldly to avow it, while at heart fully thinking it. In that day the critics of this class talked in perfect accordance with their convictions. They consequently patronized Shakespeare. There was a general tone of condescension in their most favorable judgments. He lived in a barbarous age. The language had not then attained that refinement which it had since been made to receive. False taste prevailed, and from the influence of it he had been unable to free himself. In fact, he lacked almost entirely the favorable conditions with which the men of the eighteenth century were profusely blessed. Yet in spite of these disadvantages his mighty powers had enabled him to accomplish much which they honestly felt bound to speak of with decided approval. "If Shakespeare's genius," wrote Lord Chesterfield, "had been cultivated, those beauties which we so justly admire in him, would have been undisguised by those extravagances and that nonsense with which they are frequently accompanied." This mingled tone of regard and regret pervades no small share of the critical utterance of this period. It is hard indeed to tell which is the more predominant feeling in the eighteenth century, its admiration of Shakespeare or its admiration of itself for admiring Shakespeare; for its broad-minded catholicity in not being so offended by his faults as to become blind to his merits.

Such was the prevalent belief about Shakespeare with the critics of the first class. But even at the era of the Restoration it came into conflict with another belief, which was from the beginning outspoken, though it did not at first speak in print. But from the time the eighteenth century opened, it gathered constantly volume and energy, and at last triumphed over the previously predominant belief, with which it had, however, much in common. Those holding it admitted the correctness of the premises laid down by the critics of the first class. What they dissented from was the conclusion. As a consequence they admired in fact what in theory they were bound to condemn. Shakespeare might be deficient in art; he undoubtedly was deficient in art. He might venture upon practices which the trained judgment of the cultivated would disapprove; but he took possession of the heart, and the heart never refused its allegiance to the great master, whatever protest the mere understanding might put forth. Others might preach the superiority of the creed of the regular school of dramatists. They might point out how free it was from the faults which deformed the writings of the great Elizabethan, and proclaim that the doctrine it taught was the only orthodox one, and could not be violated with impunity. But there remained the disagreeable fact that the writers of this school, while observing all the laws, committed the one unpardonable sin of being uninteresting. Those who censured the dramatist for his irregularities, and then subjected themselves to comparison with him by producing regular plays of their own, had without exception exposed themselves to the malediction pronounced by Dryden in the prologue to his last play, —

> " To Shakespeare's critic he bequeaths the curse,
> To find his faults, and yet himself make worse;
> A precious reader in poetic schools,
> Who by his own examples damns his rules." [1]

[1] Prologue to ' Love Triumphant,' 1694.

Here in truth thrusts in its ugly face the ever-recurring difficulty which besets literary as well as religious movements. The creed of the gospel which is preached is brought into disrepute by the acts of its apostles.

As a result, the men who could not tolerate the plays of the orthodox pattern were glad to shelter themselves under the broad and unimpeachable heterodoxy of Shakespeare. Still they had been brought up to believe in the rules they disliked. In theory they recognized their binding force, though there was always likelihood that in the heat of controversy they might speak of them disparagingly and question their value. As therefore they had a sort of faith in these rules, and full faith in the man who disregarded them, they were obliged to resort to the further theory that Shakespeare was somehow above art; that he had received a special commission from Nature to do as he pleased, and that the mighty mother, in allowing him to penetrate into her profoundest mysteries, had absolved him from the necessity of paying heed to the restraints which held inferior men in check, — had permitted him to pass unharmed the bounds of space and time, beyond whose confines others could not venture with safety. The special exemption of the great dramatist from the operation of general law is a distinctive feature of the dramatic criticism of the eighteenth century. It has been more than once conveyed in passages which have been cited in preceding pages for a totally distinct purpose. It rarely if ever occurred to the men who held this view that the law itself might not really be binding. They rarely drew the inference that the art which Shakespeare had neglected to observe might not be art at all, but merely a parcel of conventions which had been dubbed with that title. They accepted, with grumbling perhaps, but still without dissent, the rules which were to regulate the practice of dramatists; but they accepted just as unflinchingly and much more ardently the writer who had persistently violated them.

It is clear that men of this stamp existed from the very beginning of the Restoration period. During the half-century that followed they may have been awed into silence by the predominance of the opposing view. It is not at least from anything they said themselves that we learn of the opinions they held; it is from what is said about them by others. Their existence cannot be questioned. Dryden tells us, in the defence of his epilogue to the second part of 'The Conquest of Granada,' that there were those then who called the Elizabethan age the golden age of English poetry. The general belief in the superiority of Shakespeare in particular, coupled with much ignorance on the part of many of what he had written, and with distinct disparagement of it on the part of a few, is conveyed unmistakably in the minor literature of the latter half of the seventeenth century. His works were sometimes plundered without acknowledgment; as frequently, however, the pillager was anxious to secure the advantage of his name. Crowne in the prologue to the first part of his 'Henry VI.' bore witness in the following words to the prejudice existing in favor of the elder dramatist: —

" To-day we bring old gathered herbs, 't is true,
    But such as in sweet Shakespeare's garden grew.
    And all his plants immortal you esteem,
    Your mouths are never out of taste with him."

This was said in 1680.   As time went on, as the eighteenth century opened, reference to these varying views
become increasingly frequent.   Dennis, in the preface
to his alteration of 'The Merry Wives of Windsor,'
tells us that in setting out to remodel this play, he
found that he should have two sorts of people to deal
with, who would equally endeavor to obstruct his success.   The one believed it so admirable that nothing
ought to be added to it; the other fancied it to be so
despicable that the time of any one would be lost in
improving it.

That the former class was steadily growing in numbers, is made evident from the increasing violence with
which its opinions were attacked.   Rowe, in his life
of Shakespeare prefixed to the first critical edition of
the plays, had intimated his belief that additional learning might have been an injury instead of a benefit to
the dramatist.   He might in consequence have become
a more correct writer, but it was not improbable that
the regularity and deference for rule which would have
attended his correctness, might have restrained some of
that fire and impetuosity and even beautiful extravagance which we admire.   This is clearly an opinion
then widely entertained.   The declaration of it by
Rowe called forth an earnest protest from Gildon.   All
through the essay which he prefixed to the supplementary volume of the minor poems runs a constant

series of attacks upon the ignorant and thoughtless men of the age who were constantly engaged in denouncing the rules, and as proof of their worthlessness pointing to the success of Shakespeare, who had either been ignorant of them, or knowing them had treated them with contempt.

Views of this sort were undoubtedly irritating to the critics of the other and then established school. In their eyes its unreasonableness was evident on its face. Of course conformity to law could not supply the place of genius. They quoted the concession of the French Academy in its controversy with Corneille that some regular pieces were very unsatisfactory. But had not this same body also pointed out so plainly that even the wayfaring man, though a fool, could not err, that in such cases it was the writers that were at fault and not the rules? In so far as he had observed these, and so far only, was Shakespeare great. It was not his disregard of the rules which had brought him success, but his excellence in the expression of manners, in the distinction of characters, in the representation of passion. If in addition to these he had only known the dramatic art, he would have occupied an altogether higher place than the one which he had actually attained. So argued, from the beginning of the eighteenth century, the adherents of the classical school. At its end we find it all repeated by Blair. But their most strenuous efforts could not uproot the lurking heresy to which some of their own side occasionally exhibited partiality. It is further manifest that there were those at that time who were disposed to push to an extreme their hostility to the so-called rules of art. They insisted that no play would please in which they were observed. They spoke of them as curbs to wit and poetry. This baleful error, as Gildon termed it, was based, in his opinion, upon the admiration which the works of Shakespeare received.

This admiration, it was further asserted, was not due altogether to his excellence, but to custom. Even early in the eighteenth century we find the same reason given for his popularity which we have found expressed in the middle of it by Goldsmith. It was definitely stated as prescription. His claim rested upon the uninterrupted enjoyment of a long reputation of conceded superiority. Even then it was the correct thing to admire Shakespeare. He who failed to do it incurred from large and steadily increasing numbers the suspicion of suffering from arrested mental development. Of this Gildon complained again and again. Rymer's charge of the gross impropriety of making the chief character in a drama a negro, as in ' Othello,' he tells us, was unquestionably just; but still, he adds, the play pleases by prescription.[1] He furthermore confessed that he did not dare to find fault with many of the speeches in ' Romeo and Juliet' as being not natural; since to do so would provoke too many who admire it as the soul of love.[2] Later in the century George III. bore unwilling witness to the existence of a sovereign whose greatness he had neither the taste to appreciate nor the ability to comprehend, but whose supremacy he was forced to recognize as being beyond the reach of criticism. Madame D'Arblay has

[1] Remarks on the Plays of Shakespeare (1710), in Shakespeare's Works, vol. x. (1728) p. 410.
[2] Ibid., p. 378.

preserved for us a few of the choice bits of wisdom which were flung forth carelessly by the royal mind. "Was there ever," he said to her, "such stuff as great part of Shakespeare? Only one must not say so! But what think you? — What? — Is there not sad stuff? — What? — What?" Miss Burney made in reply the usual admission of the imperfections of the dramatist, but attempted to put in also the usual feeble defence of his possession of great counterbalancing excellences. "O!" broke in the monarch, good-humoredly. "O, I know it is not to be said! but it is true! Only it is Shakespeare, and nobody dare abuse him." Then he proceeded to enumerate many of the characters and parts of plays to which he objected. These remarks the diarist unfortunately did not put down; but the words with which the King concluded reveal that he felt that no one, even though holding his own exalted position, could safely venture to attack the dramatist. His criticisms were just, "but," he added, "one should be stoned for saying so." [1] In this matter the King agreed with one of his most unruly subjects. Cobbett never read a line of the poet until 1797, when he was thirty-five years old; and he formed then a low opinion of him. The admiration expressed for him he attributed to mere caprice of fashion.

It is Dennis and Gildon who naturally furnish us with the fullest information as to the opinions of this earlier period; for they were the two who then concerned themselves directly in Shakespearean criticism. We find them — especially the latter — perpetually

[1] Diary of Madam D'Arblay, vol. ii. p. 398.

clamoring against a certain body of men who maintained that if Shakespeare had been more of a critic, he would have been less of a poet. These persons could not be persuaded out of the belief that his monstrous irregularities were really conducive to the shining beauties that abounded in his plays. This was a state of mind which naturally strengthened as the rules were enforced upon the writer with increasing rigidity, but with results correspondingly depressing to both spectator and reader. It was to some extent shared in by those whose practice would rank them as belonging to the classical school. Rowe was certainly not deterred by the criticism his remarks in his life of Shakespeare had received, from continuing to express the same views. In the prologue to his tragedy of 'Jane Shore,' brought out in 1714, he spoke of the superiority in certain particulars of the past to the present. Then he added the following comment : —

> " In such an age immortal Shakespeare wrote,
>   By no quaint rules or hampering critics taught ;
>   With rough majestic force he moved the heart ;
>   And strength and nature made amends for art."

It would, perhaps, not have done just then to maintain extravagant heretical opinions like these in sober prose. Men could venture upon them in the freedom of conversation ; in poetry, furthermore, they felt themselves at liberty to avow them audaciously. The sentiment already indicated, which soon came to be widely prevalent, is represented very satisfactorily in a few lines from a then somewhat popular though now long-forgotten piece, entitled 'The Progress of Poesy.' [1] It was published at least as early as 1731, and was the production of Mrs. Madan, a daughter of Spencer Cowper, and aunt of the poet of that name. In giving a running characterization of the great writers of the past and the present, she called special attention, in the case of Shakespeare, to the success he had met with in spite of having violated the laws of the drama. It was in these lines that she began her description: —

> "Exalted Shakespeare, with a boundless mind,
> Ranged far and wide, a genius unconfined;
> The passions swayed, and captive led the heart,
> Without the critic's rules or aid of art."

Many years later the portion of the poem which dealt with the dramatist was taken apart from the rest — possibly by the authoress herself — and with great additions was published in a periodical under the title of 'Verses on Reading Shakespeare.' The same sentiment was expressed even more strongly in the following words: —

> "What though by judgment's frigid rules he fails,
> Resistless still o'er passion he prevails,
> And spite of all his faults, the wise admire
> The daring bard and kindle at his fire." [2]

Then followed without acknowledgment some lines taken from Dryden; and the writer went on to pay the highest of tributes to Shakespeare, and to Garrick as his interpreter. Later in the century the feeling was ex-

---

[1] This poem was printed in 'The Flower-piece,' 1731; in the 'London Magazine' for February and March, 1759; in 'Fawkes and Woty's Poetical Calendar,' March, 1763; and it was reprinted in 1783 in a separate volume. The part on Shakespeare, much enlarged, can be found in the 'Gentleman's Magazine' for June, 1753.

[2] Gentleman's Magazine, 1753, vol. xiii. p. 287.

pressed still more strongly by Colman in his prologue to the revived 'Philaster,' in which he spoke with a good deal of contempt of the regular tragedies then produced on the English stage, and exclaimed, —

> " Say, where 's the poet, trained in pedant schools,
> Equal to Shakespeare, who o'erleaped all rules."

Several of the citations given in preceding chapters to illustrate other points express an opinion not dissimilar to the foregoing. It crops out so constantly in the literature of the eighteenth century that it would swell this work to disproportionate limits to attempt to give even a partial representation of the wealth of material illustrating it which exists. Two further passages are all that need be cited here, and they are cited not for their merit, but on account of the frequency with which they were reproduced in the periodical literature of the time. The first is a passage from a poem comparing Shakespeare and Jonson, written by Samuel Rogers, rector of Chellington in Bedfordshire. The lines are dreadful as literature, but they do more than convey the estimate of the superiority of the former author to the latter, which had long been universally accepted. They express the then widely prevalent sentiment, that Shakespeare owed nothing whatever to art. In these lines we find the view which had come to displace the one that had at first held supremacy : —

> " Great Shakespeare with genius disdaining all rules,
> Above the cold phlegm or the fripp'ry of schools,
> Appeal'd to the heart for success of his plays,
> And trusted to nature alone for the bays." [1]

[1] This poem first appeared in the 'St. James's Magazine,' vol. ii. p. 63 (1763), and afterward in a volume of collected poems by the author.

A few years later George Keate, the friend of Voltaire, addressed a poetical epistle to that author entitled ' Ferney.' In this he warmly defended Shakespeare from the strictures of the French writer, and spoke of him as

> " Above control, above each classic rule,
> His witness nature, and the world his school."

Here then have been given the views of these two classes of critics. According to the one Shakespeare was irregularly great, but he would have been far greater, had he only known and practised the poetic art. According to the other, he was great because he did not know and practise it, because he was above it. In each case his incorrectness was assumed. It was conceded by his admirers as freely as it was strongly insisted upon by his severest judges. He was unquestionably guilty of absurdities, only they were glorious absurdities. Colman, for instance, wrote an essay containing an account of various geniuses who are represented as sacrificing in the temple of Fame those portions of their works which have been preserved to their discredit. Among these Shakespeare appears, carrying to the altar a long string of puns, marked ' The Taste of the Age,' a small parcel of bombast, and a pretty large bundle of incorrectness. Yet a further remark in this same essay is noticeable, not only as indicating a view of the greatness of the dramatist now becoming universal, but some faint conception of the fact that the criticism to which he had been constantly subjected was based upon a false theory. Aristotle is represented as saying that " although Shakespeare was quite ignorant of that exact economy of the stage which is so remarkable in the Greek writers, yet

the mere strength of his genius had in many points carried him infinitely beyond them." [1]   It was a conviction
of the same sort that led some at about the same time
to avow openly an opinion which had long been held by
many in secret.   This was that Shakespeare was a far
greater dramatist than Sophocles or Euripides.   His
superiority to Corneille and Racine was assumed by
most Englishmen as not worth discussing.   But the
remark of Colman shows that, without being aware of
it, men were blindly feeling their way to that position,
which Lessing was soon to state definitely, that genius
laughs away all the boundary lines of criticism, and that
there is much which it has first to create before we can
recognize it as possible.   The modern view was slowly
taking outline and form.

It was the growth of this feeling which was under-
mining the whole foundation upon which the censure of
Shakespeare's methods had been based.   This was not
uprooted until the following century; but it was permanently impaired.   Boswell tells us in his life of Johnson
that a blind, indiscriminate admiration of Shakespeare
had exposed the British nation to the ridicule of foreign-
ers.   That commentator had rescued him from the injury wrought by his panegyrists in consequence of the
masterly display he had furnished of his excellences and
defects.   Boswell's testimony is of value as to the existence of the admiration; but he forgot to mention that
the defects which Johnson pointed out had come to be
recognized, even in the time of his biographer, not as
defects in the poet, but defects in the vision of his edi-

[1] The Adventurer, No. 90, September 15, 1753.

tor. In the last quarter of the eighteenth century there
was, furthermore, less and less disposition to heed foreign
opinion, which itself was now beginning in turn to feel
the weight of Shakespeare's influence. The disposition
further manifested itself not to stand on the defensive,
but to attack the holders of the opposite view. In truth,
the advocates of the doctrines of the French school came
to have a hard time of it in England as the eighteenth
century drew towards its close. Even as early as 1784
there is a scornful reference in a poem on Shakespeare
to

> " The self-plumed tribe of modern Gaul,
> Whose powdered critics join at fashion's call
> To mock with feeble light thy noon-tide rays." [1]

The one conclusion which the survey of eighteenth-
century criticism brings out, above all, is that the
appreciation of Shakespeare's art was a growth which
steadily increased as a consequence of the increase of
familiarity with his plays. In the latter half of the preceding century any real knowledge of his writings was
limited to but few. His works were not accessible to
the generality of men. They were contained as a whole
in large and necessarily expensive folios, incorrectly
printed, and, strictly speaking, not edited at all. These
volumes not many had the means to buy, and none had
the now existing aids to understand. Furthermore the
editions were too limited in the number of their copies
to give a large circulation to his works. For most

[1] From a 'Rhapsody' on Shakespeare, written at Stratford-on-Avon,
and published in a volume (1784) containing as the principal poem
'Abelard to Eloisa,' by T. Warwick. It is printed in full in the 'European Magazine' for July, 1784, vol. vi. p. 55.

men acquaintance with his plays was made through the medium of stage representation, and was restricted to the comparatively few which were then acted. This state of things made it possible for writers to steal much from his less-known pieces with little fear of detection, and then imply or openly assert that they had stolen nothing. The impudence and audacity with which this was occasionally done is so great as to awaken a certain feeling of respect. In 1682 Durfey converted 'Cymbeline' into a play entitled 'The Fatal Wager.' Not the slightest indication was given of its origin. The name of Shakespeare appears neither on the title-page nor anywhere else. Even the effect of the intimation in the prologue that the play was a revived one was destroyed by the statement in the epilogue that the piece had been written nine years before. Similarly the version of 'The Taming of the Shrew,' attributed to the actor, Lacy, which was entitled 'Sawney the Scot,' contains no reference whatever to the original author. This may have been accident; for the reputed adapter had been long dead when the comedy was printed. But in this matter the palm for bold impudent lying must be awarded to Crowne. In the dedication of the first part of his 'Henry VI.' to Sedley, he declared that he used his patron's name to support his venture through the press, as he had previously used Shakespeare's to support it on the stage. Yet Shakespeare, he added, had no title to the fortieth part of the play. As even the slightest comparison would have disclosed the falsity of the statement, its utterance must be regarded both as a tribute to the influence of Shakespeare's name with the public, and as a testimony to their ignorance of his less-known writings.

All this condition of things underwent change, as soon as critical editions of Shakespeare plays began to follow one another, beginning with Rowe's of 1709. As these became more numerous, the ability to have his works in one's own possession came within the reach of all. Hence the critical cant which had once run almost unchallenged began to come in contact with the independent judgment of a cultivated class who formed their opinions by a direct study of the writings of the dramatist. To this was due the growing dislike of the alterations which has been already mentioned. To it was due the growing recognition of his greatness as a writer of comedy as well as of tragedy. For a long period ' The Merry Wives of Windsor' was frequently, perhaps usually, spoken of as his best work in the former kind of composition. This was partly because in character and treatment it approaches nearer to that Plautian and Terentian model which the classicists held sacred than plays like ' The Tempest,' ' Twelfth Night,' and ' As You Like It,' which ascend wholly or at intervals into a higher spiritual atmosphere.

Still how late was the development of the critical appreciation of Shakespeare can be seen in the view taken at different periods of his female characters. One can hardly enlarge upon the beauty of these now without subjecting himself to the reproach of uttering commonplace. In foreign as well as English-speaking lands men of the highest order of mind have paid them the tribute of unquestioning homage. No literature of

369

the imagination presents a gallery of portraits like those of Miranda, Juliet, Portia, Imogen, Isabella, and a score besides, each one distinctly different from the rest, but in their different ways all alike beautiful. We recognize their charm so plainly that it would seem a matter of wonder that it could escape the notice of the blindest observer. Yet a view which appears to us a mere matter of course did not so strike our ancestors. The admiration now so universally felt is but a little more than a century old, at least as regards its expression. Venturesome as it is to affirm a negative — I therefore speak it under correction — I am fairly confident that critical literature for the more than hundred years which followed the Restoration will be searched in vain for a passage implying the slightest recognition of the purity, the delicacy, and the loftiness of the female characters of Shakespeare. He received unbounded credit for his skill in characterization, but it was always the characterization of his masculine heroes.

In truth, for a long period either nothing whatever is said about the heroines, or what is said is distinctly derogatory. Rymer's contemptuous mention of Desdemona has already been given.[1] She fared no better at the hands of Gildon. He looked upon Otway, whom he called his master, as unquestionably superior in the portrayal of female character. " 'T is true," he wrote, " every man can not succeed in every passion; some that touch those that are the more manly with energy and force enough, are awkward and calm in the more tender. Shakespeare that drew Othello so finely has

[1] See p. 278.

made but a scurvy piece of Desdemona; and Otway alone seemed to promise a master in every kind." [1] He reiterated this view a few years later in his remarks on the plays of Shakespeare. "It must be owned," he wrote, "that Shakespeare drew men better than women, to whom indeed he has seldom given any considerable place in his plays." No one needs to be told that the criticism in the first clause is as well founded as the fact asserted in the last. Yet neither is by any means unexampled. Years before Rowe had implied a not dissimilar view of the dramatist's powers in the prologue to his tragedy of 'The Ambitious Stepmother.' In that occur the following lines: —

> "Shakespeare, whose genius to itself a law,
> Could men in every height of nature draw
> And copied all but women that he saw."

Ridiculous as this opinion may seem to us, it was long the belief of many and possibly of most. Montesquieu, who was in England in 1730, records a conversation in which Queen Caroline took part on occasion of his presentation at the court. It turned on the dramas of Shakespeare. The queen asked Lord Chesterfield, who was present, why it was that Shakespeare had made his women talk so wretchedly and act so like fools. Chesterfield had his answer ready, and Montesquieu regarded it as satisfactory as far as it went. Women, he said, did not appear on the stage in the time of Elizabeth. Their parts were taken by bad actors, and therefore the writers did not put forth any pains to make them speak well. For good all-round ignorance

[1] Preface to 'Love's Victim' (1701).

this explanation is hard to equal. Montesquieu thought he could better it by contributing still another reason. In order to make women talk well, he observed, it is necessary to know the usages of the world and the manners of good society. To have men talk like heroes, it is only necessary to study books.[1] This conclusion left Shakespeare in what he himself would have called a parlous case. According to the general opinion of his critics, he knew nothing worth speaking of about books. As a consequence he could not draw men. On the other side he was shut out from high society. Accordingly he could not draw women.

Montesquieu can be excused for accepting and even improving upon the opinion of others in a matter about which he himself knew nothing at all. It is clear that the views he reported were current. They strike us now as almost inconceivably silly. Yet Queen Caroline was very far from being a fool. In the knowledge of literature we know that she surpassed immeasurably her grandson who thought that so much of Shakespeare was sad stuff. Chesterfield too, limited in many ways as was his taste, was destitute of neither sense nor insight. We can in truth almost pardon the lack of appreciativeness in them when we find a professed student of the dramatist expressing not essentially dissimilar views. "Shakespeare," wrote Upton, "seems to me not to have known such a character as a fine lady; nor does he ever recognize their dignity. . . . Instead of the Lady Bettys and Lady Fannys, who shine so much in modern comedies, he brings you on the stage plain Mrs. Ford and

[1] Œuvres de Montesquieu, vol. vii. p. 358 (ed. of 1822).

Mrs. Page, two honest good-humored wives of two plain country gentlemen. His tragic ladies are rather seen than heard; such as Miranda, Desdemona, Ophelia, and Portia." [1] Further he observed that the less that women appear on the stage, generally the better is the story; and unmarried women are left entirely out in his best plays, as in ' Macbeth,' ' Othello,' ' Julius Cæsar.' This must be regarded as most extraordinary criticism, that is, if anything in criticism can be deemed extraordinary. There is a hopeless, helpless imbecility about it which makes us realize that Shakespeare did not have to wait till later times to exercise his peculiar power of turning the brains of even sensible men and making them talk unmitigated drivel. For Upton was a scholar and in some ways a man of decided ability. He had read, furthermore, the works he thus criticised, even though he had read them to so little purpose. If such a man could entertain such an opinion, we need not wonder at the prevalence of mistaken beliefs on the part of others who derived the little knowledge they had of Shakespeare from hearsay.

It is not until 1775 that I have come across a view of Shakespeare's female characters at all resembling the one now universally held. It occurs in a fragmentary poem contained in a novel which came out that year entitled ' The Correspondents.' This consisted of letters which purport to have passed between Lord Lyttleton, who had died two years before, and the woman who became the wife of his son. The correspondence was spurious, but for a while was deemed genuine in certain

---

[1] Critical Observations on Shakespeare (1746), p. 83.

quarters, and on that account occasioned a certain degree of interest. But it excited then more attention and deserves more now for the tribute it paid to the skill of the dramatist in delineating female character. The writer of the work was probably a woman; but whether so or not, the poem mentioned celebrated in the most glowing terms the fact that wise unerring nature had made Shakespeare both the judge and friend of womankind. The innocence of Miranda, the virgin-honor of Isabella, the filial affection of Cordelia, the wisdom of Portia, in fine, all the characteristics of the various female characters that appear in his pages, are made the subject of recognition and of eulogy. Contemporary criticism in the leading magazine of the day spoke of this piece of poetry as having placed Shakespeare "in a new point of view." [1]

Undoubtedly similar opinions had been entertained long before, even though not expressed. They were, so to speak, in the air. Le Tourneur, about this time engaged in the translation of Shakespeare into French, and a man evidently of peculiar delicacy and refinement, was struck by the beauty of these female characters, and so expressed himself when his version appeared. Even the year before the novel just mentioned came out, Richardson had devoted to Imogen one of the essays in his volume on the characters of Shakespeare. It was not indeed a very illuminating or inspiring treatise. We hardly feel ourselves much advanced when we are told, as he tells us, that " if we

---

[1] Gentleman's Magazine, August, 1775, vol. xlv. p. 371. The poem can be found on p. 394.

see a man deeply affected, we are persuaded that he has suffered some dreadful calamity or that he believes it to be so." Still these occasional outbreaks of the platitudinous ought not to hinder our recognition of the fact that he regarded the heroine of Cymbeline as more distinctly worthy of study than the men who appear in that play. Some years later to his treatise dealing with certain other personages of the Shakespearean drama, Richardson appended a general disquisition about the female characters found in it, in the guise of a letter to a friend. The friend, whether real or imaginary, had taken the then common ground that these characters were inferior to the male ones portrayed by the poet. It was a view which Richardson stoutly combated. His antagonist, it must be confessed, was an easy prey; and some of the opinions ascribed to him are so absurd that it seems as if they could not have been invented, but must have been the production of a real personage. It was not, however, the contents of this so-called letter that make it noteworthy. It is the fact that it is the first professional estimate of the kind in our literature; that it is the first instance in which criticism exhibits perception of an excellence which it would seem to have required peculiar dulness to miss.

The growth of the appreciation of Shakespeare was far from being confined to the estimate taken of the female characters he had portrayed. It extended all along the line. We have seen how belief in the cardinal principles of the school which upheld the regular drama had been slowly but steadily sapped during the eighteenth century, and maintained nothing but a lingering life as it reached its close. But though the house was being swept and garnished, its rightful occupant had not yet come to take possession. It is only in Maurice Morgann's essay on the dramatic character of Sir John Falstaff that I seem to see indicated dimly the view of Shakespeare which was developed in the nineteenth century, and which reigns triumphant to-day. The agencies which had been working for it had been in existence from the beginning, but they then worked under the surface rather than in the open day. It was not advocated by any body of persons like the two just described, constituting distinct critical classes. Yet its influence can be traced even when it was least apparent. Animated by that ardent devotion with which a great writer inspires his adherents, it took the ground, either avowedly or by implication, that the censures passed upon Shakespeare were unjustifiable; that the things for which he was condemned were the things for which he should be praised; and that the criticism which represented him as being deficient in art was itself based upon ignorance of what really constituted art. It must be admitted that it was at first a blind faith rather than one which rested upon knowledge. It contented itself with believing in Shakespeare; it rarely went farther than to maintain that anything which Shakespeare did was right because it was what Shakespeare did.

From the very outset, however, this view was felt even where it was not distinctly perceived. While it did not proclaim itself openly, it exhibited the disposition to resent any attack that was made upon its favorite. Dryden, full of praise as he was for his great predecessor, fell under severe censure for the attitude which he at first occasionally ventured to take. As time passed on, this disposition became more pronounced. Pope complained of it. Whether he did so in pretence or earnest is of no consequence, so long as his words bear witness to the fact itself. In what seems to us a peculiarly unnecessary protest against the preference exhibited in his own day for the writers of the past, he took occasion to pay his respects to those who insisted that Shakespeare should receive praise for practices which really merited condemnation. He professed indignation that men should censure modern works, not because they were bad, but because they were new;

> " While if our elders break all reason's laws,
>   These fools demand not pardon, but applause."

That the allusion was here to the dramatist is made further evident by the fact that these lines immediately precede the following passage in which direct reference is made to the criticism to which those became subject who presumed to point out errors in Shakespeare's writings : —

> " On Avon's bank, where flowers eternal blow,
>   If I but ask if any weed can grow;
>   One tragic sentence if I dare deride
>   Which Betterton's grave action dignified,
>   Or well-mouthed Booth with emphasis proclaims,
>   Though but perhaps a muster-roll of names,
>   How will our fathers rise up in a rage,
>   And swear all shame is lost in George's age !"[1]

The necessity of conforming the sentiments of his imitation to those of the Latin original compelled Pope

[1] Imitations of Horace, Epistle to Augustus (1737), lines 119–126.

to ascribe to the fathers what could have been true of his immediate contemporaries only, and to give to their feelings also too heightened a color. But, however exaggerated his words may be as a representation of the view generally entertained in his age, as unquestionably they are exaggerated, they had a certain foundation of fact then, and have now become essentially exact as a representation of the view prevalent to-day. The sweep of the revolution which has taken place during the more than one hundred and fifty years that have gone by since they were written, could find no better illustration of itself than in the reception which would now be accorded to criticisms of the kind which have been quoted in the preceding pages. No one is likely at the present day to entertain the opinions contained in the passages cited; at least he can be relied on, in that case, not to express them, if he has any regard for his own reputation. For the feeling that with us holds Shakespeare as practically faultless is even more tyrannical than that which once pronounced him as abounding in faults. It endures no contradiction. It is inclined to be impatient with anything which savors of even the mildest form of criticism. Nor does it base itself any longer upon mere sentiment. It rests, according to its own full conviction, upon scientific demonstration. It insists that Shakespeare's work was not, as was one time the common cry, a result due to the agency of a gigantic natural force, acting independently of law, but of one in which truth to nature has had added unto it the perfection of highest art.

CHAPTER X

SHAKESPEARE AS DRAMATIST AND MORALIST

HARDLY a generation passes in which some one —
frequently some one of considerable ability and reputation — does not come forward to show us the utter
insufficiency of Shakespeare; to inform us that he is
obsolete; to demonstrate in the most incontrovertible
way that the interest in his productions is purely factitious, begotten of traditional beliefs and prejudices, kept
alive not by any real liking, but by a blind unreasoning
faith in the duty to admire. Were his works now
brought out for the first time, divested consequently of
the repute which has gathered about them from the com-
mendations of successive generations, we are assured
that they would meet with scant success upon the stage,
if indeed with any success at all. A modern audience
would not care for them; in all probability it would
refuse to give them more than a single trial.

This is the doctrine which has been preached at frequent intervals during the past two hundred years.
Two or three illustrations of it have been given in the
course of this work. It turns up, indeed, with the regularity of certain epidemics. It is preached, too, with all
that fervor of conviction which so often does duty for
reason and truth. Occasionally some are impressed by
it; at least they think they are. Its futility, however,

is shown by the fact that nobody ever takes serious offence at it or at him who proclaims it. One would as soon think of feeling indignation at the man who denies the doctrine of gravitation or insists that the sun revolves about the earth. The world accordingly listens with a sort of pleased wonder at this regularly recurring exposure of Shakespeare's pretensions as a dramatist. It is inclined to approve of the utterance of these speculations which disturb temporarily the monotony of established beliefs. It is entertained for a while by the criticism; it is often struck with an honest admiration for the cleverness of the critic. Then it proceeds to forget what is written, and in process of time to forget its writer.

In contrast with all the other writers for the English stage one fact in the case of Shakespeare stands out conspicuously. No year goes by without witnessing the performance of some of his plays somewhere. We do not need to stop even here. Not a year has gone by since the theatre was re-opened at the Restoration, which has not seen pieces of his acted. No other playwright of our tongue has such a record. The assertion used once to be made, and is sometimes repeated now, that Garrick was the first to make Shakespeare popular. Nothing could be farther from the truth. That greatest of actors undoubtedly did much to deepen the impression which the greatest of dramatists had already made upon the theatre-going public. His wonderful impersonations of certain characters gave to many a clearer and higher conception of the meaning and power that lay in the words he recited. But while he strengthened the interest men felt, he was very far from being the first to create it. Long before Garrick was born, Shakespeare had been constantly styled the matchless, the inimitable, the divine. Ample testimony can be produced from the latter part of the seventeenth century to establish the fact of his increasing popularity; to prove how steadily he had even then passed all other playwrights in the general estimation, leaving behind him in particular, Fletcher, who for a while had been preferred by the ordinary mass of theatre-goers, and Ben Jonson, whose superiority had been insisted upon by the select few. Early in the eighteenth century the dramatist, John Hughes, bore witness to the still earlier reputation of the great master. Writing to the 'Guardian' in the character of an old man, he expressed his pleasure above all things "in observing that the tragedies of Shakespeare, which in my youthful days have so frequently filled my eyes with tears, hold their rank still and are the great support of the theatre." [1]

Every generation has its temporary dramatic favorites; at times, even every year. They come and go. Shakespeare always remains. They are cried up for a while and then neglected. He alone endures. His greatness as a poet will explain the constantly increasing circulation of his works in the world of readers. In that as in other things he has broken all records. It was as true of him at the beginning as it is now. That he was the most popular dramatist of his time, while he was writing for the stage, admits of no real question, though it has sometimes been questioned. But it is further true that his plays, so far as they were allowed to be printed,

[1] No. 37, April 23, 1713.

proved as successful with readers as they were with auditors. It is to be kept in mind that not only was the population of England then comparatively small, but also that the proportion of those interested in books was comparatively smaller than now. Nearly all the dramatists whose productions were published had to be content with a single edition. Occasional exceptions there are in the case of particular plays: but they are only occasional. The fact was true in most instances of Ben Jonson, at the very time he ranked at the head of English men of letters. It was not true of Shakespeare. Of the sixteen plays which were published in quarto form during his lifetime, the large majority appeared before his death in more than one edition, five of them in several. The only author of the whole period who has approached anywhere his success in this respect was Fletcher; and Fletcher's success, so far as it went, did not take place until he had been some time in his grave. A like statement is true of the complete editions of the plays. Shakespeare was the first dramatist of his time whose works public interest caused to be brought out in a collected form; for the production of the Ben Jonson folio of 1616 was the act of the author himself, and not of his admirers. Furthermore, when once published, no one of his contemporaries equalled him in the frequency of republication during the century in which his death took place. Since that century no one has approached him even distantly. He is so far first that there is no second in sight.

But while the inherent worth of his matter will account for his popularity with those who read, it cannot altogether explain the hold which he has retained upon those who come merely to hear. The recital of beautiful poetry is sure to be attractive to a certain limited number, but unaided it will never keep long the attention of the great mass of men. How then shall we account for the continued success of Shakespeare as a writer not for the closet but for the stage? For even here he has done much more than retain the grasp which he early acquired over the prepossessions of his own race in his favor. Interest in his pieces as acting pieces has extended over no small share of the civilized world. It has triumphed over the disadvantage of translation. And desirous as are men to see his works played, equally desirous are men to play them. No aspiring actor of our race feels that he has won his spurs, that he has achieved the highest distinction in his art, until he has made his mark in some Shakespearean character. This is true at least of the tragic stage. Other playwrights make demand upon histrionic ability: to gain pre-eminent success in Shakespearean representation evinces histrionic genius. So it has been in the past; so it will be in the future. In the history of the English theatre there is not a tragedian of the first rank, from the days of Betterton to the present time, whose name is not associated with some of the plays of the greatest of English dramatists. None the less his total unfitness to satisfy the requirements of the modern audience will be demonstrated again and again. But his works will continue to be performed long after these successive demonstrations of his unfitness to please have passed entirely from the memory of men.

For this world-wide and constantly increasing success there is but one rational explanation. I have sought to show in the preceding chapters that Shakespeare was not only a great dramatic artist, but that—so far at least as English literature is concerned—he is the great dramatic artist. In that fact lies the secret of his hold upon successive generations of the men of his own race, and of the extension of it over the men of alien races. It is the perfection of his art which has enabled his productions to outlive the hostile criticism which once decried his methods as irregular, and the results as monstrous. Of all the idle suppositions, in the infinite number of idle suppositions which have been put forth about Shakespeare, none is more baseless than the one which so long held sway, that he was an intellectually irresponsible man of genius, who wrote solely under the pressure of circumstances, or under the compulsion of a momentary overwhelming inspiration, doing his work without being conscious of what it was he did or why he did it. It almost passes human comprehension to imagine how any one could have read with care the second scene of the second act of 'Hamlet' and not have recognized the profound interest the dramatist took in his art, as well as his knowledge of its theory. Yet this indifference and ignorance on his part was the cant of the one hundred and fifty years that followed the Restoration. Nor has it yet died out entirely, though uttered now with bated breath and faltering voice. We begin at last to recognize the applicability to Shakespeare of Lessing's dictum, that while the great critic may not be a great poet, the great poet is invariably a great critic.

By this he means he judges scrutinizingly the methods he adopts, and does not adopt them unless approved by his judgment. Whatever he does, therefore, is done consciously. The conclusions he reaches may be wrong. If wrong, he must abide by the consequences of his mistakes. But if the great artist choose erroneously, he likewise chooses deliberately. It is never with him a haphazard blundering either upon the wrong or the right.

Time has largely swept away the cloud of learned detraction which once gathered about the name of Shakespeare under the guise of upholding art. We are coming to recognize that the course he followed was not due to his ignorance of the rules upon which his critics insisted, but upon his knowledge of their inapplicability. His independence he showed in other ways. We have the right, for instance, to infer, not merely from his general but from his particular conduct, that he cared nothing for that laborious and pedantic trifling which aims to make the creations of the imagination conform to the results — the frequently changing results also — of the latest historical and archæological investigation. It is quite clear from Ben Jonson's words that his endowment of Bohemia with a sea-coast had provoked contemporary criticism. It is hardly possible to suppose him to have remained ignorant of the mistake. Yet he clearly did not take it to heart: he certainly never troubled himself to have the passage altered. Greene's authority was enough for him, as it was for putting Delphos on an island. Unquestionably there is a point beyond which the defiance of the known and actual ought never to go.

But it is a point that varies from age to age. It must always be fixed by the knowledge which the ordinary reader or hearer may be presumed to have then, not by the more accurate knowledge of which later times may become possessed. This view needs to be insisted upon in an age like the present, when writers of works of imagination seem too often to feel themselves constrained to make their facts accord precisely with the conclusions of scholarly research, and in consequence spend strength upon collecting tithes of mint and anise and cumin, with the inevitable result of neglecting the weightier matters of the law. It is the business of the poet or the novelist to paint men; it is of altogether secondary importance to paint their costumes.

But if time has vindicated the artistic truthfulness of Shakespeare's practice, the vindication it has brought does not involve the assumption that he invariably lived up to his own ideals. However conformable to the highest art were his general methods, few there are who will be disposed to maintain that he committed no errors of detail. His most enthusiastic admirers have not sought to deny the occurrence in his writings of things reprehensible and indefensible. All which they have protested against is the disposition to attach to these lapses a consequence which is out of all proportion to their real importance. Shakespeare's indulgence in that lowest form of intellectual depravity, quibbles and plays upon words, cannot be questioned. It was the literary vice of his time. Several of his greatest contemporaries were addicted to it also. But in an age where most men were vicious, he was the most vicious of all. Furthermore, this belief in the conformity of his methods with the requirements of the highest art is consonant with the admission that inaccuracies and inadvertences appear not unfrequently in his works. There are a number of instances where, owing either to rapidity of composition, or to inattention, or to subsequent alteration, a fact or a condition of things in one part of the play is not made congruous with a fact or condition in another part. To reconcile these discrepancies commentators have felt themselves obliged to put forth labored explanations. It was at one time not an unfrequent practice with them to impute inconsistencies of this sort — in fact, anything else to which they took a dislike — to the unauthorized interpolations of actors. This may have been true in some instances; it can hardly have been true in all. At best the assumption is a purely conjectural one ; and so long as not a particle of evidence can be adduced in its support, we are forbidden to plead any such defence for what appears.

Far worse than these — which even when taken collectively are of little real importance — are occasionally found serious violations of the truth of life. These abound in the works of many, one might fairly say of most, dramatists. They are infrequent in Shakespeare ; but they nevertheless occur. Such, for instance, is the offer of Valentine to surrender the woman he loves and who loves him to the faithless Proteus who has deserted his own mistress and acted a treacherous part towards his friend.[1] The conviction of the impropriety of this representation has been so general that efforts of all

[1] Two Gentlemen of Verona, act v. sc. 4.

387

sorts have been put forth to explain away a proceeding which is as indefensible dramatically as it is morally. The jurist Blackstone proposed to transfer the speech to Thurio. Coleridge had no doubt of the passage being corrupt, or at least unfinished. By others we are told that the offer is characteristic of the romantic ideas prevalent in that day as to the obligations which the tie of friendship imposed. But this is a tribute which love could never have paid to friendship in any period. Furthermore, it would have been morally wrong to have paid it here; for it affected the lives of others as well as that of the man who makes the offer. Even could it be accepted as a true picture of the feelings and ideas of some particular century, its appearance in this place gives it a character of universality. It is therefore inexcusable. Shakespeare was not of an age, but for all time. His representation of life should in consequence be true of all time. Such it usually is; and it has survived because it is independent of changes of taste or custom.

There are found in his works a few such variations from what we feel to be just and natural, though perhaps none so noticeable as this. They belong to details, and not to any single work as a whole. To this there is one exception, — the comedy of ' All 's Well that Ends Well.' It is a play which has never met with much favor on the modern stage. First revived by Giffard, in 1741, at his theatre in Goodman's Fields, it was acted, a few times after that, during the rest of the century, at both Drury Lane and Covent Garden. But the success it met with, such as it was, came mainly

from the representation of Parolles and the episode of
his exposure and disgrace. It was but little due to the
interest inspired by the story itself or by its chief characters. Not even the genius of Shakespeare has been
equal to making men accept with pleasure the plot of
this comedy, or to respond very warmly to the eulo-
giums passed upon the heroine, worthy of admiration
as she is in many ways. Of the hero hardly any one
has ever been found to say a good word. "I cannot
reconcile my heart to Bertram," wrote Dr. Johnson:
" a man noble without generosity, and young without
truth; who marries Helen as a coward, and leaves her
as a profligate: when she is dead by his unkindness,
sneaks home to a second marriage, is accused by a
woman he has wronged, defends himself by falsehood,
and is dismissed to happiness." This hostile estimate,
in spite of its injustice, has set the style of most of the
comment upon the hero of the piece; while no amount
of praise has been thought too lavish to spend upon the
heroine.

As Bertram is drawn, it must be admitted that he
is not a highly estimable personage. Morally the best
thing to his credit is a high degree of merely brute
valor, while intellectually his lack of perspicacity makes
him an easy prey to the pretensions of a braggart and
a coward. But so far as his relations with the heroine
are concerned, there is a good deal to be said on his
side. He has forced upon him a wife he does not
desire. Not merely are his own inclinations disregarded, but his pride of birth is outraged. He is a
victim, and by no means a willing victim. He natu-

rally hates the chains which have been imposed upon him by a power to which he is constrained to submit. Nor can any excellence in Helen's character counterbalance the fundamental fact that she has been untrue to her sex. She persistently pursues a man who is not merely indifferent but averse. The situation is not made less, but even more disagreeable by its being a chase on her part of a man not worth following. All the explanations given of her conduct, all the tributes paid to her character, cannot veil the fact that she takes advantage of the favor of the king to do an essentially unwomanly act. Higher station or great superiority of fortune might justify a woman in going a long way in making advances to a lover of lower position, who for that very reason would naturally be reluctant to put forward his pretensions. But Helen has no such excuse. Whatever be her intellectual and moral excellence, she has nothing which he cares for to give to the husband upon whom she has forced herself in the face of his outspoken unwillingness. In real life we know how we should all think and feel in such a case. Our sympathies would not go out to the successful schemer, but to the hunted man who is compelled to have associated with him in the closest relation of life a woman for whom he feels dislike. So far from believing with Johnson that Bertram is dismissed to happiness, we may be sure that under ordinary conditions nothing but misery will be the fate of a couple where the consciousness of difference of station would add to the estrangement produced by difference of character, and where fraud has been the only agency to bring about the consummation of a union which could never have been effected in the first place save by force.

It is rarely the case, however, that Shakespeare outrages our feelings, as in the two instances just described. On the other hand, we have constant occasion to observe how vigilantly everything has been foreseen and cared for, so that nothing may jar upon our conceptions of the natural and the proper. Upon all the acts and actors in his drama was almost invariably fixed the keenest critical sense, though it was sometimes not the sense of later and inferior critics. No other dramatist in our tongue, in dealing with his characters, has been so uniformly consistent in the adaptation of means to ends, so solicitous to order events that nothing shall seem improbable or out of the way. In reading the works of many of his contemporaries we feel that the personages of their plays talk and act as in real life no rational beings could be expected to talk and act under the circumstances. They resort to the most unheard of and unnatural devices to bring about the results at which they aim. The moment, indeed, we subject to scrutiny a scene of Shakespeare's with a similar one attempted by an imitator, we recognize at once that careful preparation in the adaptation of means to ends which is characteristic of the highest art.

Contrast in this matter his ' Tempest ' with ' The Sea Voyage ' of Fletcher. In both plays it is necessary that the audience should be informed of how the situation depicted came to exist. In ' The Tempest ' it is done with the perfection of naturalness. Miranda has never heard the circumstances under which as a child she has been brought to the island. It is something which we should expect her to have learned long before. It was natural that she should have sought to know it; she tells us that she has made inquiry about it time and again. But the information has been withheld for satisfactory reasons until it became necessary that the audience should possess it as well as she. Accordingly nothing is said or done which is not fitting in itself and fitting to the occasion. In ' The Sea Voyage,' on the contrary, there is no trace of this careful art. There Sebastian proceeds in the crudest way to give Nicusa, his companion in misfortune, the fullest information as to how they both came there, though the one who is told knows just as much about it as the one who is telling him. In such a case it is really the author who is usurping a part for the benefit of the audience, not a character who is carrying on the proper business of the play.

Of this most common of sins against dramatic propriety — one indeed most difficult of all to shun — Shakespeare is very seldom guilty in even a venial form. His freedom from it was not the result of mere lucky accident. It was due to nothing less than the skilful evolution of a plot carefully planned and thoroughly thought out. It was this which led him to refrain from the introduction of speeches or circumstances that offend our sense of the congruous or fitting. He had not simply an intuitive perception of the minds of the personages he set out to portray, but a strength and sweep of imagination which enabled him to project himself into any situation in which they might be placed, to share their feelings, to think their thoughts, and to say their words. Hence it was that his contemporaries, as well as we, recognized the perfect propriety of everything that took place in his dramas. Hence it was that from the outset he came to be considered the representative of nature. The story he adopts for his theme may be improbable; it may even be impossible. That it should be one which would be accepted by his audience was all that he asked. So much given, he made no further demand upon human credulity. Every one acts as it is right and suitable he should act under the circumstances. He recognized that there is a limit in this respect beyond which the dramatist ought never to go. We accept the improbability of the plot. We give our faith to the fable, however extravagant, because the author has a prescriptive right to require it; because, furthermore, fiction cannot assume anything stranger than what fact actually presents. But while we accept improbability in the plot as a whole, what we do not accept is improbability in the details. We demand that the characters shall act in accordance with the motives which under the given conditions would and should dominate their conduct. The author must not seek to impose upon our belief a course of proceeding which experience and reason both teach us the character would never have adopted in real life.

Of course there is always danger of our being misled by our own limited knowledge and observation. Because a particular line of conduct would not be taken by men, as we see them about us, under ordinary conditions, it by no means follows that it would be unnatural in persons who are operated upon by agencies whose scope and power nothing in our own experience has furnished us with the means of judging. Much of the mistaken criticism which has been applied to the acts of Shakespeare's characters is due either to imperfect comprehension of the personage portrayed, or to imperfect acquaintance with the behavior of men under exceptional circumstances. The commentator too frequently considers ordinary course of conduct as universal, and ordinary feelings as ruling ones under extraordinary conditions. One critic accordingly takes exception to the naturalness of certain proceedings in one place; another critic to something else in another place. These are usually the misapprehensions of those who draw their inferences from their own limited observation of life, and not from Shakespeare's limitless knowledge.

Of the scores of mistaken judgments of this sort that might be cited, let us take one from ' Lear.' Joseph Warton, in the course of a criticism upon that tragedy, brought as an objection to it the utter improbability of Gloucester's imagining, though blind, that he had thrown himself from the summit of Dover cliff.[1] The objection has been repeated in the present century by a commentator generally so clear-headed as Hunter.[2] It was regarded at the time by Colman as a just exception, and affected his action. In his adaptation of ' Lear ' he threw out this scene, though he retained the description of the cliff, which had really

[1] The Adventurer, No. 122, Jan. 5, 1754.
[2] Illustrations of Shakespeare, vol. ii. p. 273.

no business in the play, if Gloucester was not supposed to leap from it. Here it is, as usual, that Shakespeare exhibits his superiority to his critics, who did not study the personages he portrayed with the insight he applied to their conception. Gloucester's character and acts are consistent throughout. He is an easy victim to superstition. His own son speaks of him as credulous by nature. He expresses faith in the effects of planetary influence at which the evil-minded but far abler Edmund scoffs. There is nothing which a man of this temperament cannot be made to believe against the evidence of his senses, even under ordinary conditions. But the conditions here are not ordinary. Gloucester has been passing through terrible experiences, which have already unsettled the powers both of mind and body. All that has happened tends to overthrow the natural conclusions of the judgment. That he could be persuaded that he had not only fallen, but that he had been tempted by a fiend to throw himself headlong from the summit of the cliff is exactly in line with his whole previous conduct. Shakespeare saw it and acted upon it. Warton, not having the ability to see it, censured him for a course he failed to comprehend.

This concludes all that need be said of Shakespeare's art, so far as the criticisms of it are concerned which have been based upon purely intellectual considerations. But there remains another point about which controversy gathered constantly during the century and more that followed the Restoration. Even to this day we find it occasionally renewed. It is the attack which has been made upon his course from the side of morality. Its character must not be misapprehended. It has nothing to do with the presence in his pages of occasional coarseness and vulgarity. It is his frequent violation of what is termed poetic justice which here comes under review. It is his practice of leaving the guilty unpunished and the innocent unrewarded that has provoked some of the severest criticism to which he has been subjected as a moral teacher. This is wholly independent of the question whether the play itself is of a virtuous or vicious tendency. It concerns itself entirely with the fate which in the catastrophe is assigned to the various personages of the drama. But before entering upon the discussion of the question itself, it is desirable to prepare the way for it by a consideration of both the specific and the general attitude which Shakespeare exhibits towards morality.

It is to be said at the outset that as Shakespeare's art was more free from offences against dramatic propriety than that of his contemporaries or of his successors, so it is of a distinctly higher moral tone. The continued increase of his fame is in no small measure due to this fact. The unchanging deference which is paid to the pure in literature is a tribute of itself to the permanent hold which high things have over the human heart. Shakespeare is pre-eminently a moral poet. This is stated with the full consciousness that there are passages in his writings — and by no means so infrequent as some think — which might fairly seem to convey an exactly opposite impression. I am not referring to the familiar fact of terms in lapse of time becoming coarse by association, though they have no essential coarseness in themselves; nor again to the use of direct and plain expressions where modern nicety demands euphemistic ones. Both these occur; but they are mere accidents of convention: in the domain of morals they deserve no attention. The fault is of an altogether different nature. It is the occurrence in his writings of gross and licentious allusions, which would be reckoned as such, no matter in what age they appeared, or in what disguise of language they were clothed.

In this he acted no differently from his fellow-dramatists. Though Shakespeare was a writer for all time, as was long ago said by the greatest of his rivals, he was likewise, in some particulars, the child of his age. He reflected occasionally the worst characteristics of his period, as more often he embodied the deepest convictions and loftiest aspirations of the race. He was influenced by the same moral or immoral forces which were operating upon all his contemporaries. In any consideration of the Elizabethan drama it will never do to lose sight of the fact that it was then the representative national literature. The writers for the stage were under the influence of every class in the community, from the highest to the lowest. It would be a gross error to assume, as was constantly assumed in the eighteenth century, that the latter made up the main or even a very important element of the audience. That matchless poetry which later times have often imitated but never equalled; those lofty passages which linger in the memory, though the truths they convey may have no influence upon the life, — these were never written for unappreciative ears; they were never delivered to men who did not acknowledge and act upon the highest motives. But while in many respects the theatre represented what was noblest and purest in the national life and character, it certainly catered at times to what was lowest. For the high it was high; for the pure it was pure; for the vulgar it was vulgar. From this point of view it did not differ essentially from the modern newspaper, which puts forward the claim, sometimes in express words, more frequently in its practice, that within certain limits it must satisfy all classes in the community. It is further to be borne in mind that while the Elizabethan age was one of greatness in many respects, it was also an age of plain-spokenness which too often assumed the nature of coarseness. Delicacy in many modern senses of the word seems to have been a thing almost unknown; while the squeamishness which with us occasionally goes under that garb was something that was not even dreamed of then.

The most ardent admirer of Shakespeare must concede that he was not wholly free from that tendency to pander at times to man's baser nature, which the Puritans regarded as the inherent vice of all theatrical representation. In him, as in other playwrights of his period, there is a certain proportion of licentious utterance, introduced apparently for no other purpose than to gratify the taste of the vilest of the populace. Attention has been called to the fact that he sometimes falls below the highest standard of art in consequence of his addiction to verbal quibbles. It is in connection with these that the matter objectionable on the score of impurity is very generally found. It is perhaps in accordance with the everlasting proprieties that the passages which are most offensive morally should be also the most execrable intellectually. Happily many of the vilest of these plays upon words escape, as a general rule, the notice of the ordinary reader. This is partly because of the inexpressible wretchedness of the verbal quibbles in which their meaning is wrapped up, and partly for the reason that changes which have taken place in the signification of words hide now the obscenity which was at the time plainly apparent. Most of us in reading them pass over them without the slightest suspicion of the nature of the ground upon which we are treading. Even great commentators have revealed both their innocence and their ignorance in laborious efforts they have put forth to explain the passages in which they are found. The indecency which lurks in them is couched in allusions which time has made so impenetrably obscure that the words give as little shock to the sense as if they were uttered in an unknown tongue.

Still this stain upon Shakespeare's writings exists, even though it does not go very deep. All students of the dramatist will concede it. But while this can be granted, it is easy to draw utterly mistaken conclusions from the admission. The passages which are objectionable on the score of their licentiousness are, in the first place, almost invariably of a low intellectual grade. There is still another gratifying tribute which morality is enabled to pay to the saving grace of stupidity. These passages have rarely any close connection with the proper business of the play. They are not essential to carrying forward its action. Hence they can usually be dropped in representation without attracting the slightest attention whatever. Their absence is not felt as an injury either to the development of the plot or to its comprehension. There is no dramatist who lends himself more easily than Shakespeare to expurgation, so far as expurgation is required, and who loses so little by it. In many of the plays of Fletcher, for instance, the indelicacy is ingrained into the very texture of the plot. It cannot be removed without utterly destroying the whole piece. This is far more visibly the fact in the comedy of the Restoration, often blazing with wit, brilliant with repartee, and alive with startling situations, but so shamelessly vicious in its whole nature that even out of detached scenes the modern stage can scarcely put together a production that would be tolerated by a modern audience. In Shakespeare, on the other hand, these offensive passages do not touch the inner life of the story. They are almost invariably excrescences upon the surface of the piece. The removal of them detracts nothing from its intellectual completeness, while it contributes to its moral perfection.

In Shakespeare, accordingly, there are coarse words which can be replaced by others equally expressive but not offensive. There are impure allusions which can be lopped away without injuring the context; and once gone they are never missed. These are the limits of his trespass. Against them can be placed, first, one merit in particular which outweighs in importance all such lapses. There are no indelicate situations. Furthermore, there is a peculiar refinement in his treatment of everything which concerns the relation of the sexes. In particular, the female characters drawn by him are of the loftiest type known to literature. In these respects he stands in sharpest contrast intellectually with all his contemporaries, and morally stands on an inconceivably higher plane than most of them. Still his greatness as a moral teacher does not consist in his conformity to conventions which, as a general rule, concern delicacy much more than virtue. It is when he comes to the consideration of questions affecting human life and conduct that we recognize his superiority as a guide. We feel then how fully he has penetrated into the most secret recesses of the heart, how intimate is his acquaintance with both the feelings and motives that influence us in what we do or fail to do, how complete is his knowledge of the real rewards and punishments which wait on human action, not on the fanciful ones which we in our shortsightedness would think proper to have bestowed. Once contemplating this side of his intellectual activity, those concessions to man's lower nature, which stain at intervals his writings, disappear alike from view and thought in the blaze of light with which he reveals to us the operation of the moral laws which regulate the government of the universe. One inevitable result of this deeper insight was his rejection of what is called poetical justice. This was something the men of the eighteenth century delighted to honor, though they honored it in a way not much to its credit. With them it had reference mainly to matters purely external. Virtue furthermore was rewarded, vice was punished, not so as to accord with what we know to be true in life, but what we should like to have true. To any such arbitrary and unreal disposition of events Shakespeare's art at once rose superior.

So far as I know, Rymer was the one who introduced into English criticism the doctrine of poetic justice, though playwrights had previously not neglected to conform to it in practice. Certainly he was the first to give it vogue. It was for their neglect of it that he found fault with the dramatists of the previous age. In his criticism of Beaumont and Fletcher's ' Rollo ' he proclaimed the superiority of poetical to historical justice. The former was to be observed, no matter how great had been the failure of the latter. Its satisfaction must be made complete before the malefactor went off the stage, and as he expressed it, "nothing left to God Almighty and another world." [1] The spectators must not trust the poet for a hell behind the scenes; its fire must roar in the faces of the criminals set before them, its fiends and furies must torture their consciences. In his preface to ' Don Sebastian ' Dryden defended his course in preserving the hero from death by appealing to this principle. An involuntary sin, of which alone this personage had been guilty, did not deserve so severe a penalty: "for," he continued, "the learned Mr. Rymer has well observed, that in all punishments we are to regulate ourselves by poetical justice." Playwrights

[1] Tragedies of the Last Age, p. 26.

indeed came to be very solicitous about conforming to this rule. In the dedicatory epistle prefixed to his 'Ambitious Stepmother' Rowe tells us that "that which they call the poetical justice is, I think, strictly observed." In truth, the doctrine once promulgated seems to have met with pretty general acceptance.

It was Dennis, however, who became its most earnest advocate. He, unlike Rymer, was a sincere admirer of Shakespeare, frequent as were his lamentations over the dramatist's ignorance of the poetic art. In nothing had the lack of this knowledge been attended with worse consequences than in his neglect to comply with the requirements of poetical justice. He pointed out in his 'Essay on the Genius and Writings of Shakespeare' how entirely that author had failed in the distribution of rewards and punishments in the tragedy of 'Coriolanus.' These errors he mentioned in detail. Coriolanus meets a deserved death, to be sure, for having been disloyal to his country. But his murderer Aufidius not only survives but survives unpunished. Though historic vengeance had never actually overtaken him, he should have been given up to poetic. Furthermore, this should have been the fate also of the two tribunes, Sicinius and Brutus, who had been instrumental by their mean and malicious artifices in bringing about the expulsion of the hero. Dennis did not content himself with criticism. In his altered version of the play he set out to remedy the oversight or neglect of the original author. This, after having been kept by him for nearly the Horatian period of nine years, was produced at Drury Lane in 1719. It ended with a duel between Coriolanus and Aufidius, in which the former kills the latter, but is in turn killed by the Volscians. Nor were the tribunes allowed to escape scot-free. The indignant citizens in the course of the play drive them towards the Tarpeian rock with the intent to hurl them from its summit. But Dennis relented before proceeding to this extremity; at least he left us in ignorance of their fate. However, he thus secured poetic justice all round; but he failed to secure favor for the altered play. To his great indignation it ran but three nights.

Dennis's criticism of this defect in Shakespeare was by no means limited to this particular production. He pointed out that the dramatist had been wanting in the exact distribution of poetical justice, not only in his 'Coriolanus,' but in most of his best tragedies. In them the guilty and the innocent perish indiscriminately. As a consequence there could be in them, in his opinion, no instruction or very weak instruction. "Such promiscuous events," he wrote, "call the government of providence into question, and by skeptics and libertines are resolved into chance." In these words lay the secret of this conventional criticism. That uneasy anxiety which besets men, even the best of them, to improve upon the methods of the Lord in the management of the universe was at the foundation of this demand for poetical justice. The effort to do for providence on the stage what providence had neglected to do for itself in real life can be traced for more than a century, not only in original pieces, but in the modifications to which the plays of Shakespeare were subjected on that account. As early as 1679 Dryden, in the preface to his alteration of 'Troilus and Cressida,' took credit to himself for having remedied some crying faults of this description. "Cressida is false," he wrote, "and is not punished." As the heroine of a tragedy ought not to be wicked, according to the critical theories then generally received, he elevated her character, and made her, though suspected, really faithful. She stabs herself in order to establish her innocence. Poetical justice is inflicted by him on the parties not merely guilty of acting, but even of thinking improperly. Diomede is killed in the play by Troilus for attempting the honor of Cressida, and for doubting it Troilus in turn is killed by Achilles.

So far as Shakespeare was directly concerned, however, the controversy on the subject concentrated itself mainly upon the treatment of the tragedy of 'Lear.' There were several violations of poetic justice committed by him in his other works. But in so doing he had followed his authorities, whether accredited history, or transmitted legend, or popular tale. His conduct could be explained either by his ignorance of the doctrine, or by his desire not to depart from the incidents of a story well known to his audience. But in the case of 'Lear' no such explanation was possible. Not only was poetic justice violated, but it was wantonly violated. The ending had been changed from a happy to an unhappy one; and changed, too, at a period when the monarch himself was still regarded by many, perhaps by most, as a genuine historical personage. The story had been first told in the twelfth century by Geoffrey of Monmouth. In his account Lear is restored to his sovereignty by the aid of Cordelia and her husband, the king of France. After his death she herself ascends the throne. This form of the legend — which for centuries was generally accepted as true history — is the only one known to the later chroniclers and poets from whom Shakespeare derived his materials. It is likewise the form followed in the old play of ' King Leir,' which had preceded his tragedy. Here was an instance where historic and poetic justice had exactly accorded. Of this agreement Shakespeare was so far from taking advantage that he may be said to have spurned it. There is no question that he deliberately altered the catastrophe. Tate in his version went back to a certain extent to the original narrative, not because he knew anything about it, but because he preferred a happy ending.

This alteration of Shakespeare's play, however well received by the theatrical public, called forth the condemnation of Addison. In one of his essays in the ' Spectator ' he censured the whole idea of poetical justice. He spoke of it most contemptuously as nothing but a ridiculous doctrine of modern criticism. Where it came from he could not tell; but he was sure it had no foundation in nature, or in reason, or in the practice of the ancients. Besides being false in theory, it was a failure in practice. The observance of the doctrine did not contribute to the favorable reception of a play. On the contrary, those in which the favorites of the audience sink under their calamities were in general more successful than those in which they emerge from them triumphant. "'King Lear,'" he continued, "is an admirable tragedy of the same kind, as Shakespeare wrote it; but as it is reformed, according to the chimerical notion of poetical justice, in my humble opinion it has lost half its beauty." [1]

Dennis by this time had come to be in a state of wrath with everything in general, and with everybody in particular who enjoyed more of the favor of the public than himself. The essay of Addison provoked at once an explosion. It ran counter to the doctrine he loved and taught and practised. He rebuked its author not only for his opinion, but for the insolent, dogmatic, and dictatorial way in which he had expressed it. To the 'Spectator' he addressed a number of letters which were appended to his 'Essay on the Genius and Writings of Shakespeare.' In the first of them he informed Addison that the person who originated this ridiculous doctrine of modern criticism was a modern who lived about two thousand years ago. It was no other than Aristotle himself. Poor Aristotle has had in his way a fortune as hard as Shakespeare's. He has been compelled to bear the repute of all the notions, whether sensible or silly, that men read into his writings or choose to infer from them. From Aristotle Dennis went on to say that the doctrine had been introduced into English by that noted authority, Mr. Rymer, "who, notwithstanding the rage of all the poetasters of the times, whom he has exasperated by opening the eyes of the blind that they may see their errors, will always pass with impartial posterity for a

[1] No. 40, April 16, 1711.

most learned, a most judicious and a most useful critic." [1]
It is fair to Dennis to add that he so broadened the
conception of poetic justice that a large number of the
instances in which Shakespeare had been charged with
its violation could have been included under his definition of the term.

To this outburst Addison, as usual, made no reply.
It was one of his most irritating characteristics. He
amused himself, indeed, in an essay, printed about a
week later than his previous one, by citing a couple of
lines which he called humorous, from a translation of
Boileau made by Dennis. [2] The reference suggested
the impression that he considered the critic a dunce;
but it could as legitimately be construed into a compliment. Dennis was puzzled by it; and though he could
not refrain from indulging in further comment, it is
clear he did not know how to take what was said.
Towards the close of the following year, when the
'Spectator' was nearing its end, Addison returned to
the subject. [3] He defended his former position, though
without mentioning his critic. Still, in spite of the
influence he wielded, men continued to respect and
writers to heed the doctrine. Long before this particular controversy Gildon in his preface to his 'Phaethon,
or the Fatal Divorce,' a tragedy brought out in 1698,
had proclaimed it the duty of the poet to reward the
innocent and punish the guilty, and by that means to
establish a just notion of providence in its most important action, the government of mankind. Twenty years

---

[1] Essay, pp. 38–48.   [2] Spectator, No. 47, April 24, 1711.
[3] Ibid. No. 548, Nov. 28, 1712.

later he patronizingly pointed out to Addison the falsity
of the criticism which had been made by him upon this
doctrine in the ' Spectator,' and quoted almost in full
Dennis's confutation, as he called it, of the error which
the essayist had fallen into in its denial.

In the case of ' Lear,' furthermore, men clung to the
altered catastrophe. This course on their part was, to
be sure, not always, or perhaps mainly, due to their
interest in this particular doctrine. "We still prefer the
happy ending," said a reviewer towards the end of the
eighteenth century; "reason opposes it; while the tortured feelings at once decide the contest." [1] Still the
idea of poetic justice involved in the alteration contributed somewhat to the favor with which it was received,
and was sometimes made prominent in the comments
upon the play. Cooke, for instance,— usually designated
as Hesiod Cooke,— devoted a number of pages to the
celebration of the moral teachings of ' Lear,' as exhibited
in Tate's version. [2] It showed, he observed, that the
all-wise disposer of things had from the beginning
annexed rewards to virtue and punishment to vice.
Such a criticism, if it proved nothing else, certainly
made clear that the all-wise disposer of things had not
thought it worth while to impart to the critic ordinary
observation of the facts of life. But throughout the
whole century discussion of poetical justice went on
more or less in connection with this play. It is evident
from the references in the periodical literature of the

---

[1] Critical Review, vol. lviii, p. 58 (1784).
[2] Considerations on the Stage, chap. ii., appended to ' Triumphs of
Love and Honour,' 1731.

time that Addison's words influenced many who would naturally have been carried by the current in the opposite direction.[1] As one illustration out of several that could be cited, Richardson, in defending the conclusion of 'Clarissa,' in the postscript to that novel, quoted in his favor the view of poetic justice taken by the essayist, and gave it his full assent.

With the opinions expressed by Addison in the 'Spectator,' a man, much more conspicuous than any of the petty critics mentioned, came forward to proclaim his disagreement. This was Dr. Johnson, the greatest moralist among the commentators of Shakespeare. The preface to his edition contained a general indictment of the course pursued by the dramatist in his distribution of rewards and punishments, and in his neglect of poetical justice. On this point, indeed, the censure culminated. Shakespeare, according to Johnson, sacrifices virtue to convenience, and is so much more solicitous to please than to instruct, that he seems to write without any moral purpose. His precepts and axioms drop from him casually. He carries his personages indifferently through right and wrong, dismisses them without care, and leaves their example to operate by chance, without having the lesson of the conduct they have displayed enforced upon the attention. Furthermore, he makes no just distinction of good and evil, nor is he always careful to show a disapprobation of the vicious on the part of the virtuous. Worse than all, he is wanting in what is termed poetic justice, according to which the evil man gets his deserts and the righteous is rewarded.

[1] For example, 'Gentleman's Magazine,' 1752, p. 253.

This had been illustrated particularly in the tragedy of 'Lear.' Johnson defended the alteration which had been made in the catastrophe of this play, and in so doing made use of an argument which, coming from another, he would have spurned contemptuously. "The public has decided," he said triumphantly. "Cordelia from the time of Tate has always retired with victory and felicity. And if my sensations could add anything to the general suffrage, I might relate, I was many years ago so shocked by Cordelia's death, that I know not whether I ever endured to read again the last scenes of the play till I undertook to revise them as editor."

It seems hard to believe that a man of Johnson's intellectual powers should have thought it desirable that Shakespeare should have "improved" — to use the technical language of homiletics — every occasion that presented itself for enforcing ethical instruction. Yet the words he employs both here and elsewhere seem naturally to bear this interpretation. In his criticism upon 'As You Like It' he remarks that in consequence of hastening to the end the great dramatist had "suppressed the dialogue between the usurper and the hermit, and lost an opportunity of exhibiting a moral lesson in which he might have found matter worthy of his highest powers." This is about on a par with the fault found by Dennis with 'Coriolanus,' that the hero of the piece takes leave of his wife and daughters out of the sight of the audience. Hence a great occasion to move had been neglected. In his alteration Dennis seized upon this occasion; but the audience was not

moved. So the course of conduct pointed out by Johnson as desirable would in the vast majority of cases
have been eminently calculated to defeat the very end
at which he aimed. Shakespeare was unquestionably
able to find sermons in stones; but he did not feel
called upon to put a sermon into a stone if it was not
there already. The dialogue between the usurper and
the hermit might have delighted the reader; but it
would have diverted the attention of both reader and
hearer from the main business of the play, and the
interests of morality would not have been enhanced by
disloyalty to art.

The truth is that Shakespeare's success as a moralist
is due to the fact that his moral is not made obtrusive.
It is the comment that rises naturally out of the situation. It makes all the more impression upon the mind
because we both recognize and feel its absolute appropriateness. It is the very reflection which in the same
situation would or should have occurred to ourselves,
though expressed with a felicity and force to which we
can lay no claim. His writings are crowded with
observations which bear directly upon the conduct of
life. They can only be said to drop from him casually
in the sense that they are never introduced save when
they can be made most effective by the example to
which they furnish the comment. In the opening scene
of ' King Lear' Gloucester is shown not only insensible
to his early sin, but jesting about it, in the very presence of the illegitimate Edmund, who could not but
resent in his heart the allusions to the position in life
in which he had been placed by his father's offence.

Through the machinations of this son he loses at once
home and sight. Yet when confronted with the calamities which have overtaken him, like most men of blunted
moral sense, he has no conception that they have come
as consequences of his own acts. What has happened
is in his view nothing but the result of inscrutable
chance.

> " As flies to wanton boys are we to the gods;
> They kill us for their sport."

This is the lesson he draws from his misfortunes. It
is the clearer mind and loftier nature of the son he has
discarded which recognizes the justice of providence.
What more impressive and at the same time more natural and apposite tribute can be paid to the inflexible
laws which pervade the moral government of the universe than the words of Edgar as he contemplates the
result, —

> " The gods are just, and of our pleasant vices
> Make instruments to scourge us."

It is not, however, in the single reflections, scattered
in profusion through his writings, and bearing directly
upon the ethical quality of almost every detail of life
and conduct, — so numerous indeed that, according to
Johnson himself, a system of social duty could be gathered from his sayings, — it is not in these that Shakespeare's surpassing greatness as a moralist consists.
That rests upon the fact that he steadily unfolds before
our eyes the inevitable results of sin, of crime, of errors
of all kinds, even of mere errors of judgment; and
upon the further fact that in so doing he pays no heed
to that so-called poetic justice which pictures as true

a condition of things that experience and observation unite in showing us to be false. He knew what his critic did not, that to observe poetic justice was to please and not to instruct. Dr. Johnson wished ' Lear ' to have a happy ending. He wished to see the virtue of Cordelia rewarded as well as the wickedness of her sisters punished. But in no such scrupulously exact manner operate the moral laws which control the results of human action. It is not alone upon the head of the man who has gone astray from the path of right that the vengeance of heaven descends. Upon the innocent, who are bound to him by ties of nature or affection, too often falls its heaviest curse. It is a spectacle our eyes witness daily. Not merely crimes but venial errors too often carry within them the seeds of a punishment which affects not only the individual transgressor, but all whom the accident of circumstance has involved in his fortunes or his fate.

We can go even farther. Mistakes of judgment as well as actual sins are subject to the operation of this same inexorable law. The lesson that responsibility for our deeds cannot be measured by the results which we ourselves willingly or unwillingly encounter, is one which impresses itself upon us more and more, as we meet in increasing numbers with instances in which the shadow of disgrace and disaster darkens the lives of those innocent and even incapable of wrong-doing. It was because Shakespeare realized fully the wide range of this law that he altered the catastrophe of Lear. The arrogant monarch, impatient of contradiction, deluded by grossest flattery, driving from his presence with contumely those most devoted to his person, must endure to the bitter end the results of his folly. Not only is he himself to become a wretched, weak, and impotent thing, exposed to the malignity of pitiless daughters and the fury of pitiless elements, and from both alike unshielded; but as inevitably is he to drag down with him in his ruin those nearest and dearest, whose loyalty and love he has learned to know too late. A happy ending was an anomaly and an impropriety to that tragedy of passion and suffering in which the weakness of man's nature amid the delirium of the moral forces finds its fitting counterpart in the helplessness of man himself amid the delirium of the forces of nature.

It would be wrong to convey the impression that the element of poetic justice is absent from Shakespeare's representation of life any more than it is from life itself. But in both it at times never appears at all; in both it acts but imperfectly whenever it does appear. In 'Macbeth' the punishment falls at last upon the guilty husband and the guilty wife. But that, after all, is a matter of subsidiary consequence; as an end in view it scarcely plays any part in the development of the drama. It is the gradual transforming power of sin, when once it has taken full possession of the soul, which here arrests the attention. It is the different character of the devastation wrought by it in different natures which furnishes a study as full of psychological interest as it is of dramatic. Macbeth, at the opening of the play, the valiant general, the loyal subject, promises even then, though unfixed in

415

principle, to end his career as honorably as it has been begun. His wife it is who at the outset is the dominant character. In her dauntless hardihood she gives courage and strength to her husband's infirm purpose, which, while longing for the fruits of crime, shrinks from its commission. But before the play approaches its conclusion, the positions of the two have been reversed. The gallant soldier of the early part has become a cruel tyrant, as inaccessible to remorse as he is to pity. The man, who at his first entrance into crime was horrified by the phantoms of his own disordered brain, comes to encounter recklessly and defy undauntedly the terrors of the visible and invisible worlds. The moral nature has become an absolute wreck. But with the hardening of the heart and the deadening of the conscience have disappeared entirely the compunctions which once unnerved the resolution and the tremors which shook the soul. Not so with Lady Macbeth. Her nature, far finer and higher strung, though at the beginning more resolute, pays at last in remorseful days and sleepless nights the full penalty of violated law. While Macbeth grows stronger as a man by the very course which destroys his susceptibility to moral considerations, this very susceptibility on her part increases with the success of the deed she has prompted and in which she has taken determined part. The woman could not unsex herself wholly, and succumbs at last to the long-continued and increasing strain of a burden she was not fitted to bear.

Pervading all these plays of Shakespeare which involve the problems that beset man's life and destiny is not the shallow conception of poetic justice, never fully realized in fact and rarely realizable even in the most imperfect way, but instead the profound conviction he inspires of the sway and sweep of those moral forces which, once set in motion, must go on to work out their inevitable course in human conduct, whether it be in itself right or wrong, whether it lead to triumph or to failure. There belongs not indeed to his drama the fatalism of the Greek tragedy in which the hero is urged on by the stress of irresistible necessity to a catastrophe at which he shudders but which he cannot shun. The idea that runs through it all, that unites its most discordant elements, that binds in one common bond its most diverse themes, is the existence of the reign of law; is the inexorable sequence of cause and effect, whether it bring with it joy or sorrow, whether it point to the serene close of happy days, or disclose itself in the ever-recurring tragedy of lives going out in noisy defeat or in countless quieter forms of failure. It is not at all that every act is followed by the specific result which is most appropriate to it, according to our imperfect conceptions of justice. It is that the general consequences of human conduct correspond in the Shakespearean drama with the consequences which we see exemplified in the life about us. In the domain of morals as in that of letters it is the art which holds the mirror up to nature.

Let us illustrate the fact by the play which has just been under consideration. Macbeth's overthrow and death is a mere accident of personal fortune. It might or might not have happened in real life. In his case a sort of poetic justice has been exemplified; but it was in no wise a necessary sequence of the crimes he has committed. That, so far as he is concerned, is found elsewhere, and would have been in active operation had he returned victorious from the battle-field on which he fell. He himself recognized it, and announced it. In the years which were coming he could not look to have that which should chiefly attend a happy old age, — "honor, love, obedience, troops of friends;"

> "But, in their stead,
> Curses, not loud but deep, mouth-honor, breath,
> Which the poor heart would fain deny, and dare not."

Upon him in the pride of power had fallen already the penalty of violated law. It is this inflexible enforcement of the genuine decrees which regulate the moral government of the universe; it is his full acceptation and adequate representation of the far-reaching consequences which follow human action, whether it be due to frailty or to fault, whether it spring from folly, ignorance, wilfulness, credulousness, irresolution, or anything contained in the darker catalogue of sins and crimes; it is his insistence upon the actual rewards and penalties that wait upon conduct: these it is that entitle Shakespeare to the position he holds of the great moral poet of humanity.

BIBLIOGRAPHY

THE following pages contain a bibliography of the works, referred to in this volume, which appeared from the Restoration to the end of the eighteenth century. For obvious reasons they have been put down in chronological order; but they are in the index with a reference to the page on which they are found here. In every instance they appear under the date of the year in which they were first published; but the full title is given only of the particular edition which has been consulted in the preparation of this volume. The prefix of an asterisk to a title signifies that the work has not been seen: that any account given of it, or of its contents, has been taken from others.

1663.

The Adventures of Five Hours. A Tragi-Comedy. Feb. 21° 1662. Imprimatur John Berkenhead. London, Printed for Henry Herringmann. 1663.

1665.

Four New Plays, viz.: The Surprisal, The Committee, Comedies. The Indian-Queen, The Vestal-Virgin, Tragedies. As they were acted by his Majesties Servants at the Theatre Royal. Written by the Honourable Sir Robert Howard. Imprimatur, March 7. 166$\frac{4}{5}$ Roger L'Estrange. London, Printed for Henry Herringmann. 1665.

1667.

Love Tricks: or, The School of Complements; as it is now acted by his Royal Highnesse the Duke of York's Servants at the Theatre in Little Lincolns-Inne Fields. By J. S. Licens'd May 24. 1667. Roger L'Estrange. London, Sold by Thomas Dring Junior. 1667.

The Indian Emperour, or, the Conquest of Mexico by the Spaniards. Being the sequel of the Indian Queen. By John Dryden, Esq; London, Printed for Henry Herringman. 1694.

BIBLIOGRAPHY

1668.

The Great Favorite, or, the Duke of Lerma. A Tragedy. As it was acted at the Theatre-Royal by His Majesty's Servants. Written by the Honourable Sir Robert Howard. London, Printed for Henry Herringman. 1692.
in Five New Plays. 1692.

Secret-Love, or the Maiden-Queen: As it is acted by his Majesties Servants at the Theater-Royal. Written by John Dryden, Esq; London, Printed for Henry Herringman, 1669.

The Sullen Lovers: or, The Impertinents. A Comedy acted by his Highness the Duke of York's Servants. Written by Tho. Shadwell. London, Printed for Henry Herringman. 1670.

Of Dramatick Poesie, an Essay. By John Dryden Esq: London, Printed for Henry Herringman, 1668.

1669.

The Wild Gallant: A Comedy. As it is acted by their Majesties Servants. Written by John Dryden, Esq; London, Printed for Henry Herringman, 1694.

1670.

Tyrannick Love; or, the Royal Martyr. A Tragedy. As it is acted by his Majestie's Servants at the Theatre Royal. By John Dryden, Servant to his Majesty. London, Printed for H. Herringman, 1686.

The Tempest, or the Enchanted Island. A Comedy. As it is now acted at his Highness the Duke of York's, Theatre. London, Printed for Henry Herringman. 1674.

1671.

Paradise Regained. A Poem. In IV Books. To which is added Samson Agonistes. The author John Milton. London, Printed for John Starkey. 1671.

1672.

The Conquest of Granada by the Spaniards: In two parts. Acted at the Theater-Royall. Written by John Dryden Servant to his Majesty. Printed for Henry Herringman. 1672.

Almanzor and Almahide, or the Conquest of Granada. The Second Part. As it is acted at the Theater-Royal. Written by John Dryden Servant to his Majesty. Printed for Henry Herringman. 1672.

1673.

The Law against Lovers, pp. 272-329
in The Works of Sr William D'Avenant Kt consisting of those which were formerly printed, and those which he design'd for the press: now published out of the Author's original copies. London: Printed for Henry Herringman. 1673.

420

1674.

Macbeth, a Tragedy: With all the alterations, amendments, additions, and new songs. As it is now acted at the Dukes Theatre. London: Printed for A. Clark, 1674.

Monsieur Rapin's Reflections on Aristotle's Treatise of Poesie. Containing the necessary, rational, and universal rules for epick, dramatick, and the other sorts of poetry. With reflections on the works of the ancient and modern poets, and their faults noted. Made English by Mr. Rymer: By whom are added some reflections on English poets.
in Rapin's Critical Works, Vol. ii. London, 1731. pp. 107–241.

1675.

The Mock-Tempest: or the Enchanted Castle. Acted at the Theatre Royal. Written by T. Duffett. London, Printed for William Cademan, 1675.
The heading of the play itself is "The New Tempest or the Enchanted Castle."

Theatrum Poetarum, or a Complete Collection of the Poets, especially the most eminent of all ages. The antients distinguish't from the modern in their several alphabets. With some observations and reflections upon many of them, particularly upon those of our own nation. Together with a prefatory discourse of the poets and poetry in generall. By Edward Phillips. London, Printed for Charles Smith, 1675.

1678.

The Tragedies of the Last Age, consider'd and examin'd by the practice of the ancients, and the common sense of all ages in a Letter to Fleetwood Shepheard, Esq: by Thomas Rymer, of Gray's Inn, Esquire. London, Printed for Richard Tonson, 1678. Licensed July 17, 1677. R. L'Estrange.

Edgar, or the English Monarch; an heroick Tragedy. By Thomas Rymer of Gray's-Inn Esq: Licensed Septemb. 13. 1677. Roger L'Estrange. London, Printed for Richard Tonson, 1678.

All for Love: or, The World Well Lost. A Tragedy, as it is acted at the Theatre-Royal; and written in imitation of Shakespeare's style. By John Dryden, Servant to his Majesty. In the Savoy: Printed for Henry Herringman, 1678.

The History of Timon of Athens, the Man-Hater. As it is acted at the Dukes Theatre. Made into a Play. By Tho. Shadwell. Licensed, Feb. 18, 167⅞, Ro. L'Estrange. London, Printed for Henry Herringman, 1678.

1679.

Troilus and Cressida, or, Truth found too late. A Tragedy as it is acted at the Dukes Theatre. To which is prefix'd, A Preface containing the Grounds of Criticism in Tragedy. Written by John Dryden, Servant to his Majesty. London, Printed for Jacob Tonson and Abel Swall, 1679.

1680.

The History and Fall of Caius Marius. A Tragedy. As it is acted at the Theatre Royal. By Thomas Otway. London, Printed for S. Flesher, 1680.

Henry the Sixth, or The Misery of Civil War, as it was acted at the Dukes Theatre. Written by Mr. Crown. London, Printed for R. Bentley and M. Magnes. 1681.

Horace's Art of Poetry,
in Poems by the Earl of Roscommon. To which is added, an Essay on Poetry, by the Earl of Mulgrave, now Duke of Buckingham. Together with poems by Mr. Richard Duke. London. Printed for J. Tonson, 1717.

1681.

Henry the Sixth, The First Part. With the Murder of Humphrey Duke of Glocester. As it was acted at the Dukes Theatre. Written by Mr. Crown. London, Printed for R. Bentley, and M. Magnes. 1681.

The Spanish Fryar, or, The Double Discovery. Acted at the Duke's Theatre. Written by John Dryden, Servant to his Majesty. London, Printed for Richard Tonson and Jacob Tonson, 1681.

The History of King Lear. Acted at the Duke's Theatre. Reviv'd with alterations. By N. Tate. London, Printed for E. Flesher, 1681.

The History of King Richard the Second. Acted at the Theatre Royal, under the name of the Sicilian Usurper. With a prefatory Epistle in Vindication of the Author. Occasion'd by the prohibition of this play on the Stage. By N. Tate. London, Printed for Richard Tonson and Jacob Tonson. 1681.

1682.

The Ingratitude of a Common-Wealth: or, the Fall of Caius Martius Coriolanus. As it is acted at the Theatre-Royal. By N. Tate. Printed for Joseph Hindmarsh, 1682.

The Injured Princes, or the Fatal Wager: as it was acted at the Theater-Royal, by his Majesties Servants. By Tho. Durfey, Gent. London: Printed for R. Bentley and M. Magnes, 1682.

1683.

The Duke of Guise. A Tragedy. Acted by their Majesties Servants. Written by Mr. Dryden and Mr. Lee. London, Printed for R. Bentley and J. Tonson. 1687.

1687.

Titus Andronicus, or the Rape of Lavinia. Acted at the Theatre Royall. Alter'd from Mr. Shakespear's works by Mr. Edw. Ravenscroft.

Licensed Dec 21, 1686. R. L. S. London, Printed for J. Hindmarsh, 1687.

Mixt Essays upon Tragedies, Comedies, Italian Comedies, English Comedies, and Opera's To his Grace, the Duke of Buckingham. Written originally in French by the Sieur de Saint Evvremont, Licensed Rog. L'Estrange. London: Printed for Timothy Goodwin, 1687.

1690.

Don Sebastian, King of Portugal: A Tragedy acted at the Theatre Royal. Written by Mr. Dryden. London: Printed for Jo. Hindmarsh. 1692.

1692.

The Gentleman's Journal: or the Monthly Miscellany. By way of letter to a Gentleman in the Country. Consisting of news, history, philosophy, poetry, musick, translations, &c. London. 1692–93.

Cleomenes, the Spartan Heroe. A Tragedy, as it is acted at the Theatre Royal. Written by Mr. Dryden. To which is prefixt the Life of Cleomenes. London, Printed for Jacob Tonson, 1692.

The Tragedies of the Last Age, Consider'd and Examin'd by the practice of the ancients, and the common sense of all ages in a Letter to Fleetwood Shepheard, Esq; By Mr. Rymer Servant to their Majesties. Part I. The second Edition. Printed and sold by Richard Baldwin. 1692.

1693.

A Short View of Tragedy; it's original, excellency, and corruption. With some reflections on Shakespear, and other practitioners for the stage. By Mr. Rymer, Servant to their Majesties. Printed and sold by Richard Baldwin. 1693.

The Impartial Critick: or some observations upon a late book entituled, A Short View of Tragedy, written by Mr. Rymer, and dedicated to the Right Honourable Charles Earl of Dorset, &c. By Mr. Dennis. London: Printed for R. Taylor. 1693.

1694.

Some Reflections on Mr Rymer's Short View of Tragedy, and an Attempt at a Vindication of Shakespear, in an Essay directed to John Dryden, Esq.

in Miscellaneous Letters and Essays, on several Subjects. Philosophical, Moral, Historical, Critical, Amorous, &c. in Prose and Verse. Directed to John Dryden, Esq; The Honourable Geo. Granvill, Esq: Walter Moile, Esq: Mr. Dennis, Mr. Congreve, and other Eminent Men of the Age. By several Gentlemen and Ladies. London: Printed for Benjamin Bragg, 1694.

The Epistle dedicatory to the Honourable Sir John Trenchard is signed by Charles Gildon.

1695.

Love for Love: A Comedy. Acted at the Theatre in Little Lincolns-
Inn Fields, by his Majestys Servants. Written by Mr. Congreve.
London : Printed for Jacob Tonson. 1695.

1696.

* The Mock Marriage. A Comedy. By Thomas Scott. London : 1696.
Letters upon Several Occasions: Written by and between Mr. Dryden,
Mr. Wycherly, Mr. ——, Mr. Congreve and Mr. Dennis.
    in The Works of John Dennis. Vol. ii. London, 1718. pp. 480–543.
Oroonoko : A Tragedy. As it is acted at the Theatre-Royal, by his
Majestys Servants. Written by Tho. Southerne. London : Printed
for H. Playford, B. Tooke, and A. Bellesworth. 1699.

1697.

A Plot, and no Plot. A Comedy, as it is acted at the Theatre-Royal in
Drury-Lane. Written by Mr. Dennis. London, Printed for R.
Parker, P. Buck, and R. Wellington. [1697.]

1698.

Sauny the Scott : or, the Taming of the Shrew. A Comedy. As it is
now acted at the Theatre-Royal. Written by J. Lacey, Servant to
his Majesty. And never before printed. London : Printed and sold
by E. Whitlock. 1698.
Phaeton : or, The Fatal Divorce. A Tragedy. As it is acted at the
Theatre Royal. In imitation of the ancients. With some reflections
on a book call'd, A Short View of the Immorality and Profaneness of
the English Stage. London, Printed for Abel Roper. 1698. [By
Charles Gildon.]

1700.

[King Richard iii. as altered by Cibber.] King Richard the Third, a
Tragedy, by Shakespeare. As performed at the Theatre-Royal,
Drury-Lane, regulated from the Prompt-Book, with permission of the
Managers, by Mr. Hopkins, prompter. An introduction, and notes
critical and illustrative are added by the Authors of the Dramatic
Censor. The Third edition. London : Printed for John Bell. 1779.
A note in this edition to the heading of the play says : " This Trag-
edy being admirably altered from the original, by that excellent judge
and ornament of the stage, *Colley Cibber*, we shall have the fewer
observations to make upon it." On this Genest in his copy writes
the following comment : " This note shows the editor a bigger fool
than Cibber himself."
Measure for Measure, or Beauty the best advocate. As it is acted at the
Theatre in Lincolns-Inn-Fields. Written originally by Mr. Shake-

spear : And now very much Alter'd ; with additions of several Entertainments of Music. London : Printed for D. Brown and R. Parker.
1700. [By Charles Gildon.]

Iphigenia. A Tragedy, acted at the theatre in Little Lincolns-Inn-Fields.
By Mr. Dennis. London. Printed for Richard Parker. 1700.

1701.

The Ambitious Stepmother. A Tragedy. As 'twas acted at the New
Theatre in Little-Lincolns-Inn Fields. By his Majestys Servants.
By N. Rowe, Esq ;. London, Printed for Peter Buck. 1701.

The Jew of Venice. A Comedy. As it is acted at the theatre in Little-
Lincoln-Inn-Fields, by his Majesty's Servants. London, Printed for
Ber. Lintott, 1701. [By Richard Granville, Lord Lansdowne.]

Love's Victim : or, The Queen of Wales. A Tragedy. As it was acted
at the Theatre in Lincolns-Inn-Fields. By his Majestys Servants.
London, Printed for Richard Parker, and George Strahan. 1701.
[By Charles Gildon.]

1702.

The Comical Gallant : or the Amours of Sir John Falstaffe. A Comedy.
As it is acted at the Theatre-Royal in Drury-lane. By his Majesty's
Servants. By Mr. Dennis. To which is added, A Large Account of
the Taste in Poetry, and the Causes of the degeneracy of it. London, Printed and sold by A. Baldwin. 1702.

A Discourse upon Comedy, in reference to the English Stage. In a
letter to a Friend.
in Farquhar's Works, tenth edition, 1772. Vol. I. pp. 69–92.

1703.

Love's Contrivance: or, *Le Médecin malgré Lui.* A Comedy. As it is
acted at the Theatre Royal in Drury-Lane,
in vol ii of The Dramatic Works of the Celebrated Mrs. Centlivre,
with a new account of her life. Complete in three volumes.
London : John Pearson. 1872.

1704.

The Grounds of Criticism in Poetry, contain'd in some new discoveries
never made before, requisite for the Writing and Judging of Poems
surely. Being a preliminary to a larger work design'd to be publish'd in folio, and entitul'd, A Criticism upon our most Celebrated
Poets deceas'd. By Mr. Dennis. London, Printed for Geo. Strahan
and Bernard Lintott. 1704.

1708.

Roscius Anglicanus, or, An Historical Review of the Stage from 1660 to
1706. By John Downes. A fac-simile reprint of the rare original
of 1708. With an historical preface by Joseph Knight. London :
Jarvis & Son. 1886.

1709.

The Works of Mr. William Shakespear; in six volumes. Adorn'd with cuts. Revis'd and Corrected, with an account of the Life and Writings of the author. By N. Rowe Esq; London: Printed for Jacob Tonson. 1709.

1710.

The Works of Mr. William Shakespear. Volume the Seventh. Containing, Venus & Adonis Tarquin & Lucrece and His Miscellany Poems. With Critical Remarks on his Plays, &c. to which is prefix'd an Essay on the Art, Rise and Progress of the Stage in Greece, Rome and England. London: Printed for E. Curll and E. Sanger. 1710.

Elfrid: or the Fair Inconstant. A Tragedy: as it is acted at the Theatre Royal, by her Majesty's Servants. To which is added the Walking Statue: or, The Devil in the Wine-Cellar. A Farce. Written by Mr. Hill, 1710. London, Printed for Bernard Lintott and Egbert Sanger.

1712.

The Distrest Mother. A Tragedy. As it is acted at the Theatre-Royal in Drury-Lane. By her Majesty's Servants. Written by Mr. Philips. London: Printed for S. Buckley and J. Tonson, 1712.

An Essay on the Genius and Writings of Shakespear: with some letters of criticism to the Spectator. By Mr. Dennis. London: Printed for Bernard Lintott. 1712.

The Perplex'd Lovers. A Comedy. As it is acted at the Theatre-Royal in Drury Lane. By her Majesty's Servants. Written by Mrs. Susanna Cent-livre. London: Printed for Owen Lloyd, William Lewis, John Graves, and Tho. Harbin. 1712.

1713.

Cato. A Tragedy. As it is acted at the Theatre-Royal in Drury-Lane, By her Majesty's Servants. By Mr. Addison. London: Printed for J. Tonson. 1713.

Remarks upon Cato, a Tragedy. By Mr. Dennis. London: Printed for B. Lintott, 1713.

1714.

The Tragedy of Jane Shore. Written in imitation of Shakespear's style. By N. Rowe, Esq;. London: Printed for Bernard Lintott. [1714.]

1718.

The Complete Art of Poetry. In Six parts. [In two volumes.] By Charles Gildon, Gent. London: Printed for Charles Rivington. 1718.

The Non-Juror. A Comedy. As it is acted at the Theatre-Royal, by his Majesty's Servants. Written by Mr. Cibber. London: Printed for B. Lintot. 1718.

1720.

The Invader of his Country: or, The Fatal Resentment. A Tragedy. As it is acted at the Theatre-Royal in Drury-Lane. By his Majesty's Servants. By Mr. Dennis. London: Printed for J. Pemberton and J. Watts. 1720.

1731.

The London Merchant: or, the History of George Barnwell. As it is acted at the Theatre-Royal in Drury-Lane. By his Majesty's Servants. By Mr. Lillo. London: Printed for J. Gray. 1731.

Considerations on the Stage, and on the Advantages which arise to a Nation from the Encouragement of Arts. London; Printed in the year 1731. A supplement — pp. 45–74 — to

The Triumphs of Love and Honour, a play, as it is acted by his Majesty's Servants, at the Theatre-Royal in Drury Lane. To which are added — (see above.) By Mr. Cooke. London, Printed for J. Roberts.

1735.

Junius Brutus, a Tragedy. As it is acted at the Theatre-Royal in Drury-Lane, by his Majesty's Servants. By Mr. William Duncombe. London, Printed; and sold by J. Roberts. 1735.

1736.

Some Remarks on the Tragedy of Hamlet, Prince of Denmark, written by Mr. William Shakespeare. London: Printed for W. Wilkins. 1736.

1737.

The Historical Register, For the year 1736. As it is acted at the New Theatre in the Hay-Market. To which is added a very Merry Tragedy, called Eurydice Hiss'd, or, A Word to the Wise. Both written by the Author of Pasquin. To these are prefixed a long dedication to the Publick, and a Preface to that Dedication. London, Printed; and sold by J. Roberts. [1737] [By Henry Fielding.]

1740.

Elmerick: or, Justice Triumphant. A Tragedy. As it is acted at the Theatre Royal in Drury-Lane. By Mr. Lillo. London: Printed for John Gray. 1740.

1745.

Papal Tyranny in the Reign of King John. A Tragedy. As it is acted
at the Theatre-Royal in Covent-Garden. By his Majesty's Servants.
By Colley Cibber, Esq; London: Printed for J. Watts. 1745.
Le Theatre Anglois. A Londres. 1745–1748. Tomes I–VIII.
[Par Pierre Antoine de la Place.]

1746.

Critical Observations on Shakespeare. By John Upton Prebendary of
Rochester. London: Printed for G. Hawkins. 1746.

1747.

The Roman and English Comedy Consider'd and Compar'd. With Remarks on the Suspicious Husband. And an Examen into the merit
of the present Comic Actors. By S. Foote, Esq: London: Printed
for T. Waller. 1747.

1749.

Q. Horatii Flacci Epistolae ad Pisones, et Augustum: With an English
commentary and notes: to which are added critical dissertations. By
the Reverend Mr. Hurd. In three volumes. The fourth edition, corrected and enlarged. London, Printed for A. Millar. 1766.

1752.

Eugenia: a Tragedy. As it is acted at the Theatre Royal, in Drury-
Lane, By his Majesty's Servants. London: Printed for A. Millar.
1752. [by Philip Francis.]
Miscellaneous Observations on the Tragedy of Hamlet, Prince of Den-
mark. With a preface containing some general remarks on the
Writings of Shakespeare. London: Printed for W. Clarke. 1752.
Elfrida, a Dramatic Poem, written on the model of the Antient Greek
Tragedy. By Mr. Mason. London, Printed for J and P. Knapton.
1752.

1753.

Boadicia. A Tragedy. As it is acted at the Theatre Royal in Drury-
Lane. By Mr. Glover. London: Printed for R and J. Dodsley and
M. Cooper. 1753.
The Gamester. A Tragedy. As it is acted at the Theatre-Royal in
Drury-Lane. London: Printed for R. Francklin. 1753.
The Rehearsal: or Bays in Petticoats. A Comedy in two acts. As it is
performed at the Theatre Royal in Drury Lane. Written by Mrs.
Clive. The music composed by Dr. Boyce. London: Printed for
R. Dodsley. 1753. [First acted March 15, 1750.]

Shakespear Illustrated: or the Novels and Histories on which the Plays of Shakespear are founded, collected and translated from the original authors. With critical remarks. In two volumes. By the author of the Female Quixote. London: Printed for A. Millar, 1753.

1754.

Philoclea. A Tragedy. As it is acted at the Theatre Royal in Covent Garden. Written by McNamara Morgan, a Student of the Middle Temple. London: Printed for R. and J. Dodsley, 1754.

Shakespear Illustrated. [Title-page same as in volumes of 1753.] The third and last volume. 1754.

1756.

Athelstan. A Tragedy. As it is acted at the Theatre Royal in Drury-Lane. London, Printed for Lockyer Davis and Charles Reymers, 1756. [By John Brown.]

1757.

Douglas: a Tragedy. As it is acted at the Theatre-Royal in Covent Garden. London: Printed for A. Millar. 1757. [By John Home.]

1758.

Agis: a Tragedy. As it is acted at the Theatre-Royal in Drury-Lane. London: Printed for A. Millar. 1758. [By John Home.]

Cleone. A Tragedy. As it is acted at the Theatre Royal in Covent Garden. Written by R. Dodsley. London: Printed for R.and J. Dodsley, 1758.

1759.

Cymbeline. A Tragedy, altered from Shakespeare. As it is performed at the Theatre-Royal in Covent-Garden. By William Hawkins, M. A. late fellow of Pembroke College, and Professor of Poetry in the University of Oxford. London: Printed for James Rivington and James Fletcher, 1759.

Caractacus, a Dramatic Poem: Written on the model of the Antient Greek Tragedy. By the author of Elfrida. London: Printed for J. Knapton and R. and J. Dodsley. 1759. [By William Mason.]

Oronooko: a Tragedy. As it is now acted at the Theatre-Royal in Drury-Lane. By his Majesty's Servants. By Thomas Southern. With alterations. London: Printed for C. Bathurst, 1759. [Alterations by John Hawkesworth.]

1760.

Dialogues of the Dead. The fifth edition, Corrected. London: Printed for J. Murray. 1768. [By George, Lord Lyttelton.]

BIBLIOGRAPHY

1762.

Elements of Criticism. The Eighth Edition. With the author's last corrections and additions. [In two volumes.] London: Printed for Vernor and Hood. 1805. [By Henry Home, Lord Kames.]
*Remarks on the Beauties of Poetry. By Daniel Webb, Esq.; London. Dodsley. 1762.

1763.

Philaster, a Tragedy. Written by Beaumont and Fletcher. With alterations. As it is acted at the Theatre-Royal in Drury-Lane. London: Printed for J. and R. Tonson, 1763.
[Alterations by George Colman.]

1764.

The Companion to the Play-House: or, An historical account of all the dramatic writers (and their works) that have appeared in Great Britain and Ireland, from the Commencement of our theatrical exhibitions, down to the present year, 1764. Composed in the form of a dictionary, for the more readily turning to any particular author, or performance. In two volumes. London: Printed for T. Becket, P. A. Dehondt, C. Henderson, and T. Davies. 1764. [By David E. Baker.]

1765.

The Castle of Otranto, a Gothic Story. Translated by William Marshall, Gent. From the original Italian of Onuphrio Muralto, Canon of the Church of St. Nicholas at Otranto. The sixth edition. Parma. Printed by Rodoni, for J. Edwards, Bookseller of London. 1791. [By Horace Walpole.]
The Comedies of Terence, Translated into Familiar Blank Verse. By George Colman. The Second Edition revised and corrected. In two volumes. Printed for T. Becket, P. A. De Hondt, and R. Baldwin. 1768.

1766.

The Earl of Warwick, a Tragedy, as it is performed at the Theatre Royal in Drury Lane. London: printed for T. Davies, R. Baldwin, and W. Griffin. 1766. [By Thomas Francklin.]

1768.

The History of King Lear. As it is performed at the Theatre Royal in Covent Garden. London. Printed for R. Baldwin & T. Becket. 1768. [Lear, as altered by George Colman.]

1769.

The Sister: a Comedy. By Mrs. Charlotte Lennox. London, Printed for J. Dodsley and T. Davies. 1769.

1771.

Timon of Athens, altered from Shakespear. A Tragedy. As it is acted at the Theatre-Royal in Drury Lane. London: printed for the proprietors of Shakespear's works. 1771. [By Richard Cumberland.]

1773.

She Stoops to Conquer: or, The Mistakes of a Night. A Comedy. As it is acted at the Theatre-Royal in Covent-Garden. Written by Doctor Goldsmith. London: Printed for F. Newbery. 1773.

1774.

Cursory Remarks on Tragedy, on Shakespear, and on certain French and Italian Poets, principally Tragedians. London: printed for W. Owen. 1774. [By Edward Taylor.]

Analysis of Shakespeare's Characters. A Philosophical Analysis and Illustration of some of Shakespeare's Remarkable Characters. By William Richardson, Esq. Professor of Humanity in the University of Glasgow. The second edition, corrected. London: Printed for J. Murray; and W. Creech at Edinburgh. 1775. [Contains the characters of Macbeth, Hamlet, Jaques, and Imogen.]

1775.

*The Correspondents. An Original Novel in a series of Letters. London, 1775.

The Rivals, a Comedy. As it is acted at the Theatre-Royal in Covent-Garden. London: Printed for John Wilkie. 1775. [By R. B. Sheridan.]

*The Elements of Dramatic Criticism; containing an analysis of the stage, &c. By William Cooke, Esq; of the Middle Temple. London, Kearsly, 1775.

1777.

Discours sur Shakespeare et sur Monsieur de Voltaire par Joseph Baretti, sécretaire pour la correspondence étrangère de l'Academie Royale Britannique. Londres, chez J. Nourse, libraire du Roi, et à Paris, chez Durand neveu. 1777.

Biographia Literaria; or a Biographical History of Literature: Containing the Lives of English, Scottish, and Irish Authors, from the dawn of letters in these Kingdoms to the present time, chronologically and classically arranged. By John Berkenhout, M. D. Volume I. From the beginning of the fifth to the end of the sixteenth century. London: Printed for J. Dodsley. 1777. [Volume I was the only one published.]

* A new Translation of the Heauton-timorumenos and Adelphi of Terence: in Prose. Together with a preface, containing a free enquiry into

Mr. Colman's arguments for translating the comedies of that author into blank verse. By a member of the University of Oxford. London. Dodsley. 1777.

An Essay on the Dramatic Character of Sir John Falstaff. London: Printed for T. Davies. 1777. [By Maurice Morgann.]

1779.

The Law of Lombardy; a Tragedy: As it is performed at the Theatre-Royal in Drury-Lane. Written by Robert Jephson, Esq. author of Braganza. London. Printed for T. Evans. 1779.

1780.

Zoraida: a Tragedy. As it is acted at the Theatre-Royal in Drury-Lane. To which is added a postscript, containing observations on Tragedy. London: Printed for G. Kearsly. 1780. [By William Hodson.]

1781.

* Nathan the Wise. A Philosophic Drama. From the German of G. E. Lessing, late Librarian to the Duke of Brunswick. Translated into English by R. E. Raspe. London, Fielding. 1781.

1782.

Biographia Dramatica, or a Companion to the Playhouse, &c. By David Erskine Baker, Esq. A new edition: carefully corrected, greatly enlarged; and continued from 1764 to 1782. [In two volumes.] Dublin, 1782. [An enlarged edition of the Companion to the Playhouse, 1764.]

1783.

Dissertations Moral and Critical. On Memory and Imagination. On Dreaming. The Theory of Language. On Fable and Romance. On the Attachments of Kindred. Illustrations of Sublimity. By James Beattie, LL. D. Professor of Moral Philosophy and Logick in the Marischal College and University of Aberdeen; and Member of the Zealand Society of Arts and Sciences. London: Printed for W. Strahan and T. Cadell; and W. Creech at Edinburgh. 1783.

Q. Horatii Flacci Epistola ad Pisones, de Arte Poetica. The Art of Poetry: an Epistle to the Pisos. Translated from Horace. With notes. By George Colman. London: Printed for T. Cadell. 1783.

The Mysterious Husband. A Tragedy in Five Acts. As it is acted at the Theatre-Royal, Covent-Garden. By Richard Cumberland, Esq. London: Printed for C. Dilly and J. Walter. 1783.

Lectures on Rhetoric and Belles-Lettres. By Hugh Blair, D.D. One of the ministers of the High Church, and professor of rhetoric and belles lettres in the University of Edinburgh. In three volumes. Dublin. 1783.

1784.

* Plays of Three Acts; written for a Private Theatre. By William Hayley, Esq. London. Cadell. 1784. [Among the comedies is The Two Connoisseurs.]

Dramatic Miscellanies: consisting of critical observations on several plays of Shakspeare: with a review of his principal characters, and those of various eminent writers, as represented by Mr. Garrick, and the celebrated comedians. With Anecdotes of Dramatic Poets, Actors, &c. By Thomas Davies, Author of Memoirs of the Life of David Garrick, Esq. In three volumes. London. Printed for the Author. 1784.

Essays on Shakespeare's Dramatic Characters of Richard the Third, King Lear, and Timon of Athens. To which are added, an Essay on the Faults of Shakespeare; and additional observations on the Character of Hamlet. The second edition: By Mr. Richardson, Professor of Humanity in the University of Glasgow. London: Printed for J. Murray. 1786.

1785.

The Mine: a Dramatic Poem. The second edition. To which are added, Two historic odes. By John Sargent, Esquire. London: Printed for T. Cadell. 1788.

1786.

* The Disbanded Officer; or, The Baroness of Bruchsal: a Comedy. As performed at the Theatre-Royal in the Haymarket. Cadell. London. 1786.

The New Foundling Hospital for Wit. Being a collection of Fugitive Pieces, in Prose and Verse, not in any other Collection. With several pieces never before published. A new edition, corrected and considerably enlarged. In six volumes. London: Printed for J. Debrett. 1786. [Edited by J. Almon. This is the second edition.]

1789.

Essays by W. Belsham. Essays Philosophical and Moral, Historical and Literary. By W. Belsham. In Two Volumes. London: Printed for G. G. and J. Robinson. 1799.

1790.

Memoirs of His own Life, by Tate Wilkinson, Patentee of the Theatres-Royal, York and Hull. In four volumes. York: Printed for the Author. Anno 1790.

28   433

1792.

Columbus : or, A World Discovered. An Historical Play. As it is performed at the Theatre-Royal, Covent-Garden. By Thomas Morton, of the honourable society of Lincoln's-Inn. London : Printed for W. Miller. 1792.

1832.

Some Account of the English Stage from the Restoration in 1660 to 1830. In ten volumes. Bath : 1832.
[By John Genest.]

1838.

The Correspondence of Sir Thomas Hanmer, Bart. Speaker of the House of Commons. With a memoir of his life. To which are added other Relicks of a Gentleman's Family. Edited by Sir Henry Bunbury, Bart. London : Edward Moxon. 1838.

INDEX

INDEX

IN this index, for the convenience of readers, the dates of
birth and death of most of the authors mentioned have been
given. When there is any doubt in the case of the English
ones, I have followed the authority of the Dictionary of
National Biography.

ADDISON, Joseph [1672–1719], 158,
190, 272, 274; his Cato, 59, 184,
226, 426; on bloodshed in stage
representation, 191, 192, 202; on
poetic justice, 406–410; on ryming plays, 217; on tragi-comedy,
136, 137.
ADVENTURES OF FIVE HOURS, by
Sir Samuel Tuke, 263, 419.
ÆSCHYLUS, 285, 346.
AGIS, Home's, 349, 429.
ALCESTIS, Euripides', 143.
ALCHEMIST, Jonson's, 33.
ALL FOR LOVE, Dryden's, 70, 95,
216, 421; account of, 97–99.
ALTERATION OF SHAKESPEARE'S
PLAYS, to produce a new play,
303–306; to introduce spectacu-
lar entertainments, 306–308; to
produce a happy ending, 308; to
introduce love-scenes, 309–313; to
hostility to, 313–318.
AMBITIOUS STEPMOTHER, Rowe's,
371, 403, 425.
ANALYSIS OF SHAKESPEARE'S
CHARACTERS, Richardson's, 152,
431.
ANTIGONE, Sophocles', 204.
APOLLONIUS Rhodius, 233.
APOLOGY FOR POETRY, Sidney's,
20, 149.
ARISTOPHANES, 4, 111.

ARISTOTLE, 226, 235, 247, 249, 282,
365, 407; his connection with the
doctrine of the unities, 16, 17,
20, 49, 250.
ARNE, Thomas Augustus [1710–
1778], 252.
ATHALIE, Racine's, 243, 251.
ATHELSTAN, Brown's, 66, 193, 429.

BACON, Francis [1561–1626], 340;
on love in stage-plays, 115.
BARETTI, Giuseppe Marc' Antonio,
[1719–1789], 64, 431.
BARRY, Lodowick, 38.
BARTHOLOMEW FAIR, Jonson's,
180.
BEATTIE, James [1735–1803], 64,
432.
BEAUMONT, Francis [1584–1616],
34, 35.
BEAUMONT AND FLETCHER, plays
of, 2, 174, 230, 265; Rymer on,
234, 235, 277, 281, 402.
BELSHAM, William [1752–1827], 65,
433.
BENTLEY, Richard [1708–1782],
208.
BERENICE, Racine's, 80.
BERKENHOUT, John [1730?–1791],
62, 66, 74, 431.
BETTERTON, Thomas [1635?–1710],
302, 377.

BIOGRAPHIA DRAMATICA, 166 *n*, 169 *n*, 319 *n*, 432.

BLACKSTONE, Sir William [1723–1780], 388.

BLAIR, Hugh [1718–1800], 64, 359, 432; on Shakespeare, 348.

BLANK VERSE, in comedy, 211, 212; in tragedy, 211, 214–216, 217.

BOADEN, James [1762–1839], 164, 165.

BOADICIA, Glover's, 428; account of, 200.

BOILEAU-DESPREAUX, Nicolas [1636–1711], 157, 408.

BOLINGBROKE, Henry St. John, Viscount [1678–1751], 43, 131; on English tragedy, 345.

BOOTH, Barton [1681–1733], 377.

BOOTH, Edwin [1833–1893], 320.

BOSWELL, James [1740–1795], 1, 366.

BROME, Richard [*d.* 1652], 34, 40.

BROWN, John [1715–1766], his tragedy of Athelstan, 66, 193, 429.

BROWNING, Robert [1812–1889], observes dramatic unities, 15.

BRUMOY, Pierre [1688–1742], 192.

BRUTUS, Voltaire's, 245.

BUCKINGHAM, George Villiers, Duke of [1628–1687], 330.

BUCKINGHAMSHIRE, John Sheffield, Duke of [1648–1721], alteration of Julius Cæsar, 310; Essay on Poetry, 310, 422.

BURNABY [*fl.* 1703], 303.

BYRON, George Gordon, Lord [1788–1824], 93, 251.

CAIUS MARIUS, HISTORY AND FALL OF, Otway's, 302, 304, 422; balcony scene in, 324.

CARACTACUS, Mason's, 246, 252, 255, 429.

CAROLINE, Queen [1683–1737], on Shakespeare's women, 371, 372.

CARTWRIGHT, William [1611–1643], 297.

CASE IS ALTERED, Jonson's, 25, 26.

CASTLE OF OTRANTO, Walpole's, 144, 430.

CATILINE, Jonson's, 32, 144, 242.

CATO, Addison's, 426; Dennis on, 59, 426; Voltaire on, 184.

CÉNIE, Madame de Grafigny's, 198.

CENTLIVRE, Mrs. Susannah [1667 ?–1723], 45, 71, 300, 425, 426.

CERVANTES SAAVEDRA, Miguel de [1547 ? –1616], 282, 289.

CHAPELAIN, Jean [1595–1674], 233.

CHAPMAN, George [1559 ?–1634], 38.

CHESTERFIELD, Philip Dormer Stanhope, Earl of [1694–1773], 63, 80, 131, 191, 192, 198, 211, 218, 317, 345, 354, 371, 372.

CHORUS, THE ANCIENT, in modern plays, adopted by Milton, 243; advocated by Roscommon, 243 — by Rymer, 243 — by Francklin, 245 — by Hurd, 245, 254 — by Duncombe, 245; denounced by Dennis, 244 — by Walpole, 245 — by Colman, 253 — by Gray, 254; Mason's attempt to introduce it, 246–255.

CIBBER, Colley [1761–1757], 195, 197, 302, 314–317, 319, 323, 424, 427, 428.

CIBBER, Theophilus [1703–1758], 315.

CINTHIO (Giovanni Battista Giraldi) [1504–1573], 290.

CLARISSA, Richardson's, 410.

CLEOMENES, Dryden's, 57, 153, 423.

CLEONE, Dodsley's, 72, 429.

CLEOPATRA, Daniel's, 206, 215; account of, 24.

CLEVELAND, John [1613–1658], 34.

CLIVE, Mrs. Catharine [1711–1785], 207, 428.

COBBETT, William [1762–1835], 361.

COLERIDGE, Samuel Taylor [1772–1834], 388.

COLMAN, George [1732–1794], 68, 89, 139, 174, 212, 218, 252, 253, 321, 364, 365, 394, 432; his alteration of Lear, 309, 312, 430; his translation of Terence, 213, 214, 430.

COLUMBUS, Morton's, 73, 434.

COMIC DRAMA OF THE RESTORATION, 257–259.

COMICAL GALLANT, Dennis, 303, 358, 425.

COMPANION TO THE PLAYHOUSE, 319, 430, 432.

COMPLETE ART OF POETRY, Gildon's, 275, 426.

CONGREVE, William [1670–1729], 121, 158, 269, 273, 339 n, 424.

CONQUEST OF GRANADA, Dryden's, 344, 357, 420.

CONQUEST OF MEXICO, Dryden's, 233, 419.

COOKE, Thomas [1703–1756], 409, 427.

COOKE, William [fl. 1775], 62, 431.

CORNEILLE, Pierre [1606–1684], 76, 80, 92, 224, 267, 300, 346, 359, 366.

CORRESPONDENTS, THE, 373, 431.

COVENTRY, Francis [fl. 1751], 227 n.

COWLEY, Abraham [1618–1667], 229.

COWPER, William [1731–1800], 212.

CROMWELL, Victor Hugo's, 14.

CROWNE, John [fl. 1665–1698], 357; his alterations of Shakespeare, 302, 309, 368, 422; on Shakespeare, 345.

CUMBERLAND, Richard [1732–1811], his alteration of Timon, 311, 318; the Mysterious Husband of, 157, 220, 432; on Shakespeare, 346.

CURSORY REMARKS ON SHAKESPEARE, Taylor's, 167, 431.

DACIER, André [1651–1722], 252.

DANIEL, Samuel [1552–1619], 24, 25, 206, 215.

D'ARBLAY, Frances (Burney) [1752–1840], 360.

D'AVENANT, Sir William [1606–1668], 229, 263, 330; alteration of Macbeth, 302, 303, 307, 421; of The Tempest, 287, 302, 305, 420; his Law against Lovers, 302, 304, 307, 420.

DAVIDEIS, Cowley's, 229.

DAVIES, Thomas [1712?–1785], 164, 165, 312, 433.

DEKKER, Thomas [1570?–1640?], 39.

DELANY, Mrs. Mary [1700–1788], 199.

DENHAM, Sir John [1615–1669], 2.

DENNIS, John [1657–1734], 225, 239, 283, 286, 288, 329, 345, 361, 409, 423, 424, 425, 426; account of, 271–275; on Addison's Cato, 59, 426; alteration of Coriolanus, 195, 301, 403, 411, 427; of Merry Wives of Windsor, 303, 358, 425; on the chorus, 244, 284; on poetic justice, 403, 404, 407, 408; on tragi-comedy, 137, 159; on the unities, 58–60.

DIALOGUES OF THE DEAD, Lyttelton's, 156, 429.

DISBANDED OFFICER, THE, 89, 433.

DISSERTATIONS, MORAL AND CRITICAL, Beattie's, 64, 432.

DISSERTATION ON ANCIENT TRAGEDY, Francklin's, 245.

DISTREST MOTHER, Philip's, 67, 426.

DODINGTON, Bubb, see Melcombe.

DODSLEY, ROBERT [1703–1764], 72, 429.

DOMESTIC TRAGEDY, 222.

DON SEBASTIAN, Dryden's, 57, 153, 402, 423.

DORSET, Charles Sackville, Earl of [1638–1706], 282.

DOUGLAS, Home's, 429; Scotch opinion of, 349, 350.

DOWNES, John [*fl.* 1662–1710], 303, 425.

DRAMATIC MISCELLANIES, Davies', 164, 312, 433.

DRUMMOND, William, of Hawthornden [1585–1649], 1, 4, 5.

DRYDEN, John [1631–1700], 70, 136, 137, 151, 153, 197, 216, 240, 241, 258, 265, 268, 273, 283, 309, 330, 339, 347, 357, 363, 376, 422, 423; his All for Love, 95, 97–99; his alteration of the Tempest, 287, 302, 305, 420; of Troilus and Cressida, 301, 302, 421; on poetic justice, 402, 405; his relations with Rymer, 232, 233, 283, 285; on Shakespeare, 269, 271, 283, 340, 344, 355; on tragi-comedy, 135, 136, 159; on the unities, 42, 47, 48, 56, 57.

DUFFETT, Thomas [*fl.* 1675], his Mock-Tempest, 302, 306, 421.

DUKE OF GUISE, Dryden and Lee's, 57, 422.

DUKE OF LERMA, Sir Robert Howard's, 47, 420.

DUNCIAD, Pope's, 275, 316.

DUNCOMBE, William [1690–1769], 245, 427.

DURFEY, Thomas [1653 – 1723], his alteration of Cymbeline, 194, 302, 368, 422.

EARL OF WARWICK, Francklin's, 45, 68, 430.

EASTWARD HO, Chapman, Jonson and Marston's, 38.

EDGAR, Rymer's, 277, 285, 421; account of, 239–241.

ELECTRA, Sophocles', 139, 244.

ELEMENTS OF CRITICISM, Kames', 51, 430.

ELEMENTS OF DRAMATIC CRITICISM, Cooke's, 62, 431.

ELFRID, Hill's, 71, 426.

ELFRIDA, Mason's, 248, 252, 254, 255, 428.

ELMERICK, Lillo's, 219, 427.

ENGLISH, their reputation for cruelty, 201–203.

EPICENE, Jonson's, 33.

EPILOGUE, in English plays, 44.

ERNANI, Victor Hugo's, 100.

ESSAY OF DRAMATIC POESY, Dryden's, 135, 265, 420.

ESSAY ON THE GENIUS AND WRITINGS OF SHAKESPEARE, Dennis', 403, 407, 426.

ESSAY ON FALSTAFF, Morgann's, 376, 432.

ESTHER, Racine's, 243, 251.

EUGENIA, Francis's, 139 *n*, 197, 198, 428.

EURIPIDES, 139, 143, 244, 286, 346, 366.

EVELYN, John [1620–1706], 293.

EVERY MAN IN HIS HUMOR, Jonson's, 19, 313; examined, 123–125; observance of unities in, 27, 28, 103.

EVERY MAN OUT OF HIS HUMOR, Jonson's, 103; observance of unities in, 29–31, 32, 33.

FAIRY QUEEN, The, 302.

FALKENER, Sir Everard [1684–1758], 190.

FALL OF MORTIMER, Jonson's, 32.

FARQUHAR, George [1678–1707], on the dramatic unities, 49, 56, 90, 104, 425.

FELTHAM, Owen [1602?–1668], 35.

FEMALE CHARACTERS IN SHAKESPEARE, 369–375.

FEMALE QUIXOTE, Mrs. Lennox's, 289.

FIELDING, Henry [1707–1754], 427; on Cibber's alterations, 314; on the dramatic unities, 50, 51, 90.

FLETCHER, John [1579–1625], 2, 174, 297, 348; popularity during Restoration period, 42, 262, 265–

267, 277, 381; his Sea Voyage contrasted with the Tempest, 391.

FLORIO, John [1553?-1625], 12.

FŒDERA, Rymer's, 227.

FOOTE, Samuel [1720-1777], 428; on the dramatic unities, 50.

FOX, Charles James [1749-1806], on Hamlet, 347.

FRANCIS, Philip [1708?-1773], 139, 198, 428.

FRANCKLIN, Thomas [1721-1784], 45, 68, 245, 430.

FRENCH ACADEMY, 41, 65, 168, 169, 359.

FULLER, Thomas [1608-1661], 103.

GAMESTER, Moore's, 219, 428.

GAMMER GURTON'S NEEDLE, 23.

GARRICK, David [1717-1779], 45, 66, 193, 199, 200, 318, 346, 363, 380, 381; his alteration of Hamlet, 161-173; his Lear, 312, 313, 321.

GENTLEMAN'S JOURNAL, Motteux's, 282, 423.

GEOFFREY OF MONMOUTH [1100?-1154], 406.

GEORGE BARNWELL, Lillo's, 218, 427.

GEORGE III. on Shakespeare, 360.

GIFFORD, William [1756-1826], 27 n.

GILDON, Charles [1665-1724], 238, 270, 271, 272, 329, 340, 358, 370, 423, 424, 426; account of, 275, 287; his alteration of Measure for Measure, 303, 307, 425; on poetic justice, 408; relations with Rymer, 285, 286; on Shakespeare, 229, 286, 287, 360, 361; on tragi-comedy, 136, 137.

GLASSE, George Henry [1761-1809], 246.

GLOVER, Richard [1712-1785], 200, 428.

GOETHE, Johann Wolfgang von [1749-1832], on the dramatic unities, 93.

GOLDSMITH, Oliver [1728-1774], 51, 125, 360, 431; on Shakespeare, 346-348.

GONDIBERT, D'Avenant's, 229.

GORBODUC, Sackville and Norton's, 20.

GRAFIGNY, Madame de [1695-1758], 198.

GRAVEDIGGERS' SCENE in Hamlet, 106, 141-143, 154, 162, 164, 166, 169.

GRAY, Thomas [1716-1771], 208, 246, 247; on the chorus, 253, 254.

GREENE, Robert [1560?-1592], 22, 385.

HALLAM, Henry [1777-1859], 231.

HAMBURGISCHE DRAMATURGIE, Lessing's, 75, 87.

HANMER, Sir Thomas [1677-1746], 60 n.

HARDY, Sir Thomas Duffus [1804-1878], 227 n.

HAWKESWORTH, John [1715?-1773], his alteration of Oronooko, 158, 429.

HAWKINS, William [1722-1801], his alteration of Cymbeline, 317, 429.

HAYLEY, William [1745-1820], 211, 218, 246, 432.

HENSLOW, Philip [d. 1616], 26, 27.

HIGGONS, Bevil [1670-1735], 331.

HILL, Aaron [1685-1750], 71, 426.

HISTORICAL REGISTER FOR THE YEAR 1736, Fielding's, 314, 427.

HISTRIOMASTIX, Dekker's, 39.

HOADLEY, John [1711-1776], 164, 166; his additions to Hamlet, 171.

HODSON, William [fl. 1780], 63 n, 431.

HOME, John [1722-1808], his Agis, 349, 429; his Douglas, 350, 429.

HOMER, Pope's and Tickell's translation of, 276.

HORACE, 54, 55, 245, 253, 254, 282, 422, 428.

HOWARD, Hon. James [*fl.* 1662–1674], 303, 309.

HOWARD, Sir Robert [1626–1698], 419, 420; on tragi-comedy, 137; on the unities, 47, 48.

HUGHES, John [1677–1720], 381.

HUGO, Victor Marie [1802–1885], 14, 100.

HUME, David [1711–1776], 64, 131; on Home's Douglas, 350; on Shakespeare, 352, 353.

HUNTER, Joseph [1783–1861], 394.

HURD, Richard [1720–1808], 254, 428; on the chorus, 245, 254.

ILIAD, translations of the, 275.

IMPARTIAL CRITIC, Dennis', 284, 423.

INGRATITUDE OF A COMMONWEALTH, Tate's, 302, 422.

INJURED PRINCESS, Durfey's, 302, 422.

INQUIRY, etc., Goldsmith's, 346.

INTERLOCKING OF SCENES, 256.

INVADER OF HIS COUNTRY, Dennis', 195, 301, 403, 427.

INVINCIBLE ARMADO, Rymer's, 285.

IPHIGENIA, Dennis', 58, 272, 425.

IPHIGENIA in Tauris, Euripides', 139.

IPHIGENIE, Goethe's, 94.

IRVING, Henry [1838–], 320.

JANE SHORE, Rowe's, 362, 426.

JEFFREY, Francis [1773–1850], 59, 93.

JEPHSON, Robert [1736–1803], 69, 432.

JERONIMO, Kyd's, 180, 181.

JEW OF VENICE, Lansdowne's, 302, 425; account of, 329–338.

JOHNSON, Samuel [1709–1784], 64,

75, 192, 290, 291, 366, 389, 390; on poetic justice, 410; on tragi-comedy, 137, 156, 157, 162; on the dramatic unities, 54, 55, 62, 70, 87, 90, 91, 101, 102, 104, 130.

JONSON, Benjamin [1573?–1637], 1, 2, 3, 4, 8, 15, 40, 47, 119, 144, 174, 180, 181, 184, 256, 262, 264, 267, 296, 340, 348, 353, 364, 381, 382, 385; on the chorus, 242; Every Man in his Humor examined, 123–125; on the unities, 19, 22, 23, 25–40, 102; his Volpone examined, 82–86.

JUNIUS BRUTUS, Duncombe's, 245, 427.

KAMES, Henry Home, Lord [1696–1782], 62, 430; on the dramatic unities, 51–54.

KEAN, Edmund [1787–1833], 309.

KEATE, George [1729–1797], 365.

KEMBLE, John [1758–1822], 72, 173.

KENRICK, William [1725?–1779], 66 *n.*

LACY (Lacey), John [*d.* 1681], 302, 368, 424.

LA MOTTE, Antoine Houdart de [1672–1731], 42.

LANSDOWNE, George Granville, Lord [1667–1735], his alteration of Merchant of Venice, 302, 319, 425; compared with original, 328–338.

LA PLACE, Pierre Antoine de [1707–1793], 80, 203, 428.

LAW AGAINST LOVERS, D'Avenant's, 302, 304, 307, 420.

LAW OF LOMBARDY, Jephson's, 69, 432.

LEE, Nathaniel [1653?–1692], 57, 422.

LEIR, KING, 406.

LE MOYNE, Pierre [1602–1671], 233.

LENNOX, Mrs. Charlotte [1720–1804], 192, 429, 430 ; account of, 289, 292.

LEONIDAS, Glover's, 200.

LESSING, Gotthold Ephraim [1729–1781], 75, 76, 82, 120, 366, 384, 432 [433] ; English estimate of, 87–90; on the unities, 53, 77–81, 90.

LE TOURNEUR, Pierre [1736–1788], 168, 374.

LILLO, George [1693–1739], 218, 219, 220, 427.

LITTLE FRENCH LAWYER, Fletcher's, 174.

LLOYD, Robert [1733–1764], 212, 213.

LOPE DE VEGA [1562–1635], 43.

LOVE, in the ancient and the modern drama, 110–114 ; intrudes into tragedy, 116, 129, 223 ; difficulty of its treatment while observing the unities, 120–128 ; not distinction between the classical and romantic dramas, 223–226 ; prominent in alterations of Shakespeare's plays, 309–313.

LOVE BETRAYED, Burnaby's, 303.

LOVE FOR LOVE, Congreve's, 121, 424.

LOVE'S CONTRIVANCE, Mrs. Centlivre's, 300, 425.

LOVE'S VICTIM, Gildon's, 371, 425.

LYLY, John [1554?–1606], 22.

LYONS MAIL, Reade's, 320.

LYTTELTON, George, Lord [1709–1773], 156, 373, 429.

MACAULAY, Thomas Babington, Lord [1800–1859], 227.

MACKLIN, Charles [1697?–1797], 319.

MACREADY, William Charles [1793–1873], 319, 321.

MADAN, Mrs. Judith (Cowper) [1702–1781], 363.

MAID OF HONOR, Massinger's, 72, 73.

MAID'S TRAGEDY, Beaumont and Fletcher's, 230.

MAIDEN QUEEN (Secret Love), Dryden's, 42, 56, 420.

MALONE, Edmund [1741–1812], 27 n, 101.

MARINI (or Marino), Giambattista [1569–1625], 233.

MARLOWE, Christopher [1564–1593], 22, 216.

MARMONTEL, Jean François [1723–1799], 168.

MARSTON, John [1575?–1634], 38.

MASON, William [1724–1797], 169, 428, 429 ; his attempt to restore the chorus, 246–255.

MASSINGER, Philip [1583–1640], 72, 73, 174, 212.

MAYNE, Jasper [1604–1672], 35.

MELCOMBE, George Bubb Dodington, Lord [1691–1762], 208.

MENÆCHMI, Plautus', 108, 118.

MERES, Francis [1565–1647], 26, 184.

MILTON, John [1608–1674], 41, 208, 230, 272, 342, 420; on the degradation of tragedy, 143–145 ; introduces the chorus, 243, 246, 251 ; on Shakespeare, 2.

MINE, Sargent's, 246, 433.

MINNA VON BARNHELM, Lessing's, 89 [433].

MOCK MARRIAGE, Scott's, 58, 424.

MOLIÈRE, Jean Baptiste Poquelin [1622–1673], 92, 300.

MONBODDO, James Burnett, Lord [1714–1799], 350.

MONTAGU, Mrs. Elizabeth [1720–1800], 340.

MONTESQUIEU [1689–1755], 371, 372.

MOORE, Edward [1712–1757], 219, 220, 428.

MORE, Hannah [1745–1833], 350.

MORGAN, McNamara [d. 1762], 72, 429.

MORGANN, Maurice [1726–1802], 376, 431.

MORTON, Thomas [1764?–1838], 73, 434.

MOTTEUX, Peter Anthony [1660–1718], 282, 423.

MURPHY, Arthur [1727–1805], 192, 200.

MUSES' LOOKING-GLASS, Randolph's, 23.

MYSTERIOUS HUSBAND, Cumberland's, 157, 220, 432.

NATHAN DER WEISE, Lessing's, 88, 432.

NEW FOUNDLING HOSPITAL FOR WIT, 167 n, 433.

NON-JUROR, Cibber's, 316, 427.

NORTHERN LASS, Broome's, 40.

OBSERVATIONS ON HAMLET, 141, 428.

ŒDIPE, Voltaire's, 42, 225, 252.

ORONOOKO, Southerne's, 139, 424; altered by Hawkesworth, 158, 429.

ORRERY, John Boyle, Earl of [1707–1762], 192, 290.

OTWAY, Thomas [1652–1685], 347, 350, 370; his use of Romeo and Juliet, 302, 304, 324.

PAPAL TYRANNY, etc., Cibber's, 314, 316, 428.

PARADISE LOST, Milton's, Dennis on, 272; Rymer on, 229.

PEELE, George [1558–1597], 22.

PEPYS, Samuel [1633–1703], 307; on the English theatre, 260, 261; on Shakespeare, 263.

PERSÆ, Æschylus', 285.

PERPLEXED LOVERS, Mrs. Centlivre's, 45, 426.

PHAETON, Gildon's, 408, 424.

PHELPS, Samuel [1804–1878], 308, 320, 321.

PHILASTER, Beaumont and Fletcher's, Colman's alteration of, 139, 364, 430.

PHILIPS, Ambrose [1675?–1749], 67, 426; his Pastorals, 276.

PHILLIPS, Edward [1630–1696?], 342, 421.

PHILOCLEA, Morgan's, 72, 429.

PHILOCTETES, Sophocles', 204.

PHILOTAS, Daniel's, 25, 215.

PHIPPS, Hon. Henry [1755–1831], 73 n.

PLAUTUS, 4, 108, 111, 112, 117, 118, 213.

PLOT AND NO PLOT, Dennis', 58, 424.

POETASTER, Jonson's, 39.

POETIC JUSTICE, doctrine of, 222, 308, 401–417.

POMPEY THE LITTLE, Coventry's, 227 n.

POPE, Alexander [1688–1744], 3, 59, 157, 192, 231, 240, 271, 275, 276, 287, 316; on Shakespeare's repute, 377, 378.

PROGRESS OF POESY, Mrs. Madan's, 363.

PROLOGUE, in English plays, 44.

PROMOS AND CASSANDRA, Whetstone's, 18, 19, 102, 215.

PROSE in tragedy, 212, 218–220; in comedy, 211.

QUINTILIAN, 283.

RABELAIS, François [1495?–1553], 282.

RACINE, Jean Baptiste [1639–1699], 67, 76, 80, 92, 224, 249, 300, 346, 349, 366; introduces the chorus, 243, 251.

RALEIGH, Sir Walter [1552?–1618], 340.

RAM ALLEY, Barry's, 38.

RAMBLER, Johnson's, 54, 137.

RANDOLPH, Thomas [1605–1635], 23.

RAPIN, René [1621–1687], 229, 233; on English fondness for blood, 201; on love in tragedy, 224.

RASPE, Rudolf Eric [1737–1794], 88, 432.

RAVENSCROFT, Edward [*fl.* 1671–1697], his alteration of Titus Andronicus, 196, 300, 302, 422.

READE, Charles [1814–1884], 320.

REED, Isaac [1742–1807], 166, 169, 172.

REHEARSAL, Mrs. Clive's, 207, 428.

REMARKS ON HAMLET, 60, 427.

RICCOBONI, Lodovico [1677–1753], 203.

RICHARDSON, Samuel [1689–1761], 410.

RICHARDSON, William [1743–1814], 64, 431, 433; on Shakespeare, 152; on Shakespeare female characters, 374, 375.

RIVALS, Sheridan's, 121, 430.

ROCHESTER, John Wilmot, Earl of [1648–1680], 330.

ROGERS, Samuel [*fl.* 1764], 364.

ROLLO (The Bloody Brother), Fletcher's, 402.

ROMANO, Giulio (Pippi) [1492–1546], 106.

ROME SAUVÉE, Voltaire's, 147, 225.

ROSCOMMON, Wentworth Dillon, Earl of [1633 ?–1685], 191, 422; on the chorus, 243, 244.

ROSCIUS ANGLICANUS, Downes's, 303, 425.

ROWE, Nicholas [1674–1718], 286, 287, 358, 362, 369, 425, 426; on Shakespeare's female characters, 371; on poetic justice, 403.

RYME, attempt to discard from English verse, 7; in comedy and tragedy, 211, 216, 217.

RYMER, Thomas [1641–1713], 202, 204, 225, 271, 272, 275, 290, 360, 370, 403, 421, 423; account of, 227–233; on the chorus, 243; his critical views, 234–239, 241; his Edgar, 239–241, 421; on poetic justice, 402, 407; on Shakespeare, 276–286, 288, 343.

ST. EVREMOND [1613–1703], 267, 283, 423; on the English theatre, 189, 190, 203.

ST. JAMES'S MAGAZINE, 208, 213.

SAMSON AGONISTES, Milton's, 41, 143, 243, 420.

SARGENT, John [*fl.* 1788], 246, 433.

SAWNEY THE SCOT, Lacy's, 302, 368, 424.

SCHOOL OF COMPLIMENT, Shirley's, 264, 419.

SCORNFUL LADY, Beaumont and Fletcher's, 174.

SCOTT, Thomas [*fl.* 1696], 58, 424.

SCOTT, Sir Walter [1771–1832], 231, 239; on the dramatic unities, 70, 97.

SEA VOYAGE, Fletcher's, 205; compared with the Tempest, 391.

SECRET LOVE, or the Maiden Queen, Dryden's, 42, 420.

SEDLEY, Sir Charles [1639 ?–1701], 135, 136, 345, 368.

SEJANUS, Jonson's, 31, 144, 242.

SELDEN, John [1584–1654], 34.

SELIMUS, 187, 215.

SÉMIRAMIS, Voltaire's, 225.

SENECA, 23, 24.

SHADWELL, Thomas [1642 ?–1692], 420; his alterations of Shakespeare's plays, 302, 310, 330; on the unities, 46.

SHAKESPEARE, William [1564–1616], Estimate of, by Blair, 348 — by Chesterfield, 345, 354 — by Cobbett, 361 — by Colman, 364 — by Crowne, 345, 357 — by Cumberland, 346 — by Dennis, 284, 286, 345, 358, 361 — by Dryden, 344 — by Fox, 347 — by George III., 360 — by Gildon, 285–288, 345, 361 — by Goldsmith, 346–348 — by Hume, 349, 351–353 — by Keate, 365 — by Mrs. Lennox, 289–292 — by Mrs. Madan, 363 — by Rogers, 364 — by Rowe, 362 — by Rymer, 276–

284, 343 — by J. Warton, 345;
his fondness for quibbles, 147,
386; his indifference to anachro-
nisms, 385; his plays plundered
without acknowledgment, 368;
his

ALL'S WELL THAT ENDS
WELL, revived by Giffard,
388; plot considered, 389–
391.

ANTONY AND CLEOPATRA, de-
scribed, 95–97.

AS YOU LIKE IT, 369; Dr.
Johnson on, 411.

COMEDY OF ERRORS, 108, 118.

CORIOLANUS, altered by Tate,
195, 300, 302, 422; by Dennis,
159, 195, 301, 427; criticised
by Dennis, 403, 411; observation of poetic justice in,
403.

CYMBELINE, 312; altered by
Durfey, 194, 302, 368, 422;
altered by Hawkins, 317,
429.

HAMLET, 60, 107 n, 293, 314,
384; alteration of, by Garrick, 161–173, 314; Charles
James Fox on, 347; Pepys
on, 263; unities disregarded
in, 13.

HENRY IV., altered by Betterton, 302; borrowed from
by Cibber, 323; Pepys on,
263.

HENRY V., defence of romantic drama in, 103–105.

HENRY VI., altered by Crowne,
302, 309, 357, 368, 422.

JOHN, KING, alteration of, by
Cibber, 314, 317, 428.

JULIUS CÆSAR, 147, 373; altered by Duke of Bucking-
hamshire, 310; criticised by
Rymer, 278, 279.

LEAR, KING, 187, 236; its relation to poetic justice, 405–

415; Tate's alteration of,
139, 194, 300, 302, 309, 313,
319, 409, 422 — described,
325–328 — condemned by
Addison, 406 — approved by
Dennis, 407, by Gildon, 408,
by Dr. Johnson, 410 — his
introduction of love-scenes
into, 117, 311–313; Colman's
alteration of, 309, 312, 430;
revival of original by Macready, 321 — by Phelps, 321;
unities disregarded in, 13.

LOVE'S LABOR'S LOST, unities
in, 100 n, 101 n.

MACBETH, 373; art of, 188,
235; D'Avenant, alteration
of, 302, 303, 307, 421; Gildon
on, 270; Pepys on, 263, 307;
poetic justice observed in,
415–418; revival of original
by Phelps, 308; unities disregarded in, 13.

MEASURE FOR MEASURE, 214;
alteration of, by D'Avenant,
302, 304, 307, 420; alteration
of, by Gildon, 288, 303, 307,
424.

MERCHANT OF VENICE, Lans-
downe's alteration of, 302,
319, 425 — described, 328–
333 — compared with original, 333–338; Macklin's restoration of original to stage,
319.

MERRY WIVES OF WINDSOR,
123, 214, 222, 369; alteration of, by Dennis, 303, 358,
425.

MIDSUMMER NIGHT'S DREAM,
altered into an opera, 302;
Pepys on, 263.

MUCH ADO ABOUT NOTHING,
214; borrowed from, by
D'Avenant, 304.

OTHELLO, 373; art of, 188;
early popularity of, 281;

never altered, 162; Pepys on, 263; Rymer on, 277–281, 290, 360; unities disregarded in, 13.

PERICLES, 242.

RICHARD II., Tate's alteration of, 302, 422; reasons given for alterations, 159, 241.

RICHARD III., 235; Cibber's alteration of, 302, 314, 319, 424 — character of alteration, 195, 323; revival of original by Macready, 319 — by Phelps, 320 — by Irving, 320 — by Booth, 320.

ROMEO AND JULIET, 312; altered into tragi-comedy by Howard, 303, 309; Gildon on, 360; Lessing on, 120; Pepys on, 263; use of by Otway, 302, 304, 422 — his version of balcony scene compared with original, 324.

TAMING OF THE SHREW, 222; alteration of, by Lacy, 302, 368, 424; Pepys on, 263; comparison of, with Fletcher's Woman's Prize, 266.

TEMPEST, 345, 369; alteration of, by D'Avenant and Dryden, 287, 302, 420 — its character, 305; alteration of, by Duffett, 302, 306, 421; converted into an opera by Shadwell, 302; its art, contrasted with Fletcher's Sea Voyage, 391; observance of unities in, 108–110, 126–128.

TIMON, alteration of by Shadwell, 302, 310, 421; alteration by Cumberland, 311, 318, 431.

TITUS ANDRONICUS, 180; alteration of, by Ravenscroft, 196, 300, 302, 422; its character, 184–186; its genuineness, 184.

TROILUS AND CRESSIDA, 340; Dryden's alteration of, 301, 302, 405, 421.

TWELFTH NIGHT, 24, 369; Burnaby's alteration of, 303; Pepys on, 263.

WINTER'S TALE, 108, 242; disregard of rules in, 22, 105–107, 110.

SHAKESPEARE ILLUSTRATED, Mrs. Lennox's, 429; described, 290.

SHAKESPEARE'S DRAMATIC CHARACTERS, Richardson's, 152, 374, 433.

SHE STOOPS TO CONQUER, Goldsmith's, 125, 431.

SHERIDAN, Richard Brinsley [1751–1816], 121, 431.

SHIRLEY, James [1596–1666], 262, 264 [419].

SHORT VIEW OF TRAGEDY, Rymer's, 277–284, 423.

SICILIAN USURPER, Tate's, 302, 422.

SIDNEY, Sir Philip [1554–1586], 7, 104, 340; on tragi-comedy, 149; on the dramatic unities, 20.

SILENT WOMAN, Jonson's, 174.

SISTER, Mrs. Lennox's, 291, 430.

SMITH, Adam [1723–1790], 350.

SOFONISBA, Trissino's, 17.

SOLIMAN AND PERSEDA, 182.

SOPHOCLES, 139, 286, 346, 349, 366; chorus in, 244.

SOUTHERNE, Thomas [1660–1746], 158, 424, 429.

SPANISH CURATE, Fletcher's, 174.

SPANISH FRIAR, Dryden's, 139, 159 n, 422.

SPANISH TRAGEDY, Kyd's, 182, 184, 185, 186; character of, 181.

'SPARAGUS GARDEN, Broome's, 40.

SPENCE, Joseph [1699–1768], 231, 271, 349.

SPENSER, Edmund [1552?–1599], 7, 24, 229, 340.

STATIUS, 233.

STEELE, Sir Richard [1672–1729], on the dramatic unities, 67.

STEEVENS, George [1736–1800], 101, 166; encourages Garrick in altering Hamlet, 162, 163.

SULLEN LOVERS, Shadwell's, 46, 420.

SWIFT, Jonathan [1667–1745], 192.

SWINBURNE, Algernon Charles [1837–], 123, 124.

TASSO, Torquato [1544–1595], 233.

TATE, Nahum [1652–1715], 330; his alteration of Coriolanus, 195, 300, 302, 422; of Lear, 139, 194, 300, 302, 319, 325–328, 406, 409, 411, 422; of Richard II., 159, 241, 302, 422.

TAYLOR, Edward [d. 1797], 167, 168, 431.

TERENCE, 4, 111, 112, 213, 430.

THEATRUM POETARUM, Phillips', 342, 421.

THEOBALD, Lewis [1688–1744], 101.

THEOCRITUS, 276.

THOMSON, James [1700–1748], 158.

THORNTON, Bonnell [1728–1768], 212, 213.

TICKELL, Thomas [1686–1740], 276.

TOM JONES, Fielding's, 51.

TRAGEDIES OF THE LAST AGE, Rymer's, 234–239, 277, 281, 421, 423.

TRISSINO, Giovanni Giorgio [1478–1550], 17.

TWO CONNOISSEURS, Hayley's, 211, 432.

TYRANNIC LOVE, Dryden's, 56, 420.

UNITIES, doctrine of, defined, 8–11; attributed to Aristotle, 16; introduced into modern plays by Trissino, 17; championed in England by Jonson, 22, 25; controversy about, in Elizabethan age, 18–25; controversy about, after the Res-
toration, 40–44, 47; decadence of belief in, 71–74; views on, of Dryden, 47, 56 — of Sir Robert Howard, 47 — of Farquhar, 49 — of Foote, 50 — of Fielding, 51 — of Kames, 51–54 — of Dr. Johnson, 54–56 — of Dennis, 57–60 — of Upton, 61 — of Webb, 61 — of Cooke, 62 — of Berkenhout, 62 — of Richardson, 64 — of Blair, 64 — of Beattie, 64 — of Baretti, 64 — of Belsham, 65 — of Sir Richard Steele, 67 — of Colman, 68 — of Jephson, 69 — of Sir Walter Scott, 70 — of Lessing, 74–82, 87 — of Byron, 93 — of Goethe, 93 — of Jeffrey, 93.

UPTON, John [1707–1760], 61, 428; on Shakespeare's female characters, 372.

VERGIL, 233, 246, 276.

VICAR OF WAKEFIELD, Goldsmith's, 347.

VICTOR, Benjamin [d. 1778], 170.

VOLPONE, Jonson's, 33; observance of unities in, 82–86.

VOLTAIRE (François Marie Arouet) [1694–1778], 19, 62, 65, 75, 129, 142, 145, 168, 175, 201, 245, 248, 251, 256, 280, 340, 345, 351, 365; on bloodshed on the stage, 190; on love in tragedy, 225; on ryme in French plays, 216; on Shakespeare, 102, 131, 184, 281; on tragi-comedy, 147; on the dramatic unities, 42, 130; Lessing on, 82, 87.

WALLER, Edmund [1606–1687], 330.

WALPOLE, Horace [1717–1797], 169, 208, 245, 430; on tragi-comedy, 144, 156.

WARTON, Joseph [1722–1800], on Lear, 394; on love in tragedy, 226; on Shakespeare, 345.

WEBB, Daniel [*fl.* 1762], 61, 430.

WHETSTONE, George [1544 ?–1587 ?], 20, 102, 215; on tragicomedy, 149; on the unities, 18, 19.

WHITE, Richard Grant [1821–1885], 100.

WIELAND, Christoph Martin [1733–1813], 76.

WILD GALLANT, Dryden's, 197, 258, 420.

WILKINSON, Tate [1739–1803], 170, 433.

WOMAN'S PRIZE, Fletcher's, 266.

WYCHERLEY, William [1640 ?–1716], 273.

YOUNG, Edward [1683–1765], 158.

ZAIRE, Voltaire, 190.

ZORAIDA, Hodson's, 63 *n*, 432.